Fodor's

LOS CABOS
& THE BAJA
PENINSULA

2nd Edition

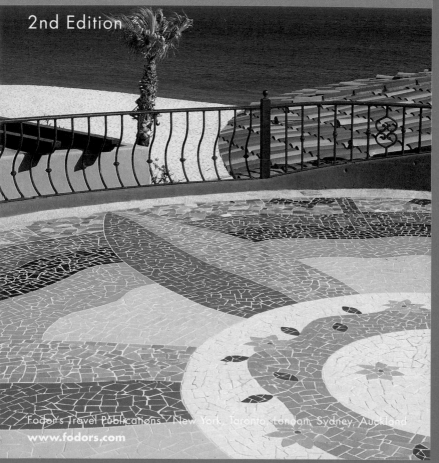

Fodor's Travel Publications · New York, Toronto, London, Sydney, Auckland
www.fodors.com

Be a Fodor's Correspondent

Your opinion matters. It matters to us. It matters to your fellow Fodor's travelers, too. And we'd like to hear it. In fact, we *need* to hear it.

When you share your experiences and opinions, you become an active member of the Fodor's community. That means we'll not only use your feedback to make our books better, but we'll publish your names and comments whenever possible. Throughout our guides, look for "Word of Mouth," excerpts of your unvarnished feedback.

Here's how you can help improve Fodor's for all of us.

Tell us when we're right. We rely on local writers to give you an insider's perspective. But our writers and staff editors—who are the best in the business—depend on you. Your positive feedback is a vote to renew our recommendations for the next edition.

Tell us when we're wrong. We're proud that we update most of our guides every year. But we're not perfect. Things change. Hotels cut services. Museums change hours. Charming cafés lose charm. If our writer didn't quite capture the essence of a place, tell us how you'd do it differently. If any of our descriptions are inaccurate or inadequate, we'll incorporate your changes in the next edition and will correct factual errors at fodors.com *immediately.*

Tell us what to include. You probably have had fantastic travel experiences that aren't yet in Fodor's. Why not share them with a community of like-minded travelers? Maybe you chanced upon a beach or bistro or B&B that you don't want to keep to yourself. Tell us why we should include it. And share your discoveries and experiences with everyone directly at fodors.com. Your input may lead us to add a new listing or highlight a place we cover with a "Highly Recommended" star or with our highest rating, "Fodor's Choice."

Give us your opinion instantly at our feedback center at www.fodors.com/feedback. You may also e-mail editors@fodors.com with the subject line "Los Cabos Editor." Or send your nominations, comments, and complaints by mail to Los Cabos Editor, Fodor's, 1745 Broadway, New York, NY 10019.

You and travelers like you are the heart of the Fodor's community. Make our community richer by sharing your experiences. Be a Fodor's correspondent.

¡Buen Viaje!

Tim Jarrell, Publisher

FODOR'S LOS CABOS & THE BAJA PENINSULA
Editors: Heidi Johansen, Alexis Kelly, Laura M. Kidder

Writers: Georgia deKatona, Larry Dunmire, Coco Krumme, Jeffrey Van Fleet

Production Editor: Carrie Parker
Maps & Illustrations: Mark Stroud, Moon Street Cartography; David Lindroth, Inc.; Ed Jacobus, *cartographers;* Bob Blake, Rebecca Baer, *map editors;* William Wu, *information graphics*
Design: Fabrizio La Rocca, *creative director;* Guido Caroti, Siobhan O'Hare, *art directors;* Tina Malaney, Chie Ushio, Ann McBride, Jessica Walsh, *designers;* Melanie Marin, *senior picture editor*
Cover Photo: (Cabo San Lucas): Philip & Karen Smith/SuperStock
Production Manager: Amanda Bullock

2nd Edition

ISBN 978-1-4000-0438-6

ISSN 1941-028X

SPECIAL SALES
This book is available at special discounts for bulk purchases for sales promotions or premiums. Special editions, including personalized covers, excerpts of existing books, and corporate imprints, can be created in large quantities for special needs. For more information, write to Special Markets/Premium Sales, 1745 Broadway, MD 6-2, New York, New York 10019, or e-mail specialmarkets@randomhouse.com.

AN IMPORTANT TIP & AN INVITATION
Although all prices, opening times, and other details in this book are based on information supplied to us at press time, changes occur all the time in the travel world, and Fodor's cannot accept responsibility for facts that become outdated or for inadvertent errors or omissions. So **always confirm information when it matters,** especially if you're making a detour to visit a specific place. Your experiences—positive and negative—matter to us. If we have missed or misstated something, **please write to us.** We follow up on all suggestions. Contact the Los Cabos & the Baja Peninsula editor at editors@fodors.com or c/o Fodor's at 1745 Broadway, New York, NY 10019.

PRINTED IN SINGAPORE

10 9 8 7 6 5 4 3 2 1

CONTENTS

Fodor's Features

MAPS

ABOUT THIS BOOK

Our Ratings

Sometimes you find terrific travel experiences and sometimes they just find you. But usually the burden is on you to select the right combination of experiences. That's where our ratings come in.

As travelers we've all discovered a place so wonderful that its worthiness is obvious. And sometimes that place is so unique that superlatives don't do it justice: you just have to be there to know. These sights, properties, and experiences get our highest rating, **Fodor's Choice**, indicated by orange stars throughout this book.

Black stars highlight sights and properties we deem **Highly Recommended**, places that our writers, editors, and readers praise again and again for consistency and excellence.

By default, there's another category: any place we include in this book is by definition worth your time, unless we say otherwise. And we will.

Disagree with any of our choices? Care to nominate a place or suggest that we rate one more highly? Visit our feedback center at www.fodors.com/feedback.

Budget Well

Hotel and restaurant price categories from ¢ to $$$$ are defined in the opening pages of each chapter. For attractions, we always give standard adult admission fees; reductions are usually available for children, students, and senior citizens. Want to pay with plastic? **AE, D, DC, MC, V** following restaurant and hotel listings indicate whether American Express, Discover, Diners Club, MasterCard, and Visa are accepted.

Restaurants

Unless we state otherwise, restaurants are open for lunch and dinner daily. We mention dress only when there's a specific requirement and reservations only when they're essential or not accepted—it's always best to book ahead.

Hotels

Hotels have private bath, phone, TV, and air-conditioning and operate on the European Plan (aka EP, meaning without meals), unless we specify that they use the Continental Plan (CP, with a continental breakfast), Breakfast Plan (BP, with a full breakfast), or Modified American Plan (MAP, with breakfast and dinner) or are all-inclusive (including all meals and most activities). We

always list facilities but not whether you'll be charged an extra fee to use them, so when pricing accommodations, find out what's included.

Listings	
★	Fodor's Choice
★	Highly recommended
✉	Physical address
✢	Directions or Map coordinates
⬛	Mailing address
☎	Telephone
🖷	Fax
⊕	On the Web
✑	E-mail
▦	Admission fee
☉	Open/closed times
Ⓜ	Metro stations
▱	Credit cards
Hotels & Restaurants	
▥	Hotel
⮡	Number of rooms
⬧	Facilities
⧦	Meal plans
✕	Restaurant
⬟	Reservations
⬜	Dress code
⬚	Smoking
⬗	BYOB
Outdoors	
丬	Golf
⛺	Camping
Other	
♨	Family-friendly
⇨	See also
✉	Branch address
☞	Take note

Experience Los Cabos and the Baja Peninsula

WHAT'S NEW IN BAJA

It happened about 30 million years ago, give or take a couple of hundred thousand.

According to seismologists, it must have been an unimaginably powerful seismic event. It happened in just seconds—a giant rift, perhaps associated with the San Andreas Fault, tore a huge finger of land miles away from the mainland. Much later the mainland would be called Mexico and the finger the Baja California Peninsula.

Perhaps not as physically jarring as that monstrous quake, the recent developments in Baja—many in Los Cabos specifically—are nothing short of an explosion of epic proportions. In Los Cabos, hotels, restaurants, bars, golf courses, and tourist-oriented businesses have sprung up seemingly overnight in recent years. And those properties that are not necessarily new are undergoing major renovations in order to keep up.

Other parts of Baja are seeing significant goings-on, too. Outside Ensenada, a burgeoning wine district, the Valle de Guadalupe, is gaining recognition. And U.S. citizens are finding themselves hit with some new restrictions on reentering the United States from Mexico by land and sea.

San José del Cabo Grows Up

The same gnawing question has always confronted visitors planning a trip to Los Cabos: do I stay in San José del Cabo or Cabo San Lucas? Most visitors have always opted for the flash and glitter of the latter. San José's hoteliers and restaurateurs have stopped trying to compete on San Lucas's terms, opting instead to market their community for what it is.

The city has truly come into its own. San José's zócalo (central plaza) has been jazzed up with a lighted fountain and gazebo; old haciendas have been transformed into trendy restaurants and charming inns. And the city's art scene is thriving with a high-season **Thursday Night Art Walk,** where those interested in art can visit participating galleries and enjoy free drinks and live music.

Greens Galore

Golf is the name of the game in Los Cabos. There are 11 courses tied to names that read like a Who's Who of golf legends and course designers: Jack Nicklaus, Greg Norman, Davis Love III, Phil Mickelson, Tom Weiskopf, Robert Trent Jones II, and Tom Fazio. Baja golf is more than just Los Cabos: courses line the entire peninsula, if not in the same density as at its southern extreme.

The Rise of Todos Santos

Once the province of surfers—the undertow is wicked here, making for some amazing waves, but risky swimming—this town overlooking the western cape about an hour north of Cabo San Lucas is home to a growing artists' community. Just don't call Todos Santos Baja's "hot" new destination, because folks here aren't interested in becoming another Los Cabos, thank you very much. But "genteel" and "refined" and "preserving Mexican culture"? Absolutely, those descriptions apply.

Baja's Boomtown

People always ask, "Is Los Cabos the next Cancún?" And that's not exactly a compliment, as potentially negative repercussions for the environment and local culture are implied. Perversely, Los Cabos did benefit from 2005's Hurricane Wilma, which battered Cancún and the Mayan Riviera, as visitors canceled plans to vacation there in the storm's aftermath. The

next three years were boom times unlike Los Cabos had ever seen.

The east–west balance has been restored and the world economy has slowed. The flurry of new construction, especially in Cabo San Lucas, has abated, but only somewhat. Even if the number of new hotels opening has subsided, many are still being remodeled and refurbished.

New Terminal at SJD
Anyone who's flown into Aeropuerto Internacional de Los Cabos—SJD in airport-code lingo—recently can tell you that the infrastructure at Mexico's eighth-busiest airport has not kept pace with the ever-rising number of visitors coming here. Relief is on the way in the form of a new terminal, expected to open in 2010. The 10 additional gates should greatly ease congestion for the nearly 3 million passengers who pass through annually.

Border Crossing 2010
U.S. citizens need to have their paperwork in order to return to the United States from Mexico by land or sea. Those aged 16 years and older need to carry a passport or passport card. Children 15 and under are only required to provide a birth certificate if traveling with their parents or an organized group.

Note that if you return from a cruise and your itinerary also took you beyond Mexico, a full-fledged passport is necessary for reentry to the United States. All travelers, regardless of age, require a passport when returning by air from Mexico. See the U.S. Department of Homeland Security's Web site (🌐 *www.dhs.gov*) for more information.

A Bit of Bad News
You've seen the reports: drug cartels are responsible for violence that has gripped pockets of Mexico, including the sliver of land just south of the U.S. border, near Tijuana. For now, we have greatly reduced our coverage of Baja's border towns, but we hope to restore that coverage in future editions. With standard travel precautions, the rest of the peninsula can present you with carefree travels.

Mexico appeared to be the epicenter of the H1N1 virus—the so-called "swine flu"—in 2009, although the outbreak centered in Mexico City. Many visitors canceled reservations to Los Cabos and Baja, possibly hastily and unnecessarily.

September 2009's Hurricane Jimena roared ashore in central Baja near Santa Rosalía and Mulegé. Repairs to damaged infrastructure began almost immediately and are ongoing at this writing.

And, to end on an upbeat note . . .

200 Proud Years
Mexico celebrates its bicentennial in 2010. (Mexico declared its independence from Spain in 1810 and marks that year as the year of its birth, although true freedom wasn't won until 1821.) A palpable sense of pride runs through the population here as the odometer reaches 200. Exuberant fiestas and delicious celebrations are sure to take place throughout the year.

WHAT'S WHERE

1 San José del Cabo.
Thirty-two kilometers (20 mi) east of Cabo San Lucas, San José, the elder sister, has remained the smaller, quieter, and more traditional of the two siblings. Its 18th-century colonial architecture, artsy vibe, and quality restaurants are great for those who like to be within driving distance, not right in the middle, of the happening spots.

2 The Corridor. Along this stretch of road, which connects San José to Cabo, exclusive, guard-gated resort complexes have taken over much of the waterfront with their sprawling villas, golf courses, and shopping centers such as **Las Tiendas de Palmilla,** an upscale, open-to-the-public mall.

3 Cabo San Lucas. Cabo San Lucas is located to the west of the Corridor at the very end of the Carretera Transpeninsular (Highway 1). Cabo has always been the more gregarious, outspoken, and,

dare we say, rowdy of the sisters. The sportfishing fleet is anchored here, and cruise ships anchored off the marina tender passengers into town. Trendy restaurants and bars line the streets and massive hotels have risen all along the beachfront. Here, you'll find Bahía Cabo San Lucas (Cabo Bay), the towering Land's End Rocks, and the famed arched landmark, El Arco.

4 Todos Santos. Only an hour north of Cabo San Lucas, Todos Santos lies close enough to be part of the Los Cabos experience—you'll find its listings within the Los Cabos chapters in this book—but still be that proverbial world away. This típico town on the West Cape is home to a growing expat community, as well as some cozy lodgings and restaurants.

5 Baja California Sur. La Paz, the capital of southern Baja, is a "big little" city, one of the most authentic on

the peninsula, and Loreto, a smaller, charming town beloved by sportfishermen, is in the process of developing a new identity. Along the Pacific Coast lie three coves, which fill with birthing gray whales and boats of whale-watchers from December to April.

6 Baja California Norte.
Drive right on through the border towns of Tijuana, Tecate, and Mexicali—safety is questionable these days—and head to the beauty and charm of towns farther south. The beaches and seafood of Rosarito, Ensenada, and San Felipe draw retirees, RVers, and, during spring break, crowds of wild college kids; the Valle de Guadalupe provides respite and fantastic wine to those willing to stray from Napa. Farther south, Highway 1 traverses vacant landscapes of mountains and cacti, then enters Baja California Sur at Guerrero Negro.

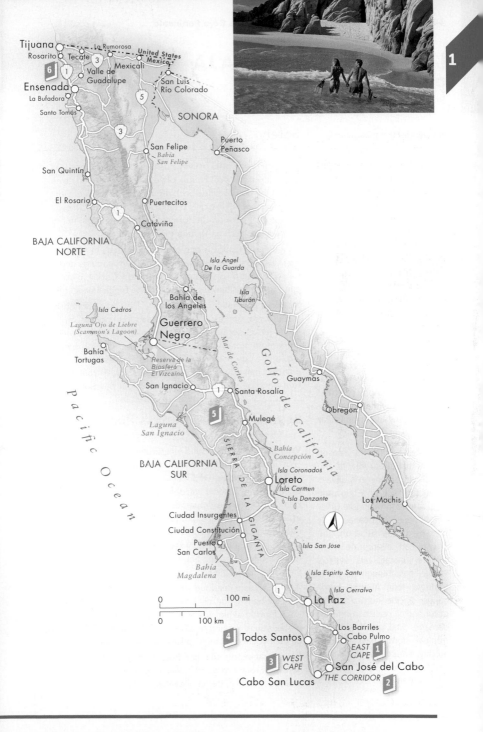

Tijuana
Rosarito
Tecate
La Rumorosa
United States
Mexico
6
1
Valle de
Guadalupe
Mexicali
Ensenada
La Bufadora
San Luis
Río Colorado
5
Santo Tomás
SONORA
3
San Felipe
Bahía
San Felipe
Puerto
Peñasco
San Quintín
El Rosario
Puertecitos
1
Cataviña

BAJA CALIFORNIA
NORTE

Isla Ángel
De la Guarda

Isla Cedros
Bahía de
los Angeles
Isla
Tiburón

Laguna Ojo de Liebre
(Scammon's Lagoon)
Guerrero
Negro

Bahía
Tortugas
Reserva de la
Biosferá
El Vizcaíno

San Ignacio
1
Santa Rosalía
Guaymas

Mar de Cortés

Golfo de California

Laguna
San Ignacio
5
Mulegé
Obregón

Bahía
Concepción

BAJA CALIFORNIA
SUR
Isla Coronados
Isla Carmen
Loreto
Isla Danzante
Los Mochis

Ciudad Insurgentes
Ciudad Constitución
Puerto
San Carlos

SIERRA DE LA GIGANTA

Isla San Jose

Pacific Ocean

Bahía
Magdalena

Isla Espirtu Santu

Isla Cerralvo

| 0 | 100 mi |
| 0 | 100 km |

1
La Paz

Los Barriles
Cabo Pulmo

4 Todos Santos
EAST
CAPE
1

3 WEST
CAPE
San José del Cabo
2
Cabo San Lucas
THE CORRIDOR

LOS CABOS AND BAJA PLANNER

When to Go

Although Los Cabos hotels are often busiest starting in mid-October for the sportfishing season, the high season doesn't technically begin until mid-December, running through the end of Easter week. It's during this busy period that you'll pay the highest hotel and golf rates. Spring break, which can stagger over several weeks in March and April, is also a particularly crowded and raucous time. Downtown Cabo gets very busy, especially on weekend nights, throughout the year. Whale-watching season (December–April) coincides with high season, but whalewatchers tend to stay in La Paz and Loreto, not Los Cabos.

The Pacific hurricane season mirrors that of the Atlantic and Caribbean, so there is always a slight chance of a hurricane from August through late October. Although hurricanes rarely hit Los Cabos head-on, the effects can reverberate when a large hurricane hits Mexico's Pacific coast. Though much less frequent than Atlantic hurricanes, Pacific hurricanes do occur and can cause significant damage. Still, most summer tropical storms pass through quickly, even during the Cape's so-called short "rainy" season, from July through October.

Safety

Mexican drug cartel activity has turned border areas into no-go areas the past couple of years. We've scaled coverage of the border cities back dramatically for this edition, but hope that will be only a temporary measure. Other than stopping for border formalities, drive through, not to, communities such as Tijuana and Mexicali.

Although Los Cabos is one of the safest areas in Mexico, it's still important to be aware of your surroundings and to follow standard safety precautions. In Los Cabos, pickpocketing and petty thievery are usually the biggest concerns.

Standard precautions always apply: Distribute your cash, credit cards, and IDs between a deep front pocket, an inside jacket pocket, and a hidden money pouch. Don't carry more money in your wallet than you plan on spending for the day or evening. And, most important, leave your passport behind, with your other valuables, in your in-room safe—and be sure to make copies of your passport.

Buying a Piece of Baja's Paradise

With an idyllic, year-round temperature averaging 78°F (26°C), and a location just hours away from many parts of the United States, who wouldn't want to own a piece of Baja? Here is some valuable advice from agent Axel Estrada of Paradise Properties (⊕ www.searchincabo.com), in Los Cabos. Having a broader view of "Los Cabos"—once delineated in the industry as the two Cabo-city bookends and the corridor between them—will open up options for you. Growth is heading up both capes: to La Ribera on the east, and on the Pacific side, up to Todos Santos.

A one-bedroom condo in a good area, but a few blocks from the beach, can still be had for $80,000–$100,000 USD, Estrada explains. For a medium-size house in the same locale, you're looking at $200,000–$400,000 USD. Being on the beachfront pushes prices up to seven or eight figures.

Since most expats who purchase Baja property don't live here year-round, a good system of property management makes it easier to be an absentee landlord.

Sportfishing Conservation

For decades, anglers wanted their trophies, a photo of themselves with their fish, and a sign showing the weight of the vanquished. Then came the realization that the fish didn't need to be killed, and the conservation movement began encouraging a "catch-and-release" program, returning to the water whatever wasn't to be eaten. In recent years, the world's sportfishing factions have been battling Mexico's powerful commercial union because the Mexican government enacted a law that would enable Mexico's many commercial long-liners, as well as gillnet and seiner boats, to fish very close to Mexico's coast, practices that would quickly decimate the fragile fish stocks off Mexico's west coast and into the Sea of Cortez. For more information, go to ⊕ www.seawatch.org. The Billfish Foundation is leading the fight against the newest Mexican shark regulation, which would allow boats within 24 km (15 mi) of the Sea of Cortez and 32 km (20 mi) of Baja's west coast, and does not restrict by catch. It supports a bill in Mexico's congress at this writing that would roll the no-commercial-fishing zones back to 80 km (50 mi) offshore, and to 161 km (100 mi) off the coast of Los Cabos. A 2009 study conducted by the foundation concluded that sportfishing provides, directly or indirectly, 24,000 jobs and an annual $630 million to Los Cabos' economy. More info can be found at ⊕ www.billfish.org.

Holidays

Banks and government offices close during Holy Week, Cinco de Mayo, Día de la Raza, and Independence Day, and occasionally for other religious holidays; hours and staff are reduced Christmas through New Year's Day.

One of Los Cabos' most enjoyable celebrations is the Festival of Rhythms, Colors and Flavors (Festival de Ritmos, Colores y Sabores), which takes place in late November/early December. It's a weeklong celebration of food, drink, and music, and showcases the area's top restaurants.

Mexico's public holidays include New Year's Day (January 1); Constitution Day (February 5); Benito Juárez's Birthday (March 21); Good Friday (Friday before Easter Sunday); Easter Sunday; Labor Day (May 1); Cinco de Mayo (May 5); St. John the Baptist Day (June 24); Independence Day (September 16); Día de la Raza (October 12); Día de los Muertos (November 2); Anniversary of the Mexican Revolution (November 20); and Christmas (December 25).

Getting Here

1

Once upon a time, the majority of Cabo's visitors were anglers primarily from Southern California and the west coast.

These days, however, they fly in nonstop to Los Cabos from all over the United States, and to Loreto and La Paz from some U.S. cities. Via nonstop service, Los Cabos is about 2½ hours from Los Angeles, 2¾ hours from Houston, 2¾ hours from Dallas/Fort Worth, and 2 hours from Phoenix.

Flying time from New York to Mexico City, where you must switch planes to continue to Los Cabos, is five hours. Los Cabos is about a two-hour flight from Mexico City.

As far as Baja Norte is concerned, you have a few options other than flying in to Tijuana (which doesn't receive many international flights). Many people buy Mexican car insurance in San Diego and drive on in.

If you don't live that close, you can fly into San Diego, rent a car, and drive down (be sure to check with rental companies as their policies differ on this).

LOS CABOS AND THE BAJA PENINSULA TOP ATTRACTIONS

Cacti Mundo, San José del Cabo, Los Cabos

(A) You've seen them everywhere in Baja, but may not know their names. The Cacti Mundo ("Cactus World") botanical gardens in San José del Cabo collect this plant group all in one place and are just the ticket for everything you want to know about cacti and succulents. The facility displays nearly 5,000 species of plants from all over the world, including many rare cacti native to Baja.

Iglesia de San Ignacio Kadakaamán, San Ignacio, Baja Sur

(B) How to choose which among the peninsula's many mission churches to visit? For both its size and ornamentation, we recommend this 1728 house of worship dedicated to the Jesuit order's very own founder, St. Ignatius Loyola, complete with elaborate facade. The structure underwent extensive restoration in the 1970s, and an active worship schedule keeps this a living, breathing church, rather than a musty museum piece.

Land's End, Cabo San Lucas, Los Cabos

(C) This is it. It's the end of the line. The sight of the towering granite formations here lets you know that you've arrived at the tip of the Baja Peninsula. El Arco ("the arch") has become Los Cabos' most iconic symbol—an odd choice, perhaps, for something so stark and natural to represent a place so entrenched in commerce. Yet all the sleek hotels and shopping malls nearby can't deflect from the end-of-the-world feel you get when you arrive.

Malecón, La Paz, Baja Sur

(D) Quick: what's Baja's best oceanside walk? The marina boardwalk in Cabo San Lucas gets most votes, but for a far more authentic Mexican experience, head three hours north to the seaside promenade in southern Baja's largest city. This is urban renewal at its best, with attractive landscaping for the entire 5 km (3 mi) of the malecón's length. The walkway comes alive as evening approaches and residents throng the walkway for their evening paseo.

Parque Nacional Marino Cabo Pulmo, Cabo Pulmo, Baja Sur

(E) The 25,000-year-old coral reef here is the only living coral reef on North America's west coast. Its eight reef fingers attract more than 2,000 different kinds of marine organisms, including almost 250 species of tropical fish. Toss in the sunken wreck of a tuna boat nearby and you have one of Baja's top snorkeling and diving destinations.

Valle de Guadalupe, near Ensenada, Baja Norte

(F) You may know about Corona beer, tequila, and margaritas, but did you know Mexico had a wine industry? An anomaly in Baja's desert climate produces the Guadalupe Valley, a cooler, Napa-like pocket that cultivates several varieties of grapes and produces some of the world's best (but not best known) wines. Many of the vineyards are open to tours and samplings, some to meals and overnight stays, and all, of course, to purchases.

TOP EXPERIENCES

Catch and Release a Marlin

Let's start with the sport that originally put Los Cabos on the map, and keeps it there—fishing! Even for someone who has never been fishing, plying the indigo seas while savoring the stunning scenery from a new perspective makes for an amazing day. Boats from 23 to 110 feet long are available, and you can pay from $250 to $5,000 for the experience. Everyone, even non-anglers, will get excited when the line goes screaming out behind a jumping marlin, as it "greyhounds" off into the ocean. Catch (and, of course, release) all billfish—e.g. marlin and sailfish—but enjoy telling your tale

"Under the Boardwalk, Down by the Sea"

If you arrive in Cabo San Lucas on a cruise, you'll first step on land at its marina boardwalk, where cruise ships tender passengers. Approach from any other direction and you'll still find your way here. Lined with restaurants and bars that are terrific for people-watching, and complete with an air-conditioned shopping mall to pop into when the afternoon heat gets you down, perhaps no place in Baja pulses to the tourist beat quite the way Cabo's marina does.

Yes, it's undeniably touristy, but we look at it this way: can all those visitors possibly be wrong? And we suspect you won't be able to get that song, released by the Drifters and covered by the Beach Boys, out of your head.

Go Whale-Watching

The giant gray whales are snowbirds, too. Thousands of these mammoth cetaceans make their lengthy migrations between December and April, swimming nearly 10,000 km (6,000 mi) from Alaska and Canada to mate and give birth in Baja's warm(ish), west-coast lagoons; they make the trip without even stopping to eat, they're in such a rush to get to Mexico (we know how they feel).

Once the whales arrive, they cavort, spyhop (poking their heads straight out of the water), and generally enjoy the seas of Baja, just like their human counterparts. A number of whale-watching tours are available, most of them centered around Scammon's Lagoon, San Ignacio Lagoon, and Magdalena Bay, where tourists go in *pangas* (small boats) out into the lagoons. Oftentimes, the whales and their new babies will approach the boat, rubbing against it, and looking with their sweet brown eyes at the people inside.

Enjoy a Maya Temazcal

Los Cabos has the spas, where giving yourself up to utter pampering and exotic treatments is just another day's vacation, but don't forget about the *temazcal*. This Maya sweat-lodge experience, at the Pueblo Bonito Pacífica Holistic Retreat and elsewhere, is spiritual in nature, working over your psyche as much as your body. Lead by a *temazcalero*, this ritual is a group experience, within a traditional enclosure, and incorporates bathing, steam at high temperatures, and medicinal plants. It requires an almost meditative commitment because extreme emotions often surface in these conditions. Your reward? A feeling of having been completely cleansed and renewed.

Art and Wine in San José del Cabo

Art lovers unite on Thursday evenings in San José del Cabo, where the Art District Association is behind the Thursday Night Art Walk. With at least 15 impressive art galleries to visit in several square blocks, the district is located north and west of the town's centuries-old church.

The art walk takes place from 5 to 9 PM, November through June. The informal, unguided tour makes for a fun opportunity to drink (free) wine, and be amazed by all forms and variations of art, from amber jewelry, photography, and Huichol beadwork to very pricey sculptures from top Mexican artists.

Hit the Surf

It's during the hot summer months, when tropical storms kick up giant waves, that you'll find the best surfing in these parts. If you are inspired to learn the sport, a number of tour operators offer lessons. By far, though, the easiest way to make this happen is to book a room at the boutique **Cabo Surf Hotel**, with perhaps the most prime Los Cabos surf location. Right out in front of the hotel are three top breaks, Old Man's, La Roca, and Acapulquito, all gentle, forgiving, feathering waves. The Mike Doyle Surf School has taken up residence in the hotel, and has 60 boards of all sizes, shapes, lengths, and compositions to encourage the beginner as well as outfit more advanced surfers.

Tequila Tasting

What better place to enjoy and learn about tequila than in festive Los Cabos? Whether it's tossing down a couple of 70¢ shots of Cuervo, ordering $2.80 shots of Don Julio with your lobster omelet at the open-air Crazy Lobster restaurant, taking a tequila class at Pancho's Restaurant & Tequila Museum from a certified "Tequila Ambassador," or enjoying the world's finest tequilas in the exclusive ambience of Las Ventanas al Paraíso resort, this is the place to put tequila to the test.

Without a doubt, every bar and restaurant in Los Cabos offers a great selection; there are at least four "local" Cabo tequilas (though they're not grown or bottled

in Baja but on Mexico's mainland, and then given company labels). Cabo Wabo makes a famed line of tequilas, the Cabo Surf Hotel has its own namesake in the tequila world, as has the Hotel California in Todos Santos. Las Varitas, a popular Cabo dance club located near ME Cabo Hotel by Meliá, also slapped its name on the stuff.

Enjoy the Fiestas

Festivals include Carnaval (February or March, before Lent); Semana Santa (March or April, the week before Easter Sunday); Día de Nuestra Señora de Guadalupe (December 12); and Las Posadas (December 16–25). Don't expect to see much folkloric tradition in avowedly secular Cabo San Lucas or the Corridor. For that festival flavor of old Mexico, head to San José del Cabo, Todos Santos, La Paz, Loreto, or other smaller, more traditional communities.

GREAT ITINERARIES

Each of these fills one day. Together they touch on some of Los Cabos' most quintessential experiences from boating out to El Arco to visiting the blown-glass factory, and from grabbing a beer at a local brewpub to discovering Cabo's "Fiesta Zone."

Learn the Lay of the Land

On Day 1 take it easy, enjoy your hotel, take a swim in the pool, and get to know the beach in your general area. If staying in Cabo, meander around town, mentally noting the many restaurants and shops on the way that you might wish to sample later. Walking the length of the marina boardwalk will introduce you to Cabo's notorious party central: From the boardwalk's western end beginning near the **Marina Fiesta Hotel**, you'll pass through the marina's "Fiesta Zone" (along which is the infamous **Nowhere ¿Bar?**). If you make it all the way to **Tesoro Hotel**, you've essentially completed the marina walk. Note that it's here where you can catch a boat for sunset cruises, whale-watching, and sportfishing.

Traversing the Corridor

To see the Corridor and make it over to San José del Cabo from Cabos San Lucas, it's most convenient and least expensive if you rent a car for a couple of days. (Taxis are frightfully expensive, and buses limit you to their schedule and stops.) Shop around for rentals and you'll be amazed at the range. Take your time driving along the Corridor, both to enjoy the sights of the coast, as well as to become accustomed to the unique traits of this quirky highway. On and off ramps are challenging, as you'll see. About mid-Corridor you pass **Santa María** and **Chileno Bay,** fun for stops to sun, swim, and snorkel. Bring your own equipment and refreshments.

As you near San José del Cabo, you can't miss the **Tiendas de Palmilla** (Palmilla Shopping Center) across from the **One&Only Palmilla Resort.** "Tiendas" comprises upscale shops and some excellent restaurants, including Nick-San. (Walmart, Costco, and Sam's Club have also set up shop along Highway 1 for more basic shopping needs.) Heading farther east, you'll shortly see a turnout and large parking lot—a great panoramic overlook of the Sea of Cortez. It's a lovely spot to watch the surf at the **Old Man's** break, to your right, in front of the **Cabo Surf Hotel.**

Beachy, Happy People

For a small deposit, many hotels provide beach towels, coolers, and umbrellas, or you can rent these from **Trader Dicks,** just west of La Jolla de los Cabos Resort near the Costa Azul beach. Dicks also fixes good box lunches. To get to the most pristine beaches along the Sea of Cortez, head east out of San José del Cabo by car. At the corner of Boulevard Mijares and Calle Benito Juárez in San José, turn east at the sign marked PUEBLO LA PLAYA. The paved street soon becomes a dirt road that leads to the small fishing villages of **La Playa** (The Beach) and **La Playita** (The Little Beach), about 1½ km (½ mi) from San José. As of this writing, construction of a marina resort complex is under way here; watch for road detours.

From La Playita, drive 60 km (37 mi) up the coast to the ecological reserve **Cabo Pulmo,** home of Baja Sur's largest coral reef. Water depths range from 15 to 130 feet, and colorful marine animals live among the reef and many shipwrecks. When hunger pangs call, stroll up the beach from Cabo Pulmo to **Tito's** for a fish taco and an ice-cold *cerveza.* Try to get back to La Playa by late afternoon to

1

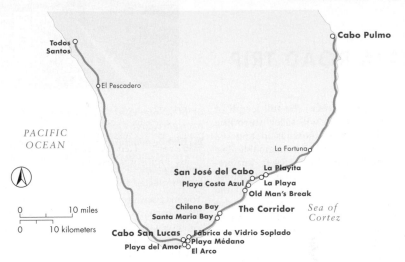

avoid driving the East Cape's dirt road at night. Stop for some fresh seafood and a frozen margarita at **Buzzard's Bar and Grill** right near the beach just north of La Playa. San José is 10 minutes away.

Artsy Los Cabos

Set out from Cabo San Lucas for the **Fábrica de Vidrio Soplado** (Blown-Glass Factory)—a bit hard to find if you're driving yourself. First head toward San José on Avenida Lázaro Cárdenas, which becomes Highway 1. Turn left at the stoplight and signs for the bypass to Todos Santos; then look for signs to the factory. It's in an industrial area two blocks northwest of Highway 1. At the factory, you can watch the talented artisans use a process little changed since it was first developed some 4,000 years ago.

From the factory, head east for the 20-minute drive to San José del Cabo. Park at the south end of Boulevard Mijares near the Tropicana Inn, since traffic tends to get congested from here on in. Grab some lunch at **Don Emiliano**, an upscale Mexican restaurant presided over by one of Mexico's top woman chefs. Then stroll through the central plaza, or zócalo, directly in front of the **Iglesia San José** (mission church) and take in the several art galleries north and west of the church.

For dinner, the **Baja Brewing Company**, located on Avenida Morelos, has a tasty San José Especial cerveza, and offers international pub fare to go along with it.

Alternatively, from the glass factory, head north on Highway 19 for the one-hour drive to the laid-back town of Todos Santos. Lunch at **El Gusto!** restaurant in the Posada La Poza hotel promises to be one of the most sumptuous you'll get in Baja. (Reservations are a must.) Spend the afternoon visiting in-town galleries near the **Misión de Nuestra Señora de Pilar** (Mission of Our Lady of Pilar) church.

Adventurous Explorations

From the Cabo San Lucas marina, board one of the glass-bottom boats that depart regularly for the dramatic **Arco** (Arch) and **Playa del Amor** (Lover's Beach), the sandy stretch in El Arco's shadow. (Or you can head out in a kayak or tour boat from Playa Médano.) The boat ride is half the fun, especially if you cruise by the sea lion colony on the rocks near the arch. Swim and snorkel only on the Sea of Cortez side; the Pacific side is too rough. When you're ready to go, board the next boat back to the marina or paddle back to shore. This is a good time to settle in for a leisurely lunch on **Playa Médano**. Order a cold drink and some grilled fish at the **Office**.

BAJA ROAD TRIP

A drive up (or down) the full length of the Baja Peninsula will surely introduce you to some of the most fascinating and unexpected desert beauty imaginable. The Baja Peninsula may be a desert, but prepare yourself for the striking turquoise lagoons of Bahía Concepción and the oddly twisted, humanlike *cirio* trees, also known as boojum trees, found in the mid-peninsula Cataviña desert region—they appear almost like apparitions along the 1,656-km-long (1,029-mi-long) highway. Driving Baja is an absolute adventure, but be forewarned and prepared. Most of the Baja highway is one lane in each direction with no shoulders.

Don't drive into Mexico without first purchasing Mexican car insurance. There are a number of reputable drive-through insurance agencies along Interstate 5 in San Diego prior to crossing the border at Tijuana. Once insured, get through Tijuana. Jump onto the *Cuota*, or Toll Road, that will take you through to Ensenada.

Enjoy this wide, well-maintained, scenic coastal highway with stunning panoramas while you can—it's the last you'll see for some 1,600 km (1,000 mi). Puerto Nuevo, or "Newport," is known for its many, and we mean *many*, lobster restaurants—perhaps 50, or maybe more.

Consider renting an auto from **CABAJA Rental Cars**, in San Diego. It's one of the few American car-rental companies that permits, and encourages, taking cars south of the border. ✉ *9245 Jamacha Blvd., Spring Valley, CA* ☎ *888/470–7368 or 619/470–7368* ⊕ *www.cabaja.com.*

For affordable insurance for your own car, that covers you in Mexico, try **Lewis & Lewis Insurance.** ✉ *8929 Wilshire Blvd., Suite 200, Beverly Hills, CA* ☎ *310/657–1112*

or *800/966–6830* ⊕ *www.mexicanautoinsurance.com.*

■**TIP→** Be mindful of the immense distance you've set out to cover and plan your stops and stays before your trip begins. Also plan for unexpected diversions.

You may wish to spend some time in festive Ensenada, shopping and strolling the large city's many colorful streets, and along the marina. Once you've passed the Tijuana border/Ensenada sprawl, you'll begin to experience the real Baja highway. It narrows, winds, and snakes up and down, into the mountains and then back down to the coast. The next stop along Highway 1 is San Quintín. (Mexico assigns its north–south federal highways odd numbers, and starts the sequence on the Pacific coast, working the way up in digits as you move east. That's why Baja's main highway gets such a premier designation.) If you find that it's getting late, don't plan to continue your drive at night.

South of San Quintín, the highway leaves the west coast and heads into central Baja, into the desert. Make sure you fuel up the car, topping off the tank, in El Rosario. It's a long way to the next gas station. The next couple of hundred miles take you right through the middle of Baja's unique Vizcaíno Desert, a biosphere reserve, and one of the world's few fog deserts.

Here you'll drive among giant boulders the size of houses, and into the Valle de los Cirios, of the oddly shaped cirio trees, likened to upside-down carrots, some of which live to be 350 years old. Much of the wild Baja interior has been set aside as national parks, biosphere reserves, and other protected areas. Rocky side roads through cirios, elephant trees, and incense trees lead to old missions and ancient cave

paintings, *pinturas repuestres,* which are older still. Use the little town of Cataviña as a headquarters for visiting this region.

You'll enjoy great views of Baja's desert flora and fauna from here south to Guerrero Negro—it's about a five- to six-hour drive from El Rosario—the town that straddles the border between Baja California (north) and Baja California Sur (south). A police checkpoint here will ask to see your Mexican tourist card, which you received when you crossed the border in Tijuana. Guerrero Negro is a large, though not very touristy, town with a nice selection of hotels and in the winter months is alive and hopping with whale-watchers. Hundreds of whales congregate in nearby Scammon's Lagoon to give birth, mate, and enjoy the warm water.

From here the highway switches southeast across the width of the peninsula, past the small oasis town of San Ignacio built alongside giant groves of date trees and the pretty Spanish mission, Misión San Ignacio Kadakkaamán. Whale-watching tours to the San Ignacio Lagoon, and ecotours, including visits to Indian cave paintings, are available here, too. On the way to Santa Rosalía, you'll encounter a severe downgrade called the Cuesta del Infierno, with wild switchbacks and few guardrails. The translation of the name, "the hill of hell," seems apt, so take your time.

Santa Rosalía has an interesting mining history, and a church designed and built by Gustave Eiffel (of the tower fame). You're now passing through areas, the highway included, that suffered damage from September 2009's Hurricane Jimena. (Repairs are ongoing.) About an hour south of Santa Rosalía is Mulegé, a tranquil town with a wealth of eco-and

adventure tours available, from whale-watching to excellent fishing.

Plan on spending a couple of hours (or a couple of days) enjoying the mesmerizing 40-km-long (25-mi-long) Bahía Concepción, just south of Mulegé. Numerous coves and inlets here make for great snorkeling, boating, camping, and hiking.

Just a few hours south is Loreto, a town going through major changes. Once the quintessential small Mexican fishing village, it's now the site of a massive resort–community development called **Loreto Bay,** whose development is languishing with the economy. At the moment, Loreto remains a quaint Baja town, with a sedate town center, and standard lodgings. For a real treat, try the charming three-room (or Mongolian-style yurt) **Sukasa;** make reservations well in advance of your drive.

From Loreto, it can be a one-day drive into Cabo San Lucas. But there's still *mucho* Baja to see and experience. So, if you still have the time, there's **Bahía Magdalena** on the west coast, another popular whale-watching stop, the peaceful capital city of La Paz (on the east), the art-gallery town of Todos Santos (on the west), and the East Cape.

Once you reach Cabo San Lucas, head straight for El Médano Beach, throw on your swimsuit, and dive into the ocean.

CRUISING TO LOS CABOS

Cruise lines with itineraries to Los Cabos and Baja California include Carnival, Celebrity, Crystal, Cunard, Holland America, Lindblad Expeditions, Norwegian, Oceania, Princess, Regent Seven Seas, Royal Caribbean, Seabourn, and Silversea. Most depart from Los Angeles (Long Beach), San Diego, San Francisco, Seattle, Fort Lauderdale, Miami, New York, San Juan, Vancouver, and even Southampton, England, or Bridgetown, Barbados. Most cruises to Baja dock at Cabo San Lucas, with a few calling at Ensenada, La Paz, and Loreto.

Carnival. Carnival is known for its large-volume cruises and template approach to its ships, two factors that probably help keep fares accessible. Boats in its Mexican fleet have more than 1,000 staterooms; the newest ship, *Splendor,* was inaugurated in 2008. Seven-night Mexican Riviera trips out of Los Angeles or San Diego hit Cabo San Lucas and, occasionally, La Paz, among other Pacific ports in Mexico. Carnival wrote the book on Baja-only cruises, with three- or four-day itineraries on *Elation* and *Paradise* out of Los Angeles or San Diego to Ensenada. Las Vegas–style shows and passenger participation is the norm. ☎ 888/227–6482 ⊕ *www. carnival.com.*

Celebrity. Spacious accommodations and the guest-lectured Enrichment Series are hallmarks of Celebrity cruises. Its *Millennium, Mercury,* and *Constellation* ply the Panama Canal east- and westbound on 13- to 17-day itineraries, hitting Cabo San Lucas along the way, with an extensive choice of departure ports (Fort Lauderdale, Los Angeles, Miami, San Diego, San Juan, or Seattle). ☎ 800/647–2251 ⊕ *www.celebritycruises.com.*

Crystal. Crystal is known for combining large ships with grandeur, opulence, and impeccable service. Its *Crystal Symphony* calls at Cabo San Lucas on a variety of itineraries from New York (19 days), Miami (13 or 14 days), and Los Angeles (10 days). Another cruise out of Los Angeles also takes in La Paz and Loreto. ☎ 800/722–0021 ⊕ *www.crystalcruises. com.*

Cunard. It's an infrequent, but festive, occasion when Cunard's luxury liner *Queen Victoria* calls at Cabo San Lucas on select 16-day Panama Canal itineraries that begin in Los Angeles and end in Fort Lauderdale. The port also features in a 40-day cruise from Los Angeles to Southampton. A return 40-day itinerary that begins in England calls at Ensenada before arrival in Los Angeles. ☎ 800/728–6273 ⊕ *www.cunard.com.*

Holland America. The venerable Holland America line leaves from and returns to San Diego. Its eight-day Sea of Cortez cruise on the MS *Veendam* calls at Cabo San Lucas and Loreto. An expanded 14-day itinerary begins in Vancouver, British Columbia. Various seven-day Mexican Riviera cruises on the *Veendam* or MS *Oosterdam* call at Cabo San Lucas and other Mexican ports. ☎ 877/932–4259 ⊕ *www.hollandamerica.com.*

Lindblad Expeditions. Lindblad's smaller *Sea Lion* and *Sea Bird* take you where the other guys can't go, for an active, nature-themed Baja cruise experience. Eight- to 15-day excursions embark in La Paz and nose around the islands of the Sea of Cortez. Its kayaks and Zodiacs launch from the ship to provide you with unparalleled opportunity to watch whales, dolphins, and seabirds. ☎ 800/397–3348 ⊕ *www. expeditions.com.*

Norwegian Cruise Lines. Its tag line is "whatever floats your boat," and Norwegian *is* known for its relatively freewheeling style and variety of activities and excursions. Seven- or 11-day cruises on the *Sun* or *Star* depart from San Francisco or Los Angeles, with full days in Cabo San Lucas and a half day in La Paz on the longer itinerary. Both include calls at other Mexican Pacific ports. ☎ 800/327–7030 ⊕ *www.ncl.com.*

Oceania. "Intimate" and "cozy" are terms that get bandied about to describe the ships of Oceania, a relative newcomer to the cruise scene. Before arrival at Cabo San Lucas or any port, you can attend a lecture to acquaint you with its history, culture, and tradition. The *Regatta* stops here on a 16-day cruise out of Miami. A 10-day Mexico-only cruise from Los Angeles stays in port overnight, giving you a rare cruise opportunity to take in nighttime Los Cabos. ☎ 800/531–5619 ⊕ *www.oceaniacruises.com.*

Princess Cruises. Not so great for small children but good at keeping tweens, teens, and adults occupied, Princess strives to offer luxury at an affordable price. Its cruises may cost a little more than others, but you also get more for the money: large rooms, varied menus, and personalized service. Seven- to 11-day Mexican Riviera cruises aboard the *Sapphire Princess, Sea Princess,* or *Star Princess* start in Los Angeles or San Francisco and hit Los Cabos and other Pacific ports. Shorter three- or four-day trips out of Los Angeles call at Ensenada. ☎ 800/774–6237 ⊕ *www.princess.com.*

Regent Seven Seas Cruises. RSSC's luxury liners *Mariner, Navigator,* and *Voyager* originate in Los Angeles or Fort Lauderdale and call at Cabo San Lucas on select Panama Canal and transpacific itineraries. Some stop here for a half day; others stay in port longer, making RSSC a rare cruise company that lets you sample Los Cabos' evening diversions. ☎ 877/505–5370 ⊕ *www.rssc.com.*

Royal Caribbean. Royal Caribbean's 7- through 12-night Mexican Riviera cruises on *Mariner of the Seas* or *Radiance of the Seas* originate in Los Angeles or San Diego and call at Cabo San Lucas, among other Mexican Pacific ports. Shorter Baja-only itineraries stop at Cabo San Lucas, and sometimes Ensenada. Striving to appeal to a broad clientele, the line offers lots of activities and services as well as many shore excursions. ☎ 800/521–8611 ⊕ *www.royalcaribbean.com.*

Seabourn. Think megayachts with sophisticated, personalized service when you hear the name "Seabourn." The line's newest ships, *Odyssey* (2009) and *Sojourn* (2010), call at Cabo San Lucas on a variety of itineraries departing from Fort Lauderdale, on a relatively brief (by Seabourn standards) 16-day cruise all the way up to a 108-day world itinerary. ☎ 800/929–9391 ⊕ *www.seabourn.com.*

Silversea. Loads of activities, including guest lectures, are the hallmark of a cruise aboard Silversea's luxury liners. Its *Silver Shadow* calls at Cabo San Lucas on 7-day itineraries from Los Angeles and 15- or 16-day cruises from Fort Lauderdale. The *Silver Cloud* plies the route between Barbados and Los Angeles, 17 days each way, with a stop at Ensenada on the eastbound cruise, and Cabo San Lucas, on the westbound. ☎ 888/722–9955 ⊕ *www.silversea.com.*

WEDDINGS AND HONEYMOONS

Mexico is a growing wedding and honeymoon destination. Many area hotels—from boutiques to internationally known brands—offer honeymoon packages and professional wedding planners. Although Mexican law dictates that an obligatory civil ceremony must accompany the Big Event, you can get married in a house of worship, on a beach, at a hotel chapel, or on a yacht or sailboat.

Choosing the Perfect Place. Los Cabos is growing in popularity as a Mexican wedding and honeymoon destination. Many couples choose to marry on the beach, often at sunset because it's cooler and more comfortable for everyone; others chuck the whole weather conundrum and marry in an air-conditioned resort ballroom.

The luxury of enjoying your wedding and honeymoon in one place has a cost: you may find it hard to have some alone time with your sweetie with all your family and friends on hand for days before and days after the main event. Consider booking an all-inclusive, which has plenty of meal options and activities to keep your guests busy. This will make it easier for them to respect your privacy and stick to mingling with you and your spouse at planned times.

Time of Year. Planning according to the weather can be critical for a successful Los Cabos wedding. If you're getting married in your bathing suit, you might not mind some heat and humidity, but will your venue—and your future mother-in-law—hold up under the summer heat? We recommend substituting the traditional June wedding that's so suitable for New England and Nova Scotia with one held between November and February. March through June is usually dry but extremely warm and humid.

By July, the heat can be unbearable for an outdoor afternoon wedding. Summer rains, rarely voluminous in Los Cabos, begin to fall here in July. Sometimes this means a light sprinkle that reduces heat and humidity; occasionally it means a downpour. Although hurricanes are rarer along the Pacific than the Caribbean, they can occur August through late October and even early November. For an outdoor wedding, establish a detailed backup plan in case the weather lets you down.

Finding a Wedding Planner. Hiring a wedding planner will minimize stress for all but the simplest of ceremonies. The slogan of one firm here is: IF YOU HAVE THE GROOM AND THE DRESS, WE CAN DO THE REST. And a planner really can. A year or more in advance, the planner will, among other things, help choose the venue, find a florist, and arrange for a photographer and musicians.

The most obvious place to find a wedding planner is at a resort hotel that becomes wedding central: providing accommodations for you and your guests, the wedding ceremony venue, and the restaurant or ballroom for the reception. But you can also hire an independent wedding coordinator; just Google "Los Cabos wedding" and you'll get tons of hits. Unless you're fluent in Spanish, make sure the person who will be arranging one of your life's milestones speaks and understands English well. (Most here do.) Ask for references, and check them.

When interviewing a planner, talk about your budget, and ask about costs. Are there hourly fees or one fee for the whole event? How available will the consultant and his or her assistants be? Which

vendors are used and why? How long have they been in business? Request a list of the exact services they'll provide, and get a proposal in writing. If you don't feel this is the right person or agency for you, try someone else. Cost permitting, it's helpful to meet the planner in person.

Requirements. Getting a bona fide wedding planner will obviously facilitate completing the required paperwork and negotiating the legal requirements for marrying in Mexico. Blood tests must be done upon your arrival, but not more than 14 days before the ceremony. All documents must be translated by an authorized translator from the destination, and it's important to send these documents certified mail to your wedding coordinator at least a month ahead of the wedding.

You'll also need to submit an application for a marriage license as well as certified birth certificates (bring the original with you to Los Cabos, and send certified copies ahead of time). If either party is divorced or widowed, official death certificate or divorce decree must be supplied, and you must wait one year to remarry after the end of the previous marriage. (There's no way around this archaic requirement, still on the books, designed to ensure that no lingering pregnancy remains from a former marriage. It doesn't matter whether you're 25 or 75.) The bride, groom, and four witnesses will also need to present passports and tourist cards. Wedding planners can round up witnesses if you don't have enough or any.

Since religious weddings aren't officially recognized in Mexico, even for citizens, a civil ceremony (*matrimonio civil*) is required, thus making your marriage valid in your home country as well. (It's the equivalent of being married in front of a justice of the peace.) Cabo San Lucas and San José del Cabo each have one civil judge who performs marriages, a good reason to start planning months in advance. Often for an extra fee, the judge will attend the site of your wedding if you prefer not to go to an office. Civil proceedings take about 10 minutes, and the wording is fixed in Spanish. Most wedding planners will provide an interpreter if you or your guests don't speak the language. For a Catholic ceremony, a priest here will expect evidence that you've attended the church's required pre-wedding sessions back home. If you're planning a Jewish wedding, you'll need to bring your rabbi with you: Los Cabos has no synagogues. Another option is to be married (secretly?) in your own country and then hold the wedding event without worrying about all the red tape.

Although same-sex civil unions are now legal in Mexico City and the northern state of Coahuila, and measures are likely or pending in six other Mexican states, Baja California Sur, where Los Cabos is located, is not one of them. A few Los Cabos wedding planners have organized same-sex commitment ceremonies, but these have no legal standing.

KIDS AND FAMILIES

Los Cabos and Baja don't necessarily leap to mind when planning a vacation with the kids. (This isn't Orlando, after all.) It's not that the region is unfriendly to children, but enjoying time with the kids here does take some advance preparation and research.

Places to Stay

Resorts: Except those that exclude children entirely, many of Los Cabos' beach hotels and all-inclusive resorts cater to families and have children's programs. A few offer little more than kid's pools, but several of the big hotels and their wealth of activities go way beyond that and make fine options for families with kids. A few of the standouts:

Dreams Los Cabos has an active Explorers Club for children ages 3–12. (The search for a beach treasure is always a crowd-pleaser.) Older kids will appreciate tennis, badminton, volleyball, and soccer.

Hilton Los Cabos's Vacation Station is geared toward kids 4–12, with bingo, painting, volleyball, piñata making, and tugs-of-war on the schedule—and that barely scratches the surface.

Villa del Palmar excels in the ages 4–12 activities program it calls its Kids Club (daily except Saturday), and its twice-a-week Kids Nights, with a special dinner, dancing, and arcade games. Ping-Pong, basketball, and volleyball will keep older kids entertained.

Those places we talked to were quick to point out that their organized kids' programs are not intended to be babysitting services. (Babysitting services are offered separately.) Most programs require reservations for participation at least 24 hours in advance. Some of the programs may entail an extra fee.

Vacation Rentals: Apartments, condos, and villas are an excellent option for families. You can cook your own food (a big money saver), spread out, and set up a home away from home, which can make everyone feel more comfortable. If you decide to go the apartment- or condo-rental route, be sure to ask about the number and size of the swimming pools and whether outdoor spaces and barbecue areas are available.

Beaches

Ah, here's the rub: if you have visions of you and your kids frolicking in the surf, revise them a bit. Many Los Cabos–area beaches are notoriously unsafe for swimming, making a day at the beach literally a day *on* the beach, rather than in the water.

Even those strands of sand that are regarded as all right for swimming have some "But don't forget" cautions: Playa Palmilla, near San José del Cabo, offers tranquil water most days, with emphasis on "most." Playa Médano, just outside Cabo San Lucas, is good for swimming, but has some very quick drop-offs. Playa del Amor, at Land's End near Cabo San Lucas, is regarded as okay for swimming on the Sea of Cortez side, but not the Pacific side. (All Pacific beaches here are no-go for swimming.)

After Dark

Nightlife here is mostly geared toward grown-ups, but a few kid-friendly dining spots do exist. Even the restaurants at Cabo Wabo and the Hard Rock Cafe have familiar food that will satisfy the most finicky of eaters, and the U.S. chains are all here, too.

All restaurants in Mexico are nonsmoking (lighting up is permitted only in outdoor-

seating areas). Both San José del Cabo and Cabo San Lucas have modern theaters that show Hollywood movies a few weeks after they premiere back home; note, though, that animated films or those rated "G" are often dubbed in Spanish.

Baja Top Five for Kids

Zoológico de Santiago, Santiago: Lions and tigers and bears, oh, my! Yes, they do exist here at this small zoo, an unexpected delight in such a remote locale. The sign shows a picture of an elephant, but don't get your hopes up on that one.

Bucaneer Queen, Cabo San Lucas: Avast ye mateys! Kids of all ages can dress up like pirates and go swashbuckling and hunting for treasure on this, one of several pirate cruises that operate out of Los Cabos. Just practice saying, "Aaaaarrrrrrrr!"

Xploration, Rosarito: Older kids and adults will enjoy the movie-themed activities here at Baja Studios, a working film studio and a branch of Fox. Moviemaking props are on display.

La Bufadora, near Ensenada: Literally "the buffalo snort," this natural tidal-wave phenomenon near Ensenada resembles a whale's blowhole. It sprays water 75 feet into the air, and everyone, no matter how curmudgeonly, delights in getting wet.

Whale-Watching, Los Cabos, Ensenada, Guerrero Negro, Loreto, Magdalena Bay: You'll find whale-watching venues up and down the peninsula. The vehicles make Baja whale-watching so special: outfitters here take you out to sea in pangas, small boats that let you get an up-close view of the magnificent beasts. We'd argue that, no matter what your age, Baja has no greater thrill.

Some Legalities

All children over the age of two require a Mexican tourist card to venture beyond the U.S. border region. Kids 15 and under require only a birth certificate to return to the United States by land from Mexico. If you fly home, everyone, regardless of age, must hold a passport to get back into the United States.

Don't forget Mexico's well-known and stringent laws regarding the entry and exit of children under 18. All minors must be accompanied by both parents. In the absence of that, the parent not present—or parents, plural, in the case of kids traveling with an organized group—must provide a notarized statement granting permission for the child to travel. Divorce, separation, or remarriage complicate these matters, but do not negate the requirement.

Even if you are traveling as a full family, we recommend erring on the side of caution if anything in your situation varies from that stereotypical 1950s *Leave It to Beaver* image of what a family looks like.

Mexican immigration officials really do know about remarriages, adoptions, blended families, multiethnic families, same-sex parents, and different last names, but copies of relevant documentation never hurt, just in case there are questions.

SNAPSHOT LOS CABOS AND BAJA PENINSULA

Where Desert Meets Sea

A visitor flying into Los Cabos will readily observe the peninsula's stark, brown terrain—indeed, it feels like you're arriving in middle of nowhere. You'll realize soon after landing that even though the tip of Baja once also resembled the rest of the dry, inhospitable, stark desert, it has been transformed into an inviting desert oasis. The desert topography, where once only cacti and a few hardy palms resided, is now punctuated by posh hotels, manicured golf courses, and brimming swimming pools. As shown by the thousands of sun-worshipping, partying people seemingly oblivious to the fact that true desert lies, literally, across Highway 1 from their beachfront hotel, Los Cabos has successfully beaten back the drylands. Pay some respect to the area's roots by taking a hike or tour around the surrounding desert landscape.

A similar phenomenon exists in the northern sector of the peninsula, with the metro area anchored by Tijuana, in reality just a continuation of U.S. Southern California. Irrigation has turned this desert into one of Mexico's prime agricultural regions.

In between far-northern Baja and Los Cabos—the peninsula logs a distance of just over 1,600 km (1,000 mi), which compares to the north–south length of Italy—expect mostly desert scrubland. Two-thirds of the land mass is desert—a continuation of the Sonora Desert in the southwest United States—and receives about 10 inches of rain per year. The remaining third of the peninsula forms a mountainous spine, technically four mountain ranges. The northernmost of these mountains are pine-forested and might make you think you've taken a wrong turn to Oregon. East of San Felipe,

Baja's highest peak, the Picacho del Diablo ("Devil's Peak"), measures 10,150 feet and is snowcapped in winter.

The Bajacalifornianos

Geography, history, and economics have conspired to give Baja California a different population mix than the rest of Mexico. The country as a whole is the quintessential *mestizo* (mixed indigenous and white/European descent) culture, but only half of *Bajacalifornianos*—the name is a mouthful—can point to any indigenous ancestry. Historically, the peninsula was a land apart, a Wild West where only the intrepid dared to venture to seek their fortunes—many Mexicans still view Baja through that prism—and has drawn a more international population. The indigenous population that does live here is a recent addition of migrants from the poorer southern states of Oaxaca and Chiapas drawn to jobs in the border cities.

Baja's population is just over 3 million according to 2009 estimates, but nearly two-thirds of that number lives near the U.S. border. The 1,600-km (1,000-mi) drive from north to south confirms this is a sparsely populated region of Mexico. The state of Baja California Sur, the southern half of the peninsula, is the country's least populous.

U.S. citizens make up around 10% of the population, with retirees, business owners who have set up shop here, or commuters who live in Mexico but work in the San Diego metro area among them.

A Multifaceted Economy

By Mexican standards, the Baja Peninsula is prosperous, but things were not always so. It was only some six decades ago that Mexico even deemed part of the region to be economically viable enough

for statehood, creating the state of Baja California north of the 28th parallel in 1953. Baja California Sur became Mexico's newest state in 1974. Prior to that, the region, once considered far-off and neglected, was administered as a territory directly from Mexico City.

This is Mexico, however, and all is relative, even today. Wages here may be double, triple, or quadruple those in the rest of the country, but you pause when you realize that $5 a day is still the national average. The presence of the maquiladora economy has brought up the on-paper average level of prosperity to the peninsula. This industry of tariff-free, export-geared manufacturing congregates on the U.S. border with more than 900 factories providing employment for more than 300,000 people, but critics decry the sweatshop conditions. Urban magnet Tijuana—whose population now stands at 1.5 million—attracts people from all over the country looking for jobs.

Agriculture and fishing contribute to Baja's economy, too. Cotton, fruit, flowers, and ornamental plants grow in the irrigated northern region. (Most of the rest of Baja California is too arid and inhospitable to support much agriculture.) Large populations of tuna, sardines, and lobster support the fishing industry.

And it goes without saying that tourism is a huge business in Baja, with an impressive $1 billion flowing into Los Cabos annually. Historically, the border region has tallied those kinds of numbers as well, but fears of drug-cartel violence have greatly eaten into tourism revenues for that area. The U.S. recession—Mexico's northern neighbor provides the bulk of Baja visitors—has dampened peninsula-wide figures somewhat, and the

well-publicized 2009 bout with H1N1 influenza, aka swine flu, kept some visitors away, although the illness was confined mostly to the central part of the country. The industry here cautiously hopes for a turnaround on both ends of the peninsula, and increased summer 2009 visitor numbers have sparked optimism.

Livin' la Vida Buena

Living the good life in Mexico—specifically in and around Los Cabos—seems to get easier year after year. Americans and Canadians are by far the biggest groups of expats, not only at the peninsula's southern tip, but in communities such as Ensenada, Rosarito, Loreto, and La Paz. In addition to those who have relocated to make Mexico their home, many foreigners have part-time retirement or vacation homes here.

Do not fall prey, though, to the dreaded "Sunshine Syndrome" that afflicts countless visitors to Los Cabos and Baja. Pause and take a deep breath if you find yourself on vacation here and starting to utter the words: "Honey, we met that nice real estate agent in the hotel bar. You know, we should buy a house here." Many succumb to the temptation, go back home and sell the farm, and return, only to find that living in Baja bears little resemblance to vacationing here. Experts suggest doing a trial rental for a few months. See if living the day-to-day life here is for you.

The sheer number of foreigners living in Los Cabos and the larger communities of Baja means that contractors and shopkeepers are used to dealing with gringos; most speak good to excellent English. Los Cabos, especially, is rich with English-language publications and opportunities for foreigners to meet up for events or volunteer work.

FLAVORS OF LOS CABOS AND BAJA

"Me sube el colesterol, mi amorcita," goes the chorus to a bouncy, popular song here. "My cholesterol's going up, my love," laments the singer about the heavy, fried Mexican food he gets at home. We take it he's never been to Baja and seen how innovative chefs here are playing around with traditional Mexican fare. Not too long ago the dining options in the Cape were pretty limited, though tastily so, with mostly *tacos de pescado y cerveza* (fish tacos and beer) or *pollo y cerveza* (chicken and beer). No longer, amigos. Walking the streets of Cabo and San José, travelers will be pleased to find grand, innovative dining experiences. Things will never go completely high-brow here because, some days, nothing beats tacos and beer.

Sibling Rivalry

The friendly inter-Cabo rivalry infuses everything—the dining scene included. Historically, it's been a comparison of quantity vs. quality: Cabo San Lucas wins hands down in sheer volume and variety of dining places. Always has, and, we suspect, always will. What San José del Cabo lacks in numbers, it makes up for with the finesse and intimacy of its dining experience. The Golden Rule of Cabo San Lucas restaurateurs was once: "As long as you keep the margaritas coming, the customer will be happy." (The mass-market eateries still adhere to this rule.) But a growing number of San Lucas dining spots have followed San José's lead and have begun to offer intimate, cozy dining experiences.

Nuevo Mexican

The terms get bandied about: "Nouveau Mexican," "Contemporary Mexican," *"Nueva Mexicana."* Ask a dozen Los Cabos chefs for a definition of today's Mexican cuisine, and you'll get a dozen different answers. Many prefer the description "Baja chic," to emphasize the peninsula's uncanny ability to find the right mix of fashionable and casual. Most experts agree that major changes have come to Mexican gastronomy in the past decade. Traditionally heavy cuisine is being altered and reinterpreted. The trend is moving toward using quality ingredients and combining traditional Mexican fare with elements of other cuisines, all the while asserting one's own interpretation. All chefs are quick to point out that they're not abandoning Mexican cooking entirely. "People visit Mexico. They do expect Mexican food," one chef told us.

Seafood

A long peninsula with 4,025 km (2,500 mi) of coastline and no point more than 110 km (70 mi) from the ocean—you do the math. Seafood figures prominently in Baja's cuisine. Baja's signature dish is the ubiquitous *taco de pescado*, or fish taco: Take strips of batter-fried fish (frequently halibut or mahimahi), wrap them, along with shredded cabbage, in a corn tortilla, and top it all off with onions, lime juice, and a dollop of sour cream. (Taco Bell will never seem the same again.) You'll find as many recipes for Baja-style seafood stew as there are cooks, who refer to the dish as or *paella* or *zarzuela*. (Ensenada is Baja's most famous spot for paella.) Any mix-and-match combination of clams, crab, shrimp, cod, sea bass, red snapper, or mahimahi could find its way into your dish, along with requisite white wine, garlic, and spices. Shellfish is frequently served here as a *coctel*, steamed with sauce and lime juice.

Beaches

WORD OF MOUTH

"Most beaches here aren't swimmable. In the town of Cabo San Lucas, Medano Beach is a fun place, with a typical set-up of beach bars and restaurants, vendors, different activities, and a beautiful view out to the rock formations."

—Suze

BEACHES PLANNER

Sun and Safety

If swimming in the ocean or the sea is important to you, be sure to research beachside resorts, as many in this region are on stretches of beach where swimming is dangerous or forbidden due to strong currents. Barely visible rocks and strong undertows make many of the beaches unsuitable for swimming. Take care when you go swimming—it can be serenely calm or dangerously turbulent, depending on the day or even the hour. The Pacific side is notorious for rogue waves and intense undertows. Also, the sun here is fierce: don't underestimate the need for waterproof sunscreen and a wide-brimmed hat.

When to Go

Nearly 360 warm and sunny days per year, few bugs, and fantastic water temperatures (70s in winter and 80s in summer) allow visitors to enjoy this natural wonderland year-round. The winter holiday season is busy, and people often book months in advance. Spring break is another busy time, though there seem to be fewer drunk college students. Late May through September is when it's hottest, and the least crowded.

Beach Etiquette

As on most beaches in Mexico, nudity is not permitted on Los Cabos beaches. If you head to a beachside bar, it's appropriate to put on a cover-up, although you'd be hard-pressed to find a strict dress code at any of these places unless you're at one of the more posh resorts. As tempting as it is to pick up seashells from the beach, be advised that U.S. Customs commonly seizes these items upon reentry to the United States. Packing a picnic or cooler for a day at the beach is a great idea, as few of the public beaches have restaurants or food vendors. A few beaches have vendors offering umbrella rentals, but if you're really keen on having one for shelter, it's best to take your own.

Beach Facilities

As a general rule, Los Cabos beaches are no-frills, with very few facilities. There is no established lifeguard program in the entire Los Cabos region. Hotels will often post a red flag on the beach to alert swimmers to strong currents and undertows, but you won't see such warnings on the stretches of public beach along the coasts.

More and more of the public beaches have toilets, but you'll still be hard-pressed to find a shower. The picnic tables, grills or fire pits, playgrounds, and other amenities common at U.S. beaches simply aren't part of the scene in Los Cabos. If you want or need anything for your day at the beach, it's best to pack it yourself. If any of the following facilities are present at a beach, we'll list it: lifeguard, toilets, showers, food concession, picnic tables, grills or fire pits, playground, parking lot, camping.

Mexican beaches are free and open to the public, although some of the resort developments along the Corridor are doing their best to keep everyone but their guests off the beaches in front of the resorts. Resort boundaries are usually very well marked; any beach after that is free for all.

2

Updated by
Georgia de
Katona

Along the rocky cliffs of the Pacific Ocean and the Sea of Cortez lie many bays, coves, and some 80-odd km (50-odd mi) of sandy beach. The waters range from translucent green to deep navy (and even a stunning turquoise on some days of the year).

Playa Médano, in Cabo San Lucas, is the most visited and active stretch of sand. Gorgeous and somewhat secluded, but by no means free of people, Playa del Amor (Lover's Beach) is five minutes across the bay by *panga* (water taxi, $7–$10). It's a great spot for swimming, although the waters can be somewhat busy with all the panga traffic. Just southwest of San José, the most popular beaches are Costa Azul and Playa Palmilla.

Most beaches in the area are seldom crowded, with the one major exception being the 3-km (2-mi) Playa Médano in Cabo San Lucas. Most people on this beach are here for the crowds, though, and there is no better place to people-watch. No other beaches are within walking distance of either Cabo San Lucas or San José del Cabo; some can be accessed by boat, but most require a car ride (unless you're staying at a Corridor hotel nearby). You can reach nearly all the beaches by bus. Taking the local public bus in Los Cabos is a safe and affordable way to access the beaches, but it takes time and it is imperative that you lug extra water if your adventuring is going to take place during the searing summer months.

SAN JOSÉ DEL CABO

Oh, the madness of it all. Here you are in a beach destination with gorgeous weather and miles of clear blue water, yet you dare not dive into the sea. Most of San José's hotels line Playa Hotelera on Paseo Malecón San José, and brochures and Web sites gleefully mention beach access. But here's the rub—though the long, level stretch of coarse brown sand is beautiful, the currents can be dangerously rough, the drop-offs are steep and close to shore, and the waves often pound brutally up onto the shore. While surfers love this type of water and flock here in droves, it's

IF YOU LIKE:	IN CABO SAN LUCAS	ALONG THE CORRIDOR	IN SAN JOSÉ DEL CABO OR BEYOND
Crystal-clear water	El Médano, Playa del Amor	Bahía Santa María	San José del Cabo's main beach (aka Playa del Sol)
Snorkeling/ Swimming	Playa del Amor (near the Sand Falls area)	Bahía Santa María, Bahía Chileno	For snorkeling, keep going to the East Cape and Cabo Pulmo area
Surfing	Monuments Beach (at eastern end of El Médano Beach)	Costa Azul stretch, Acapulquito Beach (at the Cabo Surf Hotel)	Shipwreck, 14½ km (9 mi) northeast of San José; Nine Palms, just beyond
Beachside or ocean-view bars	The Office, Mango Deck, Billygan's at El Médano Beach	Zipper's at Costa Azul, 7 Seas at Cabo Surf Hotel	Buzzard's Bar & Grill (east of La Playita)
Undiscovered beaches	El Faro Viejo Beach is difficult to access, with dangerous waves, but is a gem for sunbathing	A drive along the highway will reveal many ACCESO A PLAYA signs—be wary of waves!	Cabo Pulmo is distant—a full day's adventure—but pristine for water activities and well worth the time

extremely dangerous for the casual swimmer. Warning signs are posted up and down the beach, just in case you happen to forget. Feel free to walk along the beach to the Estero San José, play some beach volleyball, or enjoy a horseback ride along the shore. But for swimming, head to protected Playa Palmilla just a few miles west, in the Corridor.

Playa Estero. A sandy beach can be enjoyed at the mouth of the Estero San José, the lush estuary that starts just east of the Presidente InterContinental hotel. This oasis is home to more than 350 species of wildlife and vegetation (200-plus species of birds alone), and can be explored on foot, or via kayaks rentable at Tio Sports, next to the Presidente. Not recommended for swimming, it is nevertheless a worthwhile trip in an area that is otherwise not known for its lushness. Public parking is available just beyond the Presidente. **Amenities:** Parking lot.

Playa Hotelera. The long stretch of beach running in front of the hotels on the coast of San José del Cabo is called Playa Hotelera. This stretch of sand isn't swimmable, but once you step off the hotel property, it is public. You can always duck into one of the hotels for a snack or a sunset drink, and there are often locals with horses to rent for a beachside

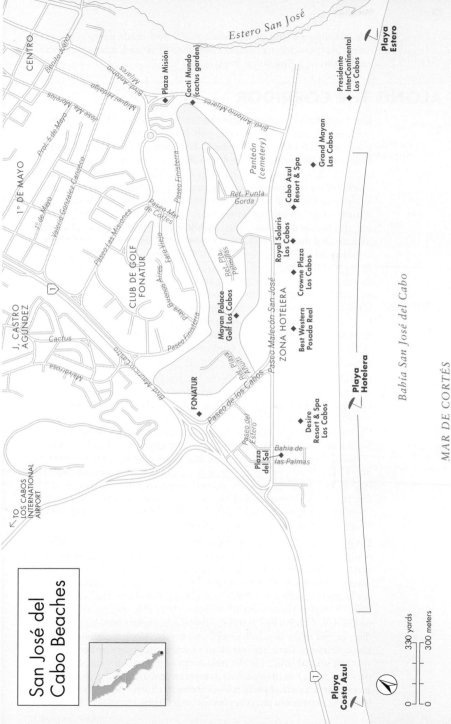

San José del Cabo Beaches

CENTRO

1° DE MAYO

J. CASTRO AGÚNDEZ

TO LOS CABOS INTERNATIONAL AIRPORT

Benito Juárez

Miguel Hidalgo

Blvd. Antonio Mijares

Prof. 5 de Mayo

José Ma. Morelos

Valerio González Canseco

1 de Mayo

Blvd. Mauricio Castro

Cactus

Marielosa

Estero San José

Plaza Misión

Cacti Mundo (cactus garden)

Paseo Finisterra

Paseo Mar de Cortés

Paseo Las Misiones

CLUB DE GOLF FONATUR

Faro Viejo

Buenos Aires

Paseo Finisterra

Ret. Playa Palmillas

Paseo Malecón-San José

ZONA HOTELERA

Ret. Playa Anuiti

Paseo de los Cabos

FONATUR

Paseo del Estero

Plaza del Sol

Bahía de las Palmas

Blvd. Antonio Mijares

Panteón (cemetery)

Ret. Punta Gorda

Presidente InterContinental Los Cabos

Playa Estero

Grand Mayan Las Cabos

Cabo Azul Resort & Spa

Royal Solaris Los Cabos

Crowne Plaza Los Cabos

Best Western Posada Real

Mayan Palace Golf Los Cabos

Desire Resort & Spa Los Cabos

Playa Hotelera

Bahía San José del Cabo

MAR DE CORTÉS

Playa Costa Azul

330 yards

300 meters

0

0

1

1

ride. At the west end of the beach you'll find shade palapas and children's play structures at Plazas Garuffi and Caracol, where there's also public parking. **Amenities:** Parking lot.

ALONG THE CORRIDOR

The Corridor's coastline edges the Sea of Cortez, with long, secluded stretches of sand, tranquil bays, golf fairways, and huge resorts. Only a few areas are safe for swimming, but several hotels have man-made rocky breakwaters that create semi-safe swimming areas when the sea is calm. Look for blue-and-white signs along Mexico 1 with symbols of a snorkel mask or a swimmer and *ACCESO A PLAYA* ("beach access") written on them to alert you to beach turnoffs. It's worth studying a map ahead of time to get an idea of where your turnoff will be. Don't hesitate to ask around for directions, and don't lose hope if you still need to circle back around once or twice. Facilities are extremely limited and lifeguards are nonexistent, though many of the beaches now have portable toilets.

⚠ The four-lane Highway 1 has more or less well-marked turnoffs for hotels. Be wary: signage as a rule appears at the very last minute, and the roads are not well lighted at night. Drivers tend to speed along most of the Corridor highway, which makes for a lot of business for the police officers who patrol the Corridor. Slow buses and trucks seem to appear out of nowhere, and confused tourists switch lanes with abandon. If you're driving, wait until you're safely parked to take in Sea of Cortez views.

Bahía Santa María and **Bahía Chileno** are two beautiful strands in the Corridor. Bahía Santa María is the less busy of the two, although there is a massive development looming over it to the west—sadly typical of nearly every inch of the Corridor. Both beaches offer fun snorkeling and safe swimming. For some truly secluded gems, drive northeast to the stunning beaches on the dirt road northeast of San José del Cabo. Soon after leaving San José you'll see mile after mile of gorgeous white sands, dotted with shade palapas and surfers looking for the next big break. Don't be put off by all of the private homes or "no trespassing" signs—beaches are plentiful and access to public ones is clear. The dirt road is well maintained and fine for passenger cars (despite dire-sounding warnings from locals who will tell you that you must have a Hummer)—but the dirt roads are best avoided if it's raining.

★ **Bahía Chileno.** A private enclave—with golf courses and residences—is being developed at Bahía Chileno, roughly midway between San José and Cabo San Lucas. The beach skirts a small, crescent-shape cove with aquamarine waters that are perfect for snorkeling and swimming (there are even restrooms). Getting here is easy, thanks to the well-marked access ramps on both sides of the road. As of this writing, construction on the new Chileno Bay project, a resort community on the rocky cliff at the east end of the beach, was well under way. Along the western edge of Bahía Chileno, some 200 yards away, are some good-size boulders that you can scramble up. On the trek down you may see some stray wrappers and cans, but the beach itself is clean and usually not too crowded. In winter, this part of the Sea of Cortez gets chilly—refreshing for a dip, but most snorkelers don't spend too much time in the water.

Continued on page 45

SURFING

CABO STYLE

by Larry Dunmire

From the gentlest of beginner waves
at Old Man's surf spot to the gnarliest winter
waves at Los Cerritos, Los Cabos has surf for everyone.
The tip of the Baja Peninsula has three key areas: the Pacific
coast (often called "the Pacific side"), the East Cape, and the Cabo
Corridor between them. This means that there are east-, west- and
south-facing beaches taking waves from just about every direction.

There are also warm, crystalline seas and great surf schools.
Friendly instructors make lessons fun and are more than willing to
tailor them to the needs of anyone—from tots to retirees, aspiring
surfers to experts. Schools also offer surf tours so you can benefit from
insider knowledge of the local waves and quirky surf spots before
heading out on your own.

LOS CABOS SURF FINDER

Surfer at a right-hand point break

Pacific Coast

Punta Conejo
Todos Santos
Punta Lobos
Playa San Pedrito
El Pescadero
El Pescadero
Playa Los Cerritos

WEST CAPE

Gentle waves during summer time.

19

PACIFIC SIDE

In winter, the Pacific from Cabo San Lucas town north to Todos Santos, often roils with rough, thundering swells. Surf spots here are only for the most accomplished although Los Cerritos, home to the Costa Azul Surf Shop and school, can have gentle waves in summer. Pacific-side beaches face essentially west and slightly north. Hence, winter swells coming from these directions (thanks to Alaskan storms) make landfall head on, creating great waves.

Punta Conejo: a rocky point break north of Todos Santos; unique in that's surfable on both north and south swells. Has good right and left breaks. *11 km (7 mi) north of Todos Santos; turn off Hwy. 19 near Km 80.*

Punta Lobos: big point breaks with south swells. *South of Todos Santos; turn off Hwy. 19 at Km 54 onto dirt road, and continue for about 2.5 km (1.5 mi).*

Surfer on the nose of his longboard on a clean wave

Perfect waves in Salsipuedes, Baja California

Playa San Pedrito: a beautiful, broad, curved, sandy beach break, surfable on both west and north swells. *About 5 km (3 mi) south of Todos Santos; turn off Hwy. 19 at CAMPO EXPERIMENTA sign, and continue about 2.5 km (1.5 mi).*

El Pescadero: fast, consistent, right reef and beach breaks; watch out for painful sea urchins in shallow water! *Hwy. 19 at Km 59.*

Playa Los Cerritos: highly versatile beach—in summer, good for beginners, with gentle breaks and a safe, sandy bottom; winter waves are gnarly. Best ones are on northwest swells, though south swells aren't bad. Both left and right beach breaks. Home to Costa Azul Surf Shop; can get crowded. *Less than a km (half a mi) south of Todos Santos; Hwy. 19 at Km 66.*

CABO CORRIDOR

The 20-mile stretch of beautiful beaches and bays between the towns of Cabo San Lucas and San José del Cabo has no less than a dozen surf spots, including some that are hard to find and access. Opportunities range from the expert-only Monuments break just outside of Cabo to the beginner-friendly Old Man's spot. For experts, surfing in the Corridor is generally best in the summer and fall, when storms as far away as New Zealand and Antarctica can send south swells all the way up here.

Playa Monumentos: powerful left point break, offering great gut-wrenching waves on south and west swells. Dangerously shallow at low tide; many sea urchins. Great surf and sunset watching from bluff near parking area. *Far south end of Cabo's El Medano Beach, east of Cabo San Lucas on Hwy 1; pull off at Misiones de Cabo, drive to gate, park at right.*

Playa El Tule: long wide beach with great right reef break in El Tule Arroyo, near highway bridge of same name. One of few places you can still camp; need 4WD to get here. *Midway btw. Cabo San Lucas and San José. East on Hwy. 1, look for EL TULE sign, pull off road and drive toward ocean on soft, sandy road.*

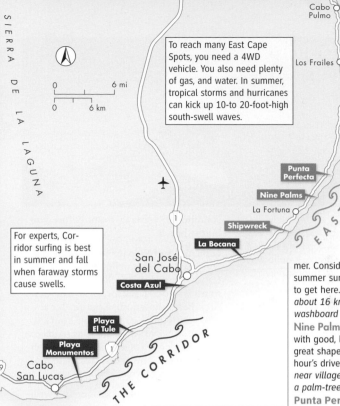

SIERRA DE LA LAGUNA

Sea of Cortez

Cabo Pulmo

Los Frailes

EAST CAPE

Punta Perfecta

Nine Palms

La Fortuna

Shipwreck

La Bocana

San José del Cabo

Costa Azul

Playa El Tule

Playa Monumentos

Cabo San Lucas

THE CORRIDOR

0   6 mi

0   6 km

To reach many East Cape Spots, you need a 4WD vehicle. You also need plenty of gas, and water. In summer, tropical storms and hurricanes can kick up 10-to 20-foot-high south-swell waves.

For experts, Corridor surfing is best in summer and fall when faraway storms cause swells.

Costa Azul: beach of choice in summer. World-famous, experts-only Zippers break often tops 12 feet. Has two other popular breaks: Acapulquito (Old Man's)—forgiving with a gentle surf break and good for beginners—and The Rock, a more challenging reef break to the east. The rocks are near the surface; quite shallow at low tide. There's a restaurant and a branch of the Costa Azul Surf Shop here. *Hwy. 1.*

La Bocana: freshwater estuary with a river mouth beach break (i.e., giant tubular waves break upon sand bars created by runoff sand deposited here after powerful summer rains). Both left and right rides. *Hwy. 1, south of Intercontinental hotel.*

EAST CAPE

North and east of San José, up the rough, unpaved East Cape Road, there are many breaks with good waves that are perpetually empty—with good reason. To get here, you need a 4WD vehicle. You also need plenty of gas, sufficient water, an umbrella, and *mucho* sun block. Waves here aren't for beginners, and some of the coast is on private property. Note, too, that locals (both Mexican and gringo) can be protective of their spots. East Cape beaches face south and east, and, in summer, tropical storms and hurricanes can kick up 10-, 15-, and even 20-foot-high south-swell waves—exciting for beginners to watch from the shore.

Shipwreck: fast, right reef break with south swells in summer. Considered the second-best summer surfing spot. Need 4WD to get here. *Off East Cape Rd., about 16 km (10 mi) up a rough, washboard road.*

Nine Palms: right point break with good, long waves and great shape but at least an hour's drive out. *East Cape Rd., near village of Santa Elena and a palm-tree grove.*

Punta Perfecta: right point break; can get big and hollow (i.e., "tubular") during summer's south swells. Out of the way (4WD required) and hard to find; territorial local surfers get testy when asked for directions. *East Cape Rd., near Crossroads Country Club and Vinorama.*

Los Frailes: Waves get big on a south swell. Down a long, dusty, pounding drive (need 4WD). Beautiful white sand beach and tranquil desert surroundings. *East Cape Rd.*

Stand-up paddling: SUPing

LEARNING TO SURF

WHAT TO EXPECT

Expect introductory classes to cover how to lie on the board, paddle properly, pop up into a surf stance, handle wave-riding, and duck incoming waves.

GEARING UP

Both surf shops and schools offer a wide selection of lessons, gear, and boards—sometimes including "skegs," soft, stable beginners's boards with safe rubber fins. Novices will want to use longboards, which offer the most stability. Rash guards (form-fitting polyester vests) protect you from board chafing and sunburn. Booties, rubberized watershoes, protect your feet from rocks, coral and sea urchins.

GETTING OUT THERE

Most agree that the best place for beginners is San José del Cabo's Acapulquito Beach, home to Old Man's surf spot. It has gently breaking, "feathering" (very forgiving) waves and the region's most understanding surfers. Acapulquito Beach is also home to the Cabo Surf Hotel, with a top school. The **Mike Doyle Surf School** (⊕ *http://cabosurfshop.com*) has three full-time teachers, certified by the NSSIA, the National Surf Schools and Instructor's Association (U.S.) and a great selection of more than 60 boards—short, long, "soft" boards for novices, and even a couple of SUP boards. The schools shows informative introductory video in the hotel's air-conditioned viewing room before you hit the beach.

Costa Azul Surf Shop (⊕ *www.costa-azul.com.mx*), with branches in San José del Cabo (near Zipper's Restaurant) and south of Todos Santos, near Los Cerritos Beach, is another option for lessons. Staff here can arrange tours to breaks so far off the path that roads to them aren't always marked on maps, let alone paved. The shop's Web site also has good interactive surfing maps.

Costa Azul's surf excursions—with guides (one guide for every two students) and two-hour lessons—cost US$85 a person.

SURF'S DOWN?

If the surf's flat, *no problema!* The latest craze is SUP-ing, or Stand-Up Paddling. It's done on flat waters using broad, long, lightweight boards that are comfortable to stand on. You paddle along, alternating sides for balance, using what resembles a single-bladed kayak paddle. SUP-ing is easy to master, great exercise, and highly enjoyable.

Accomplished surfers have pushed the SUP-ing envelope, paddling their boards into the surf line (or surf zone) and right into the waves, be they small or large. The paddle is then used to steer, almost like a boat's rudder. One step at a time, though—this type of SUP-ing is *not* as easy as the masters make it look!

Surf's up: you can really ride the waves in Los Cabos.

BOARD SHAPES

Longboard: Lengthier (about 2.5–3 m/9–10.5 feet), wider, thicker, and more buoyant than the often-miniscule shortboards. Offers more flotation and speedier paddling, which makes it easier to get into waves. Great for beginners and those with relaxed surf styles. **Skill level:** Beginner to Intermediate.

Funboard: A little shorter than the longboard with a slightly more acute nose and blunt tail, the funboard combines the best attributes of the longboards with some similar characteristics of the shorter boards. Good for beginners or surfers looking for a board more maneuverable and faster than a longboard. **Skill level:** Beginner to Intermediate.

Fishboard: A stumpy, blunt-nosed, twin-finned board that features a "V" tail (giving it a "fish" like look, hence the name) and is fast and maneuverable. Good for catching small, steep slow waves and pulling tricks. At one point this was the world's best-selling surfboard. **Skill level:** Intermediate to Expert.

Shortboard: Shortboards came on the scene in the late '60s when the average board length dropped from 9'6" to 6'6" (3m to 2m) and changed the wave riding forever. This short, light, high-performance board is designed for carving the wave with a high amount of maneuverability. These boards need a fast steep wave, completely different from the a "longboard" break, which tends to be slower with shallower wave faces. **Skill level:** Expert.

Beginner — **Expert**

Fish

Funboards

Longboards

Shortboards

Shallow wave faces, easiest surfing — Steeper wave faces, difficult surfing

SURF SLANG

By Leland Baxter-Neal and Larry Dunmire

Barrel: The area created when a wave breaks onto itself in a curl, creating a tube that's the surfer's nirvana. Also called the green room.

Beach break: The safest, best type for beginners. Waves break over sandy beaches. Found at Acapulquito (Old Man's), San Pedrito, and Los Cerritos.

Drop in: To stand up and drop down in the face of a wave. Also used when one surfer cuts another off: "Hey, don't drop in on that guy!"

Duck dive: Maneuver where the surfer first pushes his or her board underwater and then dives with it, ducking under waves that have broken or are about to break. Difficult with a longboard.

Turtle roll: the surfer rolls over on the surfboard, going underwater and holding the board upside down. Used by longboarders and beginners to keep from being swept back toward shore by breaking waves.

Goofy foot: Having a right-foot-forward stance on the surfboard. The opposite is known as natural.

Close out: When a wave or a section of a wave breaks all at once, rather than steadily in one direction. A frustrating situation for surfers; there's nowhere to go as the wave crashes down.

Ding: A hole, dent, crack or other damage to a board.

Outside: The area farther out from where waves break most regularly. Surfers line up here, and begin their paddling to catch waves.

Point break: Created as waves hit a point jutting into the ocean. With the right conditions, this can create very consistent waves and very long rides. Punta Lobos, Punta Conejo, and Monuments are examples.

Reef break: Waves break as they pass over reefs and create great (but sometimes dangerous) surf. There's always the chance of being scraped over extremely sharp coral or rocks. Found at El Tule, Shipwreck, and The Rock in Costa Azul.

Right/Left break: Terms for which direction the surfer actually travels on the wave, as seen from his or her perspective. Think of break direction in terms of when you're actually surfing the wave.

Set: waves often come in as sets, or groups of five to seven, sometimes more, in a row.

Stick: A surfboard.

Stoked: really, totally excited—usually about the surf conditions or your fantastic wave ride.

Swells: created by wind currents blowing over the sea's surface. The harder and the longer the winds blow, the larger the waves, and the longer the swell lasts.

Tubed: becoming totally enclosed inside the wave's barrel during a ride. The ultimate "stoke!" Getting "tubed" is also sometimes known as spending time inside the "green room."

Wipeout: a nasty crash off your board, usually having the wave crash down upon you.

(top) A surfer rips it up in Mexico (bottom) Baja California Sur sunset.

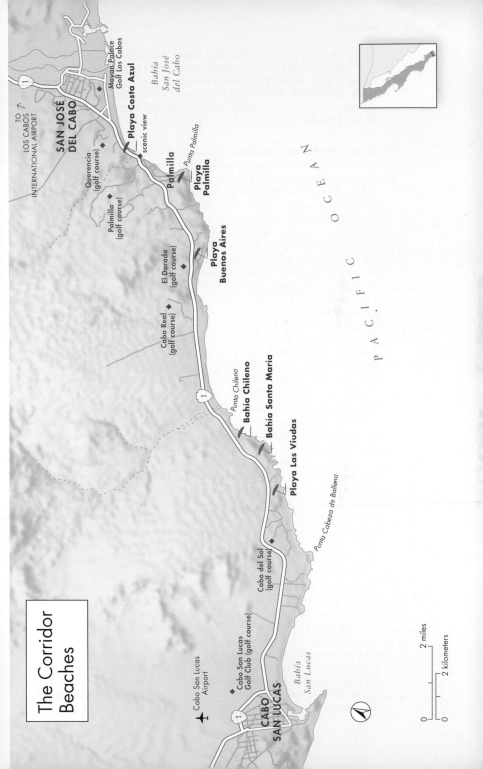

The Corridor Beaches

Mayan Palace
Golf Los Cabos

Playa Costa Azul

SAN JOSÉ
DEL CABO

TO LOS CABOS
INTERNATIONAL AIRPORT

*Bahía
San José
del Cabo*

scenic view

Querencia
(golf course)

Punta Palmilla

Palmilla

**Playa
Palmilla**

Palmilla
(golf course)

El Dorado
(golf course)

**Playa
Buenos Aires**

Cabo Real
(golf course)

P   A   C   I   F   I   C   O   C   E   A   N

Punta Chileno

Bahía Chileno

Bahía Santa María

Playa Las Viudas

Cabo del Sol
(golf course)

Punta Cabeza de Ballena

Cabo San Lucas
Airport

Cabo San Lucas
Golf Club (golf course)

*Bahía
San Lucas*

CABO
SAN LUCAS

2 miles

2 kilometers

0

0

The only business on the beach is **Cabo Acuadeportes** (☎ 624/143–0117), which rents snorkel equipment and offers scuba diving and snorkeling trips to nearby sites; hours are erratic and depend on the beach traffic (or the lack thereof). ✛ *The turnoff for the beach is at Km 14.5 on Hwy. 1. Look for the signs whether driving west from San José or at Km 16 when driving east from Cabo San Lucas.* **Amenities:** Toilets, parking lot.

↻ **Bahía Santa María.** This wide, sloping, horseshoe-shape beach is surrounded by cactus-covered rocky cliffs; the placid waters here are a protected fish sanctuary. The bay is part of an underwater reserve and is a great place to snorkel: brightly colored fish swarm through chunks of white coral and golden sea fans. Unfortunately, this little slice of paradise offers no shade unless you sit in the shadows at the base of the cliffs, so you may want to bring a beach umbrella. In high season, from November to May, there's usually someone renting snorkeling gear for $10 a day or selling sarongs, straw hats, and soft drinks. It's best to bring your own supplies, though, including lots of drinking water, snacks, and sunscreen. Snorkel and booze-cruise boats from Cabo San Lucas visit the bay in mid-morning through about 1 PM. Arrive midafternoon if you want to get that total Robinson Crusoe feel. The parking lot is a quarter mile or so off the highway and is sometimes guarded; be sure to tip the guard. The bay is roughly 19 km (12 mi) west of San José and 13 km (8 mi) east of Cabo San Lucas. Heading east, look for the sign saying *PLAYA SANTA MARÍA AND ACCESO A PLAYA.* ✛ *19 km (12 mi) west of San José del Cabo, 13 km (8 mi) east of Cabo San Lucas* **Amenities:** Toilets, parking lot.

Fodor's Choice
★

Playa Buenos Aires. This wide, lengthy, and accessible stretch of beach is one of the longest along the Cabo Corridor. Reef breaks for surfers can be good, but the beach is also known for its riptides, making it unswimmable. It's a great beach for long, quiet runs or walks, and it's not uncommon to find locals with horses to rent for a beachside ride. Whales can easily be spotted from the beach from January through March. ✛ *Near the Marquis Hotel Los Cabos/Hilton and stretching down to Meliá Cabo Real* **Amenities:** Toilets, parking lot (exit at Km 22 or 24).

Playa Costa Azul. Cabo's best surfing beach runs 3 km (2 mi) south from San José's hotel zone along Highway 1. Its Zipper and La Roca breaks (the point where the wave crests and breaks) are world famous. Surfers gather here year-round, but most come in summer, when hurricanes and tropical storms create the year's largest waves, and when the ocean is at its warmest. This condo-lined beach is popular with joggers and walkers, but swimming isn't advised unless the waves are small and you're a strong swimmer. If you do decide to take a plunge, be wary of surfers riding into the shore—it's hard to spot a swimmer from on top of a surfboard. The turnoff to this beach is sudden and only available to drivers coming from Cabo San Lucas (not from San José del Cabo). It's on the beach side of the highway, at Zipper's restaurant, which is on the sand by the surf breaks. ✛ *Just over 1 km (½ mi) southwest of San José* **Amenities:** Toilets, food concession, picnic tables, parking lot.

Bahía Santa María (Santa Maria Bay) is a popular swimming and snorkeling spot along the Corridor.

Playa Las Viudas *(Widow's Beach).* Located just west of Santa María Bay, this small public beach is also called Twin Dolphin Beach after the Twin Dolphin Hotel, a longtime landmark that was demolished in mid-2007. This is a great place for snorkeling (bring your own gear), but it is open to the ocean and all the inherent dangers that entails, so swim with extreme caution, or not at all if the water is rough. Low tides reveal great tidal pools filled with anemone, starfish, and other sea creatures (please leave these creatures in the sea). The huge development going up along the eastern end of the beach has rerouted the access road, but it is a well-graded dirt road, with a sign along the highway demarcating it. ⊠ *Hwy. 1, Km 12* **Amenities:** Toilets, parking lot.

Playa Palmilla. Check out the impressive multimillion-dollar villas on the road to Playa Palmilla, the best swimming beach near San José. Turn off the highway as if you're going to the One&OnlyPalmilla and then cross over the highway on an overpass. Continue about half a mile. The entrance is from the side road through the ritzy Palmilla development; take a left before you reach the guardhouse of the One&Only Hotel. There are signs, but they're not exactly large. The beach is protected by a rocky point, and the water is almost always calm. A few thatched-roof palapas on the sand provide shade; there are trash cans but no restrooms. Panga fishermen have long used this beach as a base, and they're still here, after winning lengthy legal battles to ensure their continued access to the beach that provides their livelihood. Guards patrol the beach fronting the hotel, discouraging nonguests from entering the exclusive resort—although the public legally has access to cross the

CLOSE UP

Don't Stop the Parade

You've heard the saying "wine, women, and song," right? Well, along the festive Médano Beach it's *"cervezas, chicas, y música"* (beers, babes, and music). A walk along this colorful, pulsating half-mile stretch of beach, on the east side of Cabo San Lucas's harbor, will reveal people checking each other out and local vendors trying to sell something to everyone. Fun-loving crowds sit and sun, and eat and drink, listening to the rock and roll from the beach

bars. Teams queue up for impromptu games of soccer and volleyball, Jet Skis roar in the distance, and Cabo's eternally ample sun beats down on it all. El Médano is essentially a daylong parade route, the parade itself fueled by buckets of beer, powerful margaritas, and that carefree feeling of being on vacation. If you don't want to be out on the beach in the thick of it, grab a table at the Office and enjoy it all from the shady haven created by its dozens of blue umbrellas.

beach in front of the resort property. ✢ *Entrance on Hwy. 1, at Km 27, 8 km (5 mi) southwest of San José del Cabo* **Amenities:** Parking lot.

CABO SAN LUCAS

Fodor'sChoice   **Playa del Amor** *(Lover's Beach)*. These days, lovers have little chance
★   of finding much romantic solitude here. The azure cove on the Sea of Cortez at the very tip of the Land's End Peninsula may well be the area's most frequently photographed patch of sand. It's a must-see on every first-timer's list. Water taxis, glass-bottom boats, kayaks, and Jet Skis all make the short trip out from Playa Médano to this small beach, which is backed by cliffs streaked white with pelican and seagull guano. Snorkeling around the base of these rocks is fun when the water's calm; you may spot striped sergeant majors and iridescent green and blue parrot fish. Seals hang out on the rocks a bit farther out, at the base of "El Arco," Cabo's famed arched landmark.

Swimming and snorkeling are best on the Sea of Cortez side of Lover's Beach, where the clear, green, almost luminescent water is unquestionably the nicest in Cabo San Lucas. The Pacific side is too turbulent for swimming but ideal for sunbathing. Vendors are usually present, but it's always best to bring your own snacks and plenty of water. The beach is crowded at times, but most people would agree that it's worth seeing, especially if you're a first-timer. To get here, take a five-minute panga water-taxi ride ($7–$10) or the half-hour glass-bottom boat tour. Opt for the latter if you wish to have some time to photograph the arch from the Pacific-side view. Both boats leave with relative frequency from the Cabo San Lucas marina or Playa Médano. Contact **Pisces Water Sports** (⊠ *Playa Médano next to Pueblo Bonito Rosé Hotel* ☏ *624/148–7530 cell phone*) for information about the glass-bottom boat tour. ⊠ *Just outside Cabo San Lucas, at El Arco* **Amenities:** None.

☺   **Playa Médano.** Foamy plumes of water shoot from Jet Skis and dozens of water taxis buzz through the water off Médano, a 3-km (2-mi) span of

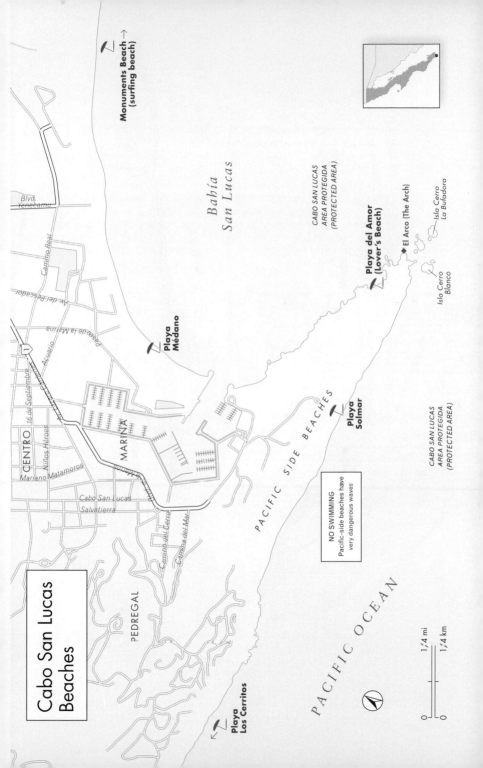

Cabo San Lucas Beaches

Monuments Beach →
(surfing beach)

*Blvd.
Yenecamu*

Camino Real

Av. del Pescador

Paseo de la Marina

Acuario

1

16 de Septiembre

CENTRO

Niños Héroes

Mariano Matamoros

Cabo San Lucas
Salvatierra

Camino del Cerro

Camino del Mar

MARINA

PEDREGAL

Playa
Los Cerritos

*Bahía
San Lucas*

Playa
Médano

CABO SAN LUCAS
AREA PROTEGIDA
(PROTECTED AREA)

Playa del Amor
(Lover's Beach)

El Arco (The Arch)

*Isla Cerro
La Bufadora*

*Isla Cerro
Blanco*

P A C I F I C   S I D E   B E A C H E S

Playa
Solmar

CABO SAN LUCAS
AREA PROTEGIDA
(PROTECTED AREA)

NO SWIMMING
Pacific-side beaches have
very dangerous waves

P A C I F I C   O C E A N

1/4 mi

1/4 km

0

0

EN ROUTE TO TODOS SANTOS

Playa Los Cerritos. This long, expansive beach on the Pacific Ocean, about 64 km (40 mi) north of Cabo San Lucas and on the way to the town of Todos Santos, is famous among surfers for its wonderful breaking waves in winter. Even if you don't ride the waves, you can watch them crash along the shore. The beach is wide, flat, and ideal for wading and swimming close to shore. Swimming farther out is not recommended because of the strong currents.

Most of the surfing crowd camps or stays in RVs near the beach. The developing area covers the basics with a few conveniences—including bustling Los Cerritos Club restaurant and two surf shops. Access to the beach is marked on Highway 19 (which connects Cabo San Lucas and Todos Santos) by a sign for Playa Los Cerritos at Km 64 (13 km [8 mi] south of Todos Santos). The graded dirt road to the beach is 2½ km (1½ mi) from Highway 19. ⟐ *64 km (40 mi) north of Cabo San Lucas, 13 km (8 mi) south of Todos Santos* **Amenities:** Toilets, showers (for restaurant patrons), food concession, parking lot, camping.

grainy tan sand that's always crowded. When cruise ships are in town, it's mobbed. Bars and restaurants line the sand, waiters deliver ice buckets filled with beer to sunbathers in lounge chairs, and vendors offer everything from silver jewelry to hats, T-shirts, and temporary henna tattoos. You can even have your hair braided into tiny cornrows or get a pedicure. Swimming areas are roped off to prevent accidents, and the water is usually calm enough for small children. But be aware: there are quick shoreline drop-offs, so life preservers are a good idea for the little paddlers in your group. Hotels line Médano, which is just north of downtown off Paseo del Pescador. Construction is constant on nearby streets, and parking is virtually impossible. The most popular spot on the beach is around the Baja Cantina Beach Club, where more than half a dozen bar-restaurants have set up beach chairs and tables. This is a hot spot for people-watching (and for singles seeking to be doubles). Be prepared to deal with the many crafts vendors cruising the beach. They're generally not pushy, so a simple head shake and "*no, gracias*" will do. ⊠ *Paseo del Pescador* **Amenities:** Food concession.

Playa Solmar. Huge waves crash onto the sand on the Pacific side of Cabo San Lucas. This wide, beautiful beach stretches from Land's End north to the cliffs of El Pedregal, where mansions perch on steep cliffs. Swimming is impossible here because of the dangerous surf and undertow; stick to sunbathing and strolling. From December to March, you can spot gray whales spouting just offshore; dolphins leap above the waves year-round. The beach is at the end of Avenida Solmar off Boulevard Marina—an easy walk from downtown Cabo San Lucas. Four resorts—Solmar, Terrasol, Playa Grande, and Finisterra—are all on this beach, making it easy to stop for a meal if you get hungry. Crowds are minimal, as guests tend to stick to the hotel pools. ⊠ *Blvd. Marina to hotel entrances* **Amenities:** None.

Sports and Outdoor Activities

WORD OF MOUTH

"Santa Maria Bay is great for snorkeling—it's between Cabo and San José. It's fairly protected and has relatively gentle surf. Your best bet is to rent a car if you don't want to go with a tour group."

—tenthumbs

Updated by
Georgia de
Katona

Long stretches of coastline along the Sea of Cortez and the Pacific Ocean make Los Cabos a beautiful spot for a beach vacation. However, you must be careful about where you take a dip, because many of those beautiful beaches border sea waters that are too dangerous for swimming due to strong undercurrents. Nearly 360 warm and sunny days per year make Los Cabos a natural wonderland, where outdoor activities—both land- and water-based—can be enjoyed year-round.

Los Cabos has something for everyone in a relatively small area to navigate. Whether you want a people-packed beach or a secluded cove, high-speed Jet Ski rides or leisurely fishing trips, deep-sea scuba expeditions or casual snorkeling, the waters off Cabo and the surrounding area offer endless possibilities.

Waterskiing, jet skiing, parasailing, and sailing are found almost exclusively at Cabo San Lucas's Playa Médano, where you can also go kayaking. At least eight good scuba-diving sites are near Playa del Amor. The East Cape, which includes the towns of Cabo Pulmo, La Ribera, and Los Barriles, is a great area for kayaking, fishing, diving, and snorkeling. In fact, Cabo Pulmo has the only coral reef in the Sea of Cortez and there are numerous spots to dive—even just snorkeling right off the beach is amazing. Both the Sea of Cortez and the Pacific provide great waves for year-round surfing whether you're a longboarder or a hotshot on a short board. Still, in the spot known as the "Marlin Capital of the World," sportfishing remains one of the most famous and popular water sports.

If you'd like to mix up your Los Cabos experience with some land-based adventures, the area's desert terrain lends itself to all sorts of possibilities, whether you're a thrill-seeker or a laid-back bird-watcher. You can explore cactus fields, sand dunes, waterfalls, and mountain forests on foot or horseback. Several tall rock faces make for great climbing and rappelling, and zip-lining (sliding across cables with a pulley) is all the rage around Arroyo Azul. Back in town, you can play beach volleyball on Playa Médano, tennis at one of hotels or at the Fonatur complex, get in a workout at your hotel or one of several gyms, or play a round of golf at one of the many courses available. If you are fortunate enough to be in Los Cabos during the whale migration (December through April)—when the weather is absolutely fantastic—a whale-watching trip with one of the many tour-boat operators is a must.

3

WATER SPORTS

BOAT TOURS

The themes of Los Cabos boat tours vary, but all tours follow essentially the same route: through Bahía Cabo San Lucas, past El Arco and the sea-lion colony, around Land's End into the Pacific Ocean, and then eastward through the Sea of Cortez along the Corridor. Costs run about $40–$50 per person; all tours include an open bar and some offer lunch and snorkel tours. Many of these operators offer whale-watching trips as well.

CABO SAN LUCAS

Cabo Adventures (✉ *Blvd. Paseo de la Marina, Lote 7a, Marina Cabo San Lucas* ☎ *624/173–9500 or 866/393–5255* ⊕ *www.cabo-adventures.com and www.cabodolphins.com*) has a three-hour sailing trip on genuine America's Cup yachts, during which the crew will teach you some basic sailing maneuvers, or you can simply sit back and enjoy the scenery—the boats pass Lover's Arch.

☾ Winter-season whale-watching in the Sea of Cortez with **Cabo Expeditions** (✉ *Behind Tesoro Hotel, Blvd. Marina* ☎ *624/143–2700* ⊕ *www.caboexpeditions.com.mx*) is done from small, customized, inflatable Zodiac boats that allow passengers to get close to gray and humpback whales. At times the whales even approach the boats with their babies. Fourteen passengers are allowed per tour.

☾ The 60-foot sailboat **Encore** (✉ *JT Water Sports, Playa Médano* ☎ *624/144–4066 or 624/144–4566* ⊕ *www.jtwatersports.com*) carries 25 passengers. Whale-watching tours are offered in the morning from January to March, and sunset cruises are offered throughout the year. *Encore* tours are more sedate than those on the party boats.

The **Jungle Cruise** (✉ *Tesoro Hotel dock* ☎ *624/143–7530 or 624/143–8150*) is both a snorkeling tour boat as well as your typical afternoon booze cruise, complete with loud reggae and other party music. It attracts a twenty- to thirtysomething crowd and heads out at 10:30 AM to 2:30 PM and 6 PM to 8 PM in summer (5 PM to 7 PM in winter months).

☾ **Kaleidoscope** (✉ *Marina near the Marina Fiesta Hotel* ☎ *624/148–7318*) is a luxurious, 100-foot power catamaran with comfortable seating inside and out. The whale-watching tour (10 AM to 12:30 PM) and the sunset cruise (5 to 7) are geared toward couples and families.

DID YOU KNOW?

Visiting El Arco, a gorgeous rock formation at the southernmost tip of the Baja Peninsula, makes for a thrilling day trip from Cabo San Lucas.

The double-decker party boat *Oceanus* (✉ *Blvd. Marina, Tesoro Hotel Dock 4* ☎ *624/143–1059 or 624/143–3929* ⊕ *www.oceanusloscabos.com.mx*) has snorkel cruises from 11 AM to 3 PM and a sunset cruise with a live band. It leaves at 5 PM (6 PM in summer) from the main dock in Cabo San Lucas. You can rent the *Oceanus* for birthdays, weddings, and other special occasions.

Pez Gato (✉ *Dock 4, behind Tesoro Hotel dock* ☎ *624/143–3797* ⊕ *www.pezgatocabo.com*) has two 42-foot catamarans, *Pez Gato I* and *Pez Gato II.* It has snorkeling cruises, a romantic sunset cruise, or the rowdier "booze cruise." Sunset cruises depart every day except Tuesday, from 5 to 7. A whale-watching cruise sails daily from 10:30 AM to 1:30 and 2 PM to 4 PM, from January through March.

☺ Cruises on the remarkable *Pirate Ship* (✉ *East end of Marina* ☎ *624/143–2714 or 624/147–5453* ⊕ *www.pirateshipcabo.com.mx*), built in 1885, are ideal for families with children. Deckhands dressed in pirate garb let kids help hoist the sail and tie knots while they learn about the rich history of pirates in Cabo San Lucas. There's even a working cannon on board. The whale-watching trip uses hydrophones to listen to the whales' song. The 105-foot ship can hold 150 people. It sails from 10:30 to 1 and includes hot dogs and hamburgers. The two-hour sunset cruise departs at 5 from Monday through Saturday. Kids under age 12 ride free.

JET SKIING AND WATERSKIING

CABO SAN LUCAS

Competition among operators in Cabo San Lucas is pretty fair, so most offer comparable, if not identical, prices. Both jet skiing and waterskiing cost about $45 for a half hour and $70 for a full hour.

For every type of water- and land-sports equipment, including diving gear, WaveRunners, and parasails, head to **JT Water Sports** (✉ *Playa Médano* ☎ *624/144–4566 or 624/144–4066* ⊕ *www.jtwatersports.com*), where WaveRunners rent for about $90 an hour; parasailing costs $40.

Omega Sports (✉ *3 locations on Playa Médano, near ME Cabo resort, Cabo San Lucas* ☎ *624/143–5519*) offers jet skiing. You might want to try a ride on the wild and crazy banana boat—a long, yellow, inflatable raft towed by high-speed motorboats.

Pisces Watersports (✉ *Far side of Playa Médano, Cabo San Lucas* ☎ *624/148–7530 cell phone*) is a large jet-skiing and waterskiing operation that also gives 12-minute banana boat rides. This is also a good place to rent Hobie Cats by the hour and other miscellaneous water-sports equipment.

Tio Sports (✉ *Playa Médano, Cabo San Lucas* ✥ *By Meliá San Lucas* ☎ *624/143–3399* ⊕ *www.tiosports.com*) was one of the original water-sports companies on El Médano Beach about 20 years ago and it's still a major operator with a sports palapa located on the beach at the ME Cabo Resort, plus stands and offices throughout Los Cabos. It provides aquatic tours, horseback rides, kayak rentals, and packages that include scuba and snorkeling.

KAYAKING

One of the most popular, practical, and eco-friendly ways to explore the pristine coves that dot Los Cabos' western shoreline is by kayak. Daylong package tours that combine kayaking with snorkeling cost anywhere from $60 to $125. Single or double kayaks can be rented by the hour for $15 to $20.

SAN JOSÉ DEL CABO

For a combined kayak and snorkeling trip, try **Baja Wild** (✉ *Hwy. 1, Km 28, s/n Local 5, Plaza Costa Azul* ☎ *624/172–6300* ⊕ *www.bajawild. com*). Daylong outdoor trips include surfing; hiking; ATV; and whale-watching trips, as well as baby sea turtle release excursions (turtle release only happens from late September through November). All trips include transportation, equipment, and lunch; you can substitute scuba diving for snorkeling. A full-day tour costs $140.

Los Lobos del Mar (✉ *Brisas del Mar RV park, on south side of San José* ☎ *624/142–2983*) rents kayaks and offers tours along the Corridor's peaceful bays. These outings are especially fun in winter when gray whales pass by offshore. Prices start at $40.

CABO SAN LUCAS

In Cabo San Lucas, Playa Médano is the beach for kayaking. A number of companies located along El Médano near the Baja Cantina Beachside, at the bottom of Cabo Villas, offer kayak rentals, and there are guided tours that go out to Lover's Beach to view El Arco, and around the Land's End Rocks. Rates are pretty uniform from one operator to the other; you don't need to waste precious time by trying to comparison shop.

The palapa for **Cabo Acuadeportes** (✉ *Playa Médano* ☎ *624/143–0117*) is right in front of the now-closed Hotel Hacienda. It offers snorkeling and waterskiing, as well as good prices on kayak rentals.

To rent a kayak or get info on boat rentals, snorkeling tours, parasailing, glass-bottom boats, and WaveRunners, try **JT Water Sports** (✉ *Playa Médano* ☎ *624/144–4566 or 624/144–4066* ⊕ *www.jtwatersports.com*).

Omega Sports (✉ *Playa Médano* ☎ *624/143–5519*) has good rates on single and double kayaks.

Tio Sports Ocean & Desert (✉ *Playa Médano* ☎ *624/143–3399* ⊕ *www. tiosports.com*) has aquatic tours, horseback riding, kayak rentals, and packages that include snorkeling.

EAST CAPE

If you have your own transportation, it is well worth driving out to Cabo Pulmo, where you can rent snorkel gear and a kayak or arrange a dive or fishing trip with one of the operators in this tiny, super-tranquilo village. In these incredible waters, you'll be able to check out everything from the smallest sea horse to a giant black sea bass.

Cabo Pulmo Dive Center (✉ *Hwy. 1 at La Ribera turnoff* ☎ *624/141–0884 or 624/141–0885* ⊕ *www.cabopulmo.com*) offers a six-hour guided tour to the sea-lion colony and environs includes lunch and snorkeling gear; tours depart at 9 AM. Cap off the tour by spending the night at this tranquil, reasonably priced resort, where rooms start at just $49 per night.

Cabo Pulmo Sport Center (⊠ *Hwy. 1 at La Ribera turnoff, at the end of the road in the waterside palapa* ⊕ *www.cabopulmosportcenter.com* has the gregarious César at the ready. He is a wellspring of knowledge and will happily advise you on the best spot to paddle, depending on the conditions of the day. He's also an expert birder. The center has a couple of very clean, simple casitas for rent ($90 per night) should you decide to extend your stay.

3

PARASAILING AND SAILING

Parasailing costs about $40 for an eight-minute flight. This is a high-risk sport, so proceed at your own risk. Sailboats and Windsurfers average about $30 per hour.

CABO SAN LUCAS

Cabo Acuadeportes (⊠ *Playa Médano* ☎ *624/143–0117* ✉ *Bahía Chileno* ✛ *16 km [9 mi] west of San José del Cabo, 16 km [9 mi] east of Cabo San Lucas*), one of the oldest operators in the area, rents Windsurfers and Sunfish sailboats. Both can be rented by the hour. This is the first shop on Playa Médano when coming from the Cabo San Lucas marina.

Arrange parasailing through any of the beachside palapas or beach salesmen at **JT Water Sports** (⊠ *Playa Médano* ☎ *624/144–4566 or 624/144–4066* ⊕ *www.jtwatersports.com*) and you'll find yourself 500 feet up in the air.

SCUBA DIVING

SAN JOSÉ DEL CABO

Expert divers head to the **Gordo Banks** (100–130 feet; also known as the Wahoo Banks), which are 13 km (8 mi) off the coast of San José. The currents here are too strong for less experienced divers. This is the spot for hammerhead sharks—which are not generally aggressive with divers—plus many species of tropical fish and rays, and, if you're lucky, dolphins. Fall is the best time to go.

THE CORRIDOR

The Corridor has several popular diving sites. **Bahía Santa Maria** (20–60 feet) has water clear enough to see hard and soft corals, octopuses, eels, and many tropical fish. **Chileno Reef** (10–80 feet) is a protected finger reef 1 km (½ mi) from Chileno Bay, with many invertebrates, including starfish, flower urchins, and hydroids. The **Blowhole** (60–100 feet) is known for diverse terrain—massive boulders, rugged tunnels, shallow caverns, and deep rock cuts—which house manta rays, sea turtles, and large schools of amberjacks and grouper.

CABO SAN LUCAS

At sites in **Bahía San Lucas** near El Arco you're likely to see colorful tropical fish traveling confidently in large schools. Yellow angelfish, green and blue parrot fish, red snappers, perfectly camouflaged

CLOSE UP

An Underwater Paradise

One of Baja's true gems is Cabo Pulmo, the raw, unspoiled national marine preserve along the Sea of Cortez. More than 8 km (5 mi) of nearly deserted rocky beach border the only living coral-reef system on the Sea of Cortez. Several dive sites reveal hundreds of species of tropical fish, large schools of manta rays, and a sea-lion colony. This is a nearly perfect place for scuba diving and snorkeling.

The village of Cabo Pulmo has 100 or so residents, depending on the season. Power comes from solar panels, and drinking water is trucked in over dirt roads.

The town has two small general stores and three restaurants. Cabo Pulmo is a magnet for serious divers, kayakers, and windsurfers and remains one of southern Baja's natural treasures.

stonefish, and long, slender needlefish share these waters. Divers regularly see stingrays, manta rays, and moray eels. The only problem with this location is the amount of boat traffic. The sound of motors penetrates deep into the water and can slightly mar the experience. **Neptune's Fingers** (60–120 feet) is a long rock formation with abundant fish. About 150 feet off Playa del Amor, **Pelican Rock** (25–100 feet) is a calm, protected spot where you can look down on Sand Falls (discovered by none other than Jacques Cousteau). **The Point** (15–80 feet) is a good spot for beginners who aren't ready to get too deep. The Shipwreck (40–60 feet), an old Japanese fishing boat, is close to Cabo San Lucas, near the Misiones del Cabo Hotel.

EAST CAPE

Cabo Pulmo/Parque Marino Nacional Cabo Pulmo, a 25,000-year-old coral reef, has been legally protected since 1995 and is home to more than 2,000 different kinds of marine organisms—including more than 230 species of tropical fish and a dozen kinds of petrified coral. The area is renowned among diving aficionados, whose favorite months to visit are June and July, when visibility is highest. The park isn't difficult to access. Head southwest from La Ribera and it's just 8 km (5 mi) from the end of the paved road; it's bordered by Playa Las Barracas in the north and Bahía Los Frailes to the south. It can also be reached by the well-maintained dirt road running along the coast from San José del Cabo. It'll take you three hours or more this way, but the coast along this route is unmatched. (Though, if it's raining, stick to the paved route.) There are two main dive centers offering full gear rentals, kayaks, snorkel gear, and sportfishing tours. (⇨ "Operators," listed below.)

FARTHER AFIELD

Well off the coast of **La Paz** (15–130 feet), you may find hammerhead and whale sharks in addition to the incredible array of colorful fish. More intrepid divers make a point of visiting the distant **Revillagigedo Islands** hundreds of miles south of the Baja Peninsula, where you can frolic with manta rays and whale sharks (some of the largest fish in the ocean). An exciting variety of diving is available in these parts.

OPERATORS

Generally, diving costs about $50 for one tank and $75 for two, including transportation. Equipment rental, dives in the Corridor, and night dives typically cost extra. Full-day trips to Gordo Banks and Cabo Pulmo cost about $150, including transportation, food, equipment, and two tanks. Most operators offer two- to four-day package deals.

Most dive shops have courses for noncertified divers; some may be offered through your hotel. Newly certified divers may go on local dives no more than 30 to 40 feet deep. Divers must show their C-card (diver certification card) before going on dives with reputable shops. Many operators offer widely recognized Professional Association of Diving Instructors (PADI) certification courses, which usually take place in hotel pools for the first couple of lessons.

The oldest (25 years in Cabo San Lucas) and most complete dive shop in Los Cabos area is **Amigos del Mar** (⊠ *Blvd. Marina, Cabo San Lucas ✚ Near harbor fishing docks* ☎ *624/143–0505, 800/344–3349 or 513/898–0547 in U.S.* ⊕ *www.amigosdelmar.com*). Its dive boats range from a 22-foot *panga* (a small, open-air unmotorized skiff) to a 25-foot runabout and 33- and 36-foot dive catamarans. The staff is courteous and knowledgeable, and all the guides speak English.

Cabo Acuadeportes (⊠ *In front of now-closed Hotel Hacienda, Playa Médano, Cabo San Lucas* ☎ *624/143–0117* ⊠ *Bahía Chileno ✚ 16 km [9 mi] west of San José del Cabo, 16 km [9 mi] east of Cabo San Lucas*) has boat dives from its shop on Playa Médano in Cabo San Lucas, and boat and shore dives from its shop at Chileno Bay in the Corridor.

Cabo Pulmo Dive Center (⊠ *Hwy. 1 at La Ribera turnoff* ☎ *624/141–0884 or 624/141–0885* ⊕ *www.cabopulmo.com*) is a full-service PADI dive shop offering a variety of trips and dive lengths. It also has the best accommodations in the village, starting at just $49 per night for the econo-option.

Cabo Pulmo Divers (⊠ *Hwy. 1 at La Ribera turnoff; at the end of the road, in the palapa right by the water on the beach, Cabo Pulmo* ⊕ *www. baja.com/cabopulmodivers*) has everything you need if you want to dive, including certification classes (multiday). This local family-run shop is right on the beach and offers full diving services, but it's most famous for excellent guided fishing trips that run $150 for three people for three hours.

Find luxury on the über-comfortable dive boat *Solmar V* (⊠ *Solmar Suites Hotel, Blvd. Marina, Cabo San Lucas* ☎ *624/143–0022, 310/455–3600 in U.S.* ⊕ *www.solmar5.com*), which takes nine-day remote adventure diving trips to the islands of Socorro, San Benedicto, and Clarion, as well as to the coral reefs at Cabo Pulmo. There are also five-day trips out of Ensenada, northern Baja. Twelve cabins with private baths serve a maximum of 24 passengers. Prices range from $1,895 to $3,095. This is one of Cabo's top diving experiences, so book well in advance.

Mutual curiosity between a scuba diver and a gentle whale shark (Rhincodon typus).

SNORKELING

Many of the best dive spots are also good for snorkeling. Prime areas include the waters surrounding **Playa del Amor, Bahía Santa María, Bahía Chileno,** and **Cabo Pulmo.** Nearly all scuba operators also offer snorkel rentals and trips. Equipment rentals generally cost $5 per hour ($15 for the day). Two-hour guided trips to Playa del Amor are about $25; day trips to Cabo Pulmo cost about $120. Most of the snorkeling and excursion boats are based in the Cabo San Lucas harbor and the best place to make reservations is along the marina walkway, near the Tesoro Hotel or at the beach palapas along El Médano Beach.

SNORKELING TOURS BY BOAT

A tall ship, once used in TV commercials, the **Buccaneer Queen** (⊠ *Blvd. Marina 39 M, Marina Cabo Plaza, Cabo San Lucas* ☏ *624/144–4217 or 624/144–4218* ⊕ *www.buccaneerloscabos.com*) now carries passengers on snorkeling and sunset cruises as well as private charters.

For a younger, party-oriented crowd, try the **Jungle Cruise Tours** (⊠ *Tesoro Hotel, 3rd fl., Cabo San Lucas* ☏ *624/143–7530 or 624/143–8150* ⊕ *www.cabobooze-cruise.com*), a slightly smaller, less luxurious boat but lots of fun. Four-hour trips cost $40 and include drinks, a light lunch, equipment, and, of course, booze.

The most upscale boat in Los Cabos is a beautiful 48-foot catamaran called **La Princesa** (⊠ *Cabo San Lucas harbor, Cabo San Lucas* ☏ *624/143–7676 or 624/147–7455* ⊕ *www.cabosanlucastours.net/ laprincesa*). Daily trips to Bahía Santa María or Bahía Chileno depart between noon and 3 PM. For $44 per person, you get a mini-Cabo adventure, drinks, a light lunch, and equipment. If *La Princesa* isn't available, there are three other yachts.

Oceanus (✉ *Blvd. Marina just in front of the Tesoro Hotel, Pier 4, Cabo San Lucas* ☎ *624/143–1059 or 624/143–3929* ⊕ *www.oceanuslos-cabos.com.mx*) leaves at 11 AM for four-hour snorkeling cruises that costs $45. It also departs at 4 PM for a $45 sunset dinner cruise.

Pez Gato (✉ *Position 1, Dock 4 at the Tesoro Hotel, Cabo San Lucas* ☎ *624/143–3797* ⊕ *www.pezgatocabo.com*) has several cruising options including a $49-per-person snorkeling trip to Bahía Santa María.

SPORTFISHING

The waters off Los Cabos are home to more than 800 species of fish—a good number of which bite all year round. It's easy to arrange charters online, through hotels, and directly with sportfishing companies along El Médano Beach and along the docks at Marina Cabo San Lucas. Indeed, to select a company yourself, consider hanging out at the marina between 1 PM and 4 PM when the boats come in, and asking the passengers about their experiences.

Prices range from $200 or $250 a day for a panga to $500 to $1,700 a day for a larger cruiser with a bathroom, a sunbathing deck, and possibly a few other amenities. The sky's the limit with the larger private yachts (think 80 feet); it's not unheard of for such vessels to cost $5,000 or $7,000 a day. All rates include a captain and crew, tackle, bait, fishing licenses, drinks, and—sometimes—lunch.

SAN JOSÉ DEL CABO

Most hotels in San José will arrange fishing trips. Fishing gear and line are available at **Deportiva Piscis Fishing Tackle Shop** (✉ *Calle Mauricio Castro near Mercado Municipal* ☎ *624/142–0332*). The pangas of **Gordo Banks Pangas** (✉ *La Playa near San José del Cabo* ☎ *624/142–1147 or 800/408–1199* ⊕ *www.gordobanks.com*) are near some of the hottest fishing spots in the Sea of Cortez: the Outer and Inner Gordo banks. The price for three anglers in a small panga runs from $210 to $290. Cruisers, which can accommodate four to six people, are available for $380 to $550 per day.

THE CORRIDOR

All of the Corridor hotels work with fishing fleets anchored at the Cabo San Lucas marina and a few with boats in Puerto Los Cabos, so any one of them can help you set up your fishing trips. The major drawback of arranging a fishing trip from one of the Corridor hotels is the travel time involved in getting down to the water. It takes up to half an hour or more to reach the docks from Corridor hotels, and most boats depart at 6:30 AM. Long a favorite for its great selection of pangas and superpangas, **Francisco's Fleet** (☎ *624/142–1152*) has boats available at both Playa Palmilla in the Corridor and La Playita in the San José del Cabo area. It has seven comfortable and speedy little rides that rent for $195 per day, not including fishing licenses, food, or drinks; it is represented by the **Jig Stop** (☎ *800/521–2281* ⊕ *www.jigstop.com*) in Dana Point, California, who also represents the Abaroa, Gaviota, and

Continued on page 70

SPORTFISHING

By Larry Dunmire

Cabo San Lucas is called both the Marlin Mecca and Marlin Capital of the World for good reason. Thanks to the warm waters of the Sea of Cortez, the tip of the Baja Peninsula has one of the world's largest concentrations of billfish. And, no matter what time of year you visit, there's a great chance—some locals say a 90% one—you'll make a catch, too.

More than 800 species of fish swim off Los Cabos, but anglers pursue only about half a dozen types. The most sought-after are the huge blue or black marlin, which have been known to fight for hours. The largest of these fish—the so-called granders—weigh in at 1,000 pounds or more. The more numerous, though smaller (up to 200 pounds), striped marlin are also popular catches.

Those interested in putting the catch-of-the-day on their table aim for the iridescent green and yellow dorado (also called mahi-mahi), tuna, yellowtail, and wahoo (also known as ono)—the latter a relative of the barracuda that can speed along at up to 50 mph. Also gaining popularity is light-tackle fly-fishing for roosterfish, jack crevalle, and pargo from small boats near the shore.

Something's always biting, but the greatest diversity of species inhabit Cabo's waters from June through November, when sea temperatures climb into the high 80s.

A billfish catch in progress (above).

WHAT TO EXPECT

You don't need to be experienced or physically strong to sportfish. Your boat's captain and crew will happily help you along, guiding you on how to properly handle the equipment.

Some of the larger boats have the so-called fighting chairs, which resemble a dentist's chair, firmly mounted to the deck. These rotate smoothly allowing you to follow the movement of a hooked fish and giving you the support you need to fight with a large black or blue marlin for an extended period of time.

Experienced fishermen sometimes forego chairs for the stand-up technique using a padded harness/fighting belt that has a heavy-duty plastic-and-metal rod holder connected to it. Though physically demanding—especially on the arms and lower back—this technique often speeds up the fight and is impressive to watch.

FISHING TWO WAYS
Most of Cabo's boats are equipped for the more traditional heavy-duty sportfishing using large, often cumbersome rods and reels and beautiful, colorful plastic lures with hooks. A modified form of fly-fishing is gaining popularity. This requires a finessed fly-casting technique and spot-on timing between crew and the fisherman. It utilizes ultra-lightweight rods and reels, relatively miniscule line, and a technique known as bait and switch.

You attract fish as near to the back of a boat as possible with hook-less lures. As the crew pulls in the lures, you cast your fly (with hooks) to the marlin. Fights with the lighter equipment—and with circle hooks rather than regular ones—are usually less harmful, enabling more fish to be released.

Sportfishing in Los Cabos; one man's catch (top)

CONSERVATION IN CABO

You're strongly encouraged to use the less-harmful circle hooks (shaped like an "O"), as opposed to straight hooks (resemble an L), which do terrible internal damage. It's now common to release all billfish, as well as any dorado, wahoo, or tuna that you don't plan to eat. Folks here frown on trophy fishing unless it takes place during an official tournament. Instead, quickly take your photos with the fish, then release it.

The Cabo Sportfishing Association has a fleet-wide agreement that no more than one marlin per boat be taken per day. Usually all are released, denoted by the "T" flags flown from a boat's bridge as it enters the marina.

The few marlin that are brought in are hoisted and weighed, photographed, and then put to good use—taken to be smoked or given to needy locals. You can ask the crew to fillet the tastier species right on your boat, and you can usually arrange for the fish to be smoked or vacuum-packed and frozen to take home. Many restaurants, especially those found marina-side in Cabo San Lucas, will gladly prepare your catch any way you like. You hook it, they cook it.

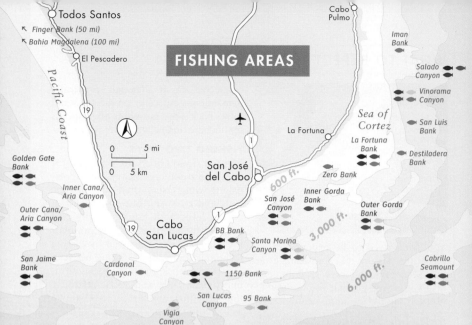

FISHING AREAS

Todos Santos
↖ Finger Bank (50 mi)
↖ Bahia Magdalena (100 mi)

El Pescadero

Cabo Pulmo

Iman Bank

Salado Canyon

Vinorama Canyon

Pacific Coast

19

0   5 mi

0   5 km

La Fortuna

Sea of Cortez

San Luis Bank

San José del Cabo

La Fortuna Bank

Destiladera Bank

Golden Gate Bank

Zero Bank

600 ft.

Inner Cana/ Aria Canyon

San José Canyon

Inner Gorda Bank

Outer Gorda Bank

Outer Cana/ Aria Canyon

Cabo San Lucas

BB Bank

3,000 ft.

San Jaime Bank

Cardonal Canyon

Santa Marina Canyon

Cabrillo Seamount

1150 Bank

San Lucas Canyon

6,000 ft.

95 Bank

Vigia Canyon

	FISH	AVAILABILITY
◄●	Billfish*	Year around
◄●	Yellowfin Tuna	Year around
◄●	Dorado	July–December
◄●	Wahoo	Year around
◄●	Yellowtail	January–May
◄●	Reef fish**	March–December

*Billfish include marlin, sailfish, and swordfish

**Reef fish include roosterfish, cabrilla, sierra, pargo, and dog snapper.

For more information on fishing locations, check out BajaDirections.com.

Although there are many great fishing areas amid the underwater canyons and seamounts off the Baja coast, there are four major spots within 40 to 50 km (25 to 30 mi) of Cabo. From north to south these banks are the Golden Gate, San Jaime, the Gordo Banks (outer and inner), and the San José Canyon. All are within an hour or so of the Marina Cabo San Lucas, if you've chartered one of the faster boats. Farther north, about 80 km (50 mi) on the Pacific side above Todos Santos, is the Finger Bank. Also on the Pacific side, more 160 km (100 mi) north of Cabo,

is Bahia Magdalena (Mag Bay), where the waters teem with marlin and game fish, and experienced anglers have been known to catch and release as many as 67 billfish in one day.

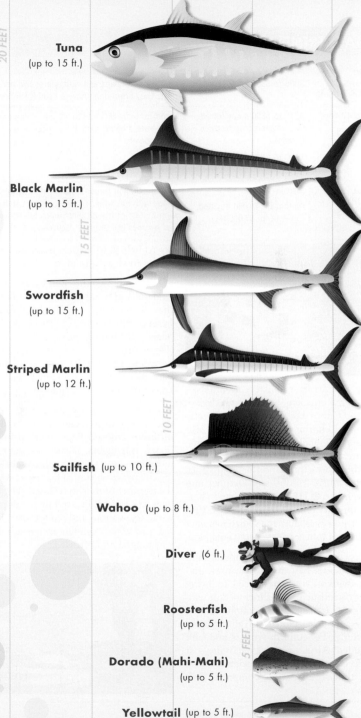

20 FEET

Tuna
(up to 15 ft.)

Black Marlin
(up to 15 ft.)

15 FEET

Swordfish
(up to 15 ft.)

Striped Marlin
(up to 12 ft.)

10 FEET

Sailfish (up to 10 ft.)

Wahoo (up to 8 ft.)

Diver (6 ft.)

Roosterfish
(up to 5 ft.)

5 FEET

Dorado (Mahi-Mahi)
(up to 5 ft.)

Yellowtail (up to 5 ft.)

CHARTERING A BOAT

TYPE OF BOAT	COST	CHARACTERISTICS
PANGAS or SUPERPANGAS	$200 to $350 for 6 hours.	Best for short trips and with one or two passengers. They often don't have a head (bathroom).
28- to 42-foot CRUISERS	$375 to $850 a day for 28 to 35 footers (two to three people).\n\n$900 to $1,700 a day for 35 to 42 footers.	Good for more-distant (30–40 mi) fishing trips. They have a head, sunbathing space, and air-conditioning.
LARGE, LUXURY CRUISERS	Start at $2,000.\n\n80-foot for $5,000 day and 111-foot for $7,000 day.	Air-conditioning through the yacht's interior, heads with hot-water showers, elegant state-rooms, state-of-the-art electronics, full kitchens, and luxuries like on-deck Jacuzzis.

You can arrange charters at hotels—through a concierge or a charter desk—at Los Cabos tackle shops, or directly through charter companies. It's also possible to make arrangements online before you arrive. Indeed, it's good to do this up to three months in advance for the busiest months of October and November. ■TIP➔ Don't arrange charters through time-share companies. They aren't always reliable and sometimes work with boats that aren't that well equipped.

Rates usually include a captain and crew, tackle, bait, fishing licenses, and soft drinks. You often need to bring your own lunch; if it is included, it usually costs extra, as do alcoholic drinks. Unless you're quoted an all-inclusive charter price, confirm what is and isn't included. Also, a tip of 15% of the cost of the charter will be appreciated. Note, too, that some charter companies will

try to help solo anglers hook up with a group to share a boat.

A walk along the perimeter of the Marina Cabo San Lucas demonstrates that Cabo really is all about fishing. Indeed, this is where most vendors are based and where most yachts set sail. (Departures are generally predawn—between 6 and 6:30 AM—so it's not a bad idea to locate your dock and boat ahead of time, in the light of day.)

It seems as if every yacht tied to the docks is a sport fisher, and you'll see different colored flags flying from the boats' outriggers. These designate the numbers and types of fish caught during the previous day of fishing as well as the number of marlin released. The blue flags are for marlin, yellow for dorado, white for wahoo, and red for tuna. Each red and white "T"-flag means a billfish was tagged and released.

A cruiser out to sea (top). Back to the marina (bottom).

SPORTFISHING TOURNAMENTS

In May, the International Game Fishing Association Offshore Championship attracts anglers from 60 countries who fish with lightweight 40-pound test line and circle hooks. Fish are caught and released, and catches are verified with cameras.

October and November are the top tournament months, with events like the fun, anything-goes Western Outdoors Tuna Tournament ($700 entry fee) and the three-day, 175-boat Bisbee Black & Blue Jackpot, whose entry fees can set a team back more than $70,000 (to enter all categories) and whose winners have taken home a pot of as much as $3,838,620 (Team Bad Company in 2007). Other events include the Los Cabos Billfish Tournament, which takes place in Cabo San Lucas, and San José del Cabo's IGT Billfish Tournament.

Money tournaments such as the Bisbee are "kill" tournaments, as fish must be brought in and weighed to win the big cash prizes. To qualify, a fish must be over 300 pounds; teams are penalized for underweight fish. In catch-and-release tournaments crews are adept at determining the weight of a fish, and the release rate is often as high as 98%.

Sailfish on deck—almost (above).

Ana Mar fleets and a total of about 30 boats. Cruisers range up to $560 per day. **Victor's Sport Fishing** (☎ 624/122–1092) has a fleet of pangas on the Palmilla resort's beach. Rates start at $180.

CABO SAN LUCAS

Most vendors are at the Marina Cabo San Lucas. Ships tend to depart from sportfishing docks at the south end of the marina, near the Puerto Paraíso Mall, or from the docks at the Tesoro Hotel. It's very important to get specific directions and departure times, since it's hard to find your spot at 6:30 in the morning.

The **Gaviota Fleet** (✉ *Docked between Gates 2 and 3 across from the Marina Fiesta Hotel* ☎ *624/145–8165 or 800/521–2281* ⊕ *www.jig-stop.com*) currently holds the record for the largest marlin caught in Cabo San Lucas's waters. The company has charter cruisers and super-pangas from 23 feet to 36 feet. Egg Harbor yachts and rates range from $200 to $755, all-inclusive for the larger boats.

Jig Stop Tours (✉ *34186 Coast Hwy., Dana Point, CA* ☎ *800/521–2281* ⊕ *www.jigstop.com*) is located in Southern California and books fishing trips for a number of Los Cabos fleets mentioned above and below. It is one of the best, and easiest, one-stop fishing shops in the United States.

Renowned tackle store **Minerva's** (✉ *Madero between Blvd. Marina and Guerrero* ☎ 624/143–1282 ⊕ *www.minervas.com*) has been around for more than 30 years and has its own fleet with three Bertram charter-fishing boats from 33 feet to 40 feet, and prices ranging from $760 to $1,250, all-inclusive.

Fodor'sChoice
★ One of the top sportfishing fleets, **Picante Fleet** (✉ *Near Harley-Davidson shop in the Puerto Paraíso shopping mall* ✦ *Puerto Paraíso Mall Local 39-A* ☎ 624/143–2474, 714/572–6693 in U.S. ⊕ *www.picantesportfish-ing.com*), offers a wide selection of 20 well-equipped, top-of-the-line, 31-foot to 45-foot Cabo sport fishers. If you prefer smaller boats, there's the Picantito fleet, with a trio of 24-foot Shamrock walk-around boats. These are primarily used for fishing close to shore. Owner Phil Gentile tells us he believes in 100% catch-and-release of billfish, and to further emphasize the point, captains are fined $50 for marlin that are not released. Renting a Picantito boat for five hours of fishing will set you back $400, plus $35 per person for fishing license, food, and beverages. Chartering a 31-footer will cost $1,100.

Fodor'sChoice
★ Some of Cabo's top hotels use the extensive range of yachts from **Pisces Sportfishing Fleet** (✉ *Cabo Maritime Center, Blvd. Marina* ☎ 624/143–1288, 619/819–7983 in U.S. ⊕ *www.piscessportfishing.com*). The fleet includes the usual 31-foot Bertrams, but also has a sizable fleet of 50- to 70-foot Viking, Mikelson, Hatteras, and Ocean Alexander yachts with tuna towers, air-conditioning, and multiple staterooms. Pisces also has luxury yachts up to 110 feet in length. Chartering a 31-foot Bertram goes for $1,195, all-inclusive, for up to six people, and trips last for around seven or eight hours.

Once the largest fleet in Cabo San Lucas, the long-established **Solmar Fleet** (✉ *Blvd. Marina* ☎ 624/122–3440 or 800/344–3349 ⊕ *www.solmar. com*) has been subdivided into several parts and its fleet representatives are now located in both the Solmar Hotel and Playa Grande Hotel. Solmar offers 13 sportfishing yachts, with superpangas at $250 for five hours, 26-footers for $325, and 36-foot Chris-Craft for $725, plus extras. Solmar boats and tackle are always in good shape, and its long-time regulars wouldn't fish with anyone else.

EAST CAPE

Outside Parque Marino Nacional Cabo Pulmo (where you aren't allowed to fish), just north of Cabo

> **MATANCITAS MAN**
>
> The remains of pre-Hispanic Indians, found in the giant sand dune region near the current Cabo San Lucas Lighthouse, were given the name of Matancitas Man by archaeologists. These people were precursors to the Pericú Indians that lived in the Cape when explorer Hernán Cortés arrived in 1535.

Pulmo there are a number of excellent spots to try your luck at hooking a marlin, tuna, giant sea bass, or snapper. It's best to stop by some of the local dive shops and make arrangements for them to take you out.

SURFING

You can rent a board right at the beach at Costa Azul in San José del Cabo, or at the Cabo Surf Hotel, and paddle right into the gentle, feathering waves at the Old Man's surf spot. If you're at the intermediate level or above, walk a short distance eastward to La Roca (The Rock) break. Big waves are best left to the experts up north, in Todos Santos.

SAN JOSÉ DEL CABO

Baja Wild (⊠ *Hwy. 1, Km 28, s/n Local 5, Plaza Costa Azul* ☎ *624/172–6300* ⊕ *www.bajawild.com*) offers daylong trips to surfing hot spots throughout the Cape region for beginners and experts. A fee of $90 per person includes transportation, equipment, and instruction for a half day at Costa Azul. Full-day surf tours on the Pacific cost $110 per person.

The **Mike Doyle Surf School** (⊠ *Cabo Surf Hotel* ✛ *On the beach at the bottom of the steps, just below the 7 Seas restaurant* ☎ *624/172–6188*) is the top "surfer-friendly" location in all of Los Cabos. If you stay at the hotel, you can check the surf conditions from the restaurant, bar, pool, or even from your balcony. The school has 60 rental boards, from soft foam boards (great for beginners and kids), to short boards, long boards, and paddleboards. There are two surf instructors available at the shop for lessons.

THE CORRIDOR

For good surfing tips, rentals, and lessons, head to **Costa Azul Surf Shop** (⊠ *Hwy. 1, Km 27.5* ☎ *624/142–2771 or 624/142–4454* ⊕ *www.costa-azul.com.mx*). Surfboard rentals are $20 a day and lessons are $55 and include the surfboard rental.

TODOS SANTOS

Todos Santos is a quick drive up the coast from Cabo San Lucas, and it offers great surfing areas for beginners to experts. The advantage here is that the crowds, including the swarming masses from the cruise ships, don't head up to these waters, which makes for a much more relaxed scene in the water and on the beach.

Los Cerritos, south of Todos Santos on Mexico 19, offers gentle waves to beginners during the summer and more challenging breaks for advanced surfers during the northwest swell from December to March. San Pedrito, also south of town, offers great surfing for experienced surfers during the winter swells, with a number of popular, low-key surf-oriented motels along the beach. In summer, the surf is generally pretty mellow along this stretch, so locals and surfers who demand greater challenge head to the Corridor or areas along the east side of the Cape for more satisfying breaks.

Costa Azul Surf Shop (☒ *Playa Los Cerritos* ☎ *624/142–2771 or 624/142– 4454* ⊕ *www.costa-azul.com.mx* is a small shop on the north end of the beach by the cliffs at Los Cerritos. The staff is friendly, and, for such a small space, there's a good selection of board rentals, as well as T-shirts, shorts, and accessories to buy. You'll see its stickers on cars all over the Cape, and the interactive map on its Web site is a great resource for information on surf spots all over Baja Sur.

You can swing by **Todos Santos Surf Shop** (☒ *Next to Shut Up Frank's on Degollado/Mexico 19 and Rangel* ☎ *612/145–0882*)on your way out of town for board rentals, to arrange a lesson, buy gear, or get that ding in your board repaired.

WHALE-WATCHING

The gray-whale migration doesn't end at Baja's Pacific lagoons. Plenty of whales of all sizes make it down to the warmer waters off Los Cabos and into the Mar de Cortés. To watch whales from shore, go to the beach at the Solmar Suites, the Finisterra, or any Corridor hotel, or the lookout points along the Corridor highway. Virtually all of the companies listed in *"Boat Tours"* offer whale-watching tours (about $30–$50 depending on size of boat and length of tour) from Cabo San Lucas. One of the biggest is **Cabo Expeditions** (☒ *Tesoro Hotel, Blvd. Marina* ☎ *624/143–2700*), which offers snorkeling and whale-watching tours in hard-bottom inflatable boats.

WINDSURFING

EAST CAPE

From mid-October through March, Cabo Pulmo, La Ribera, and Los Barriles have excellent windsurfing conditions, with breaks up to 10 to 12 feet high—recommended only for experienced windsurfers.

VelaWindsurf (☎ *800/223–5443* ⊕ *www.velawindsurf.com*) offers windsurfing and kite-boarding lessons and trips to Los Barriles in winter and fall; its center is located in front of the Hotel Playa del Sol.

Continued on page 76

A WHALE'S TALE   by Kelly Lack and Larry Dunmire

Seeing the gray whales off Baja's western coast needs to be on your list of things to do before you die. "But I've *gone* whale watching," you say. Chances are, though, that you were in a big boat and might have spotted the flip of a tail 100 yards out. In Baja your vessel will be a tiny panga, smaller than the whales themselves; they'll swim up, mamas with their babies, coming so close that you can smell the fishiness of their spouts.

Grey Whales Guerrero Negro

WHEN TO GO

Gray whales and tourists both head south to Baja around December—the whales in pods, the snowbirds in RV caravans—staying put through to April to shake off the chill of winter. So the beaches, hotels, restaurants, and bars during whale-watching season will be bustling. Book your room five to six months ahead to ensure a place to stay. The intense experience that awaits you at Magdalena Bay, San Ignacio, or Scammion's Lagoon is worth traveling in high season.

Though the average life span of a gray whale is 50 years, one individual was reported to reach 77 years of age—a real old-timer.

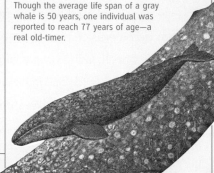

THE GRAY WHALE:
Migrating Leviathan

Yearly, gray whales endure the longest migration of any mammal on earth—some travel 5,000 miles one way between their feeding grounds in Alaska's frigid Bering Sea and their mating/birthing lagoons in sunny Baja California. The whales are bottom-feeders, unique among cetaceans, and stir up sediment on the sea floor, then use their baleen—long, stiff plates covered with hair-like fibers inside their mouths—to filter out the sediment and trap small marine creatures such as crustaceanlike Gammarid amphipods.

DID YOU KNOW?

Gray whales' easygoing demeanor and predilection for near-shore regions makes for frequent, friendly human/whale interactions. Whalers, however, would disagree. They dubbed mother grays "devilfish" for the fierce manner in which they protect their young.

WHALE ADVENTURES

Cabo Expeditions (*www.caboexpeditions.com.mx*) was the first with whale watching tours more than a dozen years ago. The staff is well-trained, and owner Oscar Ortiz believes not only in seeing the whales, but also saving them. Last year his Zodiacs rescued two grays from entanglement in giant fishing nets. Boats depart from the Cabo San Lucas Marina, near Dock M.

You've seen whales, but how about swimming with them? **Baja AirVentures** (*www.bajaairventures.com*) arranges weeklong trips to Bahia de los Angeles where you can swim with whale sharks daily. (Don't worry—the toothless plankton eaters are much more like whales than sharks.)

You fly from San Diego to the secluded Sea of Cortez fishing village, then take pangas out to Las Animas Wilderness Lodge, where you stay in spacious, comfortable yurts.

WHALE NURSERIES: THE BEST SPOTS FOR VIEWING

If you want an up-close encounter, head to one of these three protected spots where the whales gather to mate or give birth; the lagoons are like training wheels to prep the youngsters for the open ocean.

Laguna Ojo de Liebre (Scammon's Lagoon). Near Guerrero Negro, this lagoon is an L-shaped cut out of Baja's landmass, protected to the west by the jut of a peninsula.

Laguna San Ignacio. To reach the San Ignacio Lagoon, farther south than Scammon's, base yourself in the charming town of San Ignacio, 35 miles away. This lagoon is the smallest of the three, and along with Scammon's, has been designated a U.N. World Heritage site.

Bahía de Magdalena. This stretch of ocean, the farthest south, is kept calm by small, low-lying islands (really just humps of sand) that take the brunt of the ocean's waves. Very few people overnight in nearby San Carlos; most day-trip in from La Paz or Loreto.

WHAT TO EXPECT

The experience at the three lagoons is pretty standard: tours push off in the mornings, in *pangas* (tiny, low-lying skiffs) that seat about eight. Wear a water-resistant windbreaker—it will be a little chilly, and you're bound to be splashed once or twice.

The captain will drive around slowly, cutting the motor if he nears a whale (they'll never chase whales). Often the whales will approach you, sometimes showing off their babies. They'll gently nudge the boat, at times sinking completely under it and then raising it up a bit to get a good, long scratch.

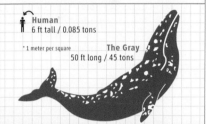

Human 6 ft tall / 0.085 tons

* 1 meter per square   **The Gray** 50 ft long / 45 tons

Baja whale watching, gray whale

LAND-BASED ACTIVITIES

AIR TOURS

CABO SAN LUCAS

One of the most spectacular ways to view Baja is from the air. **Aereo Calafia** (✉ *Blvd. Marina at Tesoro Hotel A-4* ☎ *624/143–4302 or 624/143–5280* ⊕ *www.aereocalafia.com.mx*) offers small-plane flights to Magdalena Bay where gray whales calve during winter months. The tours include the flight, a boat tour among the whales, and lunch, for $425 per person. Aereo Calafia also offers air charters and specialized tours.

Caborey (✉ *Tesoro Hotel A-4* ☎ *624/105–1976, 866/460–4105 in U.S.* ⊕ *www.caborey.com*) lets you personalize your flight path to Los Cabos over El Arco, along the beautiful Corridor coast, as well as offers sunset tours in R44 helicopters. Rides are $110 per person, but the flight only lasts 12 minutes.

Cabo Sky Tours (☎ *624/144–1294 office, 624/166–1990 cell* ⊕ *www. loscabosguide.com/caboskytours*) offers exciting aerial tours over Los Cabos in gas-powered hang gliders. A 20-minute flight costs $75 for an adult under 200 pounds.

ATV TOURS

Riding an ATV across the desert is a thrill, but it is one of the more dangerous things you can do in this area. As fun as these tours may be, it is worth thinking about the destruction these vehicles cause to the fragile desert terrain. Additionally, many of the companies do not have insurance, and will make you sign explicit release-of-liability forms before going. They do issue helmets, goggles, and handkerchiefs to protect you from the sand and dust.

When ATV trips are properly conducted, they can be safe and fun. The most popular trip passes first through Cabo San Lucas, continues through desert cactus fields, and arrives at a big play area of large sand dunes with open expanses and specially carved trails, at the foot of **El Faro Viejo**, the old lighthouse. You can reach frighteningly high speeds as you descend the tall dunes. Navigating the narrow trails in the cactus fields is exciting but not for the fainthearted or steering-impaired. Another favorite trek travels past interesting rock formations, little creeks, and the beach on the way to a small mountain village called **La Candelaria**.

A three-hour trip costs about $60 for a single or $80 for a double (two people sharing an ATV). Six-hour trips to La Candelaria include lunch and cost about $110 for a single and $130 for a double. Wear tennis shoes, clothes you don't mind getting dirty, and a long-sleeve shirt or sweatshirt for afternoon tours in winter.

CABO SAN LUCAS

Tours are almost always full at **Baja's ATVs** (✉ *Blvd. Marina, behind Tesoro Hotel* ☎ *624/143–2050*), so reserve a day in advance. Try the 9 AM or 12:30 PM departure for the lighthouse tour; the 4 PM tour is the most crowded and it returns at dark along some main roads. (ATVs kick up a lot of dust, reducing night visibility considerably.) A Candelaria trip leaves at 9 AM daily.

Cabo's Moto Rent (✉ *Av. Cárdenas in front of Puerto Paraíso* ☎ *624/143– 0808*) offers a desert tour and a beach tour at Playa Migriño on the Pacific, along with the lighthouse and Candelaria tours. ATV rentals are available. **Tio Sports** (✉ *Playa Médano* ☎ *624/143– 3399*) has tours that take you out to the lighthouse and trips out to La Candelaria.

> **THE WORLD OF CACTUS**
>
> It's easy to drive right by Cacti Mundo (Cactus World) botanical gardens in San José—but you should make a point of stopping. There are thousands of species of the prickly plants from all over the world, including many rare cacti unique to Baja. The displays are beautifully landscaped in pleasing patterns and the staff is happy to answer questions. You'll come away with a different perspective on the environment off the beach in this desert clime. Cacti Mundo is open every day from 8 AM to 6 PM, and admission costs $3.
> ✉ *Blvd. Mijares 3* ☎ *624/146– 9191* ⊕ *www.cactimundo.com.*

BACKCOUNTRY TOURS

SAN JOSÉ DEL CABO

★ **Baja Outback** (☎ *624/142–9215* ⊕ *www.bajaoutback.com*). offers a variety of drive-yourself trips (with a guide in the passenger seat) that range from four hours to several days long. The routes run through Baja backcountry, where you have the opportunity to explore the Cape's rarely seen back roads while learning desert lore from a knowledgeable guide-cum-biologist. One option takes you to a remote mountain ranch before lunching and snorkeling at Cabo Pulmo. Day trips range from $165 to $220 per person. It also offers multiday tours exploring cave paintings and whale-watching at Magdalena Bay.

★ **Baja Wild** (✉ *Hwy. 1, Km 28, s/n Local 5, Plaza Costa Azul* ☎ *624/172– 6300* ⊕ *www.bajawild.com*) has a number of adventure packages including the "Six Day Inn-to-Inn Hiking, Biking, Kayaking, Snorkeling, Surfing, and Whale-Watching Adventure" that cost between $645 and $1,040, depending on the accommodations you choose. You'll see the natural side of Cabo, with hikes to canyons, hot springs, fossil beds, and caves with rock paintings. Backcountry jeep tours start at $420 per vehicle. Full-day kayak tours at Cabo Pulmo run $140. Half-day ATV tours in the desert cost $80.

THE CORRIDOR

Baja Bora (☎ *624/105–1812 or 866/422–0130* ⊕ *www.bajabora.com*) offers challenging tours in two-passenger jeeps for 1½-, 2½-, and 4-hour trips. Trips are billed as "the ultimate off-road adventures" and cost from $150 to $325.

CABO SAN LUCAS

Another sports-and-adventures operator with a wide variety of unusual activities is **Cabo Adventures** (✉ *Blvd. Paseo de la Marina, Lote 7a, Marina Cabo San Lucas* ☎ *624/173–9500 or 866/393–5255* ⊕ *www.cabo-adventures.com and www.cabodolphins.com*). Along with its popular Dolphin Encounters program are the Desert Safaris, which take you into the Sierra Mountains by Unimog; half the fun here is jaunting along in these Swiss vehicles. Four-hour Desert Safaris cost $75 per person.

FLUTTER BY

Walk amid hundreds of butterflies at Sia Tikuva, a butterfly farm. Learn about the life of the flitting mariposas, and the magnificent flight of the monarchs here in the Baja Peninsula and Mexico. Move slowly and relax and you'll have dozens of these magical creatures landing on you in no time. ✉ *Ocotillo 1701, near the San José hotel beaches* ☎ *624/105–2414 or 624/122–2955.*

BIKING

Bicycling isn't a major activity in Los Cabos. The absolute lack of bike paths and the dangerous road conditions make it difficult to use bikes as a mode of transportation, and the summertime heat saps energy more quickly than you might imagine.

ECOTOURS

CABO SAN LUCAS

☺ ★ **Eco Tours de Baja** (✉ *Zaragoza at 5 de Febrero* ☎ *624/143–0775*) organizes a tour that includes a bumpy, exciting ride in a four-wheel-drive vehicle to a region rich with fossils, some millions of years old—you may even see a fossilized whale skeleton. Guides are knowledgeable and speak English. The area is protected by INAH, Mexico's National Institute of Anthropology and History, and several sites are being explored by scientists. During the ride you pass small ranches and vast fields of cardon cacti. Bird-watching is excellent early in the morning. Other tours include visits to the woodworking and leather factories in Miraflores and to waterfalls and lakes in the mountains. Trips, which cost about $85, include a barbecue lunch at a small ranch, as well as hotel pickup and drop-off.

TODOS SANTOS

Todos Santos Eco Adventures (✉ *La Poza neighborhood, go west on Calle Olachea and follow signs toward La Poza. It's best to call for detailed directions* ☎ *612/145–0189 or 612/145–0780* ⊕ *www.tosea. net*) offers a number of land- and water-based adventures, including culinary ones. Choose from cliff walks, mountain treks, or fishing trips. Friendly guides pride themselves on thorough knowledge of the area, the environment, and the culture of the region. You'll feel like you're traveling with a savvy friend. The Jauregui family runs the operation with great care, and it's apparent. Ask about the casitas if you need overnight accommodations.

GO-CARTS

THE CORRIDOR

High-performance outdoor go-carting has come to Cabo with Wide Open's **Cabo Karting Center** (✉ *Hwy. 1 across from Los Patios Hotel* ☎ *624/144–7073*. Here you can race high-speed go-carts on a professionally designed formula racecourse for $29 for a 14-lap race, with discounted prices for members and various combo packages available.

GOLF

Los Cabos has become one of the world's top golf destinations, thanks to Fonatur, Mexico's government tourism development agency. In 1988 it expanded Los Cabos' appeal beyond sportfishing by opening a 9-hole course in San José. Green fairways now appear like oases in the middle of the desert, with breathtaking holes alongside the Sea of Cortez. Many more courses are slated for construction in the next couple of years.

Some courses in Cabo offer memberships, but most allow nonmembers to play. The exceptions are Querencia, designed by Tom Fazio, and El Dorado, designed by Jack Nicklaus. These courses, while said to be spectacular, are only open to members and their guests.

About a million gallons of water a day is required to maintain each course, which partially explains why courses here charge some of the highest greens fees in the world. The cost usually includes access to the driving range, a golf cart, and bottled water. Some courses offer reduced rates for twilight play (after 3 PM). Greens fees are exorbitant—up to $350 in winter and $220 in summer. Rates given here are for high season, approximately November to May. Most hotels near the courses offer packages and reduced fees. Reservations are essential at all courses unless noted otherwise.

SAN JOSÉ DEL CABO AND THE CORRIDOR

On the inland side of the Corridor, **Cabo del Sol Desert Course** (✉ *Hwy. 1, Km 10.3* ☎ *624/145–8200 or 800/386–2405* ⊕ *www.cabodelsol.com*) is said to be "user-friendly": the longest hole is 625 yards, par 5. The course was designed by Tom Weiskopf. Special rates are available if you play both this and the Cabo del Sol Ocean Course. Greens fees start at $99 for low-season play and twilight times, and $220 for high season during the day.

Cabo del Sol Ocean Course (✉ *Hwy. 1, Km 10.3* ☎ *624/145–8200 or 800/386–2405* ⊕ *www.cabodelsol.com*) has been included in *Golf Digest*'s "Top 100 Courses in the World." According to designer Jack Nicklaus, it has the best three finishing holes in the world. On the par-3 17th hole, you drive over an ocean inlet with waves crashing below. The 18th hole is a mirror image of the 18th at Pebble Beach, California. Five holes are seaside. It was the site of the 1998 Senior Slam. Greens fees start at $195 for twilight times, $250 during low season, and $350 for high season.

The challenging **Cabo Real Golf Course** (✉ *Hwy. 1, Km 19.5* ☎ *624/173–9200 or 877/795–8727* ⊕ *www.caboreal.com*), designed by Robert Trent Jones II, has straight and narrow fairways, difficult slopes, and

3

strategically placed bunkers. The first six holes are in mountainous terrain, working their way up to 500 feet above sea level. Recovering from mistakes here can be quite difficult. Three holes are oceanfront. The course played host to the PGA Senior Slam in 1996 and 1999. Greens fees for 18 holes are $280, and $180 at twilight.

Although most of the area's best golf courses are in the Corridor, Los Cabos' original course, the renamed **Mayan Resorts Golf Los Cabos** (✉ *Hwy. 1, Km 31.5* ☎ *624/142–0900*), has wide fairways and few obstacles or slopes. It's good for beginners or as a warm-up. The well-maintained 9-hole course is lined with residential properties (broken windows are not unusual). Some holes have nice ocean views, and there's a large lake near the bottom. It costs $116 to play 9 holes; twilight rate is $69 including cart rental.

The 27-hole, Jack Nicklaus–designed **One&Only Palmilla Golf Course** (✉ *Hwy. 1, Km 7.5* ☎ *624/144–5250* ⊕ *www.palmillagc.com*) has wide fairways, gentle slopes, and large, challenging greens. On the 10th hole, you drive from a cliff, with the sea at your back; on the famous par-4 14th, you drive onto an island fairway. One hole borders the Sea of Cortez, and 12 holes have excellent sea views. The Palmilla course was the site of the '97 Senior Slam. It costs $269 to play, and after 1 PM it's $170. You can make reservations up to 60 days in advance.

CABO SAN LUCAS

Most of the courses in Los Cabos are attached to the large resorts in the Corridor. **Cabo San Lucas Country Club** (✉ *Hwy. 1, Km 3.6* ☎ *624/143–4653 or 888/328–8501* ⊕ *www.golfincabo.com*), the lone course actually in Cabo San Lucas, is renowned for spectacular views of the Sea of Cortez and El Arco—especially from the 18th hole— and has seven man-made lakes. The course was designed by Ron Dye, and the signature hole is the par-5 7th. Eighteen holes are $185, with a twilight rate of $95.

HIKING

SAN JOSÉ DEL CABO

Trips with **Baja Wild** (✉ *Hwy. 1, Km 28, s/n Local 5, Plaza Costa Azul* ☎ *624/172–6300* ⊕ *www.bajawild.com*) include hikes to canyons, small waterfalls, hot springs, a fossil-rich area, and caves with rock paintings. You can also take customized jeep expedition trips to La Sierra de la Laguna, a series of mountain peaks submerged in water millions of years ago. The highest peak, at 7,000 feet above sea level, is ringed by pure pine forests. Rock-climbing and rappelling trips are also available. An all-day hiking trip includes lunch, guide, equipment, and transfer and goes for $110 per person.

HORSEBACK RIDING

Cantering down an isolated beach or up a desert trail is one of the great pleasures of Los Cabos (as long as the sun isn't beating down too heavily). The following companies have well-fed and well-trained

Horseback riding along stretches of desolate Los Cabos beaches is a treat not to be missed.

horses. One-hour trips generally cost about $35 per person, two-hour trips about $65.

THE CORRIDOR

The **Cuadra San Francisco Equestrian Center** (⊠ *Hwy. 1, Km 19.5, across from Casa del Mar and Las Ventanas al Paraíso hotels* ☎ *624/144–0160* ⊕ *www.loscaboshorses.com*) offers trail rides and lessons on 50 beautiful and extremely well-trained horses. Trail rides go into the hills overlooking the Cabo Real property or to the San Carlos arroyo; both focus on the flora as much as the riding. Trips are limited to 20 people, with one guide for every 6 or 7 people. Cuadra also specializes in private trail rides. Reserve at least a day in advance and request an English-speaking guide. Note that you must query them for rates.

CABO SAN LUCAS

Horses are available for rent near the Playa Médano hotels, in the arroyo just east of Club Cascadas, near Villa del Arco, for about $25 per person for a 1¼-hour ride; contact **Rancho Collins Horses** (☎ *624/143–3652 or 624/127–0774*).

The popular **Red Rose Riding Stables** (⊠ *Hwy. 1, Km 4* ☎ *624/143–4826*) has healthy horses for all levels of riders. The outfitter leads trips to the beach and the desert. Groups are sometimes too large to suit all riders' levels of expertise; consider this if you're an expert rider, or a newbie riding with a bunch of experts.

WHICH WAY TO THE GYM?

If your hotel or resort doesn't have a gym, a few in Cabo San Lucas allow short-term memberships. Fees average about $8 a day, $25 a week, and $45 a month.

Club Fit (✉ *Plaza Nautica, Blvd. Marina* ☎ *No phone*) has excellent facilities, including a pool, free weights, and a variety of exercise machines. The club also has aerobics and yoga classes and a health bar.

Hours are weekdays 6 AM–9:30 PM, Saturday 8–8, and Sunday 10–5.

The locals work out at **Gimnasio Rudos** (✉ *Av. Cárdenas and Guerrero 23410* ☎ *624/143–0077*), a basic gym with free weights and machines. There are showers for men but not for women. It's open weekdays 6 AM–10 PM, Saturday 6 AM–8 PM.

MOTORCYCLING

Hop on a hog and live your own *Easy Rider* fantasy, Baja style. Do yourself and the bike a big favor and avoid the dirt roads, though.

CABO SAN LUCAS

The **Harley-Davidson Los Cabos** (☎ *624/143–3337*), in the Puerto Paraíso Entertainment Plaza, rents Fatboys, Electric Glides, Road Kings, and Heritage Classics. Ask the shop employees for suggestions on scenic tour routes. Rentals are $200 a day; additional days are $180.

ROCK CLIMBING

SAN JOSÉ DEL CABO

Three-hour trips with **Baja Wild** (✉ *Hwy. 1, Km 28, s/n Local 5, Plaza Costa Azul* ☎ *624/172–6300* ⊕ *www.bajawild.com*) follow one of six routes. Four focus on rock climbing and two are dedicated to rappelling. Rock faces range from 120 feet to 320 feet, and some have extraordinary views of the ocean. Trips are designed for beginners to experts, and can include as few as two people.

Where to Eat in Los Cabos

WORD OF MOUTH

"For breakfasts I loved Mama's Royal Cafe downtown or The Office on Medano Beach. My favorite places for dinner were Misiones de Kino (seafood) and Capo San Giovanni (Italian), which are a bit more high-end but lovely—both with outdoor seating."

—Suze

WHERE TO EAT IN LOS CABOS PLANNER

In This Chapter

Eating Out Strategy

Although Mexicans often prefer dining late into the evening, be warned that if you arrive at restaurants in Los Cabos after 10 PM, you're taking your chances. Most places are open year-round, sometimes closing for a couple of weeks—or even a month—in the middle of the hot Baja summer, and nearly all of Los Cabos restaurants close one night a week, typically Sunday or Monday. Unless otherwise noted, the restaurants listed in this guide are open daily for lunch and dinner.

Smoking and Drinking

Mexican law prohibits smoking in all enclosed businesses, including restaurants. The drinking age here is 18. Establishments do ask for IDs.

Reservations

Reservations are mentioned when essential, but are a good idea during high season (mid-November to May). Restaurant Web sites are common, and many let you make online reservations.

What to Wear

Dress is often casual. Collared shirts and nice slacks are fine at even the most upscale places; shirts and shoes (or sandals) should be worn any time you're away from the beach.

Tipping

You won't find much consistency in tipping expectations among Los Cabos restaurants. Some upscale places automatically add a 15% service charge (or even up to 18%) to the bill—look for the word "servicio"—but no one will object if you leave a few pesos more for good service. If a service charge is not included in your bill, a tip of 15% is common.

Prices

Restaurants in Los Cabos tend to be pricey, even by U.S. standards. Some add a fee for credit card usage. If you wander off the beaten path—often only a few blocks from the touristy areas—you can find inexpensive, authentic Mexican fare (though still more expensive than elsewhere in Mexico), although these spots may not accept credit cards.

WHAT IT COSTS IN DOLLARS

	¢	$	$$	$$$	$$$$
At Dinner	under $8	$8–$12	$12–$20	$20–$30	over $30

Prices are per person for a main course at dinner, excluding service charges or taxes.

THE SCENE

4

Updated by
Jeffrey Van
Fleet

Prepare yourself for a gourmand's delight. The competition, creativity, selection, and, yes, even the prices are utterly beyond comprehension. From elegant dining rooms to casual seafood cafés to simple *taquerías,* Los Cabos serves up anything from standard to thrilling fare.

In the past, some restaurants have tried to please everyone and overcome fierce competition by offering similar menus with often-mediocre results. But a number of the chefs and restaurateurs are settling into their niches and subsequently delighting their audiences. The food scene changes fairly quickly, so it's always a good idea to ask fellow travelers or locals about their dining experiences.

Seafood is the true highlight here. Fresh catches that land on the menus include dorado (mahimahi), *lenguado* (halibut), *cabrilla* (sea bass), *jurel* (yellowtail), wahoo, and marlin. Local lobster, shrimp, and octopus are particularly good. Fish grilled over a mesquite wood fire is perhaps the most indigenous and tasty seafood dish, while the most popular may be the tacos *de pescado* (fish tacos); traditionally a deep-fried fillet wrapped in a handmade corn tortilla, served with shredded cabbage, cilantro, and salsas. Beef and pork—commonly served marinated and grilled—are also delicious. Many restaurants import their steak, lamb, duck, and quail from the state of Sonora, Mexico's prime pastureland, and also from the United States.

In San José, international chefs prepare excellent Continental, French, Asian, and Mexican dishes in lovely, intimate restaurants. The Corridor is the place to go for exceptional hotel restaurants. Intense competition for business in Los Cabos means many restaurants go through periodic remodels and reinvention, the Corridor restaurants included. Cabo San Lucas is where the major portion of the area's explosion in new eateries has occurred. To be expected, also, Cabo has comfort food covered, with franchise eateries from McDonald's, Subway, and Domino's to Carlos 'n' Charlie's, and Ruth's Chris Steakhouse.

BEST BETS FOR LOS CABOS DINING

With hundreds of restaurants to choose from, how will you decide where to eat? Fodor's writers and editors have selected their favorite restaurants by price, cuisine, and experience in the Best Bets lists below. In the first column, Fodor's Choice properties represent the "best of the best" in every price category. You can also search by neighborhood for excellent eats—just peruse our reviews on the following pages.

Lorenzillo's, $$$$
p. 105
Mariscos Mocambo,
$$ p. 106
Marisqueríaa Mazatlán, $ p. 106

Fodor'sChoice ★

Casiano's, $$$$ p. 89
Crazy Lobster Bar &
Grill, ¢ p. 104
Don Emiliano, $$$
p. 91
El Gusto! $$$ p. 111
Marisquería Mazatlán,
$ p. 106
Market, $$$$ p. 96
Mi Cocina, $$$ p. 94
Miguel's, ¢ p. 112
Nick-San-Cabo, $$$
p. 107
Nick-San-Palmilla,
$$$ p. 99
Pitahayas, $$$ p. 99
Sunset Da Mona Lisa,
$$$ p. 99

By Price

¢

Crazy Lobster's Bar
and Grill, p. 104
Miguel's, p. 112

$

Marisquería Mazatlán,
p. 106

$$

7 Seas Restaurant,
p. 96

$$$

Don Emiliano, p. 91
El Gusto!, p. 111
Mi Cocina, p. 94
Nick-San-Cabo, p. 107
Nick-San-Palmilla,
p. 99
Pitahayas, p. 99
Sunset Da Mona Lisa,
p. 99

$$$$

Casiano's, p. 89
Market, p. 96

By Cuisine

BEST ASIAN

Baan Thai, $ p. 89
Market, $$$$ p. 96

Michael's, $ p. 112
Piatahayas, $$$ p. 99

BEST ITALIAN

La Dolce, $ p. 93
Salvatore's, $$ p. 110
Sunset Da Mona Lisa,
$$$ p. 99

BEST MEXICAN

La Fonda, $$ p. 105
Los Adobes, $$ p. 111
Miguel's, ¢ p. 112
Salsitas, $ p. 95
Tequila Restaurante,
$$ p. 95

BEST SEAFOOD

Crazy Lobster Bar &
Grill, ¢ p. 104
La Panga Antigua,
$$$$ p. 93

By Experience

BEST FOR ROMANCE

Don Emiliano, $$$
p. 91
El Galeón, $$ p. 104
El Gusto!, $$$ p. 111
Mi Cocina, $$$ p. 94
Voilá Bistro, $$$ p. 95

BEST FOR MAKING THE SCENE

Local Eight, $$ p. 93
Nikki Beach, $$ p. 107

BEST LOCAL FLAVOR

El Ahorcado, ¢ p. 91
Tropicana Inn, $$
p. 95

BEST BEACHY VIBE

Baja Cantina Beach,
$ p. 101
The Office, $$ p. 108
Zipper's, $ p. 100

SAN JOSÉ DEL CABO

San José's downtown is lovely, with adobe houses fronted by jacaranda trees. Entrepreneurs have converted many of the old homes into stylish restaurants, and new and inventive cuisine abounds—fitting for a town with an art district that is burgeoning as well. Simply meander down the rows of restaurants to find one that will thrill your taste buds and delight your senses.

$

THAI

✕ **Baan Thai.** The aromas alone are enough to bring you through the door, where you'll be greeted with visual and culinary delights. The small, comfortable, formal dining room has Asian antiques, and a fountain murmurs on a patio in the back. The chef blends Asian spices with aplomb, creating sublime pad thai, lamb curry, Thai lamb shank, and the catch of the day with lemon–black bean sauce. New favorites are mussels in a coconut broth, and wok-seared scallops. To wash it all down? Try the Ginger Martini. Prices are reasonable for such memorable food. ⊠ *Morelos and Obregón, across from El Encanto Inn, Centro* ☎ *624/142–3344* ▭ *AE, MC, V* ✆ *No lunch Sun.* ✛ *1:C2.*

$

AMERICAN

✕ **Baja Brewing Company.** Los Cabos has its own brewery, right in the middle of San José del Cabo. This fun, upbeat brewpub has great music, and serves up satisfying pub meals. Burgers, shepherd's pie, soups, salads, and pizza—and more elegant entrées such as filet mignon—should be washed down with a pint of any of the special San José cervezas, brewed within sight of the bar and restaurant. A branch opened in Cabo San Lucas in 2009. ⊠ *Morelos 1277, Comonfort and Obregón, Centro* ☎ *624/146–9995* ⊕ *www.bajabrewingcompany.com* ▭ *MC, V* ✛ *1:C2.*

$

AMERICAN

✕ **Buzzard's Bar & Grill.** Fronted by miles of secluded beach, this casual seaside cantina (with cheap cervezas) gets rave reviews from locals who make the slightly involved drive out of San José del Cabo. Former Southern California restaurant owners Denny and Judie Jones serve up hefty, reasonably priced New York steaks; seafood entrées, such as coconut shrimp; "burritos like bombs"; hefty burgers; and, without a doubt, *lo mas grande* (the biggest in the world) flan. Indeed, this custardlike dessert could easily be enough for two or three—try it with a shot of Kahlúa poured over the top. Also, Sunday breakfast is a big hit. To get here, turn off Boulevard Mijares at the signs for Puerto Los Cabos and follow the road up the hill, around the small traffic circle, and continue out into the desert, toward the sea. You'll find the restaurant about 5 km (3 mi), about a 10-minute drive, from San José in the Laguna Hills neighborhood. Check out the Web site for more detailed directions before you head out. ⊠ *Old East Cape Rd., Laguna Hills* ☎ *951/302–1735 in U.S.* ⊕ *www.buzzardsbar.com* ▭ *No credit cards* ✆ *Closed Mon. and Aug.* ✛ *1:D5.*

$$$$

ECLECTIC

Fodor's Choice

★

✕ **Casiano's.** A colorful interior of bold red-and-blue stripes and a very graphic-chic aesthetic beguile you as you enter this inventive restaurant. "No menu, no rules" is the way it describes the "spontaneous cuisine" dining experience you're about to enjoy here. If you're an open-minded, trusting, and adventurous eater, you'll enjoy this restaurant, which is full of surprises. Give yourself up to top chef Casiano Reyes, who's

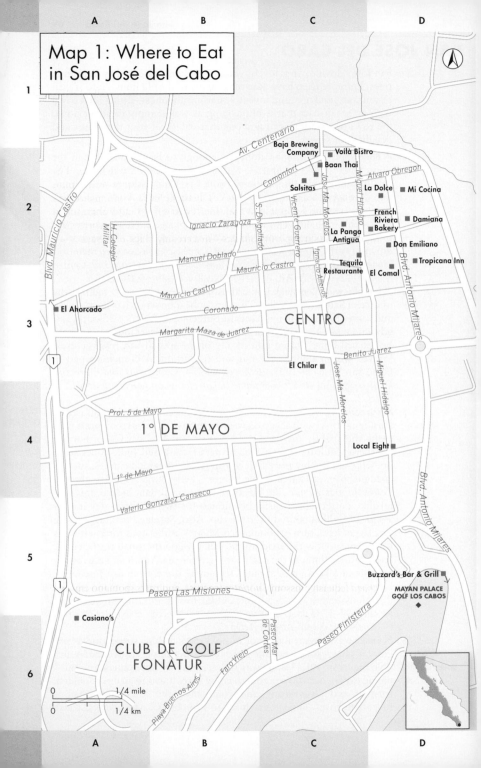

worked at both Las Ventanas and El Chilar. Your waitperson will provide you with a general list of ingredients available for the day, such as Brie, goat cheese, heirloom tomatoes, shrimp, lobster, scallops, snapper, prime beef fillet, and foie gras. Give him or her an idea of your tastes, and let the kitchen create the perfect surprise dish. Five-course meals and food-wine pairings are the specialties. Reservations are strongly recommended. ⊠ *Bahia de Palmas s/n, Local 2, 4 and 6, Plaza del Mar, Fonatur* ☎ *624/142–5928, 866/440–0073 in U.S.* ⊕ *www.casianos.com* ⊟ *AE, MC, V* ✛ *1:A6.*

$$
CONTINENTAL

✕ **Damiana.** At this small hacienda beside San José's town plaza, bougainvillea wraps around tall pines that surround wrought-iron tables, and pink adobe walls glow in the candlelight. Start with mushrooms *diablo* (steeped in a fiery-hot sauce), then move on to tender chateaubriand steak or charbroiled lobster. For more traditional seafood preparations, order the shrimp *enfrijolladas*—in a creamy black bean sauce—or the shrimp with a mild cactus sauce. If you like your dining experiences to come with a side of adventure, Damiana has created a "steak" out of ground shrimp in its signature Imperial Steak Shrimp. During peak season a trio of guitarists serenades the guests. ⊠ *Blvd. Mijares 8, Centro* ☎ *624/142–0499* ⊕ *www.damiana.com.mx* ⊟ *AE, MC, V* ۞ *Closed Aug. and Sept.* ✛ *1:D2.*

$$$
MEXICAN
Fodor's Choice
★

✕ **Don Emiliano.** One of the few woman chefs in Los Cabos area, Margarita Carrillo de Salinas is often considered one of the top chefs in Mexico. Carrillo de Salinas taps into the quality cooking that has run in the family for generations, and her menu shows it. The restaurant's signature dish is the complex Pescado Tikin-Xic (try to pronounce this Mayan recipe correctly after a shot or two of tequila). Tikin-Xic is the local catch of the day that is prepared in the Yucatecan style, with an achiote salsa and wrapped in banana leaves. For dessert the simple grilled mangoes, filled with spices and nuts and smothered in a rich orange-juice reduction, is a delectable choice. ⊠ *Blvd. Mijares 27, Centro* ☎ *624/142–0266* ⊕ *www.donemiliano.com.mx* ⊟ *MC, V* ۞ *No lunch* ✛ *1:D2.*

¢
MEXICAN

✕ **El Ahorcado.** By day it looks like a hole-in-the-wall, but when the sun goes down, this open-air eatery really comes to life. And if you can get beyond the ghoulish silhouette logo—*ahorcado* means "hangman" in Spanish—the food is great. This is one of the few area restaurants open late, and it stays packed until closing (usually around midnight). Old pots, baskets, antique irons, sombreros, and the like hang from the walls and rafters. Tacos and enchiladas come with such tasty fillers as *flor de calabaza* (squash blossom), *nopales* (cactus), and *rajas* (poblano chilies). Be sure to sample the empanadas *huitlacoche* (a savory fungus that usually grows on corn). ⊠ *Paseo Pescadores and Marinos* ☎ *624/172–2093* ⊟ *No credit cards* ۞ *Closed Mon.* ✛ *1:A3.*

$$
MEXICAN

✕ **El Chilar.** Set just a few blocks south of mainstream of San José, this spot is worth the search. The fine selection of Mexican wines and tequilas suits the stylish menu in this small, bustling space, where murals of the Virgin of Guadalupe adorn bright orange walls. In his open kitchen, chef Armando Montaño uses chilies from all over Mexico to enhance traditional and Continental dishes, coating rack of lamb with

4

Fodor's Choice ★

Don Emiliano is run by the uber-talented Margarita Carrillo de Salinas.

Mi Cocina is the restaurant at Casa Natalia.   Jean-Georges Vongerichten opened Market in 2008.

ancho chili and perking up lobster bisque with smoky *chiles guajillos.* The management refuses to stagnate, however, and changes the menu every month. One mainstay has been the Oaxacan *tlayudas* (similar to tostadas), possibly the most asked-for item of the last half dozen years here. After dinner, retire to the wine-and-tequila tasting room, admiring the service that brought it the "Distintivo T" award for tequila knowledge. ✉ *Calle Juárez at Morelos, Centro* ☏ *624/142–2544* ▭ *No credit cards* ☺ *No lunch* ✦ *1:C3.*

$$ ✕ **El Comal.** Without argument, Boulevard Mijares is San José's Restau-
MEXICAN rant Row. There are more than enough places to satiate your dining desires along this quaint street. Nestled in "La Casa de don Rodrigo" building, El Comal serves up affordable dishes such as fresh fish, carne asada à la Tampiqueña, flank steak, and cabrilla (sea bass) with mango sauce on a bed of mashed potatoes. There is also live music Thursday evening from 7:30 to 10. ✉ *Blvd. Mijares across the street from Tropicana Inn, Centro* ☏ *624/142–5508* ⊕ *www.restaurantelcomal.com* ▭ *MC, V* ☺ *Closed Sun* ✦ *1:D3.*

$ ✕ **French Riviera Bakery.** We challenge you to try to ignore the croissants
CAFÉ and éclairs beckoning to you from their glass cases beside displays of candies and ice cream here. In the creperie area, the cook tucks fresh crepes around eggs and cheese, ground beef and onions, or shrimp and pesto. If you choose to sit down, chicken salad, quesadillas, and other more standard fare are served at both the tall and short tables. The patisserie also has a well-thought-out drink menu of fine wines and tequilas, and now it also has a dinner menu that is as impressive as its similarly named sister restaurant along the Corridor. ✉ *Manuel Doblado at Av. Hidalgo, Centro* ☏ *624/142–3350* ⊕ *www.frenchrivieraloscabos.com* ▭ *AE, MC, V* ✦ *1:D2.*

$ ✕ **La Dolce.** Located literally right in the middle of everything in San José,
ITALIAN La Dolce is on the town's *zócalo* (square), near the cathedral. This spot is known for authentic and affordable Italian fare, serving antipastas, meats, wood-fired oven pizzas, and seafood, such as Calamari Trifolati, for less than $10. Both locals and visitors alike call this a favorite. ✉ *Av. Zaragoza and Av. Hidalgo, Plaza Jardin, Centro* ☏ *624/142–6621* ▭ *MC, V* ☺ *Closed Mon.* ✦ *1:D2.*

$$$$ ✕ **La Panga Antigua.** An ancient wooden *panga* (small skiff) hangs above
MEXICAN the door at this intriguing restaurant, located just across from San José's historical mission. Tastefully decorated, La Panga has tables on a series of patios, one with a faded mural, another with a burbling fountain. Chef Jacobo Turquie prepares a superb catch of the day, drizzled with basil-infused oil and served with sautéed spinach and mashed potatoes. His regional seafood dishes, *pollo con mole,* gazpacho, and creamed carrot soup are also exceptional. ✉ *Av. Zaragoza 20, Centro* ☏ *624/142–4041* ⊕ *www.lapanga.com* ▭ *AE, MC, V* ✦ *1:C2.*

$$ ✕ **Local Eight.** This is a comfortable and relaxing eatery, with soft light-
ECLECTIC ing, and bamboo decor flourishes. The soothing sound of a gurgling fountain makes you feel as if you're dining in a friend's garden. Local Eight's globally inspired cuisine is inventive, especially the pecan-and-Gorgonzola salad, rack of lamb marinated in tasty herbs, and the cabrilla (sea bass), grilled Sicilian style. In the mood for Japanese? Try the

CLOSE UP

Dining In

Eating every meal in a Los Cabos restaurant can devour your dollars quickly. Most food and liquor is shipped from the mainland or imported from the United States, resulting in higher prices than the rest of Mexico. Many hotel rooms have small refrigerators and coffeemakers, and more and more of the popular time-share units becoming available in Los Cabos are equipped with completely stocked kitchens. By stocking up on groceries you can save your pesos for splurges. Watch out for the prices on imported goods—a box of imported cereal can cost $5 or more. Stick with Mexican brands, or the many U.S. brands that are manufactured in Mexico. (It'll look just like the Kellogg's Corn Flakes box, but it will say HOJUELAS DE MAÍZ.)

Supermarkets such as Cabo San Lucas's longtime standby **Aramburo** (⌧ Av. Cárdenas across from Hard Rock Cafe, Cabo San Lucas ☎ 624/143–1450 ⌧ Hwy. 1, Km 17, Cabo San Lucas ☎ 624/143–4292), and neighborhood markets sell the basics for quick meals. Aramburo keeps a good stock of items that appeal to foreigners. Newish to the area is **Soriana** (⌧ Hwy. 19 just outside Cabo San Lucas ☎ 624/105–1290 ⌧ Hwy. 1, Km 34.5, San José

del Cabo ☎ 624/142–6132), a Mexican supermarket chain that resembles a Wal-Mart Supercenter. The stores have terrific prices and great produce selection, but fewer U.S. brands than at Aramburo. At **Costco** (⌧ Hwy. 1, Km 4.5, just outside Cabo San Lucas ☎ 624/146–7180), members can stock up on inexpensive supplies. **Tutto Bene** (⌧ At the western end of Marina San Lucas, Blvd. Marina and Camino del Cerro, Cabo San Lucas ☎ 624/144–3300) has a great selection of beer and wines—more than 450 different labels from Australia, California, Chile, Italy, and Spain—as well as organic and frozen foods, healthy and low-calorie offerings, and cheese, all at prices that can be even lower than those at Costco. Tutto Bene offers free delivery throughout Cabo San Lucas, and people even drive in from La Paz to shop here. Located in the Puerto Paraíso Mall, on the lower, marina level, **La Europea Deli and Grocery** (☎ 624/105–1818) also has good prices for food, drinks, grocery items, beer, wine, champagne, spirits, and varied food staples. For liquor in particular, stock up at the airport's duty-free shop at your departure airport. Liquor stores are generally less expensive than supermarkets and stay open until 11 PM (earlier on Sunday).

tagarashi tuna. ⌧ *Plaza Misión, Blvd. Mijares and Finisterra, Fonatur* ☎ *624/142–6655* ⊕ *www.localeight.com* ▭ *MC, V* ✛ *1:D4.*

$$$
ECLECTIC
Fodor's Choice
★

✕ **Mi Cocina.** Traveling foodies, visiting chefs, and locals in the know favor this chic outdoor restaurant at Casa Natalia, San José del Cabo's loveliest boutique hotel. Torches glow on the dining terrace, and the tables are spaced far enough apart so that you don't have to share your whispered sweet nothings with neighbors. Chef-owner Loic Tenoux plays with his ingredients, calling the new approach at Mi Cocina "Euro-Mexican Bistro-style." He mixes marinated octopus with Chinese noodles in a to-die-for salad, and stuffs poblano chilies with lamb and Oaxacan cheese. Tenoux also serves classic onion soup; the homemade focaccia bread is great for dipping. Fried Camembert goes well with many of the imported wines on the extensive list. ⊠ *Casa Natalia, Blvd. Mijares 4, Centro* ☎ 624/146–7100 ⊕ *www.micocinaloscabos.com* ▤ *AE, MC, V* ⊘ *No lunch* ✢ *1:D2.*

WORD OF MOUTH

"We ate at Salsitas—very cute restaurant and food was reasonable—the burritos were huge and would very easily feed 2. It's close to the Plaza area." —sunbum1944

$ MEXICAN ✕ **Salsitas.** One of San José's newest eateries is the offspring of the elegant Tequila Restaurante a couple of blocks away. The owners have gone for a more traditional Mexican menu here rather than the Mexican-plus-highbrow-international selection at the original restaurant. You get the same attention to detail and quality, though, along with a stone- and stucco-walled coziness—all for lower prices. The fare is standard: tacos, chiles rellenos, and enormous burritos. There's a full bar, but consider washing down your meal with a refreshing *agua de Jamaïca* (hibiscus-flavored drink). There's a small artisan shop in the restaurant, so feel free to browse while you wait for your meal. ⊠ *Obregón 1732, Centro* ☎ 624/142–6787 ▤ *MC, V* ✢ *1:C2.*

$$ ECLECTIC ✕ **Tequila Restaurante.** A beautifully redone old adobe home sets the stage for this classy dining experience. A lengthy tequila list tempts diners to savor the finer brands of Mexico's national drink, and an extensive wine cellar will make it difficult to choose what to sip as you sup. The menu is a creative blend of Mediterranean, Asian, and Mexican influences; select from excellent regional meat dishes and innovative Pacific Rim spring rolls, salads, and seafood with mango, ginger, and citrus sauces. Take your time and sample all you can. ⊠ *Manuel Doblado 1011, Centro* ☎ 624/142–1155 ⊕ *www.tequilarestaurant.com* ▤ *AE, D, MC, V* ⊘ *No lunch* ✢ *1:C2.*

$$ AMERICAN ✕ **Tropicana Inn.** Start the day with coffee and French toast at this enduringly popular restaurant. The back garden patio quickly fills up with a loyal clientele every meal; the front sidewalk seating is a great space to survey the world going by. The menu includes U.S. cuts of beef along with fajitas, chiles rellenos, and lobster—always in demand. San José's nightlife scene revolves around the comfortable second-story bar. Latin bands and other musicians play nightly. Service can be slow at times, so be prepared to be patient, especially when you're trying to get the bill. ⊠ *Blvd. Mijares 30, Centro* ☎ 624/142–1580 ⊕ *www.tropicanainn. com.mx* ▤ *AE, MC, V* ✢ *1:D2.*

$$$ ECLECTIC ✕ **Voilà Bistro.** Sharing a space and creative environment with an art gallery and an interior decorator has rubbed off on this restaurant, *sin duda* (without a doubt). Here you'll find an anything-goes style of Mexican cuisine. You could order *sopa de tortilla* or a traditional Caesar salad, but opt instead for the lobster burrito, served with avocado, chipotle, and mango, along with rice and black beans. And then dessert: pistachio crème brûlée or a coconut tart, perhaps? Or both? Daily lunch specials go for about $8. Live Latin music reigns supreme on Friday night from 7:30 to 10:30, when the menu goes ever more

4

tropical; try the pistachio-macadamia-crusted sea bass. ⊠ *Plaza Paulina, Morelos and Comonfort, Centro* ☎ *624/130–7569* ⊕ *www.voila-events. com* ▤ *MC, V* ⊙ *No lunch Sun.* ✢ *1:C2.*

THE CORRIDOR

Dining along the Corridor between San José del Cabo and Cabo San Lucas was always restricted to the ever-improving hotel restaurants. But with the addition of the Tiendas de Palmilla shopping center, just across from the One&Only Palmilla resort, top-notch eateries are establishing a new dining energy along this stretch of highway, giving drivers along the Corridor a tasty reason to slow down, and maybe even stop.

$$
ECLECTIC

✕ **7 Seas Restaurant.** It's quite soothing to sit in this restaurant, in the Cabo Surf Hotel, at the ocean's edge, smelling the sea breezes. Stop off after your morning surf session to munch on *machaca con huevos* (eggs scrambled with shredded beef) washed down with a fresh-fruit smoothie; or drop in after you've enjoyed the evening surf to dine on blue crab tostadas and tricolor shrimp ravioli. Your entertainment is simple: a wonderful view that never stops changing. ⊠ *Cabo Surf Hotel, Km 28* ☎ *624/142–2666* ⊕ *www.7seasrestaurant.com* ▤ *MC, V* ✢ *2:B6.*

$$$
AMERICAN

✕ **French Riviera.** Jacques Chretien's popular bistro has terrific views of El Arco and Land's End. The restaurant is upstairs, with the lounge-bar on the ground floor. The menu is airy and eclectic: a spinach, egg, and bacon burrito could be breakfast, and lunch and dinner might consist of a gourmet pizza, Cajun chicken salad, or sushi. For a special treat, ask the restaurant to pack you a picnic meal that you can bring to the beach. Though the dinner menu changes every day, look for braised red snapper with Provençale gratin potatoes and zucchini in a basil reduction. Finish with melt-in-your-mouth chocolate cake with pear puree or strawberries napoleon. ⊠ *Hwy. 1, Km 6.3* ☎ *624/104–3125* ⊕ *www. frenchrivieraloscabos.com* ▤ *MC, V* ✢ *2:C4.*

$$
ECLECTIC

✕ **Manuel's.** Owner-chef Manuel Arredondo has opened the Corridor's newest restaurant. Sample the shrimp fettuccine with saffron or the panfried chicken with capers, artichokes, and cherry tomatoes. Menu selections change almost daily. If you're having trouble deciding, the tasting menu lets you sample eight appetizer-size portions—a good option if you come here with a group. ⊠ *Las Tiendas de Palmilla mall* ☎ *624/144–6170* ⊕ *www.manuelsrestaurant.com.mx* ▤ *MC, V* ⊙ *Closed Sun.* ✢ *2:B5.*

$$$$
ECLECTIC
Fodor's Choice
★

✕ **Market.** Charlie Trotter's now-closed "C" restaurant in the One&Only Palmilla resort was replaced in late 2008 by a new offering from three-star Michelin chef Jean-Georges Vongerichten—his first in Latin America. The roast veal chops with chipotle glaze, Chilean salmon with lemon and dill, crab-stuffed squash blossoms, and cornmeal ravioli with cherry tomatoes all exemplify the "European with Mexican flair" description that Market gives its menu. While the consensus is that Market's contemporary furnishings in warm, inviting earth tones are more casual than those of its predecessor, this could well be one of your more expensive dinners in already pricey Los Cabos. You can bring

Enjoy out-of-this-world sushi at Nick-San–Palmilla, in the Tiendas de Palmilla shopping center.

Sunset Da Mona Lisa offers up a romantic atmosphere, amazing views and an inventive Italian menu.

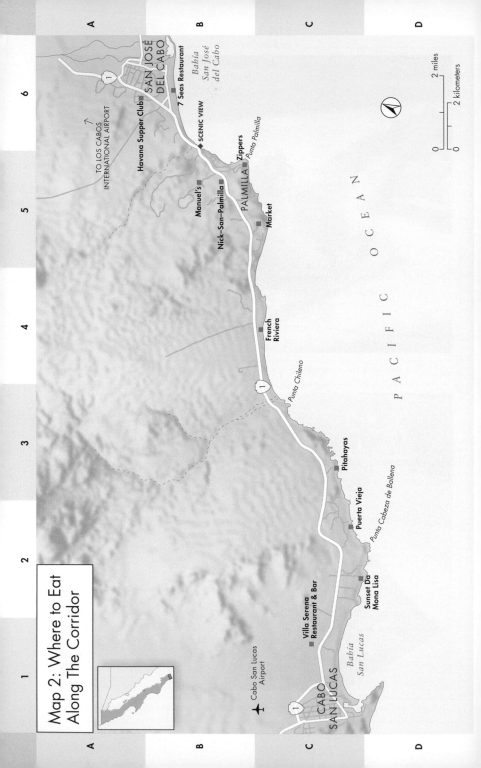

Map 2: Where to Eat Along The Corridor

A
TO LOS CABOS
INTERNATIONAL AIRPORT

SAN JOSÉ
DEL CABO

7 Seas Restaurant

Havana Supper Club

SCENIC VIEW

Manuel's

Nick-San-Palmilla

PALMILLA

Zippers

Punta Palmilla

Market

French
Riviera

Punta Chileno

Pitahayas

Puerta Vieja

Punta Cabeza de Ballena

Villa Serena
Restaurant & Bar

Sunset Da
Mona Lisa

Cabo San Lucas
Airport

CABO
SAN LUCAS

Bahía
San Lucas

Bahía
San José
del Cabo

P A C I F I C   O C E A N

2 miles

2 kilometers

your bill down slightly by opting for a fine Baja wine from the extensive wine list rather than a European one. ⊠ *One&Only Palmilla, Hwy. 1, Km 27.5* ☎ *624/146–7000* ⊕ *www.oneandonlyresorts.com* ⚲ *Reservations essential* ☰ *AE, D, MC, V* ⊘ *No lunch* ✛ *2:C5.*

$$$ ✕ **Nick-San–Palmilla.** The sky's the
ASIAN limit here at this out-of-this-world-
Fodor'sChoice inventive sushi den in the Tiendas
★ de Palmilla shopping mall. Pair each of your selections with an exceptional wine or liquor, and let chef Abel and floor manager Mauricio help you make the choices.

Favorites include the lobster roll (with cilantro, mango, mustard, and roe) with a 2005 Chateau Montalena; lobster *sambal* (marinated in sake with soy, ginger, and garlic) with Kikusi sake; and the Hamachi belly cake and tuna tostadas with a Chilean Casas del Bosque Sauvignon Blanc. ⊠ *Las Tiendas de Palmilla mall* ☎ *624/144–6262* ⊕ *www. nicksan.com* ☰ *MC, V* ✛ *2:B5.*

$$$ ✕ **Pitahayas.** In this elegant niche above the beach in the resort com-
ASIAN munity Cabo del Sol, chef Volker Romeike blends Thai, Polynesian,
Fodor'sChoice and Chinese ingredients into artful, award-winning Asian fusion. He
★ matches lobster with a vanilla-bean sauce, scallops with a sweet chili glaze, and the catch of the day with Thai curry. Soft jazz plays in the background, and the service is impeccable. The restaurant has been enlarged with a terrace and lounge, and now seats up to 500—it claims to be the largest restaurant in Los Cabos. On offer is one of the largest wine selections in all of Mexico. Dress to impress. ⊠ *Sheraton Hacienda del Mar, Hwy. 1, Km 10* ☎ *624/145–8010* ⊕ *www.pitahayas.com* ☰ *AE, MC, V* ✛ *2:C3.*

$$ ✕ **Puerta Vieja.** Puerta Vieja translates into "Old Door." The beautiful
ECLECTIC old door you walk through to enter this restaurant is actually from India. Service here includes both affordable lunches and glorious dinners. We suggest dinner at sunset, when the view of El Arco is the most impressive. The cuisine pulls from Continental, Latin, and Mexican traditions, with a touch of Asia. Entrées feature lobster, shrimp, and Sonoran cuts of meat. ⊠ *Hwy. 1, Km 6.3* ☎ *624/104–3252 or 624/104– 3334* ⊕ *www.puertavieja.com* ☰ *MC, V* ✛ *2:C2.*

$$$ ✕ **Sunset Da Mona Lisa.** Cocktail tables along the cliffs have panoramic
ITALIAN views of El Arco, making this the best place to toast the sunset and
Fodor'sChoice another beautiful day in Los Cabos before moving to the candlelit din-
★ ing room. Or remain outside, and enjoy dining alfresco. Italian chef Emanuele Olivero has paid his dues in Los Cabos, with time at La Dolce in San José, at C in the Palmilla, and also at Pitahayas. Now he has brought his ideas to full fruition here at the Mona Lisa. The restaurant's four seasonal menus all rely on ever-changing seasonal ingredients. How about ravioli filled with pumpkin, or La Paz blue crab covered with a

4

cinnamon white sauce? Or seared halibut with crunchy polenta, sun-dried tomatoes, and asparagus tempura? You can also go all out with the Grand Mona Lisa Tasting Menu, which allows you to try just about everything on the extensive menu. The restaurant is not really in the Corridor, but not really in town either; it's just a couple of miles up the hill—a short and relatively inexpensive taxi ride, well worth the trip for a sunset cocktail and dinner. Make sure you appreciate the Mona Lisa tile artwork both close up and from a distance—it's an interesting optical illusion. ⊠ *Hwy. 1, Km 5.5* ☎ *624/145–8160* ⚐ *Reservations essential* ▤ *MC, V* ☉ *No lunch* ✛ *2:C2.*

$$ ✗ **Villa Serena Restaurant & Bar.** Open for almost 20 years in the Villa Ser-
ECLECTIC ena neighborhood along the main highway, this quiet, open-air, palapa-covered restaurant offers standard fare, from shrimp cocktail to chicken Caesar salad and T-bone steak, with some Mexican specialties thrown in. If you grab an ocean-facing table, you can watch the cruise ships glide past. This restaurant has what most don't: a pool—perfect for dipping your feet while sipping a fruity concoction. ⊠ *Hwy. 1, Km 7.5* ☎ *624/145–8244* ▤ *MC, V* ✛ *2:C1.*

$ ✗ **Zippers.** Home to the surfing crowd and those who don't mind a bit
AMERICAN of sand in their burgers (well . . . not really), this casual palaparoof
☺ restaurant is on Costa Azul Beach, just south of San José. Come for the sea breezes, the delicious wafting smell of grilling lobster and tacos, and a sound track of surf tunes. Casual doesn't begin to describe the crowd, which can get downright raunchy. But hey, have fun, amigo, you've entered Los Cabos Surf Zone! There's no question that owner "Big Tony" feeds you well for your pesos. With half-pound burgers, slabs of prime rib, or steak and lobster for two at just $40, you'll leave the beach a glutton, albeit a jolly one. Bring the kiddos in the daytime; they'll enjoy running from the dining table to the sand between every couple of bites. Sporting events sometimes blare on the TV, and Friday nights bring live music. ⊠ *Hwy. 1, Km 18.5* ☎ *624/172–6162* ▤ *No credit cards* ✛ *2:B5.*

CABO SAN LUCAS

Cabo San Lucas is *in*—especially for its rowdy nightlife and slew of trendy restaurants. A pedestrian walkway lined with restaurants, bars, and shops anchored by the sleek Puerto Paraíso mall curves around Cabo San Lucas harbor, itself packed with yachts. The most popular restaurants, clubs, and shops are along Avenida Cárdenas (the extension of Highway 1 from the Corridor) and Boulevard Marina, paralleling the waterfront. As the Cabo Explosion continues, seemingly unstoppable, even more impressive restaurants and bars are opening their doors every week.

$$$ ✗ **Al Caravea.** One diner called this spot "the parking-lot restaurant,"
ECLECTIC and, yes, this eatery is carved out of such a space. But put in a raised floor, a roof, some heavy cloth hangings to serve as walls, some plants, and a scant eight tables, and you've got a surprisingly intimate and cozy place that makes you forget this was a parking lot. On the menu are items such as scalloped beef with prosciutto and *pescado con*

champiñones (fish with mushroom sauce), plus a good selection of wine and beer—it's small and modest, but what is done here, is done well. ✉ *Zaragoza and 16 de Septiembre, Centro* ☎ *624/164–2939* 🚫 *No credit cards* 🕐 *Closed Sun.* ✛ *3:B4.*

$$ ✕ **Alexander's Restaurant.** Ideally located along Cabo San Lucas's busy
ECLECTIC marina walkway, Alexander's is where Switzerland meets Mexico. Pull up a chair at one of the sidewalk tables and start with a meat-and-cheese fondue, for which Swiss chef Alex Brulhart is known. His tempura prawns served in a half coconut are mythical, and the portobello mushrooms and mixed greens with goat cheese and light balsamic dressing have critics eating out of his hands. ✉ *Plaza Bonita 7, on the Marina walkway, Marina* ☎ *624/143–2022* ⊕ *www.alexanders-restaurant-cabo.com* ▭ *MC, V* ✛ *3:B4.*

4

$$$ ✕ **Amarone Ristorante.** No, you're not in Italy, New York, or even Los
ITALIAN Angeles, but in Cabo San Lucas. But who would know? This fine-dining experience is top-drawer, no matter what country you've flown in from. From the formally attired waiters to the phenomenal selection of imported Italian products including *vinos,* cheeses, meats, olives, and olive oils, the service, presentation, and meals are as slick as it gets in Los Cabos. Everything's handmade, from the pastas, such as ravioli and gnocchi, to the desserts, such as tiramisu and a chocolate torte. ✉ *At Puerto Paraíso shopping center, lower level marina, Marina* ☎ *624/105–1035* ⊕ *www.ristoranteamarone.com* ▭ *AE, MC, V* ✛ *3:B4.*

$ ✕ **Baja Brewing Company.** This branch of the established San José del
AMERICAN Cabo microbrewery opened here in 2009, boasting the same menu—burgers, soups, salads, and pizza—same prices, and the same tasty selection of freshly brewed beers. Those beers are still brewed in San José, meaning what you get here is "20 minutes fresh," as the manager says. No quibbles with the system; these beers are a flavorful change from the ubiquitous Tecate. What's not the same is the semi-open-air venue on the rooftop of the Cabos Villas hotel on Médano Beach with a view of the ocean. ✉ *Rooftop of Cabo Villas, Médano Beach, Playa Médano* ☎ *624/143 9199* ⊕ *www.bajabrewingcompany.com* ▭ *MC, V* ✛ *3:C4.*

$ ✕ **Baja Cantina Beach.** Lighted by torches at night, with mesquite grilled seafood and sushi bar specials, as well as USDA meats, this restaurant is warm, casual, and even slightly romantic here on busy Médano Beach. You'll hear relaxing music from breakfast on at this well-run cantina. Mexican music takes center stage on Wednesday nights; live beachfront jazz is on the schedule Thursday. Check out the excellent variety of sushi, or try a tasting dinner. Wi-Fi is accessible here. ✉ *Playa Médano, next to Cabo Villas, Playa Médano* ☎ *624/143–1591* ⊕ *www.bajacantina.com.mx* ▭ *AE, D, DC, MC, V* ✛ *3:C4.*

$$ ✕ **Baja Cantina Marina.** This large, casual, sportfishing-oriented cantina,
ECLECTIC in the Tesoro Hotel, has it all (if you're looking for this type of "all"): a top marina location near M Dock, yielding an excellent view of the sportfishing and megayachts; $2 cervezas all day; affordable eats; and American sports on TV. Many of the sportfishing deckhands and boat captains eat here. In the morning, enjoy a Captain's breakfast special for $2.99. Try the $3 afternoon appetizer menu, or splurge a little with

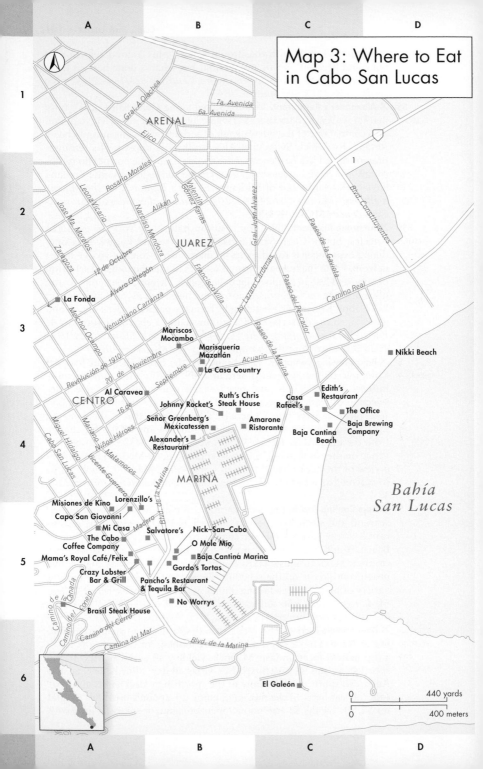

Map 3: Where to Eat in Cabo San Lucas

ARENAL

7a. Avenida
6a. Avenida

Gral. A Olachea
Elico
Rosario Morales

JUAREZ

Leona Vicario
Jose Ma. Morelos
Zaragoza
12 de Octubre
Alvaro Obregón
Narciso Mendoza
Alikan
Gómez Farías
Valentín
Francisco Villa
Av. Lázaro Cárdenas
Gral. Juan Alvarez

Blvd. Constituyentes

Paseo de la Gaviota

Camino Real

Paseo del Pescador

La Fonda

Melchor Ocampo
Venustiano Carranza

Revolución de 1910
20 de Noviembre
Paseo de la Marina

Mariscos
Mocambo
Marisquería
Mazatlán
Acuario
La Casa Country

Nikki Beach

CENTRO
16 de Septiembre

Al Caravea
Johnny Rocket's
Ruth's Chris
Steak House
Casa
Rafael's
Edith's
Restaurant

Señor Greenberg's
Mexicatessen
Amarone
Ristorante
The Office
Baja Brewing
Company

Miguel Hidalgo
Mariano Matamoros
Niños Héroes
Cabo San Lucas
Vicente Guerrero

Alexander's
Restaurant

Baja Cantina
Beach

MARINA

Bahía
San Lucas

Lorenzillo's
Misiones de Kino
Capo San Giovanni
Mi Casa
The Cabo
Coffee Company
Mama's Royal Café/Felix

Blvd. de la Marina
Madero

Salvatore's
Nick-San-Cabo
O Mole Mio
Baja Cantina Marina
Gordo's Tortas

Crazy Lobster
Bar & Grill
Pancho's Restaurant
& Tequila Bar
No Worrys

Camino de la Canada
Camino del Conejo
Camino del Cerro
Camino del Mar
Brasil Steak House
Blvd. de la Marina

El Galeón

0   440 yards
0   400 meters

the seafood and steak specials. Friday night is Ladies' Night, meaning ladies drink free from 9:30 to 11:30 PM. Stay late for the DJ and dancing. Wi-Fi is accessible throughout the restaurant, so bring your laptop. ✉ *On the marina, Marina* ☎ *624/143–1591* ⊕ *www.bajacantina.com.mx* ⊟ *AE, D, DC, MC, V* ✛ *3:B5.*

$$ ✕ **Brasil Steak House.** Although this
STEAKHOUSE architecturally impressive, bright Amazon-green restaurant is primarily for meat eaters, with meat galore roasted in the Rodicio-style (Brazilian rotisserie), it also offers a surprisingly wide-ranging salad bar. Begin with chicken wings, fried plantains, or the soup of the day. A full selection of meats includes top sirloin, filet mignon, Mexican sausages, rib eye, chicken, ham with pineapple, turkey with bacon, and lamb. If you're really hungry, eat as much as you can or want for $25. ✉ *Zapata between Hidalgo and Guerrero, Centro* ☎ *624/143–8353* ⊕ *www.brasilcabo.com* ⊟ *MC, V* ⊘ *No lunch* ✛ *3:A5.*

¢ ✕ **The Cabo Coffee Company.** We think we've found Los Cabos' best coffee
CAFÉ and best coffeehouse, and it's a twofer, depending on your mood. Locals hang out at the original branch on Hidalgo. A second, newer installment at Plaza Nautica draws the tourists. Either way, you get a terrific selection of gourmet coffee drinks that are made with beans from the Mexican state of Oaxaca and roasted fresh at Cabo Coffee's own facility just outside town. Bring your laptop; there's free Wi-Fi. ✉ *Hidalgo at Madero, Marina* ✉ *Plaza Nautica Blvd. Marina, Marina* ☎ *624/105–1130* ⊕ *www.cabocoffee.com* ⊟ *No credit cards* ✛ *3:A5.*

$$$ ✕ **Capo San Giovanni.** The sound and smell of rich sauces simmering
ITALIAN in the open kitchen blends with strains of opera at this intimate Italian restaurant. Owner Gianfranco Zappata and his wife, Antonella, a master pastry chef, perform a culinary concert that keeps you coming back for encores. Try the green salad with lobster, cioppino Calabrese, spaghetti with crab, and *mela* (an apple-and-nut pastry topped with caramel). For a little romance, dine on the starlit back patio. You'll hear soft live music most evenings. There's a 10% discount for paying with cash. ✉ *Guerrero at Av. Cárdenas, Centro* ☎ *624/143–0593* ⊕ *www.caposangiovanni.com* ⊟ *MC, V* ⊘ *No lunch* ✛ *3:A5.*

$$$ ✕ **Casa Rafael's.** The Casa, within a boutique hotel of the same name,
ECLECTIC has been a popular *restaurante* near the beach for over a dozen years, but it refuses to rest on its laurels. It continues its popular live piano-bar music, and has a nice selection of Cuban cigars for sale in the Cigar Room. But it's in the liquor-and-wine department that it really shines,

EAT, DRINK, AND SMOKE

If you're in the mood to eat, drink, and smoke a good Cuban cigar, then head to Cabo's Hemingway's Cigar & Tequila Lounge (✉ *Calle Vicente Guerrero* ☎ *624/143–6061* ⊕ *www.hemingwayscabo.com*). With a killer sound system; a fine selection of 400 tequilas; a large, aromatic cigar humidor; and a selection of top Cuban rums, this place has got a bar that would make Papa himself proud. Hemingway's also mixes up Big Papa's Mojitos and Floridita Daiquiris, and some munchies are available. There's live Cuban music from 9 to midnight. You'll find Hemingway's across from Cabo Wabo.

with an impressively updated wine list with first-growth French Bordeaux, an off-the-charts selection of American wines, a worldwide beer menu of 50 brews, a well-rounded Scotch list, and a spirits flight menu. The food is extremely varied and uses myriad ingredients. There's fresh Malaysian tuna, escargot, Casa Rafael's Greek salad, and pasta dishes. The heavenly Chicken Allison is a boneless breast sautéed in Beaujolais with mushroom sauce. There are many freshly made desserts, too. ⊠ *Calle Médano and Paseo del Pescador, Playa Médano* ☎ *624/143–0739* ⊕ *www.casarafaels.com* ▭ *MC, V* ⊗ *No lunch* ✛ *3:C4.*

¢ ✕ **Crazy Lobster Bar & Grill.** Open for breakfast, lunch, and dinner, this
MEXICAN typical Mexican sit-down locale has a happy hour that runs from 10
Fodor'sChoice AM to 6 PM. Prices here are super-cheap: You can get a lobster tail for
★ less than 10 bucks; Cuervo tequila shots are a mere 70¢; and Don Julio tequila shots are $2.80. And as you sit under the open-air palapa, strolling mariachis will pass by, providing your dining sound track. ⊠ *Hidalgo and Zapata, Centro* ☎ *624/143–6535* ▭ *MC, V* ⊗ *Closed Sept.* ✛ *3:A5.*

$$ ✕ **Edith's Restaurant.** The Caesar salad and flambéed banana crepes are
SEAFOOD prepared tableside at this colorful, classy, and popular restaurant. The
⊛ Disca de Mariscos, with lobster, shrimp, and fish, is Baja's representative dish. Here even the simplest choices are special: quesadillas are homemade tortillas wrapped around Oaxacan cheese; meat and fish dishes are doused in chili or tropical fruit sauces. Edith's air-conditioned Wine Cellar offers a large selection of domestic and imported wines, and is ideal for hosting small intimate dinners for up to 10. Families dine in early evening, so come in later if you're looking for a more romantic atmosphere when you'll hear soft, live Mexican music. ⊠ *Paseo del Pescador near Playa Médano, Playa Médano* ☎ *624/143–0801* ⊕ *www.edithscabo.com* ▭ *MC, V* ⊗ *Closed Sept. No lunch* ✛ *3:C4.*

$$ ✕ **El Galeón.** Considered by some to be one of the most distinguished
ECLECTIC dining rooms in town, this eatery has been popular for more than 20
years. El Galeón serves traditional Italian, Mexican, and American fare. One enduring favorite is the Caesar salad prepared tableside, with all the proper flourishes. Dishes are expertly prepared, with an emphasis on thick, tender cuts of beef. The osso buco Milanese is a local favorite. The choice seats look out upon the marina, with heavy wooden furnishings and white linens lending a sense of formality. Stop off at the piano bar afterwards, and enjoy Ronald Valentino's music over a late-night brandy. Or perhaps sip one last tequila with a dessert from the cart. ⊠ *Across from marina by the road to Finisterra Hotel, Playa Médano* ☎ *624/143–0443, 624/145–7576 for reservations* ⊕ *www.restaurant-galeon.com* ▭ *AE, MC, V* ⊗ *No lunch Mon.–Sat.* ✛ *3:C6.*

¢ ✕ **Gordo's Tortas.** Ready for a floor show along with your *tortas?* Lis-
MEXICAN ten for the blaring Beatles' tunes, then watch Javier don his tattered Beatles wig and strum his battered, two-stringed ukulele to "I Wanna Hold Your Hand." You've found Gordo's tiny sidewalk stand. Javier's tacos and *tortas* (sandwiches) are made with loving care, and his fans are loyal enough to chow down while standing, as there are only two small plastic tables by the stand. You can have two or three ham-and-cheese tortas for the price of one anywhere else. ⊠ *Guerrero at Zapata,*

across the street from Cabo Wabo, Centro ☎ *No phone* ▬ *No credit cards* ✚ *3:B5.*

¢ ✕ **Johnny Rocket's.** The red, white,

AMERICAN chrome, and Formica here evoke a California diner, circa 1964, and, indeed, this spot on the marina is part of a small (U.S.) California chain. There's little Mexican about it, but the burgers, chili dogs, onion rings, root beer, and malts taste air-conditioning-ly refreshing on a warm afternoon. Fiddle with the individual jukebox controls at your table—we found some Beach Boys tunes—while you partake. ✉ *Puerto Paraíso at San Lucas Marina, Marina* ☎ *624/143–9891* ⊕ *www.johnnyrockets.com* ▬ *AE, D, DC, MC, V* ✚ *3:B4.*

> **FRUITY FLAN**
>
> Flan is usually sinfully, sweetly caramel flavored. But guava? Guava flan is actually *delicioso*, and to be found at hot spot, La Fonda restaurant, in Cabo San Lucas.

$$ ✕ **La Casa Country.** If you're in the mood for a nice steak, and would

STEAKHOUSE enjoy a Mexican floor show to go with that sizzle, try La Casa Country. It's like a localized Ballet Folklorico in Cabo San Lucas. Come here for toothsome steaks, a wide variety of Mexican fare, and fun footstomping *música* in the evenings. If you come for lunch, don't arrive too early; it opens at 1 PM. ✉ *In the Plaza Las Californias, on Av. Cárdenas, Centro* ☎ *624/105–1999* ▬ *MC, V* ✚ *3:B3.*

$$ ✕ **La Fonda.** Finally, a restaurant that's all about genuine Mexican reci-

MEXICAN pes. Chef and owner Christophe Chong Boone has searched high and low, including through his mother's extensive recipe book, to offer traditional Mexican fare, down to the tasty maguey worms, ant eggs, and grasshoppers, from around the entire country. You'll receive an education in Mexican gastronomy here. Boone is quite young, but has already received a degree from the Culinary Institute of America, and is currently working towards his Master Chef Degree. Try the *tortas horgadas* (a Mexican sandwich filled with carnitas and dipped in tomato sauce) from Guadalajara, *chalupas* from Puebla, or several incarnations of mole. The slightly crunchy maguey worms, wrapped in tortillas with guacamole and lime, are surprisingly tasty, as are the ant eggs (*escamoles*) and grasshoppers (*chapulines*). Oh yes, you'll have tales to tell from Cabo. ✉ *Av. Hidalgo near 12 de Octubre, Centro* ☎ *624/143–6926* ▬ *AE, MC, V* ✚ *3:A3.*

$$$$ ✕ **Lorenzillo's.** Gleaming hardwood floors and polished brass give a nauti-

SEAFOOD cal flair to this dining room, where fresh lobster is king. Lorenzillo's has long been a fixture in Cancún, where lobster is raised on the company's farm. That Caribbean lobster is shipped to Los Cabos and served in 14 ways (the simpler preparations—steamed or grilled with lots of melted butter—are best). Menu items are named after pirates and Caribbean marine history, so Sir Francis Drake is the rib-eye steak, El Barbolento is abalone sashimi with spicy diablo sauce, and El Doblón is a giant chop on the bone. If you desire a major lobster splurge, a 2-pounder served with spinach puree and linguine or potato sets you back more than $66. Other options—Alaska king crab, conch, coconut shrimp, or beef medallions—are more moderately priced. The dessert list is lengthy and mouthwatering. A less formal oyster bar with a limited selection of the same menu sits on the pier near the entrance. ⊠ *Av. Cárdenas at Marina, Marina* ☎ *624/105–0212* ⊕ *www.lorenzillos.com.mx* ▭ *AE, MC, V* ⊹ *3:A5.*

$$
MEXICAN

✕ **Mama's Royal Café (by day)/Felix Fine Mexican & Seafood Restaurant (by night).** You can't possibly accuse this restaurant of modesty. But it does exhibit a sense of humor, claiming on the menu to be "probably the best breakfast restaurant in the whole country." Mama's serves up bountiful breakfasts of omelets, and poached eggs with avocado and ham. It also claims to serve the "World's Best French Toast"—a treasure stuffed with cream cheese, strawberries, mangoes, or bananas, along with pecans. It's then topped off with an orange liqueur, so it may just be deserving of this claim. The fried potatoes are also superb. At night, the colorful restaurant becomes Felix, serving *chiles en nogada* (chilies in walnut sauce), *pozole* (pork soup with hominy, onion, garlic, dried chilies, and cilantro), and other Mexican specialties along with a lineup of more than 30 unusual salsas daily (the owner is a salsa pro). Owner Spencer Moore shares all the cooking and salsa "secrets" on the restaurant's Web site. ⊠ *Hidalgo at Zapata, Marina* ☎ *624/143–4290* ⊕ *www.mamascabosanlucas.com* ▭ *MC, V* ⊘ *Closed Sun. and Sept.* ⊹ *3:A5.*

$$
SEAFOOD

✕ **Mariscos Mocambo.** Veracruz—a region known for its seafood preparations—meets Los Cabos in an enormous dining room packed with appreciative locals. The menu has such regional dishes as octopus ceviche, shrimp empanadas, and a heaping mixed-seafood platter that includes sea snails, clams, octopus, lobster, and shrimp. Musicians stroll among the tables and the chatter is somewhat cacophonous, but you're sure to have a great local dining experience here. ⊠ *Leona Vicario at Calle 20 de Noviembre, Centro* ☎ *624/143–2122* ⊕ *www.mariscosmocambo.com* ▭ *MC, V* ⊹ *3:B3.*

$
SEAFOOD
Fodor's Choice
★

✕ **Marisquería Mazatlán.** The crowds of locals lunching at this simple seafood restaurant are a good sign—as are the huge glass cases packed with shrimp, ceviche, and other seafood cocktails. You can dine inexpensively and quickly on wonderful seafood soup, or spend a bit more for tender *pulpo ajillo* (marinated octopus with garlic, chilies, onion, and celery) and enjoy some great people-watching as you eat. ⊠ *Mendoza at Calle 16 de Septiembre, Centro* ☎ *624/143–8565* ▭ *MC, V* ⊹ *3:B3.*

$$
MEXICAN
☾

✕ **Mi Casa.** One of Cabo's top restaurants is in a cobalt-blue adobe building painted with murals. The place is huge: Mi Casa can now seat up to 600. The fresh tuna and dorado, served with tomatillo salsa or Yucatecan achiote, both impress, as does the sophisticated *poblano chiles en nogada* (chilies stuffed with a meat-and-fruit mixture and covered with white walnut sauce and pomegranate seeds). If you're in the mood for something resembling a Mexican luau, try the *barbacoa borrego*, or barbecued goat. It's done à la Hawaii, cooked in the ground (luau olé?). Mi Casa also offers an incredible selection of 20 different fruit margaritas. The large back courtyard glows with candlelight at night, and mariachis provide entertainment. ⊠ *Av. Cabo San Lucas at Lazaro Cardenas, Centro* ☎ *624/143–1933* ⊕ *www.micasarestaurant.com* ▭ *MC, V* ⊹ *3:A5.*

$$
MEXICAN

✕ **Misiones de Kino.** You may feel like you've discovered a well-kept secret when you find, and enter, this palapa-roof house with adobe

Enjoy creative seafood and meat dishes, lively salsas, and expertly made margaritas at Mi Casa.

walls, just a few blocks off the main strip and around the corner from the Mar de Cortez Hotel. Sit on the front patio or in a backyard hut strung with weathered lanterns and photographs of the Mexican Revolution. Menu highlights include *cabrilla con salsa de frambuesa* (sea bass with raspberry sauce), *camarón coco* (coconut shrimp with mango sauce), and the crab or fish with garlic sauce. A second menu, called Pasta Bella, offers a wide range of pastas and Italian dishes. ⊠ *Guerrero and 5 de Mayo, Centro* ☎ *624/105–1418* ⊕ *www.misionesdekino.com* ⊟ *No credit cards* ☼ *Closed Sun. No lunch* ✛ *3:A5.*

$$$ ✕ **Nick-San–Cabo.** Dare we make such a claim: That Nick-San may very
ECLECTIC possibly be Cabo San Lucas's top restaurant. Owner Angel Carbajal
Fodor'sChoice is an artist behind the sushi counter (he also has his own fishing boats
★ that collect fish each day). A creative fusion of Japanese and Mexican cuisines truly sets his masterpieces apart. The sauce on the cilantro sashimi is so divine that some say diners sneak in bread to sop up the sauce (rice isn't the same). You can run up a stiff tab ordering sushi here. The mahogany bar and minimalist dining room are packed most nights, but the vibe is upbeat. Many diners eat here so frequently they've become family friends. There's also a second Nick-San on the Corridor in the Tiendas de Palmilla shopping center. Reservations are recommended, especially on weekend nights and during high season. Otherwise, be prepared for a wait. ⊠ *Blvd. Marina, Plaza de la Danza next to Tesoro Hotel, Marina* ☎ *624/143–4484* ⊕ *www.nicksan.com* ⊟ *MC, V* ✛ *3:B5.*

$$ ✕ **Nikki Beach.** Undoubtedly one of the hippest places in Cabo, by day
ECLECTIC or by night, this restaurant by the pool of the ME Cabo Hotel is really more than just a place to eat—it's a chic and sophisticated scene in and

of itself. Surrounded by chill music and many beautiful people, you'll be tempted by appetizers such as wild-salmon-and-crab cakes, fried octopus with wonton, and raspberry gazpacho. For dinner choose from chicken satay, seafood tabule, or *pankoco* shrimp with risotto, shiitake mushrooms, mango, and coconut. The restaurant turns into more of a club as the night goes on. ⊠ *Playa Médano* ☎ *624/145–7800 Ext. 741* ⊕ *www.nikkibeach.com* ⊟ *MC, V* ✦ *3:D3.*

$ ✕ **No Worrys.** Just look for the 200-foot-tall lighthouse along the north-
AMERICAN   western side of the marina boardwalk, and you've found No Wor-
rys. (Okay . . . Spelling might not be their forte.) Everything in this restaurant-shop in the Tesoro Hotel Lighthouse is served large and in charge, from the cold beers in the buckets to the huge burgers, ribs, and sandwiches. Eat, drink, and be merry while you shop till you drop in the boutique to the sounds of classic rock and roll. ⊠ *Marina Cabo San Lucas, Marina* ☎ *624/143–8575* ⊕ *www.noworrys.com* ⊟ *AE, D, DC, MC, V* ✦ *3:B5.*

$$ ✕ **The Office.** Playa Médano is lined with cafés on the sand, some with
ECLECTIC   lounge chairs, others with more formal settings. At least once during your visit to Los Cabos, you must visit the Office, the original break-fast spot on Médano Beach. This place has a huge sign, blue umbrellas (the perfect photo backdrop), and great view of Land's End. There's no better way to start out the morning in Cabo than enjoying a *sabroso* (tasty) lobster omelet, fresh-fruit smoothie, and powerful cup of Mexi-can coffee, with your toes in the sand, of course. Another favorite menu item is the French toast. The service is friendly, the menu a bit expensive, but hey, amigo, you're on vacation. Cold beer (later in the day, of course), ceviche, nachos, fish tacos, french fries, and burgers are served in portions that somewhat justify the high prices. You can split most entrées. Dinners of grilled shrimp, fish with garlic, and steaks are popular. ⊠ *Playa Médano* ☎ *624/143–3464* ⊕ *www.theofficeonthebeach.com* ⌖ *Reservations essential* ⊟ *MC, V* ✦ *3:C4.*

$$ ✕ **O Mole Mío.** A stylish little café near the marina, O Mole is filled
MEXICAN   with traditional arts and crafts and offers contemporary Mexican fare. Inexpensive breakfasts are $3 to $5; quick appetizers such as *quecas de tingas,* small quesadillas, are tasty ways to start; and dinners such as El Baile de O Mole Mío (The Dance of O Mole Mío), a chicken-mole concoction, will delight your taste buds. This spot is also great for just a quick cocktail while shopping in downtown Cabo, and is a favorite with the cruise crowd. ⊠ *Plaza del Sol shopping center, Francisco Madero and Blvd. Marina, Marina* ☎ *624/143–7577* ⊟ *AE, MC, V* ✦ *3:B5.*

$$ ✕ **Pancho's Restaurant & Tequila Bar.** Owner John Bragg has an enormous
MEXICAN   collection of tequilas, and an encyclopedic knowledge of the stuff. The
☾   restaurant is nothing short of a tequila museum, with a colorful dis-play of many hundreds of the world's top tequilas—many no longer available—displayed behind the bar. Sample one or two of the nearly 1,000 labels available, and you'll appreciate the Oaxacan tablecloths, murals, painted chairs, and streamers even more than you did when you first arrived. Try regional specialties like tortilla soup, chiles rellenos, or *sopa de mariscos* (seafood soup). The breakfast and lunch specials are a bargain. Pancho's offers special and private tequila tastings; you'll leave

MENU GLOSSART

Aguacate	avocado
Ajo	garlic
A la parrilla	cooked on the grill
Almuerzo	lunch
Arrachera	flank steak
Arroz	rice
Atún	tuna
Azúcar	sugar
Barra de ensaladas	salad bar
Cabrilla	sea bass
Camarones	shrimp
Carnes	meats
Carta de vinos	wine list
Cebolla	onion
Chalupas	stuffed tortillas
Champiñones	mushrooms
Cocida en horno de Lena	cooked in a wood-burning oven
Con queso	with cheese
Cuchara	spoon
Cuchillo	knife
Desayuno	breakfast
Enegrecido	blackened
Ensalada	salad
Frijoles	beans
Frito	fried
Fruta	fruit
Helados	ice cream
Hielo	ice
Huitlacoche	corn fungus
Langosta	lobster
Leche	milk
Mariscos	seafood
Menu degustación	tasting menu
Ostiones	oysters
Pescado	fish
Picante	hot sauce, spicy
Pollo	chicken
Postres	desserts, sweets
Servilletas	napkins
Tenedor	fork
Totopos y salsa	chips and salsa

with a greater appreciation of this piquant liquor from Jalisco. ⊠ *Hidalgo between Zapata and Serdan, Centro* ☎ *624/143–2891* ⊕ *www.panchos.com* ⊟ *AE, MC, V* ⊙ *Closed Sept.* ✢ *3:B5.*

$$$ ╳ **Ruth's Chris Steak House.** If you've eaten enough fish tacos for a while,
STEAKHOUSE and are hankering for a steak like they cook 'em back home, there's Ruth's restaurant in the upper level of the Puerto Paraíso mall. It's known for its wide range of meaty cuts, and also serves veal and lamb. Not finished yet? There's a chocolate espresso cake and pecan pie, freshly baked. If you stop by for lunch, know that the place doesn't

Budget Bites

CLOSE UP

You can dine reasonably in Los Cabos if you're not scared by the myth that the food at mom-and-pop operations or at street stands will send you running for the bathroom. These places usually cook to order, so you can tell if something has been sitting out too long or hasn't been cooked well. If there's a crowd of locals, the food is probably fresh and well prepared. Safe bets include quesadillas, fish tacos, corn on the cob, and tortas (sandwiches). Some restaurants have a *comida corrida* (prepared lunch special), a three-course meal that consists of soup or salad, an entrée with rice and vegetables, coffee, and a small dessert. It's not gourmet, but you'll be sated economically.

In Cabo San Lucas, head for the taco stands in the couple of blocks behind Squid Roe and Avenida Cárdenas and the backstreets inland from the marina. **Carnitas El Michoacano** (⊠ *Leona Vicario between Carranza and Obregon, Cabo San Lucas*) sells savory roasted pork served in tacos or tortas for about $3 each. At **Pollo de Oro** (⊠ *Morelos at Av. Cárdenas, Cabo San Lucas*), a half-chicken meal costs about $5.

For inexpensive Mexican eateries close to the marina and hotels, try the juice stands. **Rico Suave** (⊠ *Av. Cárdenas between Av. Hidalgo and Calle Guerrero, Cabo San Lucas*) makes great smoothies with yogurt, as well as cheese tortas. **Oye Como Va** (⊠ *Calle Guerrero and Blvd. Zapata, Cabo San Lucas*), a juice stand, also serves *molletes* (sliced rolls with beans and cheese) for $1.50. **Café Europa** (⊠ *Blvd. Marina, Cabo San Lucas*) has a big breakfast burrito for $5 and quesadillas for $1.50.

In San José del Cabo, there are at least a dozen stands at the **Mercado Municipal,** a couple of blocks west of the heart of San José, near El Chilar Restaurant. You may be the only gringo at the tables—a great way to practice your Spanish. Stock up on fresh papayas, mangoes, melons, and other peelable fruits. Look for reasonably priced restaurants on Zaragoza and Doblado by the market. Good taco stands line streets on the inland side of Highway 1. **Super Tacos Indios** has filling baked potatoes. **Las Ranas,** a *taquería* (taco eatery), has a full bar.

open until 1 PM. ⊠ *Puerto Paraíso, 1st fl., Marina San Lucas, Marina* ☎ *624/144–3232* ⊕ *www.ruthschris.com* ▭ AE, MC, V ✛ 3:B4.

$$ ✗ **Salvatore's.** The local gringo cadre has nothing but *bueno* things to
ITALIAN say about this affordable and dependable little Italian spot, located by the pool at the Siesta Suites Hotel, in downtown Cabo San Lucas. Mussels with marinara, pork scaloppine, and calamari Italiano are just the beginning. Finish dinner off with a chocolate flan, and you'll be saying "¡Ciao, y muchísimas gracias, amigo!" ⊠ *Zapata between Guerrero and Hidalgo,Centro* ☎ *624/143–2773* ▭ AE, MC, V ✛ 3:B5.

$ ✗ **Señor Greenberg's Mexicatessen.** Pastrami, chopped liver, knishes,
CAFÉ bagels, lox, cheesecake—you can find them all, and much, much more behind the glass counters of this Mexican incarnation of a New York deli. Greenberg's serves all three meals and has an extensive menu that ranges from soups, salads, and sandwiches to smoothies, steaks, and

desserts. Fishermen get their box lunches here, and you can also arrange party platters. The air-conditioning, stacks of newspapers, and soft music might pull you back more than once. You'll find this spot in Puerto Paraíso, overlooking Cabo's marina. It has a huge dining room and patio, the entirety of which is outfitted with Wi-Fi, and there are several Internet-connected computers set up on dining tables, for a reasonable charge. ⊠ *Puerto Paraíso on Blvd. Marina, Marina* ☎ *624/144– 3804* ▭ *MC, V* ✛ *3:B4.*

TODOS SANTOS

Todos Santos's dining selection echoes the town—stylish expat with traditional Mexican—and makes a nice outing from any Los Cabos–area stay. Restaurants here do a brisk business at lunch, less so at dinner. It's a real treat to drive up from Los Cabos or down from La Paz for a special meal. At an hour each way, that's easier to do before dark.

$$$
ITALIAN
✕ **Café Santa Fe.** The setting, with tables situated in an overgrown courtyard, is as appealing as the food, which includes salads and soups made with organic vegetables and herbs, homemade pastas, and fresh fish with light sauces. Many Cabo-area residents lunch here regularly. The marinated seafood salad is a sublime blend of shrimp, octopus, and mussels with olive oil and garlic, with plenty for two to share before dining on lobster ravioli. ⊠ *Calle Centenario* ☎ *612/145–0340* ▭ *MC, V* ☉ *Closed Tues. and Sept. and Oct.*

$
ECLECTIC
✕ **Caffé Todos Santos.** Omelets, bagels, granola, and whole-grain breads delight the breakfast crowd at this small eatery; deli sandwiches, fresh salads, and an array of burritos, tamales, *flautas* (fried tortillas rolled around savory fillings), and combo plates are lunch and dinner highlights. Check for fresh seafood on the daily specials board. ⊠ *Calle Centenario 33* ☎ *612/145–0787* ▭ *No credit cards* ☉ *No dinner Mon.*

$$$
ELCECTIC
Fodor'sChoice
★
✕ **El Gusto!.** Even if you don't stay at the sumptuous Posada La Poza just outside town, lunch or dinner at its equally lovely restaurant will be one of the highlights of your Los Cabos vacation. Owners Jürg and Libusche Wiesendanger call their offerings "Swiss-Mex"—Mexican food with European touches, and careful attention to detail. Start with the vegetarian-based tortilla soup with three different types of dried chilies to give it just enough kick. Then sample the smoked-tuna flautas with raspberry-chipotle sauce, quesadillas with mushroom or shrimp, or marinated *arrachera* (flank steak) strips. You'll find dishes such as lamb shoulder in winter. Believe it or not, there is enough of an evening chill in the air that time of year that dining next to the fireplace feels cozy. Top your meal off with a sorbet, flan, or mousse, and possibly the best selection of wines in the region (all Mexican from northern Baja's Guadalupe Valley). Dinner is served from 6 to 8, which gives you time to catch the sunset. ⊠ *Follow signs on Hwy. 19 and Benito Juárez to beach* ☎ *612/145–0400* ⊕ *www.lapoza.com* ⌦ *Reservations essential* ▭ *MC, V* ☉ *Closed Thurs.*

$$
MEXICAN
✕ **Los Adobes.** Locals swear by the fried, cilantro-studded local cheese and the beef tenderloin with huitlacoche at this pleasant outdoor restaurant. The menu is ambitious and includes tapas and several organic,

¿Y LO DESEA CON PAPAS FRITAS?*

*Translation: And would you like fries with that?

We understand. Sometimes the siren's call of a U.S. chain is too tempting to ignore, especially if you're traveling with kids. Several have set up shop here in Los Cabos.

Applebee's (✉ Plaza Península, Hwy. 1, Km 29.5, San José del Cabo ☎ 624/172-6472).

Burger King (✉ Blvd. Marina 17, Cabo San Lucas ☎ 624/143-5727 ✉ Aeropuerto Internacional de Los Cabos, San José del Cabo ☎ 624/146-5452).

Dairy Queen (✉ Plaza de la Danza, Blvd. Marina, Cabo San Lucas ☎ 624/143-2858).

Domino's (✉ Centro Comercial Posada, Cabo San Lucas ☎ 624/143-3999).

McDonald's (✉ Av. Lázaro Cárdenas and Paseo de Marina, Cabo San Lucas ☎ 624/143-8101 ✉ San José Mega Mall, San José del Cabo ☎ 624/130-7526).

Subway (✉ Plaza Nautica, Blvd. Marina, Cabo San Lucas ☎ 624/143-0924 ✉ Aeropuerto Internacional de Los Cabos, San José del Cabo ☎ 624/146-5283).

vegetarian options—rare in these parts. At night the place sparkles with star-shape lights. An Internet café within the restaurant offers high-speed access. ✉ *Calle Hidalgo* ☎ *612/145–0203* ⊕ *www.losadobes-detodossantos.com* ⊟ *MC, V* ⊗ *Closed Sun.*

$ **✕ Michael's.** Everybody who dines here seems to know each other—the
ASIAN clientele is mostly the foreigners who live in town—but visitors are always welcome. The attraction at Michael's—not to be confused with Miguel's, the equally recommended Mexican place as you come into town—is the Asian menu, predominantly Vietnamese, but with a few Thai dishes, too. Share a big order of Vietnamese sweet-potato fritters and shrimp, or Vietnamese crab cakes. You'll dine on the patio behind one of Todos Santos's many art galleries; you can browse while you wait for your food. Michael's keeps very limited hours, open just three evenings, for a total of 12 hours per week, and sometimes cuts back a bit more during the slow summer season. Calling ahead is always a good idea. ✉ *Juárez and Topete* ☎ *612/145–0500* ⊟ *No credit cards* ⊗ *Closed Mon.–Wed. No lunch Thurs.–Sat.*

¢ **✕ Miguel's.** Deliciously prepared chiles rellenos are the attraction at
MEXICAN Miguel's. The sign out front says so, and it speaks the truth. Hearty
Fodor's Choice bell peppers, almost any way you like them, stuffed with fish, lobster,
★ shrimp, pork, beef, or veggies, make up the bulk of the lunch and dinner menu. Breakfast consists of burritos and eggs or Baja's ubiquitous fish tacos. A copy of *The New York Times* arrives later in the day for your perusal. Don't confuse this semi-outdoor place on the edge of town with Michael's, the Asian restaurant several blocks away near the church. ✉ *Degollado at Hwy. 19* ☎ *612/145–0733* ⊟ *No credit cards* ⊗ *Closed Sun.*

5

Where to Stay in Los Cabos

WORD OF MOUTH

"I would classify Cabo San Lucas as a spring break crowd—think bars like Cabo Wabo, El Squid Roe, Mango Deck, The Monkey Bar. Fun for one or two nights. San Jose del Cabo—much more "refined" town—smaller. Nice shopping, art galleries, and restaurants."

—jbass

5

WHERE TO STAY IN LOS CABOS PLANNER

What to Expect

Bargains here are few; rooms generally start at $200 a night and can climb into the thousands. For groups of six or more planning an extended stay, condos or villas can be a convenient and economical option, though you should always book early.

Hotel rates in Baja California Sur are subject to a 10% value-added tax and a 2% hotel tax for tourism promotion. Service charges (at least 10%) and meals generally aren't included in hotel rates. Several of the high-end properties include a daily service charge in your bill; be sure you know the policy before tipping (though additional tips are always welcome). We always list the available facilities, but we don't specify extra costs; so always ask about what's included.

Hotels operate on the European Plan (EP, with no meals) or Continental Plan (CP, with a continental breakfast), Breakfast Plan (BP, with a full breakfast), Modified American Plan (MAP, with breakfast and dinner), or the Full American Plan (FAP, with all meals). A number of properties throughout Los Cabos have gone all-inclusive (AI, with all meals and drinks).

Which Region Is for You?

San José del Cabo is the closest to the international airport, and it's here and in Todos Santos that you'll be farthest from the crowds that gravitate toward downtown Cabo San Lucas's fiesta atmosphere. These towns have retained their Mexican colonial roots and are the most charming of Los Cabos region. It's worth noting that Todos Santos—though still quite warm—can have the coolest temperatures in Los Cabos during the hot summer months. Some small hotels and bed-and-breakfasts lie in or near the town centers of these very walkable towns, and others are more remote. For high-season stays, try to make reservations at least three months in advance, and six months in advance for holidays. Precious few lodgings serve travelers on a budget.

The Corridor—the stretch that connects San José with Cabo San Lucas—has seen the growth of several megaresorts. These microcosms contain two or more hotels, throughout which golf courses, private villas, and upscale condo projects are interspersed. ⚠ If you are planning a vacation in Los Cabos, do keep in mind that most of the beaches at the resorts along the Corridor are not swimmable.

Cabo San Lucas continues its meteoric climb into the five-star stratosphere. Nearly every hotel in Cabo has undergone some kind of renovation, from minor to complete makeovers. The ME Cabo by Meliá is one such example. When Casa Dorada Resort opened, smack in the middle of busy El Médano Beach, it raised the bar in regards to rooms, services, and pampering.

The rate of development in the area is astonishing, and begs the question of sustainability. As developable space in Los Cabos region diminishes and becomes prohibitively expensive, the newest expansions are moving beyond the Sea of Cortez coastline north of San José del Cabo, known as the "East Cape," and north of Cabo San Lucas along the Pacific coast. For years, building restrictions have been discussed, but money talks in every language. The only "restrictions" seem to be how much actual land is left.

All About All-Inclusives

All-inclusives are like all-you-can-eat buffets—with all the positive and negative aspects included. You fork over the cash and just have at it, from the food and drink to an expansive pool complex and often water sports and excursions, too. You might consider this as one way for first-time visitors (especially families) to experience Los Cabos and not break the bank. The all-inclusive concept has come a long way since Club Med launched the concept decades ago. These days, all-inclusive properties are becoming more and more sophisticated, offering an impressive array of restaurants, bars, activities, and entertainment—and often striving to keep some local flavor present in the process.

Going to the Chapel

If you decide to get married in Los Cabos, you'll be able to enjoy nuptials with friends and family in a gorgeous setting, and there'll be no worries about heading out for the honeymoon the morning after—you're already there. Los Cabos has a bevy of choices, and prices, for dream destination weddings. If money is no object, look into the big-name properties such as One&Only Palmilla, Las Ventanas al Paraíso, Esperanza, and the Marquis Los Cabos, where celebs often say "I do." Palmilla even has an official Director of Celebrations to assist. At Las Ventanas, hire its *caballero anillo,* "ring bearer on horseback." But the true champion of weddings has got to be the Dreams Los Cabos property, where as many as five couples get hitched each week. Let anyone concerned about the legitimacy of a Mexican wedding know that as long as you satisfy a few easy requirements, the ceremony will be legally binding.

WHAT IT COSTS IN DOLLARS

	¢	$	$$	$$$	$$$$
Hotels	under $100	$100–$200	$200–$300	$300–$399	over $399

Hotel prices are for two people in a standard double room in high season, excluding tax.

When to Go

With its growing popularity, Los Cabos has a high season that seems to keep gaining months. It's been said that high season is now mid-November through May, though the crowds are a bit more manageable in October and after mid-April. Summers can be scorchers in this desert landscape, reaching temperatures in the 90s and above. Book early—as many as six months in advance for top holidays such as Thanksgiving, Christmas, New Year's, and Easter, and at least three months in advance for other high-season stays.

Traveling with Kids

If you're heading down to Los Cabos with the little ones in tow, you're in luck, because many properties are kid-friendly. A number of them welcome children with Kids' Clubs, including the Royal Solaris in San José del Cabo and the Hilton Los Cabos in the Corridor. In Cabo San Lucas, the time-share properties Villa del Palmar, Villa del Arco, and neighboring Club Cascadas will keep your little ones busy with fun activities. The properties that go out of their way to provide entertainment for kids are marked with a ducky symbol in this chapter. Many of the independent hotels listed don't restrict children, but their size and arrangement suggest more adult-oriented accommodations. We've mentioned these factors in our reviews.

THE SCENE

Updated by
Georgia de
Katona

Expect high-quality accommodations wherever you stay in Los Cabos—whether at a huge resort or a small bed-and-breakfast. Much of the area's beaches are now backed by major properties, all vying to create the most desirable stretch on the sand; for the privilege of staying in these hot properties, you'll pay top dollar—and more for oceanfront rooms with incredible views. Prices at accommodations off the beach reflect the popularity of the area and may surprise travelers used to spending much less in other areas of Mexico—even in the hot summer months which are, technically, the low season.

Sprawling Mediterranean-style resorts of generally 200 to 400 rooms dominate the coastline of Los Cabos, especially on the 29-km-long (18-mi-long) Corridor, but also on the beaches in Cabo San Lucas and San José (the town of San José is not on the coast, but inland just a bit). These resorts have lavish pools and lush grounds in addition to their beachfront access, although the majority of beaches on the densely developed coastline, with the notable exception of Playa Médano in Cabo San Lucas, can have an oddly deserted appearance because of the dangerous currents in the water and the predominance of luxurious pools.

Many of the resorts along the Corridor offer all-inclusive plans if you want to check into your hotel and stay put for the duration of your stay, but choosing that option means you'll have little reason to venture out and taste some of the diverse and remarkable food available in this region. These huge resorts offer high-quality facilities and pleasant service, to be sure, but guests looking to get a feel for the local culture

BEST BETS FOR LOS CABOS LODGING

Fodor's offers a selective listing of quality lodging experiences in every price range, from the city's best budget beds to its most sophisticated luxury hotels. Here, we've compiled our top recommendations by price and experience. The very best properties—in other words, those that provide a particularly remarkable experience in their price range—are designated in the listings with the Fodor's Choice logo.

Fodor's Choice ★

Cabo Cush, $ p. 141
Casa Dorada Los Cabos Resort & Spa, $$ p. 142
Casa Natalia, $$$ p. 120
Casa Rafael Hotel, ¢ p. 144
Esperanza, $$$$ p. 126
Finisterra, $ p. 146
Hilton Los Cabos, $$$ p. 126
Hotelito, $ p. 152
Las Ventanas al Paraíso, $$$$ p. 128
Marbella Suites, $ p. 128
One&Only Palmilla, $$$$ p. 130

Posada La Poza, $$ p. 154
Posada Terranova, ¢ p. 122
Pueblo Bonito Pacifica Holistic Retreat & Spa, $$$ p. 149
Royal Solaris Los Cabos, $$ p. 122
Sheraton Hacienda del Mar Resort, $$ p. 131
Todos Santos Inn, $ p. 156
Tropicana Inn, $ p. 123

By Price

¢
Casa Rafael Hotel, p. 144
Posada Terranova, p. 122
San Pedrito Surf Retreat Hotel, p. 154

$
Cabo Cush, p. 141
Finisterra, p. 146

Hotelito, p. 152
Marbella Suites, p. 128
Todos Santos Inn, p. 156
Tropicana Inn, p. 123

$$
Casa Dorada Los Cabos Resort & Spa, p. 142
Posada La Poza, p. 154
Royal Solaris Los Cabos, p. 122
Sheraton Hacienda del Mar Resort, p. 131

$$$
Casa Natalia, p. 120
Hilton Los Cabos, p. 126
Pueblo Bonito Pacifica Holistic Retreat & Spa, p. 149

$$$$
Esperanza, p. 126
Las Ventanas al Paraíso, p. 128
One&Only Palmilla, p. 130

By Experience

Cabo Surf Hotel, $$ p. 125
El Encanto, ¢ p. 121
Las Ventanas al Paraíso, $$$$ p. 128
Posada La Poza, $$ p. 154
San Pedrito Surf Retreat Hotel, ¢ p. 154
Todos Santos Inn, $ p. 156

BEST SPA

Esperanza, $$$$ p. 126
Las Ventanas al Paraíso, $$$$ p. 128
Marquis Los Cabos, $$$$ p. 128
One&Only Palmilla, $$$$ p. 130
Villa del Arco Beach Resort & Spa, $$ p. 150

MOST KID-FRIENDLY

Casa Dorada Los Cabos Resort & Spa, $$ p. 142
Hilton Los Cabos, $$$ p. 126
Playa Grande Resort, $ p. 148
Pueblo Bonito Rosé, $$ p. 149
Sheraton Hacienda del Mar, $$ p. 131

5

may find the generic, chain-hotel atmosphere frustrating. For those wanting less Westernized slickness, and a more intimate experience of Mexican hospitality, checking into one of the many excellent smaller properties is the way to go.

If you're inclined to go beyond the beach-and-party vibe of Cabo San Lucas, it's well worth spending time in Todos Santos and San José del Cabo. Both towns offer exceptional independent hotels and inns, as well as burgeoning arts scenes, great restaurants, and ambience you won't find elsewhere.

SAN JOSÉ DEL CABO

Updated by
Georgia de
Katona

If being in Mexico, not the thick of a hopping resort scene, is more your speed, Cabo San Lucas's sister city San José del Cabo is the place to base your stay. Its restored downtown, with century-old buildings and many elevated sidewalks, is a delight to explore on foot. Plaza Mijares, the open and popular *zócalo*, is graced by a "dancing waters" fountain, lighted at night, and a stage where live music takes place frequently for the crowds who gather to stroll, enjoy ice cream, and relax after the heat of the day has let up. Several streets fronting the square are pedestrian-only, giving this historic downtown a lush and leisurely feel. Just beyond the center of town, and a bit farther south, is the ever-expanding Zona Hotelera, where a dozen or so new hotels, time-shares, and condo projects face the long stretch of beach (also referred to as Playa Hotelera) on the usually placid Sea of Cortez.

$$–$$$ 🖫 **Best Western Posada Real.** One of the better values in the hotel zone, this tranquil beachside property consists of two tri-level, Santa Fe–style buildings, nice cactus gardens, and has, like its neighbors, joined the all-inclusive world. Every room has a balcony and at least a partial ocean view, a bathtub and shower, and a refrigerator. The large, heated pool has a palapa-roof swim-up bar. This Best Western is ultraquiet compared to its super-size neighbors. It frequently draws business travelers. **Pros:** the hotel maintains an intimate feeling with a friendly staff; the price is very reasonable compared to all of its neighbors. **Cons:** fairly standard, slightly outdated rooms, many of which have a lingering smell of cigarette smoke; staff isn't welltrained in handling booking errors or other snafus. ⊠ *Malecón, Zona Hotelera* ☎ *624/142–0155, 800/528–1234 in U.S.* ⊕ *www.posadareal.com.mx* ⟿ *156 rooms* ⚴ *In-room: Safe, kitchen (some), Wi-Fi. In-hotel: 2 restaurants, room service, bars, tennis courts, pool, beachfront, laundry service, Internet terminal* ▤ *AE, MC, V* ⦿ *AI* ✛ *1:B5.*

$$$$ 🖫 **Cabo Azul Resort & Spa.** A relative newcomer on the beach in San José del Cabo, the exceptional Cabo Azul is still partially under construction, but you would never know it. Azul seems destined to be one of Los Cabos' top hotels, with two restaurants on the premises: the gorgeous Javier's Cantina & Grill and the posh palapa-style Flor de Noche. This hotel-and-time-share hybrid, despite the sophistication and elegance, has a friendly, relaxed atmosphere with spacious one- to three-bedroom villas and more than a dozen giant penthouses. The Paz Spa offers luxe indoor and outdoor treatments. You'll find that most of

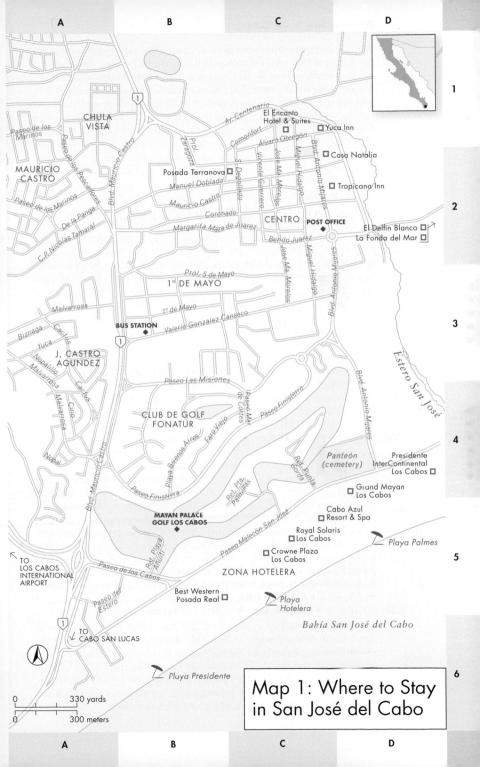

Map 1: Where to Stay in San José del Cabo

the action is centered on the giant asymmetrical pool, with a swim-up bar adjacent to the Flor de Noche Restaurant & Lounge. **Pros:** beautiful, distinctive rooms; professional and friendly staff keep it all running smoothly. **Cons:** the time-share aspect is difficult to avoid—with tours and salespeople nearly always present with hordes of prospective buyers; incomplete construction; no shallow pool for kids. ☒ *Desarrollo Cabo Azul, Paseo Malecón #11, San José del Cabo, Zona Hotelera* ☏ *624/163–5100, 877/216–2226 in U.S.* ⊕ *www.caboazulresort.com* ⊐ *332 villas ☆ In-room: Safe, kitchen, DVD. In-hotel: 2 restaurants, room service, bars, pools, gym, spa, laundry service, Internet terminal, parking (free)* ☐ *AE, MC, V* ✛ *1:C5.*

$$$–$$$$
Fodor's Choice
★
⚏ **Casa Natalia.** An intimate, graceful boutique hotel, Casa Natalia is in the heart of San José's downtown and opens onto the zócalo. Rooms are decorated in regional Mexican motifs and have king-size beds, soft robes, remote-controlled air-conditioning, and private patios screened by bamboo and bougainvillea. Suites have hot tubs and hammocks on large terraces. A free shuttle takes you to a beach club in the Corridor. Natalia's cozy little bar offers hotel guests afternoon happy-hour specials, including *dos por uno*, or two-for-ones. The in-patio restaurant, Mi Cocina, is fabulous. Staffers are helpful and welcoming. Casa Natalia is the most luxurious option for those who wish to spend time enjoying the culture of this tranquil town. **Pros:** lovely, oasis-like location in the heart of downtown; fantastic complimentary breakfast; excellent staff. **Cons:** no bathtubs in the standard rooms; noise from music and fiestas on Plaza Mijares can be disturbing; beach shuttle only runs twice per day. ☒ *Blvd. Mijares 4, Centro* ☏ *624/146–7100, 888/277–3814 in U.S.* ⊕ *www.casanatalia.com* ⊐ *14 rooms, 2 suites ☆ In-room: Safe. In-hotel: Restaurant, bar, pool, laundry service, Wi-Fi hotspot, no kids under 13* ☐ *AE, MC, V* ⅩⅠ*CP* ✛ *1:C2.*

$$–$$$
☺
⚏ **Crowne Plaza Los Cabos.** Another all-inclusive on Playa del Sol, along San José del Cabo's hotel zone, this five-story hotel caters to both business and fun, with five restaurants, four bars, and massive meeting rooms. The rooms are standard, though some have private balconies perched above the pool complex and looking out over the ocean. **Pros:** friendly service and reasonable rates for the beach; La Tortuga kids' club keeps tots busy; no time-shares, hence no time-share salespeople. **Cons:** food is standard, American-buffet style; housekeeping can be an issue. ☒ *Paseo Malecón, San José del Cabo, Zona Hotelera* ☏ *624/142–9292, 800/496–7621 in U.S.* ⊕ *www.crowneplaza.com* ⊐ *222 rooms, 22 suites ☆ In room: Safe, kitchen (some), Wi-Fi (some). In-hotel: 5 restaurants, room service, bars, pool, gym, children's programs (ages 4–12), laundry facilities, Wi-Fi hotspot, parking (free)* ☐ *AE, MC, V* ⅩⅠ*AI* ✛ *1:C5.*

¢
⚏ **El Delfin Blanco.** This is an affordable alternative for travelers who don't want all the hoopla of a highly developed, all-inclusive–style resort. The emphasis at El Delfin Blanco is on natural beauty, which is abundant, and the sweet community of people, travelers, and residents who congregate here. It's a short stroll to La Playita beach, which seldom has more than a few fishermen on it and seems to stretch for miles and miles. **Pros:** this is a place to get away from it all; the shared

kitchen is super for cooking your catch of the day; wonderfully attentive innkeepers; three restaurants within walking distance. Cons: 10-minute drive to San José del Cabo; taxis only by arrangement; saggy mattresses; slightly ramshackle facilities. ⊠ *Pueblo La Playita, La Playita* ☎ *624/142–1212* ⊕ *www.eldelfinblanco.net* ↝ *4 casitas, 1 cabana* ⚭ *In-room: No phone, refrigerator, no TV, Wi-Fi. In-hotel: Wi-Fi hotspot, parking (free)* ☰ *MC, V* ✛ *1:D2.*

¢–$ 🏨 **El Encanto Hotel & Suites.** Located in the heart of San José's Historic Arts District, and near many bars and great restaurants, this gorgeous and comfortable inn has two separate buildings—one looks onto the verdant gardens and pool; the other one, across the street, is in a charming, historic building with a narrow courtyard. All guest quarters are immaculate and are impeccably decorated, and both buildings are surrounded by gardens and adorned with climbing vines. This intimate hotel makes for a great wedding property, and the on-property wedding chapel harkens back to the Mexico of years gone by. Pros: lush, Mexican-hacienda feeling; sunny pool area; excellent location that is central but quiet. Cons: service may be friendly, but staffing is minimal. ⊠ *Morelos 133, Centro* ☎ *624/142–0388* ⊕ *www.elencantoinn. com* ↝ *12 rooms, 14 suites* ⚭ *In-room: Kitchen (some). In-hotel: Pool, laundry service* ☰ *AE, MC, V* ✛ *1:C1.*

$$$–$$$$ 🏨 **Grand Mayan Los Cabos.** As soon as you see the enormous twin Mayan statues that stand in the dimly lighted lobby entrance, you'll feel as if you've entered another world. This ultraglitzy, exotic resort offers vibrant, spacious suites, all with a view of the enormous pool and the Sea of Cortez beyond. Water flows out of the mouths of giant rattlesnake sculptures into the pool, which is decked out with lights that change colors at night. Early-morning yoga classes greet the sunrise near the beach. Pros: children's programs; Grand Mayan golf course; guests can opt out of all-inclusive plan. Cons: no coffeemakers or refrigerators in standard rooms; views of sea vary from panoramic to none at all. ⊠ *Paseo Malecón, San José del Cabo, Zona Hotelera* ☎ *624/163–4000* ⊕ *www.wyndam.com* ↝ *172 rooms, 86 suites* ⚭ *In-room: Safe, kitchen (some). In-hotel: 2 restaurants, bars, gym, spa, beachfront, laundry services, Wi-Fi hotspot, parking (free)* ☰ *MC, V* ⏹*AI* ✛ *1:D4.*

¢ 🏨 **La Fonda del Mar.** If you're looking for a peaceful back-to-nature retreat, check out this hotel on a long, secluded beach that straddles the line between desert and ocean. And once the diners clear out of the adjacent and very popular Buzzard's Bar & Grill, La Fonda is even more tranquil. The three thatch-roof cabañas and one cabaña/suite are in heavy demand by both surfers and the more adventurous in high season. Cabañas have en suite toilets and sinks but share a hot-water shower; the suite has standard in-room facilities. The whole operation runs on solar power. To get here, turn off Boulevard Mijares at the signs for Puerto Los Cabos, continue past PLC and follow the road up the hill, around the mini-circle, and continue out into the desert; it's about 5 km (3mi; 10 minutes) outside town. Pros: fantastic location on the beach; excellent full breakfast included in room rate. Cons: not within walking distance to town; difficult to find; shared shower facilities. ⊠ *Old East Cape Rd.* ☎ *624/113–6368 cell, 624/110–6454, 951/303–9384 in*

5

U.S. ⊕ *www.vivacabo.com or www.buzzardsbar.com* ⤵ *3 cabañas, 1 suite* ⚘ *In-hotel: Restaurant, bar, pool, beachfront* ⊟ *No credit cards* ⊙ *Closed Aug.* ⏐◎⏐*BP* ✚ *1:D2.*

¢

Fodor's Choice

★

⊞ Posada Terranova. People return to San José's best inexpensive hotel over and over again. Terranova's large rooms have two double beds, tile bathrooms, and Mexican art. Its restaurant serves quality Mexican cuisine for all three meals; the diverse clientele makes dining an international event. Yet, whether you congregate with other guests at the front patio tables or within the restaurant, it still feels like a private home. **Pros:** friendly staff; immaculate rooms; easy walk to Plaza Mijares. **Cons:** no pool; check the bed if a firm mattress is a necessity for you. ⊠ *Calle Degollado at Av. Zaragoza, Centro* ☎ *624/142–0534* ⊕ *www. hterranova.com.mx* ⤵ *25 rooms* ⚘ *In-hotel: Restaurant, room service, bar* ⊟ *AE, MC, V* ⏐◎⏐*CP* ✚ *1:C2.*

$$–$$$

☾

⊞ Presidente InterContinental Los Cabos. Cactus gardens surround this low-lying hotel, one of the originals in what has become a lineup of massive all-inclusives along the beach. There's an attentive, friendly, old-world Mexican attitude among the staff members, many of whom have been here for decades. Each of the hotel's three sections is centered on pools and lounging areas, and the ground-floor rooms, which have terraces, are the best; ask about the patio rooms with hammocks for tranquil, retreat-like stays. All accommodations have showers but no bathtubs. Try Napa, the property's top restaurant, part of the resort's all-inclusive plan. **Pros:** Chiqui Kids' Club (ages 5–12); adults-only restaurant and pool; generally mellow atmosphere is good for families and those looking for a getaway. **Cons:** rooms tend to be basic, without refrigerators; food is run-of-the-mill buffet style, except at Napa. ⊠ *Paseo San José, at end of hotel zone, Zona Hotelera* ☎ *624/142–0211, 800/424–6835 in U.S.* ⊕ *www.ichotelsgroup.com* ⤵ *390 rooms, 7 suites* ⚘ *In-room: Safe, Internet. In-hotel: 6 restaurants, room service, bars, tennis courts, pools, gym, beachfront, children's programs (ages 5–12), laundry service* ⊟ *AE, MC, V* ⏐◎⏐*AI* ✚ *1:D4.*

$$–$$$

Fodor's Choice

★

⊞ Royal Solaris Los Cabos. This was the first all-inclusive in Los Cabos—it runs smoothly, although the resort feels a bit like an amusement park. You'll be entertained with four major dinner shows per week in the Teatro (theater) Teotihuacan, a casino night, a Latin Show, and other themed nights. A complete Kids' Mini-Club area includes toboggan waterslides, dancing lessons, kites, and crayons. Adults can play tennis, basketball, and beach volleyball. **Pros:** Kids' Club entertains kids 4–12 years old from 9 to 9; there is something for everyone at this busy resort, from cooking classes to dancing lessons; this is the best value for the money of the all-inclusives. **Cons:** the accommodations and food veer toward only adequate here, despite the volume of options; this is not the place to go for romance-seeking couples; time-share salespeople are pushy. ⊠ *Lote 10, Colonia Campo de Golf, San José del Cabo, Zona Hotelera* ☎ *624/145–6800, 281/288–9747 in U.S.* ⊕ *www. hotelessolaris.com* ⤵ *389 rooms* ⚘ *In-hotel: 5 restaurants, room service, bars, gym, spa, children's programs (ages 4–12), Wi-Fi hotspot, parking (free)* ⊟ *MC, V* ⏐◎⏐*AI* ✚ *1:C5.*

Cabo Condos

If you're planning to stay a week or more, renting a condo can be much more economical and convenient than staying in a hotel. Los Cabos has countless condominium properties, ranging from modest homes to ultra-luxurious villas in such exclusive areas as Palmilla near San José del Cabo and the hill-clinging Pedregal neighborhood above Cabo San Lucas and its marina. Many private owners rent out their condos, either through the development's rental pool or property management companies. The price is the same for both, but with the latter you might get a better selection.

Nearly all condos are furnished and have a fully equipped kitchen,

a television, bed and bath linens, laundry facilities, and maid service. Most are seaside and range from studios to three-bedroom units. A minimum stay of one week is typically required, though rules can vary by property. Start the booking process at least four months in advance, especially for high-season rentals. **Cabo Homes and Condos** (☎ 624/142–6244 ⊕ www.cabohome-sandcondos.com) handles a large number of vacation rentals. **Cabo Villas** (☎ 831/475–4800, 800/745–2226 in U.S. and Canada 🖶 831/475–4890 ⊕ www.cabovillas.com) represents several properties including the high-end homes at Villas del Mar in the One&Only Palmilla compound.

5

$ **Tropicana Inn.** It's not directly on the beach, but this hotel in a quiet **Fodor'sChoice** enclave along one of San José's main boulevards is a delightful find. The ★ hotel restaurant faces the street, with the guest quarters tucked away at the back of the property. The warm yellow buildings frame a pool and palapa bar in a quiet, verdant enclave. The rooms were all renovated in mid-2007 and outfitted with fine Mexican artwork and textiles. Two suites, El Troje and El Jacaranda, are situated poolside. In its previous life, El Troje was a hand-carved, dark wood, Tarascan Indian bungalow that the Tropicana transplanted here from Michoacán. Compared to the rates typical of Los Cabos properties, the rates for El Troje make for a very special and very romantic find. The hotel is steps from great shopping, across the street from several top restaurants (including Don Emiliano's), and a stone's throw from the zócalo. The Tropicana is clearly a favorite among locals, and it is common to see businesspeople having breakfast and lunch meetings in the restaurant. **Pros:** very good on-site restaurant and bar with live entertainment on the weekends; the bands pack in the dancers but the music is not heard back in the hotel rooms; rooms are immaculate, and beds extremely comfortable; staff is attentive and courteous. **Cons:** kids are allowed, even though the hotel is clearly oriented to adults seeking peace and relaxation; Wi-Fi is only available around the pool. ⊠ *Blvd. Mijares 30, Centro* ☎ *624/142–1580* ⊕ *www.tropicanainn.com* 🛏 *37 rooms, 4 suites* ♦ *In-room: Refrigerator. In-hotel: Restaurant, room service, bar, pool, parking (free), Wi-Fi hotspot* ▤ *AE, MC, V* ❘◎❘ *CP* ✛ *1:C2.*

¢   **Yuca Inn.** Accommodations at this friendly, funky place are clean and simple, and each room has a private bathroom. There's a small

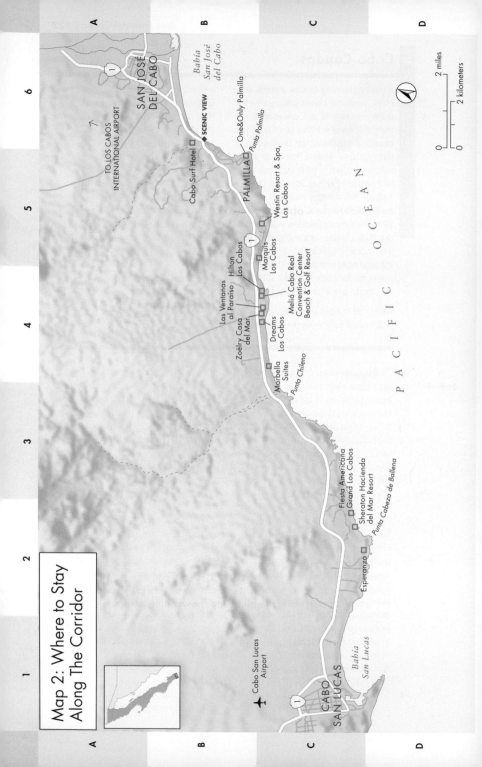

Map 2: Where to Stay Along The Corridor

A B C D
1 2 3 4 5 6

TO LOS CABOS INTERNATIONAL AIRPORT

SAN JOSÉ DEL CABO

Bahía San José del Cabo

Cabo Surf Hotel

◆ SCENIC VIEW

PALMILLA

One&Only Palmilla

Punta Palmilla

Westin Resort & Spa, Los Cabos

Marquis Los Cabos

Hilton Los Cabos

Meliá Cabo Real Convention Center Beach & Golf Resort

Las Ventanas al Paraíso

Zoëtry Casa del Mar

Dreams Los Cabos

Marbella Suites

Punta Chileno

PACIFIC OCEAN

Fiesta Americana Grand Los Cabos

Sheraton Hacienda del Mar Resort

Punta Cabeza de Ballena

Esperanza

Cabo San Lucas Airport

CABO SAN LUCAS

Bahía San Lucas

0   2 miles
0   2 kilometers

swimming pool, hammocks for lounging, and a library. You can store food and prepare meals in the communal kitchen. **Pros:** unbeatable price; just steps away from the zócalo; the gregarious manager, Rogelio, is happy to advise on activities and sights. **Cons:** mattresses can be soft; this is not the choice for those looking for any kind of luxury accommodations—this is a budget hotel all the way. ⊠ *Alvaro Obregón #1 L-B, by Casa de la Cultura, Centro* ☎ *624/142–0462* ⊕ *www.yucainn. com.mx* ⊷ *8 rooms, 1 suite* ♿ *In-room: No TV. In-hotel: Pool* ⊟ *MC, V* ⦿ *CP* ⊹ *1:C1.*

THE CORRIDOR

Even before the Corridor had an official name or even a paved road, the few hotels here were ritzy and elite; one even had its own private airstrip. As the saying goes, the more things change, the more they stay the same—developers have deliberately kept this area high-end and private. The Corridor is the most valuable strip of real estate in the region, with guard-gated exclusivity, golf courses, luxury developments, and unsurpassed views of the Sea of Cortez.

$$–$$$ 🏨 **Cabo Surf Hotel.** Legendary and amateur surfers alike claim the prime break-view rooms in this small hotel on the cliffs above Playa Costa Azul. They mingle by the swimming pool and in the cozy Seven Seas restaurant (which is a great place to enjoy a wonderful meal and stunning views), and they schedule their day's activities around the daily surf report. Rooms are spacious enough for two wave-hounds to spread out their gear; some have French doors that open to the sea breezes. The hotel offers its own label of Cabo Surf Tequila, a surf school, and surfboard rentals. The small Sea Spa & Salon, adjacent to the lobby, offers massages developed specifically for surfers' wave-taxed muscles, with many other treatments for nonsurfers to enjoy, as well. Book early at this popular spot. **Pros:** if surfing is your thing, then you can't get any closer than this while having all your basic needs covered; celebrity sightings are frequent; in-room iPod players. **Cons:** traffic from the highway can be noisy; musty smells in the rooms. ⊠ *Hwy. 1, Km 28* ☎ *624/142–2666, 858/964–5117 in U.S.* ⊕ *www.cabosurfhotel.com* ⊷ *22 rooms* ♿ *In-room: Kitchen (some), refrigerator, Wi-Fi. In-hotel: Restaurant, bar, pool, gym, spa, Wi-Fi hotspot* ⊟ *MC, V* ⊹ *2:B6.*

$$$$ 🏨 **Dreams Los Cabos.** If there's one Los Cabos property that gets a nod ☾ for the most weddings per year, it would have to be the all-inclusive Dreams, which averages as many as five weddings per week. This property is touted as a romantic getaway, but it really seems to have become a destination for families and for wedding parties with all ages of guests in attendance. It is a casual, unfussy resort, where guests simply check in at the restaurant or bar of their choice, rather than having to wear the brightly colored wristbands synonymous with all-inclusives. Dreams has three huge pools, with one set aside just for kids. Wedding and honeymoon packages are offered. **Pros:** Explorer's Club for kids ages 3–12; access to Cabo Real golf course; golf concierge; complimentary shuttle to and from the airport. **Cons:** resort can feel overrun with children; food is abundant but cuisine is only average; staff often seems overwhelmed and uninterested in service. ⊠ *Hwy. 1, Km 18.5* ☎ *866/237–3267 or 624/145–7600* ⊕ *www.dreamsresorts.com or www.amresorts.com* ↪ *308 suites* ☖ *In-room: Safe, kitchen (some), DVD, Wi-Fi. In-hotel: 5 restaurants, room service, tennis courts, pools, gym, Wi-Fi hotspot, parking (free)* ⊟ *AE, MC, V* 🍴 *AI* ✥ *2:C4.*

$$$$
Fodor's Choice
★

🍽 **Esperanza.** This is an utterly polished inn with a focus on exquisite privacy and truly luxurious, but not over-the-top, accommodations. Some suites are right on a secluded beach; all have handcrafted furnishings, Frette linens, and dual-head showers. Even the smallest suite is still a heavyweight at 925 square feet. Villas take the luxe even further with private pools and butler service. The Penthouse Suite (which will run you a minimum of $2,500 per night) offers one of the most stunning views of El Arco imaginable. Californian and Mexican recipes get a Baja twist in the restaurants, which generally get high ratings. The spa, which is our favorite in the region, takes treatments to a whole new level, with 12 individual and two couples treatment cabins, steam caves, and a waterfall. Treatments with novel ingredients leave even the most sun-beaten skin soft and rejuvenated. An on-site art gallery showcases local painters and sculptors. **Pros:** service and amenities are virtually flawless; the physical setting is exquisite; every room has an ocean view; resort is for adults and children 16 and over only (families with younger children are welcome in the Villas). **Cons:** the high cost of everything at this property can get exhausting, even for guests used to luxury accommodations; wind can be fierce on the rocky cliffs that the resort is set on. ⊠ *Hwy. 1, Km 7* ☎ *624/145–6400, 866/311–2226 in U.S.* ⊕ *www.esperanzaresort.com* ↪ *57 suites* ☖ *In-room: Safe, DVD, Wi-Fi. In-hotel: 4 restaurants, pool, gym, spa, beachfront, laundry service* ⊟ *AE, MC, V* ✥ *2:C2.*

$$$–$$$$

🍽 **Fiesta Americana Grand Los Cabos.** The dramatic lobby of the Fiesta is eight stories above the beach, and every room looks out onto the Sea of Cortez. Stone walls, rich marble floors, and abundant art make for an elegant and contemporary atmosphere. As part of the Cabo del Sol development, the Fiesta also offers guests access to the 18-hole Jack Nicklaus Ocean Golf Course, in addition to the luxurious spa. **Pros:** a good choice for couples wanting a relaxing getaway; though the beach is rocky, this is one of the few hotels on a stretch of water that is safe to swim and snorkel in. **Cons:** not the place for people looking for Cabo's infamous party scene; expensive to get back and forth to town, whether in a cab or the resort's shuttle; food quality doesn't match expensive dining costs; service is notoriously spotty. ⊠ *Hwy. 1, Km 10.3, Cabo del Sol* ☎ *624/145–6200, 800/345–5094, or 800/343–7821* ⊕ *www. fiestamericanagrand.com* ↪ *288 rooms* ☖ *In-room: Safe, refrigerator, Wi-Fi. In-hotel: 3 restaurants, bars, golf courses, pools, spa, beachfront, children's programs (ages 5–12)* ⊟ *AE, DC, MC, V* ✥ *2:C2.*

$$$–$$$$
☾
Fodor's Choice
★

🍽 **Hilton Los Cabos.** Rooms are spacious at this hacienda-style Hilton built on one of the Corridor's few swim-friendly beach lagoons. It's a multipurpose, business-friendly, wedding-friendly, kids-friendly hotel, with Hilton's famous high standard of service. Four meeting rooms will accommodate up to 600. In the guest rooms, elaborate headboards, luxurious linens, and L'Occitane bath products are lovely touches to a

The Hilton Los Cabos, on the Corridor, offers up a swimmable beach and attentive service.

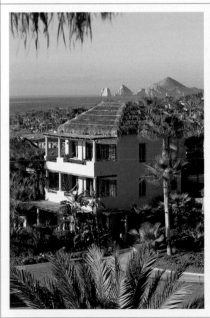

Esperanza is synonymous with luxury and seclusion.   Casa Natalia is decorated with authentic Mexican flair.

resort that has an edge on most properties in this price category. **Pros:** professional, attentive staff stands out among Corridor hotels; the infinity pool is dramatic and relaxing; excellent golf concierge service can make arrangements at the area's best courses. **Cons:** spa services aren't up to par with the rest of the resort; resort is not within walking distance to any towns or other sights. ⊠ *Hwy. 1, Km 19.5* ☎ *624/145–6500 or 800/522–2999* ⊕ *www.hiltonloscabos.com* ⤳ *309 rooms, 66 suites* ♿ *In-room: Safe, refrigerator, Wi-Fi. In-hotel: 2 restaurants, bars, tennis courts, pools, spa, beachfront, children's programs (ages 5–12), laundry facilities, parking (free)* ☰ *AE, D, DC, MC, V* ✛ *2:C4.*

$$$$
Fodor'sChoice
★
🏨 **Las Ventanas al Paraíso.** Despite the high room rates at this ultraprivate, ultraluxe hotel, it's often hard to get a reservation. This hotel continues to garner awards in every category, making it a standout in the region. Guests luxuriate in suites that have hot tubs, fireplaces, and telescopes for viewing whales or stars. Newer hotels have attempted to copy such Ventanas touches as handcrafted lamps and doors, inlaid stone floors, and tequila service, but the original remains the best. Service is sublime, with a knowledgeable butler assigned to each suite; the restaurants are outstanding; and the spa treatments reflect the latest trends. The three spa suites (really more like individual villas) have private spa butlers and separate in-suite treatment rooms. **Pros:** this is the place to escape any semblance of the all-inclusive scene; restaurants are excellent and are worthy of a visit to the hotel even if you're not a guest; children under 12 not allowed. **Cons:** there can be a minimum night stay for weekends depending on the season; the resort is more formal than many in the area. ⊠ *Hwy. 1, Km 19.5* ☎ *624/144–2800, 888/767–3966 in U.S.* ⊕ *www.lasventanas.com* ⤳ *68 suites, 3 spa suites* ♿ *In-room: Safe, refrigerator, Internet. In-hotel: 3 restaurants, room service, bar, tennis courts, pools, gym, spa, beachfront, water sports, laundry service, some pets allowed, no kids under 12* ☰ *AE, MC, V* ✛ *2:C4.*

$–$$
Fodor'sChoice
★
🏨 **Marbella Suites.** With all the sophisticated properties in Los Cabos, it's a treat to discover little Marbella Suites, which still retains the flavor of the peaceful and romantic East Cape properties. A rental car is mandatory, though, if you wish to stay here and also explore Los Cabos and beyond. As stated on its brochure, Marbella is "located halfway between the shopping of San José and the nightlife of Cabo San Lucas." It's a good spot for inexpensive weddings, as wedding party, friends, and family can easily fill the hotel and have it to themselves. **Pros:** large rooms with kitchenettes; gracious, friendly staff; homey, relaxed atmosphere; hot tubs perched on a cliff above the beach. **Cons:** lobby is three floors above lowest level; not accessible for guests with wheelchairs; most rooms open onto a central garden courtyard with only minimal ocean views. ⊠ *Trans. Hwy. 17* ☎ *624/144–1060* ⊕ *www. marbellasuites.com* ⤳ *40 suites* ♿ *In-room: Safe, no phone, no TV, kitchen. In-hotel: Restaurant, bar, pool, beachfront, Internet terminal, Wi-Fi hotspot* ☰ *AE, DC, MC, V* ✛ *2:C4.*

$$$$
🏨 **Marquis Los Cabos.** An impressive art collection, noticeable attention to detail, and luxurious touches make the Marquis stand out. A serpentine swimming pool, running the length of the hotel, curves along the edge of the sand. The Marquis has developed a number of custom-

The intimate, 40-suite Marbella Suites is known for its laid-back atmosphere.

Las Ventanas al Paraíso is stylish and ultra-luxurious, with in-room fireplaces and an unforgettable spa.

tailored packages, such an Elopement Package, which includes, among other things, the rental of a Mexican wedding dress and tux, and a Hummer with a "Just Married" sign that whisks the newly married couple back to the airport. Other packages include the Surf & Turf—essentially rounds of golf, cigars, and surfing lessons; and multiday digital photography and painting trips that allow visitors to delve into unique aspects of Los Cabos. The Marquis recommends that you book these packages online, and well in advance of the dates of your planned visit. Food

> ### AN ADVENTURE-A-DAY
>
> The Marquis has implemented a program that might just lure even its least activity-oriented patrons off their beach chairs. The year-round Adventure-A-Day program offers trips and activities around the area that range from an easy visit to San José's Art Walk, to hikes in the Sierras and horseback rides through the desert. The adventures range in price from $15 to $220 and can be booked when reserving your room.

is excellent and reasonably priced. **Pros:** rooms have Bulgari toiletries, reversible mattresses (hard or soft), and original art; the 28 casitas, at 1,600 square feet each, are great for families—with private pools and refrigerators—and are right on the beach; all rooms have ocean views. **Cons:** highway noise is apparent in rooms; suites are smaller than might be expected; not a good choice for children (no activities). ⊠ *Hwy. 1, Km 21.5* ☎ *624/144–2000, 877/238–9399 in U.S.* ⊕ *www.marquisloscabos.com* ↪ *209 suites, 28 casitas* ⚐ *In-room: Safe, refrigerator, Internet, Wi-Fi. In-hotel: 3 restaurants, bar, pool, gym, spa, beachfront* ⊟ *AE, MC, V* ⦵Ⓞ⦵ *CP* ⊹ *2:C5.*

$$–$$$ ⊞ **Meliá Cabo Real Convention Center Beach & Golf Resort.** Whether you're traveling for a business meeting or a family get-together, this all-inclusive property is fun. The resort offers one of the largest meeting centers in the Corridor, holding up to 1,200. In winter, it's family oriented, with nightly shows in the Vallarta Theater, along with a Bingo Night, two Kids' Clubs, a rock-climbing wall, and even a whale-watching bell down by the pool—ring it when you spot a whale! Rooms have basic furnishings, with no nod toward luxury, and bathrooms generally need updating. **Pros:** near golf courses; low prices make this attractive for budget-oriented travelers looking for an all-inclusive. **Cons:** housekeeping standards tend to be lax, at best; facilities are not designed for people with small children. ⊠ *Hwy 1, Km 19.5* ☎ *624/144–2222 or 800/336–3542* ⊕ *www.meliacaboreal.com* ↪ *305 rooms* ⚐ *In-room: Safe. In-hotel: 5 restaurants, bars, pool, beachfront, water sports, children's programs (ages 4 months–12 yrs), laundry facilities, laundry service, Wi-Fi hotspot* ⊟ *AE, DC, MC, V* ⦵Ⓞ⦵ *AI* ⊹ *2:C4.*

$$$$ ⊞ **One&Only Palmilla.** Built in 1956 by the son of the then-president of
Fodor's Choice   Mexico, the One&Only was the first resort built in Los Cabos area,
★   and it retains an old-world ambience and elegance that is without match in the region. This world-class resort is home to renowned chef Jean-Georges Vongerichten's new Market restaurant. Also on offer are a Jack Nicklaus golf course and a top spa that offers such special treatments as an exclusive Bastien Gonzalez pedicure. The hotel also employs a

Director of Celebrations in order to help guests further enjoy their stay. Two pools seem to flow over low cliffs into the sea, and each of the 13 beach casitas has its own infinity pool. Hand-painted tiles edge stairways leading to rooms and suites, where beds are overloaded with pillows, bathtubs are deep, and the water from the shower truly rains down upon you. Your quarters also have Bose sound systems, flat-screen TVs, and wireless Internet access. Some patios and terraces have daybeds and unobstructed sea views. **Pros:** from beginning to end, Palmilla has already thought of everything, even offering "Air to Go" meals: quality, custom-made box lunches to take along with you on the flight home. **Cons:** prices are exorbitant; increasing numbers of large, boisterous groups in the past few years mar the otherwise genteel atmosphere. ⊠ *Hwy. 1, Km 27.5* ☎ *624/146–7000, 866/829–2977 in U.S.* ⊕ *www.oneandonlyresorts. com* ☞ *61 rooms, 91 junior suites, 20 one-bedroom suites* ♿ *In-room: Safe, refrigerator, DVD, Internet, Wi-Fi. In-hotel: 2 restaurants, bars, golf course, tennis courts, pools, gym, spa, beachfront, water sports, laundry service* ⊟ *AE, MC, V* ✛ *2:B5.*

> ## STARRY STARRY NIGHT
>
> Every Friday night, customized desert vehicles transport One&Only Palmilla guests and the hotel's astronomer into the desert mountain region to enjoy the Baja desert at night under the star-filled sky. The unique mountain background sets the stage for an evening of exciting entertainment including fire dancing and song as well as a sumptuous Mexican feast.

5

$$–$$$
☕
Fodor's Choice
★

🖥 **Sheraton Hacienda del Mar Resort.** Small tiled domes painted red, orange, and pink top eight buildings at this majestic resort. Rooms have white walls, cobalt textiles, and terra-cotta floors; whirlpool tubs and large balconies with ocean views take the hotel beyond chain standards. Huge, luxurious pools are surrounded by palms and all the chaise lounges guests need. The 450-yard beach is beautiful to stroll on, and sometimes the sea in this sheltered cove is calm enough for a swim. Top this all off with the Sheraton's famous service and you've got all the makings for a fantastic beach vacation. **Pros:** rooms, whether on the golf course or with a view of the ocean, are serene and quiet; as part of the Cabo del Sol development, the Sheraton has access to amazing local golf courses. **Cons:** beach is not good for swimming; the mostly mediocre restaurants are expensive. ⊠ *Hwy. 1, Km 10* ☎ *624/145–8000, 888/672–7137 in U.S.* ⊕ *www.sheratonloscabos.com* ☞ *270 rooms, 31 suites* ♿ *In-room: Safe, kitchen (some), refrigerator (some), Internet. In-hotel: 4 restaurants, room service, bars, pools, gym, spa, beachfront, children's programs (ages 5–12), laundry service, Wi-Fi hotspot* ⊟ *AE, DC, MC, V* ✛ *2:C2.*

$$$–$$$$
☕

🖥 **Westin Resort & Spa, Los Cabos.** The stunning architecture of the Westin is a magnificent conglomeration of colors, shapes, and views. The rooms, some set high above a man-made beach, are among the best in this price range and have Westin's trademark "Heavenly Beds," with cushy pillows and comforters. Villas have full kitchens and whirlpool tubs that face the sea. The dramatic setting of the hotel means you'll get plenty of exercise moving from one area to another, which is good for some and less appealing for those not in good physical condition. The restaurants receive mixed reviews, with most leaning toward the expensive but mediocre end—if you're a foodie, you'll need to make arrangements to get into Cabo or San José for satisfying meals. **Pros:** the children's center is clean and well staffed; great spa and gym; excellent pools. **Cons:** it's a trek from the parking lot and lobby to the rooms and pools, making this a poor choice for those with disabilities; cliff setting means the property has many steep stairs and precipitous walkways; time-share salespeople are pushy. ⊠ *Hwy. 1, Km 22.5* ☎ *624/142–9000, 888/625–5144 in U.S.* ⊕ *www.starwood.com/westin* ↘ *243 rooms* ⑆ *In-room: Safe, refrigerator (some). In-hotel: 5 restaurants, room service, bars, tennis courts, pools, gym, spa, beachfront, children's programs (ages 5–12), laundry service* ⊟ *AE, MC, V* ⑆ *EP* ✛ *2:C5.*

$$$$ ⌕ **Zoëtry Casa del Mar.** It's all about comfort and privacy at this award-winning, hacienda-style hotel. An ancient hand-carved door leads into the courtyard-lobby, and stairways curve up to the spa, library, and guest rooms—each of which has a view of the sea and the beautiful white-sand beach stretching in front of it. A few steps above the main bedroom, guest quarters have bathrooms with whirlpool bathtubs. Streams, fountains, and gardens lead around the pools and across verdant grounds. Golfers are well taken care of at this genteel property, as are, increasingly, wedding parties. The staff here is notable for its hospitality and attentiveness. **Pros:** access to the fantastic Cabo Real golf course; gorgeous views of the Sea of Cortez; adults-only Beach Club with pool and restaurant. **Cons:** the hotel is technically 56 rooms/suites, but it's surrounded by 220 time-share condos; time-share salespeople can be annoyingly pushy and omnipresent. ⊠ *Hwy. 1, Km 19.5* ☎ *624/145–7700, 888/227–9621 in U.S.* ⊕ *www.casadelmarmexico.com* ↘ *56 suites* ⑆ *In-room: Safe, Wi-Fi. In-hotel: 2 restaurants, room service, bars, tennis courts, pools, gym, spa, beachfront, laundry service* ⊟ *AE, MC, V* ✛ *2:C4.*

CABO SAN LUCAS

In Cabo San Lucas, there's a massive hotel on every available plot of waterfront turf. A pedestrian walkway lined with restaurants, bars, and shops anchored by the sleek Puerto Paraíso mall curves around the entire perimeter of Cabo San Lucas harbor, itself packed with wall-to-wall sportfishing and pleasure yachts. Unfortunately, a five-story hotel complex at one edge of the harbor blocks a small portion of the water view and sea breezes from the town's side streets, but it can't be denied that Cabo is a carnival and a parade, all at once. The short Pacific coast beach just over the rocky hills at the west end of the marina has a more peaceful ambience, though monstrous hotel projects have gobbled up much of the sand here, too. If being right on the water isn't a primary concern, it is well worth checking out some of the smaller, independently owned hotels sprinkled around the downtown area. Several offer gracious, hacienda-style accommodations with a personal touch that huge hotels cannot match.

Continued on page 141

The first major resort to be built in the area, the One&Only Palmilla retains its old-world glamour.

Stylish, quiet rooms and world-class golf await at the Sheraton Hacienda del Mar Resort.

Cabo San Lucas

San José del Cabo

THE CORRIDOR

↗ Los Cabos International Airport

Pacifica Holistic Retreat & Spa

Villa del Arco

Cabo Surf Hotel

Playa Grande

Esperanza

Fiesta Americana Grand

Las Ventanas al Paraíso

Marquis Los Cabos

One&Only Pamilla

PACIFIC OCEAN

BAJA REJUVENATION

Updated by Heidi Johansen and Georgia de Katona

A spa vacation—or even a single treatment—is the perfect way to kick-start a healthier lifestyle, slow a hectic routine, or simply indulge in a little pampering.

There are more treatment choices than ever before. Los Cabos, the land of sybaritic pleasures, has no shortage of resorts where you can be smeared with rich mud, plunge into a series of hot and cold baths, or simply enjoy a traditional facial.

Although spas once drew upon European traditions, they now offer treatments from around the globe: Japanese shiatsu, Indonesian jasmine-oil rubdowns, deep-tissue Thai massage, and the temazcal, or Maya sweat-lodge experience. Often you can follow an herbal wrap or mud bath with yoga or tension-relieving classes. The small Sea Spa at the Cabo Surf Hotel even offers a Surfer's Massage for those who've overdone it in the waves.

Self care is a growing trend, with custom prescriptions for upkeep between facials and massages and advice on holistic approaches to living to help keep you healthy and sane between spa visits.

All Los Cabos resort spas have packages—whether for a day of beauty or for a long weekend of treatments. Most spas are also open to nonguests of the resorts, and some properties allow you to use the fitness facilities if you've booked a spa treatment. Always call ahead.

Resort Name	Body Treatments	Facials	Seaside Treatments	Treatments For Two	Fitness Day Pass	Sauna	Steam Room
Cabo Surf Hotel	$60–$125	$80–$120	yes	yes	yes	yes	no
Esperanza	$160–$335	$185–$295	yes	yes	no	no	yes
Fiesta Americana Grand	$100–$250	$140–$290	yes	yes	yes	yes	yes
Marquis Los Cabos	$115–$195	$115–$170	yes	yes	yes	no	yes
One&Only Palmilla	$150–$350	$140–$250	yes	yes	$120	yes	yes
Pacifica Holistic Retreat & Spa	$110–$300	$80–$250	yes	yes	yes	yes	yes
Playa Grande Resort	$120–$250	$130–$165	yes	yes	no	no	yes
Las Ventanas al Paraíso	$145–$300	$180–$215	yes	yes	yes	yes	yes
Villa del Arco	$52–$290	$90–$120	no	yes	yes	yes	yes

(opposite page) Esperanza Resort

TOP SPOTS

ESPERANZA	MARQUIS LOS CABOS

ESPERANZA

Luxury continues to soar to great heights at this exclusive 17-acre resort between the towns of Cabo San Lucas and San José del Cabo where the spa doubled its size in 2007. At check in you're presented with an *agua fresca*, a healthy drink made with papaya or mango, or other fruits and herbs.

Before your treatment, enjoy the *Pasaje de Agua* (water passage) therapy, which includes steam caves and a waterfall. Treatments incorporate local ingredients, tropical fruits, and ocean-based products. Look for such pampering as the papaya-mango body polish, the grated coconut and lime exfoliation, and the Corona beer facial. Two free yoga classes are offered at 9 and 10:15 each morning.

BODY TREATMENTS. Massage: Agua, hot stone, essential oil, Thai (stroke techniques vary). **Exfoliation:** Body polish, salt glow. **Wraps/baths:** Aloe wrap, floral bath, herbal bath, mud bath, thalassotherapy. **Other:** Outdoor shower, steam room, warm soaking pool, waterfall rinse.

BEAUTY TREATMENTS. Facials, hair/scalp conditioning, manicure, pedicure, peels.

PRICES. Body Treatments: $160–$335. **Facials:** $185–$295. **Mani/Pedi:** $45–$200.

Hwy 1, Km 3.5. Tel. 624/145–6406. ⊕ *www.esperanzaresort.com. Parking: Valet (free, but please tip).* ⊟ *AE, MC, V.*

MARQUIS LOS CABOS

Known as the "Resort for All Senses," the Marquis is the only member of Leading Spas of the World in Los Cabos. You'll enjoy the open-air hot tubs that face the Cape's blue sky and overlook the Sea of Cortez. Lounge chairs draped with thick towels tempt you to linger by the hot tubs. Noteworthy is the Quetzalcoatl Oxygenating Experience: a eucalyptus foot bath, marine-salt exfoliation, herbal purification bath, and light massage with cucumber-milk lotion.

A hallway connects the spa with the Marquis' fitness center with its sky-high ceiling and wall-to-wall windows looking out to the pool slithering above the sand along the ocean.

BODY TREATMENTS. Massage: Aromatherapy, ayurvedic, deep tissue, essential oil, hot stone, pregnancy, reflexology, shiatsu, sports, Thai. **Exfoliation:** salt glow. **Wraps/baths:** herbal bath, mud wrap, thalassotherapy. **Other:** Ayurvedic treatments, hot tub, sauna, steam room.

BEAUTY TREATMENTS. Facials, manicure, pedicure, waxing.

PRICES. Body Treatments: $115–$195. **Facials:** $115–$170. **Mani/Pedi:** $39–$79.

Hwy 1, Km 21.5. Tel. 624/144–0906. ⊕ *www.marquisloscabos.com. Parking: Valet (free, but please tip).* ⊟ *AE, MC, V.*

ONE&ONLY PALMILLA

Treatment villas are tucked behind white stucco walls, ensuring privacy. Therapists lead you through a locked gate into peaceful palm-filled gardens with a bubbling hot tub and a day bed covered with plump pillows.

Treatments blend Mexican, Asian, and other global accents; using cactus, lime, and a variety of Mexican spices. Each session begins with a Floral Footbath—a symbolic Balinese ritual, which represents a cleansing of life's tensions to prepare you for total relaxation. One signature treatment is the Aztec Aromatic Ritual, a spicy body wrap that uses an ancient village recipe of clove, ginger, and cinnamon.

BODY TREATMENTS. Massage: Aromatherapy, Balinese, chocolate synergy, deep tissue, essential oil, hot stone, pregnancy, reflexology, sports, Swedish, Thai, watsu. **Exfoliation:** Body polish, dry brush, salt glow. **Wraps/baths:** Floral bath, herbal wrap, milk bath. **Other:** Anticellulite, colon therapy, pools, sauna, steam.

BEAUTY TREATMENTS. Anti-aging, peels, facials, hair styling, scalp conditioning, makeup, manicure, pedicure, waxing.

PRICES. Body Treatments: $150–$350. **Facials:** $140–$250. **Mani/Pedi:** $55–$150.

Hwy. 1, Km 7. S. Tel. 624/146–7000. ⊕ *www.oneandonlyresorts.com.* ***Parking:*** *Valet (free, but please tip).* ▭ *AE, MC, V.*

LAS VENTANAS AL PARAÍSO

The resort's bi-level spa is surrounded by serene cactus gardens and has both indoor and outdoor facilities. It's known for innovative treatments—skin resurfacing facials, nopal (cactus) anticellulite and detox wrap, crystal healing massages, and raindrop therapy.

Some of the eight treatment rooms have private patios; massages are available in a pavilion by the sea; and body wraps and massages are also performed on the hotel's 55-foot yacht.

BODY TREATMENTS. Massage: Aromatherapy, ayurvedic, deep-tissue, hot stone, reflexology, Reiki, shiatsu, shirodhara, sports, Swedish, watsu. **Exfoliation:** Body polish, dry brush, loofah scrub, salt glow. **Wraps/baths:** Herbal wrap, milk bath, mud wrap, cactus wrap. **Other:** Acupuncture, anticellulite, aromatherapy, Ayurvedic treatments, crystal therapy, hydrotherapy pool, sauna, steam room.

BEAUTY TREATMENTS. Facials, hair cutting/styling, manicure, pedicure, waxing.

PRICES. Body Treatments: $145–$300. **Facials:** $180–$275. **Mani/Pedi:** $45–$145.

Hwy. 1, Km 19.5. Tel. 624/144–0300. ⊕ *www.lasventanas.com.* ***Parking:*** *Valet (free, but please tip).* ▭ *AE, MC, V.*

TOP SPOTS

VILLA DEL ARCO	FIESTA AMERICANA GRAND

The Desert Spa on the beach in Los Cabos is also the area's largest, with 17 treatment rooms and two suites comfortably spread through three airy, sunny floors; the entire complex totals 31,000 square feet. With Los Cabos' largest hydrotherapy "wet" circuit, improve your circulation with dips in hot tubs followed by plunges in cold. The spa has the biggest fitness center in Cabo, and the beauty salon has a perfect view of the sea.

Treatments tend to utilize fruits, plants, and herbs that can be found in the area. Indulge in an organic succulent cactus facial or an after-sun soothing mint and eucalyptus treat.

BODY TREATMENTS. Massage: Deep tissue, reflexology, aromatherapy, couples. **Exfoliation:** Body scrub, fruit polish. **Wraps/baths:** Tequila wrap, fruit wrap, melon wrap, mineral bath. **Other:** Facials, hot-stone treatments Solo pare Caballeros treatments for me.

BEAUTY TREATMENTS. Facials, hair/scalp conditioning, hair cutting/styling, manicure, pedicure, waxing.

PRICES. Body Treatments: $52–$290. **Facials:** $90–$120. **Mani/Pedi:** $36–$46.

Camino Viejo a San José, Km 0.5. ☎ *624/145–7000.* ⊕ *www.-villadelarcoloscabos.com.* ***Parking:*** *Valet (free, but please tip).* ▭ *MC, V.*

The Fiesta's SOMMA Wine Spa uses grapes from the up-and-coming Valle de Guadalupe wine region. It's an unusual experience blended with classical treatments, focusing on the calming, cosmetic, and antioxidant properties of grapes and wine, or vinotherapy.

The spa is the only one of its kind in Mexico, with only six others throughout the entire world. It towers high above the Sea of Cortez with 15 treatment rooms, both indoor and open-air, and offers more than 30 facial and body treatments.

BODY TREATMENTS. Massage: Classic, deep tissue, sports, aromatherapy, hot stone, relaxing, Swedish, Chardonnay foot. **Exfoliation:** Salt body scrub. **Wraps/baths:** Mud wrap, chocolate wrap, Chardonnay wrap, clay wrap, honey and fruit wrap, seaweed wrap, green coffee wrap, water lily wrap. **Other:** Facials, cellulite firming.

BEAUTY TREATMENTS. Hair/scalp conditioning, hair cutting/styling, manicure, pedicure, waxing.

PRICES. Body Treatments: $100–$250. **Facials:** $140–$290. **Mani/Pedi:** $40–$60.

Hwy. 1, Km 10.3. ☎ *624/145–6200, or 800/FIESTA.* ⊕ *www.fiestaamericanagrand.com.* ***Parking:*** *Valet and self parking.* ▭ *MC, V.*

HONORABLE MENTIONS

PLAYA GRANDE RESORT

The meaning of the word thalassotherapy comes from the practice of using seawater baths and seaweed-based treatments for preventive and curative purposes. Playa Grande's spa is said to be the finest thalasso center in North America. They often use combinations of seaweed and seawater and the minerals in both will rejuvenate and renew your skin like you've never experienced.

BODY TREATMENTS. **Massage:** Hot stone, shiatsu, Swedish, four hands, foot reflexology, **Exfoliation:** Honey body polish, seaweed polish, sea-salt glow, cinnamon-sugar scrub, pomegranate/cranapple scrub. **Wraps/baths:** Thalassotherapy bath, seaweed bath, hydrotheraphy bath, seaweed body mask, honey/almond/buttermilk wrap.

PRICES. **Body Treatments:** $120–250. **Facials:** $130–165. **Mani/Pedi:** $35–$65.

Avenida Playa Grande No. 1, Playa Solmar ☎ *624/145-7575* ⊕ *www.playagrande-sort.com* **Parking:** *Valet (free, but please tip).* ▭ *MC, V.*

PACIFICA HOLISTIC RETREAT & SPA

This small, tranquil hotel on the Pacific side of Cabo is an adults-only property, filled with feng shui design, immaculately kept cactus gardens, and water, water, everywhere. The treatments at their Armonia (Harmony) Spa run the gamut from crystal reiki healing to a yogurt and violet exfoliation to temazcal.

BODY TREATMENTS. **Massage:** Hot stone, Swedish, sports, deep tissue, shiatsu, four hands, couples, expectant mother, ayurveda, shirobyhanga, Thai, reflexology, aromatherapy. **Exfoliation:** Honey sugar glow and amazing array of scrubs. **Wraps/baths:** Bamboo/alfalfa/aloe/chamomile, detox, Dead Sea mud, revitalizing.

PRICES. **Body Treatments:** $110–$300. **Facials:** $80–$250. **Mani/Pedi:** $35–$62.

Cabo Pacifica s/n ☎ *624/143-9696.* ⊕ *www.pueblobonitopacifica.com.* **Parking:** *Valet, (free, but please tip).* ▭ *AC, MC, V.*

ALSO WORTH NOTING

The boutique Cabo Surf Hotel's Sea Spa caters to its athletic guests with, among others, a Surfer's Sports Package and Day at the Beach massage and facial. *Playa Acapulquito Km 28, San Jose del Cabo* ☎ *624/142-2676.* ⊕ *www.seaspacabo.com.*

GLOSSARY

acupuncture. Painless Chinese medicine during which needles are inserted into key spots on the body to restore the flow of *qi* and allow the body to heal itself.

aromatherapy. Massage and other treatments using plant-derived essential oils intended to relax the skin's connective tissues and stimulate the flow of lymph fluid.

ayurveda. A traditional Indean medical practice that uses oils, massage, herbs, and diet and lifestyle modification to restore balance to the body.

body brushing. Dry brushing of the skin to remove dead cells and stimulate circulation.

body polish. Use of scrubs, loofahs, and other exfoliants to remove dead skin cells.

hot-stone massage. Massage using smooth stones heated in water and applied to the skin with pressure or strokes or simply rested on the body.

hydrotherapy. Underwater massage, alternating hot and cold showers, and other water-oriented treatments.

reflexology. Massage on the pressure points of feet, hands, and ears.

reiki. A Japanese healing method involving universal life energy, the laying on of hands, and mental and spiritual balancing. It's intended to relieve acute emotional and physical conditions. Also called radiance technique.

salt glow. Rubbing the body with coarse salt to remove dead skin.

shiatsu. Japanese massage that uses pressure applied with fingers, hands, elbows, and feet.

shirodhara. Ayurvedic massage in which warm herbalized oil is trickled onto the center of the forehead, then gently rubbed into the hair and scalp.

sports massage. A deep-tissue massage to relieve muscle tension and residual pain from workouts.

Swedish massage. Stroking, kneading, and tapping to relax muscles. It was devised at the University of Stockholm in the 19th century by Per Henrik Ling.

Swiss shower. A multijet bath that alternates hot and cold water, often used after mud wraps and other body treatments.

Temazcal. Maya meditation in a sauna heated with volcanic rocks.

Increasingly popular at Mexico spas is the traditional sweat lodge, or *temazcal*. Herb-scented water sizzles on heated lava rocks, filling the intimate space with purifying steam. Rituals blend indigenous and New Age practices, attempting to stimulate you emotionally, spiritually, and physically. For the sake of others, it's best to take a temazcal only if you're committed to the ceremony, or at least open-minded, and not claustrophobic.

Thai massage. Deep-tissue massage and passive stretching to ease stiff, tense, or short muscles.

thalassotherapy. Water-based treatments that incorporate seawater, seaweed and algae.

Vichy shower. Treatment in which a person lies on a cushioned, waterproof mat and is showered by overhead water jets.

Watsu. A blend of shiatsu and deep-tissue massage with gentle stretches—all conducted in a warm pool.

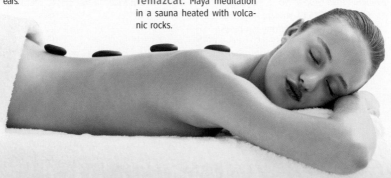

$ ⊡ **The Bungalows Hotel.** If solitude in comfortable hacienda-style surroundings and a reasonable room rate are more important than being in the center of the action, this is your place. Rooms are simply decorated with Mexican textiles and art; a cluster of two-story buildings frame a small, heated pool with lush landscaping. The hotel offers a complete, cooked-to-order Mexican breakfast in the morning that could include banana-walnut pancakes or a mushroom omelet. The Bungalows Hotel is about 10 blocks from the beach, and a 15-minute walk from Cabo San Lucas town—pleasant if you're in the mood. **Pros:** oasis-like property is a nice way to escape the constant hustle of Cabo; caring, personalized service encourages lingering and relaxation. **Cons:** hot water can be in short supply; there is noise from traffic and surrounding neighborhood. ⊠ *Blvd. Miguel Angel Herrera, 5 blocks from main plaza* ☎ *624/143–5035, 888/424–2252 in U.S.* ⊕ *www.cabobungalows.com* ⟳ *16 suites and bungalows ₺ In-room: Kitchen (some), DVD (some). In-hotel: Pool, Wi-Fi hotspot* ☰ *MC, V* ⟨◯⟩ *BP* ✛ *3:A4.*

$ ⊡ **Cabo Cush.** By far one of the most affordable hotels in Cabo, this **Fodor's Choice** little gem is reminiscent of courtyard hotels in mainland Mexico, with ★ a central breezeway running between the low-slung two-story buildings. Owner Jeff Layton has created a serene little spot in the heart of town. Upon entering the rooms, you'll find top-of-the-line pillow-top mattresses with soft cotton sheets; sleek, contemporary furniture; and bathrooms with beautiful Talavera tiling. There is a midcentury-meets-Mexico feel to this place, and, though it's simple, it's quite comfortable. If you're in Cabo to get out and do things and you want an extremely comfortable and affordable rest when you finally lay your head down, this is the place for you. **Pros:** fantastic price for a simple, comfortable room; easygoing, friendly staff will offer all sorts of recommendations; cheap, tasty meals available from the on-site eatery. **Cons:** no swimming pool or gardens—not really a hangout spot; no view. ⊠ *Calle Zaragoza between Revolucion and Carranza* ☎ *624/143–9300* ⊕ *www.cabocush. com* ⟳ *19 rooms ₺ In-room: No phone, Wi-Fi. In-hotel: Restaurant, gym, laundry service, Wi-Fi hotspot, parking (free)* ☰ *MC, V* ✛ *3:A3.*

¢–$ ⊡ **Cabo Inn.** The small, comfortable rooms at this affordable palapa-roof, cactus-lined, and jungle-like hotel have tangerine-and-cobalt sponge-painted walls and stained-glass windows above the headboards. The eight rooms on the lower level have refrigerators; and the two top-floor palapa suites are playful and funky, if a little bit noisy, due to their slightly open-air construction and the hotel's close proximity to downtown Cabo's festivities. Palapa #2 has a king bed and hot tub. A young, hip, international clientele frequents the Cabo Inn, with guests from Argentina, Germany, Ireland, Spain, and Sweden signing the guest book. **Pros:** very affordable hotel right in the thick of things and only a few minutes' walk to the beach; communal kitchen, barbecue, and dining area mean you can cook here and save on expensive meals out. **Cons:** some rooms are dark and cramped; upper rooms can get very noisy during high season when downtown revelers are at their wildest. ⊠ *Calle 20 de Noviembre and Vicario, Centro* ☎ *624/143–0819, 619/819–2727 in U.S.* ⊕ *www.caboinnhotel.com* ⟳ *20 rooms ₺ In-room: Refrigerator (some), no TV. In-hotel: Wi-Fi hotspot* ☰ *MC, V* ✛ *3:A3.*

5

$$$$ ⊡ **Capella Pedregal Resort.** Just when we thought there was no more room for a top resort in Los Cabos' five-star universe, along comes the small, stylish, hidden Capella Pedregal. You'll reach this newest (July 2009) beachfront boutique through a stunning tunnel, which was dynamited through a quarter-mile of Land's End bedrock. The open and airy resort is located near the tip of the Baja Peninsula, with 66 ultra-stylish rooms, suites, casitas, and a 4,000-square-foot presidential suite. The large staff provides personable service. On-site you can enjoy the Julian Farel Salon in the award-winning Auriga Spa, which integrates "uniquely Bajan visions of water, local Mexican healing traditions and the phases of the moon." Hear, hear. **Pros:** hidden away through a tunnel, but still quite near Cabo San Lucas town and marina; every room has a plunge pool. **Cons:** Pacific-side beach is not swimmable. ⊠ *Camino del Mar 1, Pedregal* ☎ *877/247–6688* ⊕ *www.capellapedregal.com* ⤳ *66 rooms* ⚐ *In-room: safe, DVD, Wi-Fi, refrigerator. In-hotel: 3 restaurants, bars, spa, beachfront, laundry facilities, laundry service, Internet terminal, pets allowed.* ⊟ *AE, MC, V* ✢ *3:A5.*

$ ⊡ **Casa Bella.** The Ungson family had been in Cabo for more than four decades before turning their home across from Plaza San Lucas into a spacious, sedate inn. It's by far the classiest and friendliest place in the neighborhood, landscaped with meandering paths leading to the pool, gazebo, and terrace. It is indeed, a *casa bella,* or beautiful house. Room furnishings are handcrafted and thoughtfully arranged. The open showers in the huge tiled bathrooms are works of art—some even have little gardens. **Pros:** no TVs in the rooms (vpro or con? You decide.); property feels totally secluded, though it's in the middle of town; ambience suggests a stay at a private home rather than a hotel. **Cons:** no TVs in the rooms (again, pro or con? Your call!); local roosters crow in the mornings. ⊠ *Calle Hidalgo 10, Centro* ☎ *624/143–6400* ⊕ *www.casabellahotel.com* ⤳ *11 rooms, 3 suites* ⚐ *In-room: No TV. In-hotel: Pool, laundry service, Wi-Fi hotspot* ⊟ *MC, V* ⊙ *Closed Aug. and Sept.* ⦿ *CP* ✢ *3:A4.*

$$–$$$ ⊡ **Casa Dorada Los Cabos Resort & Spa.** Through the dramatic, drawbridge-
Ⓒ   like entry on the stone facade you'll find this seven-floor, all-suites com-
Fodor'sChoice   bination hotel–time-share has it all. In addition to the standard one-,
★   two-, and three- bedroom suites, there are 13 impressive penthouse suites, which range from 920 to 4,500 square feet. To relax, head to the 7,000-square-foot Saltwater Spa, where you can partake in such treatments as Chinese Ball Stimulating Massage and Couleur de Vie therapy, which combines color, aroma, and saltwater therapies. Casa Dorada's lounge offers a selection of 50 beers, including a signature mango-flavor brew; the 12 Tribes restaurant has creative dishes from just about every corner of the world. **Pros:** beautifully appointed rooms here are suggestive of a much higher-priced hotel; huge jetted tubs in bathrooms; ocean views from every room; located at the heart of Playa Médano. **Cons:** the beach in front of the hotel is host to noisy bars and clubs; time-share salespeople are aggressive. ⊠ *Av. del Pescador* ☎ *624/143–9167, 866/385–0256 in U.S.* ⊕ *www.casadoradaloscabos.com* ⤳ *186 suites* ⚐ *In-room: Safe, kitchen (some), Wi-Fi. In-hotel: 2 restaurants, room service, bars, pools, gym, spa, water sports, children's programs (ages 4–12), laundry service, parking (free)* ⊟ *AE, MC, V* ✢ *3:B3.*

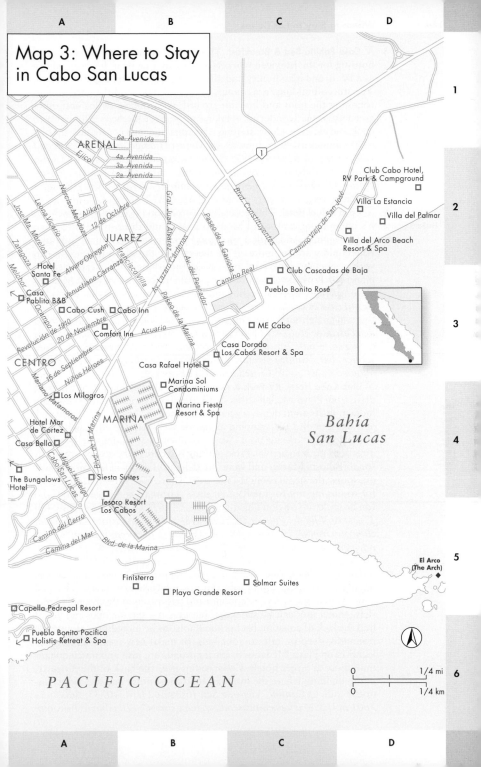

Map 3: Where to Stay in Cabo San Lucas

A **B** **C** **D**

1

ARENAL
6a. Avenida
4a. Avenida
3a. Avenida
2a. Avenida
Ejico
Narciso Mendoza
Alikan
12 de Octubre
Leona Victoria
Jose Ma. Morelos
Zaragoza
Blvd. Constituyentes
Paseo de la Gaviota

Club Cabo Hotel,
RV Park & Campground □

Villa La Estancia □
Villa del Palmar □

2

JUAREZ
Gral. Juan Álvarez
Francisco Villa
Alvaro Obregón
Venustiano Carranza
Camino Viejo de San José

Villa del Arco Beach
Resort & Spa □

Hotel
Santa Fe □
Casa
Pablito B&B □
Camino Real
Av. del Pescador
Camino Real

Club Cascadas de Baja □

Pueblo Bonito Rosé □

Meltchar
Ocampo
Revolución de 1910
20 de Noviembre
Cabo Cush □ □ Cabo Inn
Comfort Inn   Acuario
Paseo de la Marina

ME Cabo □

3

CENTRO
Mariano Matamoros
16 de Septiembre
Niños Héroes
Casa Rafael Hotel □
Casa Dorado
□ Los Cabos Resort & Spa

□ Los Milagros

Hotel Mar
de Cortez □
Casa Bella □
Cabo San Lucas
Miguel Hidalgo
Blvd. de la Marina
MARINA

Marina Sol
Condominiums □

Marina Fiesta
Resort & Spa □

*Bahía
San Lucas*

4

The Bungalows
Hotel
□ Siesta Suites

Tesoro Resort
Los Cabos
Camino del Cerro
Camino del Mar
Blvd. de la Marina

5

Finisterra
□
□ Playa Grande Resort
□ Solmar Suites

El Arco
(The Arch)
◆

□ Capella Pedregal Resort

Pueblo Bonito Pacifica
Holistic Retreat & Spa □

PACIFIC OCEAN

0		1/4 mi
0		1/4 km

6

A **B** **C** **D**

$ 🍽 **Casa Pablito Bed & Breakfast.** This cozy establishment started out as housing for the Mexican workers at Cascadas de Baja. It's been reborn as a B&B, and it's a homey and affordable option in an expensive town. The stucco buildings are orange, pink, and blue, and the gardens surrounding the pool and hot tub are lush with bougainvillea and other greenery. **Pros:** wonderful, relaxing pool area; kitchens allow you to cook and eat here. **Cons:** staffing is minimal (though courteous); marina is 30 minutes away on foot. ⊠ *Av. Miguel Hidalgo, between 1906 and Felix Ortega* ☎ *624/143–1971* ⊕ *www.casapablitoscabo.com* ⟿ *15 studio condos* ♿ *In-room: No phone (some), safe (some), kitchen, refrigerator, DVD (some). In-hotel: pool, laundry service, Wi-Fi hotspot, parking (free), some pets allowed* ▭ *MC* 🍽 *CP* ✛ *3:A3.*

¢–$ 🍽 **Casa Rafael Hotel.** This centrally located hotel is close to everything:
Fodor'sChoice it's one-minute walk to El Médano Beach, and three minutes to town
★ and shopping. And with a very good restaurant-bar-lounge in-house, who could want for more? It's a cheery little thing, painted bright teal with a shocking-pink pool area, sweet furnishings, and a rather gaudy piano bar. **Pros:** excellent price for a room in the heart of Playa Médano action; serene, tropical-feeling pool area; fantastic staff that embodies the *mi casa es su casa* ethos. **Cons:** the ocean view was taken away by a towering neighbor; furnishings are basic. ⊠ *Calle Médano and Camino del Pescador* ☎ *624/143–0739* ⊕ *www.casarafaels.com* ⟿ *10 rooms* ♿ *In-room: Safe, no phone, refrigerator. In-hotel: Restaurant, room service, bar, laundry service, Wi-Fi hotspot, parking (free), some pets allowed* ▭ *MC, V* ☉ *Closed Sept.* 🍽 *EP* ✛ *3:B3.*

$ 🍽 **Club Cabo Hotel, RV Park & Campground.** Though only a five-minute drive from Playa Médano, this small complex is quiet and remote—even hidden. It sits amid dense vegetation between the beach and Highway 1 and has tent and RV camping alongside well-maintained motel rooms and a long, sparkling pool. We recommend contacting the hotel for directions prior to arrival. **Pros:** parking is secure and prices are very reasonable; hosts Martin and Irene are delightful and will happily answer questions; the steam room is a real treat. **Cons:** reservations are accepted for rooms but not for the RV/tent sites; getting to and from Club Cabo can be tricky if you don't have a vehicle. ⊠ *Off Old Rd. to San José, Km 3, east of Villa del Palmar* ☎☎ *624/143–3348* ⊕ *www.mexonline.com/ clubcabo.htm* ⟿ *10 rooms, 18 tent/RV sites* ♿ *In-room: Kitchen (some), refrigerator (some). In-hotel: Pool, laundry facilities, Wi-Fi hotspot, parking (free), some pets allowed* ▭ *No credit cards* ✛ *3:D2.*

$$ 🍽 **Club Cascadas de Baja.** While surrounding properties have gone up, up, up, the two-story, palapa-roof villas of Club Cascadas haven't changed a bit. At first, the lack of telephones and televisions at this friendly timeshare–hotel mix can be shocking, but give it a day or two, and you'll find the lack of constant background noise to be incredibly calming. Be romantic, sleep in, talk to your kids, or make new friends. **Pros:** nice location on Playa Médano; tropical grounds are lush and much quieter than those at larger hotels. **Cons:** rooms near the back of the property, in the building where the lobby is, tend to be noisy and are more run-of-the-mill. ⊠ *Camino Viejo de San José* ☎ *624/143–0738, 800/365– 7601 in U.S.* ⊕ *www.clubcascadasdebaja.com* ⟿ *110 villas* ♿ *In-room:*

Casa Dorada Los Cabos Resort & Spa is home to the 7,000-square-foot Saltwater Spa.

Pueblo Bonito Pacifica Holistic Retreat & Spa incorporates feng shui elements throughout the resort.

No *phone, safe, no TV, kitchen. In-hotel: 2 restaurants, room service, bars, tennis court, pools, gym, beachfront, laundry service, Wi-Fi hotspot* ⊟ *MC, V* ✚ *3:C3.*

¢ ☎ **Comfort Inn.** This tidy little hotel is several blocks from the marina and about a five-minute walk to the beach. There is nothing fancy here,

but the rooms are clean, the beds are comfortable, and the interior courtyard, where the pool is, has lush palms and flowers in addition to a palapa-roof swim-up bar. The pool is a good size, and it's sparkling and refreshing, with plenty of chaise lounges surrounding it. You'll find lots of families here, with a friendly vibe prevailing. **Pros:** very safe-feeling hotel; attentive staff; reliable budget option. **Cons:** rooms are small; furnishings somewhat flimsy. ✉ *Leona Vicario and Revolucion 20 de Noviembre* ☎ *624/143–7501* ⊕ *www.choicehotelsmexico.com* ↘ *95 rooms* ⚭ *In-hotel: Bar, pool, laundry service, parking (free), some pets allowed* ⊟ *AE, D, DC, MC, V* ⃝CP ✚ *3:A3.*

$–$$
Fodor's Choice
★

☎ **Finisterra.** One of the first hotels built in Cabo, the Finisterra, perched on a hill overlooking the marina and the Pacific, was an architectural marvel back in the 1960s. The hotel has grown over the years and the two towers of the newer Palapa Beach Club overlook their gorgeous pools and the Pacific. An eight-story palapa roof covers the restaurant and bar on the sand next to the hotel's three giant free-form swimming pools and eight hot tubs. Rooms in the new Palapa Beach Club buildings are by far the nicest; they are large and have oceanfront balconies—where, from the upper floors, it's not uncommon to spot whales during the winter months. The stone buildings of the less expensive, older section of the hotel are simpler and evoke the early days of Cabo's popularity. The Blue Marlin Restaurant is good, and the Whale Watcher bar that sits perched high atop the cliff behind the Finisterra has one of the best views in town, especially when the wintering whales are in town. A café-deli overlooking the marina side of Cabo San Lucas offers a great view of the Cabo Adventures Dolphin experience below. **Pros:** fantastic location, short walk to the marina and Cabo's action, but very quiet, as well; great beach access for walking on the Pacific side; attentive but unobtrusive staff. **Cons:** restaurants (except at the pool) and older sections of the hotel are closed during the summer months; beach is not swimmable at all due to rough waves and undertow. ✉ *Blvd. Marina* ☎ *624/143–3333, 800/347–2252 in U.S.* ⊕ *www. finisterra.com* ↘ *286 rooms* ⚭ *In-room: Safe. In-hotel: 2 restaurants, bars, tennis courts, pools, gym, beachfront, Internet terminal, Wi-Fi hotspot* ⊟ *AE, MC, V* ✚ *3:B5.*

$ ☎ **Hotel Mar de Cortez.** Another one of Cabo's original hotels, this colonial-style property has been operating for 37 years, and remains one of the most affordable in all of Los Cabos. Great for fishermen with buddies, and travelers on a budget, the suites have up to four beds (and are quite reasonably priced in high season). Located in the very middle of the downtown Cabo San Lucas action, Hotel Mar is only a few blocks from the marina, a block from the main square, near *muchos* restaurants, bars, clubs, and shopping. **Pros:** clean rooms and pleasant surroundings; refreshing pool. **Cons:** noisy air-conditioning units; surrounding streets are busy and loud; beds and pillows are too hard; towels are limited. ⊠ *Lazaro Cardenas and Guerrero* ☎ *624/143–0032, 800/347–8821 in U.S.* ⊕ *www.mardecortez.com* ⇥ *65 rooms, 16 suites* ⚎ *In-room: No phone, refrigerator, no TV, Wi-Fi. In-hotel: Restaurant, room service, bar, pool, laundry service, parking (free)* ☰ *MC, V* ✛ *3:A4.*

¢–$ 🖼 **Hotel Santa Fe.** A make-yourself-at-home feeling pervades this small, colonial-style hotel that resembles a two-story apartment building. It's managed by the Villa Group, which also operates three major properties on El Médano Beach. Room service is provided by the deli at the adjacent market. Rooms have sofa beds and cable TV. **Pros:** rooms are large and clean; rates are reduced if you stay one week or longer. **Cons:** pool isn't heated; beach is a 10-minute walk away; service is minimal. ⊠ *Av. Zaragoza and Obregón* ☎ *624/143–4401, 877/845–5247 U.S.* 🖷 *624/143–4402* ⊕ *www.hotelsantafeloscabos.com* ⇥ *46 rooms* ⚎ *In-room: Kitchen, refrigerator. In-hotel: Restaurant, room service, pool, laundry facilities, laundry service, parking (free)* ☰ *MC, V* 🍽 *EP* ✛ *3:A3.*

¢–$ 🖼 **Los Milagros.** A mosaic sign (crafted by co-owner Ricardo Rode) near the entrance hints at the beauty inside this small inn. Brilliant purple bougainvillea and orange lipstick vines line the patio, which showcases more of Rode's works by the fountain and small pool. *Bóveda*-style (arched brick) roofs top the rooms, which have terra-cotta tile floors and handmade Mexican furniture. Co-owner Sandra Scandiber dispenses budget travel tips while visiting with guests in the courtyard, and is always ready to lend books from her huge library. Checks or cash are accepted at the hotel; to use a credit card, you must pay prior to arrival through PayPal. **Pros:** quaint, quiet inn located close to everything in Cabo; one room is accessible to travelers with disabilities. **Cons:** air-conditioning units in rooms can be loud; pool is small and not heated. ⊠ *Matamoros 116* 🖷 *718/928–6647 in U.S., 624/143 4566* ⊕ *www.losmilagros.com.mx* ⇥ *12 rooms* ⚎ *In-room: Wi-Fi In-hotel: Pool, laundry service, Wi-Fi hotspot, parking (free)* ☰ *AE, D, MC, V* ✛ *3:A4.*

$–$$ 🖼 **Marina Fiesta Resort & Spa.** Though this colonial-style building is not ocean-side, most rooms have a pleasant view of the cloverleaf-shape pool and out to the yacht-filled marina. Rooms are designed for practicality, with stain-proof floral textiles, tile floors, and plenty of space to spread your stuff about. The hotel is on the Golden Zone walkway adjacent to the Puerto Paraíso Mall. **Pros:** close to popular bars and shops, and a quick walk from popular Playa Médano. **Cons:** staff is not trained to deal with problems or guest concerns; there is no buffer between guests and aggressive time-share salespeople. ⊠ *Marina, Lot 37, Marina* ☎ *624/145–6020* ⊕ *www.marinafiestaresort.com* ⇥ *155 rooms* ⚎ *In room: Safe, kitchen (some), refrigerator (some). In-hotel: 4 restaurants, room service, bar, pools, gym, spa, laundry service, Wi-Fi hotspot* ☰ *AE, MC, V* ✛ *3:B4.*

$ 🖼 **Marina Sol Condominiums.** Good bargains can be found here—especially for groups. Most of the condos hold two bedrooms, but some have one, three, or five bedrooms. Furnishings vary widely due to private ownership—ask to see photos if you are particular about decor. There are dozens of dining options on virtually every block surrounding this property. Reserve at least three months in advance for high season. **Pros:** only a few blocks from the town center and just a quick walk to Playa Médano, this is a good spot if you like being close to the action. **Cons:** but be sure to ask for an "inside" garden condo, as the outside rooms are noisy, due to the never-ending construction and traffic in this, one of the busiest parts of town; Internet connectivity is spotty; this property may just have the pushiest time-share salespeople in the area. ⊠ *Paseo del Pescador* ☎ *624/143–3231, 877/255–1721 in U.S.* ☎ *624/143–6286* ⊕ *www.marinasolresort.com* ⋼ *52 condos* ♿ *In-room: Kitchen, refrigerator, DVD (some). In-hotel: Restaurant, bar, pool, spa, laundry service, Wi-Fi hotspot* ▤ *MC, V* ✛ *3:B4.*

$$–$$$ 🏨 **ME Cabo.** In the middle of the most popular beach in Los Cabos, El Médano, is where you'll find the ME—Sol Meliá's entrée into this lively W-style hotel brand. With its huge, bustling pool areas, more daybeds than you can imagine, and hot tubs under the palms, the ME Cabo is a playground for adults. The hotel's swim-up pool bar is the favorite in Cabo. At poolside is the fun and friendly Nikki Beach Restaurant, serving its culinary blend of Asian and Mediterranean dishes, along with chill music, often spun by a DJ. Rooms are chic, ultra-comfortable, and have easygoing wood furnishings and breezy, flowing drapes. A wide range of creatively designed suites is on offer, with names like Energy, Chic, and Nikki. Early reservations are essential here. **Pros:** great for adults and singles looking for a hopping social scene; ME's Passion Night Club (open Thursday–Saturday) is a popular Cabo destination; iPod docking stations and plasma TVs in every room. **Cons:** rooms in the high $200s are limited and rates jump up quickly after that; rooms anywhere near the Passion club are noisy; though not advertised as "adults only," this is not the hotel to take children. ⊠ *Playa Médano* ☎ *624/145–7800, 800/336–3542 in U.S.* ⊕ *www.solmelia.com* ⋼ *88 rooms, 62 suites* ♿ *In-room: Safe, Wi-Fi. In-hotel: 3 restaurants, bars, pools, beachfront, laundry service* ▤ *AE, MC, V* ✛ *3:C3.*

$–$$ 🏨 **Playa Grande Resort.** This large, multicolor time-share–hotel complex located on the beach next to the original Solmar Suites looks a bit Las Vegas, even by Cabo standards, but it's got all kinds of activities and facilities, making it a great family vacation option. The quarters in the 100-room Ridge wing offer eagle's eye views of both the marina and the Pacific beyond, and the mostly two- and three-bedroom suites are beautifully decorated with tasteful, modern Mexican decor. **Pros:** the Thalasso Spa is huge and gets rave reviews; putt-putt golf course and play structures, in addition to fabulous pools, will keep your kids entertained. **Cons:** getting to and from rooms in the Ridge is time-consuming and confusing; aggressive time-share salespeople. ⊠ *Av. Playa Grande #1* ☎ *624/145–7575, 800/344–3349 in U.S.* ⊕ *www.playagranderesort.com* ⋼ *358 rooms* ♿ *In-room: Safe, refrigerator, Wi-Fi. In hotel: 4 restaurants, room service, bars, pools, gym, spa, beachfront, laundry service* ▤ *MC, V* ✛ *3:B5.*

$$$-$$$$ 🖫 **Pueblo Bonito Pacifica Holistic Retreat & Spa.** Soothing waterfalls, glass-
Fodor's Choice   domed ceilings, and pebbled floors bring nature indoors to complement
★   this holistic approach to vacationing. The emphasis here is on health
and wellness, peace and tranquillity. No children are permitted. A phy-
sician who works with natural therapies oversees the Armonia spa,
where treatments include *watsu* and an outdoor, beachside *temezcal*, or
native Mayan sweat lodge. It's a refreshingly small hotel by Los Cabos
standards, and rooms have minimalist decor with cream fabrics, cedar-
and-straw accents, and ocean views. The designers incorporated feng
shui elements throughout the resort and grounds, which are stunning,
with patterned cactus gardens designed by the talented Cacti Mundo
team from San José del Cabo. **Pros:** adults only; truly tranquil lodgings;
entire hotel is no-smoking. **Cons:** the extremely sedate atmosphere can
be shocking for guests; charges apply for use of beach beds and gym;
beach is not swimmable; pushy time-share salespeople; you must have a
car or take a cab to get to town. ⊠ *Cabo Pacifica s/n* ☎ *624/142–9696,
866/585–1752 in U.S.* ⊕ *www.pueblobonitopacifica.com* ⌁ *140 rooms,
14 suites* ⚫ *In-room: Safe, refrigerator, Internet. In-hotel: 2 restaurants,
room service, bars, pools, gym, spa, beachfront, laundry service, Inter-
net terminal, no kids under 16* ⊟ *AE, MC, V* ✛ *3:A6.*

$$-$$$ 🖫 **Pueblo Bonito Rosé.** Mediterranean-style buildings curve around ele-
☾   gant grounds; imitations of Roman busts guard reflecting pools, and
Flemish tapestries adorn the lobby—this is definitely not your typi-
cal Cabo hotel. Even the Rosé's smallest suites can accommodate four
people, and all have private balconies overlooking the grounds. Staff is
gracious and attentive, and many guests return year after year because
of this. **Pros:** there are two Pueblo Bonito hotels on El Médano Beach
in San Lucas and two other properties, the Pueblo Bonito Pacifica
Holistic Resort and Pueblo Bonito Sunset, out on the Pacific coast—a
shuttle bus travels between them, and guests have signing privileges at
all four; booking online often gets significant discounts on rates. **Cons:**
pushy time-share salespeople; thin walls mean you may have to endure
all the noises of your neighbors. ⊠ *Playa Médano* ☎ *624/142–9898,
800/990–8250 in U.S.* ⊕ *www.pueblobonito.com* ⌁ *260 suites* ⚫ *In-
room: Safe, kitchen, refrigerator. In-hotel: 2 restaurants, room service,
bars, pools, gym, spa, beachfront, laundry service, Internet terminal*
⊟ *AE, MC, V* ✛ *3:C3.*

¢   🖫 **Siesta Suites.** The proprietors keep a close eye on this three-story
hotel—a calm refuge two blocks from the marina, ideal for lengthy
stays—and they can offer great advice to visitors. The simply furnished
suites have full-size refrigerators, and between the bedrooms with two
double beds and living rooms with wide padded couches, there's room
to sleep quite a crew. Salvatore's Restaurant, an Italian eatery, is situ-
ated poolside; it's widely acclaimed by resident gringos in the know.
The owners also have a condo on the beach in San José for rent by the
week. **Pros:** great rates for stays of a week or longer; friendly staff really
takes care of guests; barbecue area great for cooking up the catch of the
day. **Cons:** town noise can sometimes be disturbing; no off-street park-
ing; pool is small and is surrounded by tables from Salvatore's restau-
rant at night. ⊠ *Calle Zapata, Apdo. 310, Centro* ☎☎ *624/143–2773,*

5

866/271–0952 *in U.S.* ⊕ *www.cabosiestasuites.com* ⤸ *5 rooms, 15 suites ♿ In-room: Kitchen (some), refrigerator. In-hotel: Pool, Internet terminal ☰ AE, MC, V ✢ 3:A4.*

$-$$ 🍽 **Solmar Suites.** The whitewashed, modern Solmar sits against the rocks at Land's End facing the surging Pacific. Rooms are done in a Mexico–Santa Fe style, with subdued green- and blue-tile baths. The oldest rooms open right onto the sand, and you literally feel the waves breaking on the nearby beach. Newer buildings run up a tiered hillside. Timeshare units (also used as hotel rooms) have kitchenettes and a private pool area. The surf here is far too dangerous for swimming, but don't miss a stroll along the wide strip of beach. The Solmar's sportfishing fleet is a longtime local favorite. **Pros:** Solmar has just added an all-inclusive meal option to its plans; secluded location; 10-minute walk to town. **Cons:** major teardown of hillside buildings for the planned construction of new time-share buildings has severely disrupted the tranquillity of this resort (completion date is unclear), and service and management seem to be suffering as a result; food is hit-or-miss. ⊠ *Av. Solmar at Blvd. Marina, Apdo. 8* ☎ *624/146–7700, 800/344–3349 in U.S.* ⊕ *www.solmar.com* ⤸ *109 suites, 14 studios ♿ In-room: Safe, refrigerator. In-hotel: Restaurant, room service, bar, pools, beachfront, laundry service ☰ MC, V ✢ 3:C5.*

¢-$$ 🍽 **Tesoro Resort Los Cabos.** The Tesoro, as it is now called, was the original hotel on the Cabo Marina, when it was known as the Costa Real. There are four categories of rooms, from penthouses to dependable standards, all with tiled floors, spacious balconies, and firm beds. Furnishings are updated and comfortable, and get reliably more so in the fancier rooms. **Pros:** the Tesoro is possibly the most centrally located hotel for fishing, restaurants, and overall fiesta atmosphere—it's literally surrounded by dozens of fun bars and restaurants; best close-up view of Marina Cabo San Lucas; free shuttle to Playa Medano. **Cons:** the grounds and pool area are basic; this is not a lounge-around-a-luxurious-pool resort, nor is it on the beach. ⊠ *Calle Marina San Lucas* ☎ *624/173–9300, 866/998–3767 in U.S.* ⊕ *www.tesororesorts.com* ⤸ *286 rooms ♿ In-room: Safe, kitchens (some), Internet. In-hotel: 2 restaurants, bars, pool, gym, laundry service, room service ☰ AE, MC, V* ⍩◯⍵ *EP, AI ✢ 3:A4.*

$$-$$$ 🍽 **Villa del Arco Beach Resort & Spa.** Another resort opened by the Villa Group on El Médano Beach, the Villa del Arco is next to Villa La Estancia. As with its sister properties, del Arco offers comfortable, stylishly decorated one-, two- and three-bedroom suites and penthouses with all the amenities, including full kitchens. And for spa aficionados, the 31,000-square-foot Desert Spa is intoxicating—the largest in Los Cabos, offering treatments that utilize desert plants and herbs. Sign up for the Mexican Tequila Body Wrap or the Organic Succulent Cactus Facial. **Pros:** an on-property deli and market lets you stock up the kitchen, saving money on meals out; rooms are large and very comfortably furnished. **Cons:** service can be spotty and is often geared more toward selling time-shares than satisfying hotel guests. ⊠ *Camino Viejo a San José, Km 0.5* ☎ *624/145–7000, 877/845–5247 in U.S.* ⊕ *www. villadelarcoloscabos.com* ⤸ *221 suites ♿ In-room: Safe, kitchen (some),*

Wi-Fi. In-hotel: 3 restaurants, room service, bars, pools ▬ *MC, V* ⦿ *EP, AI* ✛ *3:D2.*

$$ 🏨 **Villa del Palmar.** The whale-shape waterslide traversing the three-level ☺ pool is perhaps the best indication that families and kids are welcome. The large marble-floored entry welcomes you into a property that is as comfortable and casual as a vacation home—if vacation homes came with a full-time staff on hand. Rooms are not cramped, but they're not as well designed as those you'll find at the sister properties (which are, admittedly, more expensive), and the comforters and furniture are more '80s than 21st century. Still, the staff is friendly and happy to help you arrange adventures in the area. **Pros:** large rooms with kitchenettes; great location on Playa Médano and near all of Cabo's offerings. **Cons:** the oldest of the Villa Group properties on Playa Medano, Palmar facilities and rooms need updating and, in fact, a major renovation began in late 2009, which should be a consideration when you're booking your stay. ✉ *Camino Viejo a San José, Km 0.5* ☎ *800/823–4488 in Mexico, 877/845–5247 in U.S.* ⊕ *www.villadelpalmarloscabos.com* ↪ *460 suites, 96 villas* ♿ *In-room: Safe, kitchen (some), Internet. In-hotel: 2 restaurants, room service, bars, pools, gym, spa, children's programs (ages 4–12), laundry service, Internet terminal* ▬ *AE, D, MC, V* ✛ *3:D2.*

$$–$$$ 🏨 **Villa La Estancia.** It's apparent that this is the Villa Group's top property as soon as you enter its suites. Located between its two sister properties, Villa del Palmar and Villa del Arco, La Estancia is the quiet one—a kids-free resort. Rooms are spacious and furnished with comfortable, contemporary furniture, and have large bathrooms, and kitchenettes. The Private Chef Service offers in-suite dining. **Pros:** beautifully maintained grounds; located on swimmable Playa Médano; small deli-market on the premises to stock up on snacks. **Cons:** restaurants on this property are expensive, and food quality varies widely; pushy time-share salespeople. ✉ *Camino Viejo a San José, Km 0.5* ☎ *624/143–8121, 619/683–7883 in U.S.* ⊕ *www.villalaestancialoscabos.com* ↪ *156 villas* ♿ *In-room: Safe, kitchen (some), DVD, Wi-Fi. In hotel: 2 restaurants, room service, bars, pools, parking (free)* ▬ *MC, V* ⦿ *EP, AI* ✛ *3:D2.*

TODOS SANTOS

The secret of the charm of Todos Santos is out, as more and more expats—American and European alike—move to the area. And there's a lot to love here: the surf on the Pacific, just a couple of miles west of town, is good; weather is always cooler than in Los Cabos; and the lush, leisurely feel of this artsy Mexican colonial town is relatively undisturbed by the many tourists who venture up from Los Cabos for the day. The quality of lodgings is surprisingly high, and are a much better value than any along the Corridor or in Cabo—and there isn't a megaresort to be found. In fact, some of the best lodging in the region is found right here, among the lush palm trees of this former sugarcane town.

$–$$ 🏨 **Hacienda Todos los Santos.** The owners of this gracious hacienda used to come here on weekends, but they loved it so much that they've expanded their old weekend home, and have decided to stay year-round.

5

TIME-SHARE BEWARE

For some families who frequently like to get away to resorts, the time-share concept can be a good, and economical, way to vacation. Time-shares are a big business in Los Cabos, and the offers are incessant, especially as you walk through the town of Cabo San Lucas. Indeed, pushy, in-your-face time-share representatives at the airport and in many hotel lobbies will try to entice you to attend a presentation by offering free transportation, breakfast, and activities, or even attractive amounts of cash. These aggressive salespeople are a major downside to many

expensive lodgings where you might assume that you won't be harassed. Don't feel obligated to accept— presentations often last two hours or more, and can be physically and emotionally draining. If you're staying in a hotel that has time-share units, aggressive salespeople may call your room every morning asking you to attend a free breakfast. If you're not interested, nicely demand to be taken off their call list.

■TIP→ If you want those time-share "sharks" off your back pronto, simply say "I live here"— and they'll leave you alone.

Within each of the three guesthouses, you'll find canopied beds and antique art. The rooms in the newer Casa de Los Santos are furnished as beautifully as the original casitas, but do not have kitchens. The three suites in Casa de Los Santos are quite different, but all have Saltillo-tiled floors, hand-carved furniture, and plenty of windows. One, Casa Santa Luz, has a wood-burning fireplace. The houses are surrounded by palms, bamboo, and flower-filled gardens. **Pros:** original three casitas have private terraces and fully equipped kitchens; the upstairs rooms have wonderful views of the lush farmland surrounding the property. **Cons:** quiet, serene lodgings not ideal for young children. ⊠ *End of Benito Juárez* ☎ *612/145–0547* ⊕ *www.todossantos.cc/haciendatodoslossantos.html* ↙ *8 rooms in 4 guesthouses* ⚲ *In room: No phone, kitchen (some), refrigerator (some), no TV (some). In hotel: Pool* ⊟ *No credit cards* ✛ *4:B2.*

$–$$$ 🖃 **Hotel California.** This handsome structure with two stories of arched terraces and rich, vibrant colors on the walls, is a testament to the artistic bent of owner Debbie Stewart. A deep-blue-and-ocher scheme runs throughout, and rooms, some with ocean views, are decorated with a mix of antiques and folk art reminiscent of Santa Fe, New Mexico. The Coronela restaurant and bar are local hot spots, and the Emporio shop is stuffed with curios, jewelry, and funky natural-fiber clothing from around the globe. **Pros:** the inn feels exotic and lush; great location in the heart of downtown Todos Santos. **Cons:** noise from town and cars can be disturbing; service not as smooth as at other hotels in town. ⊠ *Benito Juárez at Morelos* ☎ *612/145–0525* ⊕ *www.hotelcalifornia-baja.com* ↙ *11 rooms* ⚲ *In-room: No phone, no TV, Wi-Fi. In-hotel: Restaurant, bar, pool* ⊟ *MC, V* ✛ *4:B1.*

$ Fodor'sChoice ★   🖃 **Hotelito.** This Mexican-modern hotel by local architect Jesus Fernando de Castro has been artfully decorated by British interior designer and owner Jenny Armit. Original art is found throughout and has been

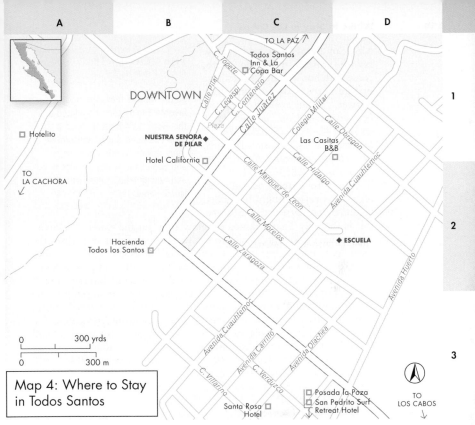

Map 4: Where to Stay in Todos Santos

A
B
C
D

TO LA PAZ

Todos Santos
Inn & La
Copa Bar

DOWNTOWN

Hotelito

NUESTRA SENORA
DE PILAR

Hotel California

Las Casitas
B&B

TO
LA CACHORA

Hacienda
Todos los Santos

ESCUELA

0   300 yrds
0   300 m

Posada la Poza
San Pedro Surf
Retreat Hotel

Santa Rosa
Hotel

TO
LOS CABOS

mixed with contemporary and antique Mexican decorative pieces; the sculptural furniture is as comfortable as it is captivating. Each room has a private patio with lounge chairs and hammocks. A variety of activities can be planned with the assistance of the friendly, accommodating staff. Beds are incredibly comfortable, linens are dreamy, robes are fluffy, and fresh flowers are always present. There is also a three-bedroom home available for rent on the property, which is lush with palms, bougainvillea, and jasmine. **Pros:** saltwater swimming pool is fabulous; generous breakfasts are delicious (mangoes right off the tree!); boogie boards, beach towels and umbrellas are available to use at the beach; five-minute walk to the beach. **Cons:** 10-minute walk to downtown; not recommended for families with young children—this is really a retreat-like property. ⊠ *Rancho de la Cachora, take Topete north from downtown toward La Cachora* ☎ *612/145–0099* ⊕ *www. hotelitotodossantos.com* ⟳ *4 rooms* ⌂ *In-room: Refrigerator, Wi-Fi. In-hotel: Bar, pool, laundry service, Wi-Fi hotspot, parking (free)* ⊟ *AE, D, DC, MC, V* ⊖ *CP* ✛ *4:A1.*

¢–$ ⊡ **Las Casitas Bed & Breakfast.** Canadian artist Wendy Faith has used her talents to turn the rustic adobe-and-wood casitas on this property into cozy, artsy lodgings set amid a lush, tropical garden. Bright walls and hand-painted murals, the owner's own glass artwork, and comfortable, well-dressed beds make this a lovely place to stay. **Pros:** generous

Mexican breakfasts, with a few favorite dishes from the north, come with house coffee; suites have private baths. **Cons:** rooms share shower; ceilings are low. ✉ *Rangel between Obregon and Hodalgo* ☎ *612/145–0255* ⊕ *www.lascasitasbandb.com* ⇆ *5 casitas In-hotel: Wi-Fi hotspot, parking (free)* ⊟ *No credit cards* ⦿| *BP* ✛ *4:D1.*

$$–$$$$
Fodor's Choice
★

☒ **Posada La Poza.** Located west of town, overlooking a bird-filled lagoon that gives way to the Pacific,

this is the only Todos Santos property right on the water. The Swiss owners have taken great care to create a property that showcases the local flora, and the results are flawless. The handsome, spacious suites have terra-cotta–color walls, modern furniture, and sumptuous Swiss linens. You'll find a CD player and binoculars on hand, but there aren't any TVs or phones in the rooms. Even if you're not staying, stop by the excellent El Gusto! restaurant (closed Thursday) for spicy tortilla soup, local scallops, organic salads, and an impressive list of Mexican wines. **Pros:** very generous, delicious breakfasts; gorgeous saltwater pool and hot tubs. **Cons:** no children under 12; no TV or phones. ✉ *Follow signs on Carretera 19 and on Benito Juárez to beach* ☎ *612/145–0400* ⊕ *www.lapoza.com* ⇆ *8 suites* ⚅ *In-room: No phone, safe, refrigerator, no TV. In-hotel: Restaurant, bar, pool, beachfront, Wi-Fi hotspot, no kids under 12* ⊟ *MC, V* ⦿| *BP* ✛ *4:C3.*

¢   ☒ **San Pedrito Surf Retreat Hotel.** Just outside Todos Santos, west of the village of El Pescadero, serious surfers and anyone else in the know gather at this cozy, family-style hotel. The attractions here are the water and the waves, and the chill community of surfers and beach lovers who now live here permanently, or who spend part of the year here, in all variety of homes. Rooms at San Pedrito are decorated simply, but have nice kitchens, stocked with coffee, cookware, and utensils. There is a large recreation room with a pool table and games, maps, fishing rods, and gear. Surfboards and wet suits are also available. It is imperative that you make reservations during high season. **Pros:** as great for families or groups as it is for couples; fabulous beach and surfing right off the patio; laid-back but helpful staff; the big casitas, which sleep up to six people, are very affordable. **Cons:** somewhat challenging to find—keep your eyes peeled for the sign at the highway; no access for people with disabilities; not within walking distance to any restaurants. ✉ *Playa San Pedrito* ⊕ *www.sanpedritosurf.com* ⇆ *6 casitas* ⚅ *In-room: No phone, kitchen, refrigerator, no TV. In-hotel: Beachfront, laundry facilities, Internet terminal* ⊟ *No credit cards* ✛ *4:C3.*

¢   ☒ **Santa Rosa Hotel.** Located on the southwest end of downtown, in a
☾   quiet residential area, just two blocks west of Highway 19, this two-story stucco hotel looks a bit more vintage Las Vegas than Todos Santos, but it's a friendly, easygoing place with a huge pool and relaxing patio. Prices are reasonable, and the staff is very courteous. The clientele tends

In addition to standard rooms, the Casa Dorada Los Cabos Resort & Spa has 13 lavish penthouses suites.

Todos Santos Inn defines understated elegance.   Posada La Poza overlooks a bird-filled lagoon.

BIKINI BOOT CAMP

Some travel for utter indulgence, using the excuse "I'm on vacation" to justify any and all excesses. However, others travel as a way to reconnect their mind and body, using vacation as time off from obligatory office happy hours, conference-room doughnuts, and I'm-exhausted-and-it's-late Chinese takeout.

The latest spin on exercising in Cabo San Lucas is the Cabo Bikini Boot Camp, offered by Lisa Mini. The BBCs are speedy four-day, four-night high-energy workout camps for the lady who wants to get in shape—and fast! These intensive workouts feature long days of yoga, Pilates, beach running, and kickboxing, finished off with relaxing massages, swims in the pool, and healthy, chef-prepared meals. Lodging is in a private home in the luxe Pedregal neighborhood of Cabo San Lucas. ☎ *624/358–8187, 707/337–0444 in U.S.* ⊕ *www.cabobikinibootcamp.com.*

to be both friendly and international. The hotel offers great rates for extended stays. **Pros:** affordable, clean, and child-friendly; spacious rooms; kitchens in rooms make it easy to save on meals; ocean views from second-story units. **Cons:** some of the details in the hotel are a bit rag-tag—loose tiles in the bathrooms, aging furniture. ⊠ *Olachea between Verduzco and Villarino* ☎ *612/145–0394* ⊕ *www.hotelsantarosa.com.mx* ⟿ *8 rooms* ♿ *In-room: Kitchen, refrigerator, Wi-Fi. In-hotel: pool, laundry facilities, Internet terminal, Wi-Fi hotspot, parking (free), some pets allowed* ⊟ *MC, V* ♦ *4:C3.*

$

Fodor's Choice

★

🖭 **Todos Santos Inn.** This converted 19th-century house, with only eight guest rooms, is unparalleled in design and comfort, owing to the loving care and attention of the owners, Todd and John. The pool deck is lined with hearty stone and brick; the painted walls of the foyer depict a fading, dusky scene; and gorgeous antiques are displayed throughout, completing the period feel in this hacienda that once belonged to a sugar baron. The absence of telephones and TVs allow for unencumbered relaxation. The attached Copa Wine Bar is open in the evening, and good restaurants are within easy walking distance. **Pros:** this is traditional Mexican elegance and hospitality at its best; the interior courtyard of this property is a verdant oasis. **Cons:** occasional noise from construction and renovation in the surrounding neighborhood; not ideal for families, as no children under 12 are allowed. ⊠ *Calle Legaspi 33* ☎ *612/145–0040* ⊕ *www.todossantosinn.com* ⟿ *8 rooms* ♿ *In-room: No phone, no TV. In-hotel: Bar, pool, Wi-Fi hotspot, no kids under 12* ⊟ *MC, V* ⍥ *BP* ♦ *4:C1.*

Shopping

WORD OF MOUTH

"When you use the ATM, enter an amount that is not divisible by 500 (like 4,800 pesos)—then you'll get smaller bills. Many ATMs have a sign saying what denominations the machine has in it; also, on the screen, it will say what the smallest amount it will deliver."

—cabron

SHOPPING PLANNER

Hours of Operation

Many stores are open as early as 9 AM, and often stay open until 9 or 10 PM. A few close for siesta at 1 PM or 2 PM, then reopen at 4 PM. About half of Los Cabos' shops close on Sunday; those that do open usually close up by 2 or 3 in the afternoon.

It's not uncommon to find some shops and galleries closed in San José del Cabo or Todos Santos during the hot season (roughly June to Sept.), though very few shops close in Cabo San Lucas.

We've noted this whenever possible; however, some shops simply close up for several weeks if things get excruciatingly slow and/or hot. In any case, low-season hours are usually reduced, so call ahead during that time of year.

Buyer Beware

One of the benefits of traveling in Los Cabos is the low crime rate, thanks in part to the large population of expats and year-round tourists, and the *tranquilo* nature of locals. That being said, it's always wise to pay attention to what's going on when money is changing hands. Some tips: Watch that your credit card goes through the machine only once, so that no duplicates of your slip are made. If there's an error and a new slip needs to be drawn up, make sure the original is destroyed. Don't let your card leave a store without you. One scam is to ask you to wait while the clerk runs next door ostensibly to use another business's phone or to verify your number—but really to make extra copies. Again, this area is refreshingly safe and incident-free compared to many areas on the mainland, but it's always wise to be aware.

Best Bring-Backs

If you travel Los Cabos with a few extra pesos in your pocket it's likely you'll want to return home with a memento, or 10, that reminds you of the spirit and vibrancy of this region.

Works of art by local artists such as **Kaki Bassi**, **Wentworth**, and photographer **Tomás Spangler** make great treasures to take back home—and galleries will usually ship the items for you. For more packable take-home goodies, the clothing options are nearly endless: T-shirts, resort wear, and clothing from hip Mexican designers will all compete for space in your suitcase. Cabo San Lucas is a great shopping town; if you've got time and some money, there's no need to worry about purchasing your beach vacation clothing before leaving home.

If you're looking for something truly authentic and *hecho en Cabo* (made in Cabo), then check out the blown glass at the intriguing **Fábrica de Vidrio Soplado**. Other fun souvenirs include the new labels of tequila offered from such outlets as Cabo Wabo, Hotel California in Todos Santos, the Cabo Surf Hotel, and Las Veritas, a popular Cabo dance club and bar.

What You Can't Bring Home

Don't buy items made from tortoiseshell or any sea turtle products: it's illegal (Mexico's turtle species are endangered or threatened, and these items aren't allowed into the United States, Canada, or the United Kingdom). Cowboy boots, hats, and sandals made from the leather of endangered species such as crocodiles may also be taken from you at customs, as will birds, or stuffed iguanas or parrots. It isn't uncommon for U.S. Customs agents to seize seashells, so those and all sea creatures are best left where you find them.

Both the U.S. and Mexican governments also have strict laws and guidelines about the import–export of antiquities. Check with customs beforehand if you plan to buy anything unusual or particularly valuable.

Although Cuban cigars are readily available, American visitors aren't allowed to bring them into the United States and will have to enjoy them while in Mexico. However, Mexico produces some fine cigars from tobacco grown in Veracruz. Mexican cigars without the correct Mexican seals on the individual cigars and on the box may be confiscated.

Tips and Tricks

Better deals are often given to cash customers—even though credit cards are nearly always accepted—because stores must pay a commission to the credit-card companies. If you are paying in cash, it is perfectly reasonable to ask for a 5%–10% discount—though you shouldn't assume you'll be given one.

U.S. dollars are widely accepted in Los Cabos, although most shops pay a lower exchange rate than a bank (or ATM) or *casa de cambio* (money exchange).

Bargaining is common in markets and by beach vendors, who may ask as much as two or three times their bottom line. Occasionally an itinerant vendor will ask for the real value of the item, putting the energetic haggler into the awkward position of offering far too little. One vendor says he asks *norteamericanos* "for twice the asking price, since they always want to haggle." The trick is to know an item's true worth by comparison shopping. It's not necessary to bargain for already inexpensive trinkets like key chains or quartz-and-bead necklaces or bracelets.

Shopping In Spanish

bakery: *panadería*

bookseller: *librería*

candy store: *dulcería*

florist: *florería*

furniture store: *mueblería*

grocery store: *abarrotes*

hardware store: *ferretería*

health-food store: *tienda naturista*

jewelry store: *joyería*

market: *mercado*

notions store: *mercería*

stationery store: *papelería*

tobacconist: *tabaquería*

toy store: *juguetería*

Sending Stuff Home

Better stores and galleries offer shipping services for large or unwieldy items.

If you are an avid shopper, it won't hurt to pack a duffel bag for all your new treasures to check as luggage on your way home.

⇨ *For more shipping info, see Los Cabos Essentials section.*

Updated by
Georgia de
Katona

Los Cabos may not have a whole lot of homegrown wares, but the stores are filled with beautiful and unusual items from all over mainland Mexico. You can find hand-painted blue Talavera tiles from Puebla; blue-and-yellow pottery from Guanajuato; black pottery from San Bartolo Coyotepec (near Oaxaca); hammocks from the Yucatán; embroidered clothing from Oaxaca, Chiapas, and the Yucatán; silver jewelry from Taxco; fire opals from Queretaro; and the fine beaded crafts of the Huichol tribe from Nayarit and Jalisco.

Los Cabos manufactures good times under plenty of sunshine but very few actual products. One exception is glassware from Fábrica de Vidrio Soplado (Blown-Glass Factory). In addition, a burgeoning arts scene has national and international artists opening galleries and, in fact, a large number of galleries now abound throughout Los Cabos, with many in San José del Cabo's rapidly evolving city center and more dotted throughout Todos Santos's historic downtown. Dozens of shops will custom-design gold and silver jewelry for you, fashioning pieces in one to two days. Liquor shops sell a locally produced liqueur called *damiana*, which is touted as an aphrodisiac. A few shops will even create custom-designed bathing suits for you in a day or so.

No longer hawking only the requisite T-shirts, belt buckles, and trinkets, Cabo's improved shopping scene has reached the high standards of other Mexican resorts. Its once-vacant streets are today lined with dozens of new shops, from open-air bazaars to souvenir shops and fine designer boutiques. To be sure, there's something for everyone here.

SAN JOSÉ DEL CABO

Cabo San Lucas's sister city has a refined air, with many shops in old colonial buildings just a short walk from the town's *zócalo* (central plaza). Jewelry and art are great buys—this is where you'll find the best shopping for high-quality Mexican folk art. Many of the most worthwhile shops are clustered within a few of blocks around Plaza Mijares, where Boulevard Mijares and Avenida Zaragoza both end at the remodeled zócalo at the center of San José. Thursday nights from November through April are designated Art Nights, when galleries stay open until 9 serving drinks and snacks, with various performances, demonstrations, and dancing—it's a fun night out!

ART GALLERIES, FOLK ART, AND CERAMICS

Amber Gallery & Fine Art Annex (✉ *Obregón 18* ☎ *624/105–2332* ⊕ *www. loscabosambergallery.com* ✛ *1:A3*) is the store to visit if you're a fan of amber jewelry, sculptures, abstract art, and collector perfume bottles.

Arenas Gallery (✉ *Obregón and Morelos* ☎ *624/142–4969* ✛ *1:B2*) displays fine jewelry, oil and acrylic paintings, and intricately painted, handmade pottery from Mata Ortiz, a small town in the state of Chihuahua that's famous for its Mesoamerican-pottery revival.

Arte de Julian Garcia (✉ *Morelos near Comonfort* ☎ *624/142–3566* ⊕ *www.juliangarciaf.com* ✛ *1:B2*) is a showplace for the dramatic forms of sculptor and painter Julian Garcia. Housed within Plaza Paulina, you'll find a number of Julian's organic pieces adorning the compound.

Casa Dahlia Fine Art Gallery (✉ *Morelos and Zaragoza* ☎ *624/132–2647, 503/922–3434 in U.S.* ⊕ *www.casadahlia.com* ✛ *1:B3*) features contemporary artists from Mexico and abroad, and invites visitors to linger in its beautifully renovated historic building with organic teas and coffee—some people even enjoy a cigar in the gallery's gardens.

Copal (✉ *Plaza Mijares* ☎ *624/142–3070* ✛ *1:D3*) has carved animals from Oaxaca, masks from Guerrero Negro, and heavy wooden furnishings, along with woven rugs and beautiful Mexican crafts and jewelry.

Curios Carmela (✉ *Blvd. Mijares 43* ☎ *624/142–1117* ✛ *1:D4*) displays an array of Mexican textiles, pottery, glassware, hammocks, and souvenirs that can be nearly overwhelming, but never fear: the prices are reasonable. You could easily find all the gifts you need right here.

El Armario (✉ *Obregón and Morelos* ☎ *624/105–2989* ✛ *1:B2*) which calls itself "the cutest shop in town," offers a selection of Mexican folk art, ceramic pottery, candles, clay figurines, papier-mâché—plus fresh coffee out on the patio.

★ **Frank Arnold Gallery** (✉ *1137 Calle Comonfort* ☎ *624/142–4422, 559/255–8273 in U.S.* ⊕ *www.frankarnoldart.com* ✛ *1:B2*) has two big draws: arguably the best gallery space in town, in a great new building by local architect Alfredo Gomez, and Frank Arnold's dramatic, widely acclaimed contemporary paintings.

6

Galería Corsica (✉ *Obregón Hidalgo* ☎ *624/128–1468* ⊕ *www.galeria-corsica.com ✛ 1:B2*) is in a spectacularly dramatic space. The gallery shows museum-quality fine art with an emphasis on paintings and large, impressive sculpture pieces.

Galería de Ida Victoria (✉ *Guerrero 1128* ☎ *624/142–5772* ⊕ *www.ida-victoriaarts.com ✛ 1:A3*) has been designed with skylights and domes to show off the international art contained within, which includes paintings, sculpture, photography, and prints.

★ **Galería Veryka** (✉ *Plaza Mijares 418* ☎ *624/142–0575 ✛ 1:D3*) is one of the best folk art shops in the region, with gorgeous embroidered clothing, masks, wood carvings, jewelry, and hand-molded black and green pottery. Most of the goods are from Oaxaca. Check out the seasonal displays, especially the Day of the Dead altar.

Gallery Casa Don Pablo (✉ *Guerrero 12, near Obregón* ☎ *624/142–2539 ✛ 1:A3*) has a little bit of everything: original Mexican art, Talavera earthenware, wood carvings, fine silver, and local historic photographs.

Gerardo Lopez Art Studio (✉ *Morelos 11* ☎ *624/142–3725 or 624/123–4078* ⊕ *www.fingerardo.com.mx ✛ 1:B3*) is colorful and quizzical, displaying works of surrealism, finger painting, and still lifes along with portraits and landscapes.

La Dolce Art Gallery (✉ *Hidalgo between Zaragoza and Obregón* ☎ *624/142–6621 ✛ 1:C2*), near San José's classic cathedral on the zócalo, specializes in modern painting styles.

La Sacristia (✉ *Hidalgo near Obregón* ☎ *624/142–4007* ⊕ *www.lasacristiaart.com ✛ 1:C3*) has a fine selection of Talavera pottery, traditional and contemporary Mexican jewelry, blown glass, and contemporary paintings. The glassware is incredible.

Muvezi (✉ *Alvaro Obregón 1523400* ☎ *24/105–2792* ⊕ *www.muvezi.com ✛ 1:B2*) presents the unexpected here in Baja Sur: fine Shona sculptures from Zimbabwe in a variety of breathtaking stones. This gallery is the public face of an economic development project working to keep the ancient tradition of stone carving alive in Zimbabwe, and to provide desperately needed funds for health care at the grassroots level there. Don't worry about the weight of the stone: sculptures come in a variety of sizes and Muvezi will ship pieces to your home.

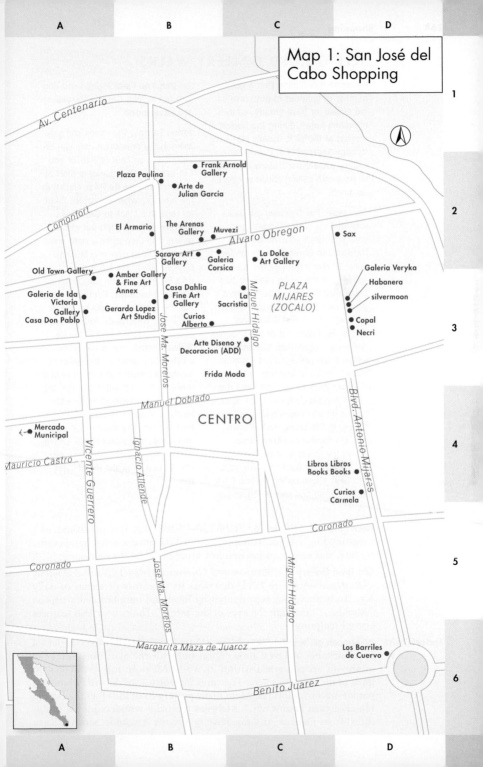

SELF-GUIDED GALLERY WALKS

It's worth mentioning that a good number of galleries in both towns are closed, or have greatly reduced operating hours, during the hottest months of the year, usually late June through September. If there is one gallery you are particularly interested in, it's worth calling ahead to check on hours.

San José. The Thursday art walks start at 5 PM, with galleries open until 9 PM. Start your walk on Hidalgo and Obregón, and wander down Obregón through the six or so galleries scattered on the next two blocks. Turning left on to Guerrero, you'll want to stop in to see **Galería de Ida Victoria** and **Casa Don Pablo**. Turn right out of the galleries and walk a block over to Comonfort, where you'll connect to Morelos in another block to find the galleries in **Plaza Paulina** awaiting, and the **Frank Arnold Gallery** a half block farther up on Comonfort. If you're hungry at this point, **Voilà Bistro** in Plaza Paulina and **Baan Thai**, across the street from each other on Morelos at Comonfort, are both excellent. Finish up by heading back to the zócalo and wandering among the shops on Plaza Mijares—making sure not to miss **Galería Veryka** and **silvermoon**.

Todos Santos. The shops and galleries in the downtown area can be explored in an hour or two, or you can easily make a day of it. Start at **Nuestra Señora de Pilar** church in the morning, when it's cooler. Head up Legaspi a block to **Galería la Coronela**. Make a left out of the gallery and then make a right onto Topete to head over one block to Centenario—to the left is **Joyeria Brilanti**, and on the corner is **Manos Mexicanas**. Continue heading south on Topete and on Juarez you'll find **Galería de Todos Santos** at the intersection, and **Fénix de Todos Santos** around the corner on the right. Between the galleries mentioned you'll find dozens of additional shops to wander through, too. Satisfy your growling tummy with lunch at **Ataxcon**, a local's favorite for fantastic, very inexpensive food on Hidalgo at Camino Militar, where you'll find a chicken, beef, and vegetarian option on the menu every day.

Necri (✉ *Blvd. Mijares 16* ☎ *624/130–7500* ✛ *1:D3*) is an offshoot of a long-standing San Lucas shop; it carries Talavera ceramics, handicrafts, pottery, and pewter pieces and hot sauce made by the owner.

Old Town Gallery (✉ *Obregón and Guerrero* ☎ *624/142–3662* ⊕ *www.oldtowngallery.net* ✛ *1:A3*) describes its inventory of scenes of daily life, landscapes, and oceanscapes by local and international artists as "Mexico . . . through the eyes of the artist." The gallery also features crystal sculptures.

Fodor's Choice
★
silvermoon gallery (✉ *Plaza Mijares No. 10* ☎ *624/142–6077* ✛ *1:D3*) is remarkable in Los Cabos region both for the assortment and the quality of art contained within its walls. Mexican folk art makes up most of the inventory here. Treasures include Carlos Albert's whimsical papier-mâché sculptures, Mata Ortiz pottery from the Quezada family, Huichol yarn "paintings," Alebrijes (colorful wooden animal sculptures) from Oaxaca, and fine jewelry. Owner Armando Sanchez Icaza

is gracious and knowledgeable; he knows volumes about the artists whose work he carries. His silversmiths can also make custom jewelry for you within a day or two.

Soraya Art Gallery (✉ *Obregón and Morelos* ☎ *624/355–2819*) sells murals, faux finish, and trompe l'oeil art by local artists.

BOOKS
Libros Libros, Books Books (✉ *Blvd. Mijares 41* ☎ *624/142–4433* ✛ *1:D4*) is a bookstore that stocks a good selection of newspapers, such as the *Wall Street Journal* and *USA Today,* and also has an extensive selection of English-language magazines, plus postcards, maps, and souvenirs.

CLOTHING
Curios Alberto (✉ *Zaragoza in front of Plaza Mijares* ☎ *No phone* ✛ *1:B3*) carries beautiful embroidered dresses for young girls amid all sorts of other fun goodies, curios, knickknacks, and clothing items to pick up for folks at home.

Frida Moda (✉ *Blvd. Mijares* ☎ *624/142–2870* ✛ *1:C3*) offers a range of mostly American sportswear and jeans.

HOME FURNISHINGS
Arte, Diseno y Decoracion (ADD) (✉ *Zaragoza at Hidalgo* ☎ *624/143–2055* ✛ *1:C3*) is an interior-design shop that has hand-painted dishes from Guanajuato, carved wood furniture from Michoacán, and an impressive selection of tempting housewares from all over Mexico.

Plaza Paulina (✉ *Morelos and Comonfort* ☎ *624/142–5555* ✛ *1:B2*) is more than just an art gallery, it's a wealth of decorating ideas and items for the home that will steal your attention for hours. Arte de Julian Garcia gallery is here, too, and, if you get hungry, the plaza is also home to the gourmet Voilá Bistro, which serves up creative Mexican fare.

JEWELRY
Ofelia's Los Castillo (✉ *In Royal Solaris Resort* ☎ *624/145–6800*) features high-quality silver jewelry from top artists in Taxco, a town halfway between Mexico City and Acapulco, that's noted for its silversmiths.

Sax (✉ *Plaza Mijares at Obregón* ☎ *624/142–6053* ✛ *1:D2*), owned by two talented sisters, is a great place to find exceptional, eclectic silver jewelry designs. The artists will create a design of your choice in 24 hours. Prices are very good here.

MARKETS
El Mercado Municipal (✉ *Castro and Coronado, off Calle Doblado* ☎ *No phone* ✛ *1:A4*) is San José's traditional market area, where you can stock up on fresh meats and produce, or visit the market's **Viva Mexico** stand for clothes, belts, spices, jewelry, and other curios—all at excellent prices.

SUNDRIES AND LIQUOR
Los Barriles de Cuervo (✉ *Blvd. Mijares and Juárez* ☎ *624/142–5322* ✛ *1:D6*) specializes in rare tequilas.

A shop in San José del Cabo displays its colorful handmade wares.

TOBACCO

Habanera (✉ *Plaza Mijares 6* ✛ *1:D3*) has a nice selection of Cuban cigars and Mexican handicrafts. Don't miss the colorful hand-embroidered bedspreads.

THE CORRIDOR

There are shopping options along the Corridor—the stretch of land between San José del Cabo to the east and Cabo San Lucas to the west—but the shops cater more to resort guests and American expats than travelers looking to experience Los Cabos. Unless you are intent on something specific at one of the shops on the Corridor, you'll have much more fun shopping in San José del Cabo, Cabo San Lucas, or Todos Santos.

HOME FURNISHINGS

★ **Artesanos** (✉ *Hwy. 1, Km 2.5* ☎ *624/143–3850* ✛ *2:D1*) is where home owners and restaurateurs go from throughout the area to shop for Mexican furnishings, dishes, and glassware, along with colorful handicrafts and ornaments.

Villa Valentina (✉ *Hwy. 1, Km 31* ☎ *624/142–6611 or 624/142–661* ⊕ *www.villa-valentina.com*) is the most notable shop on the Corridor, with impressive and unique home furnishings, from rustic antiques to custom-made pieces.

MALL

Las Tiendas de Palmilla (⊠ *Hwy. 1, Km 27.5* ☎ *624/144–6999* ⊕ *www. lastiendasdepalmilla.com*) is located just across from the posh Palmilla Resort. There are a smattering of shops and galleries, a couple of restaurants, a coffee shop, a nice terrace with a peaceful fountain, and a view of the Palmilla development with the tranquil, turquoise Sea of Cortez beyond. **Antigua de México** is a branch of the famous Tlaquepaque store, and shoppers will discover distinctive furniture and bedding supplies, and many Mexican-flavor interior-decorating items. **Pez Gordo Art Gallery** is artist Dana Leib's second location, and offers her pieces, as well as those by other artists. You'll find beautifully designed silver tableware pieces from Taxco at **Prestige Designs**. Tiki Lounge is one of the Tommy Bahama "lifestyle" boutiques for men only, with silk and other natural-fiber clothing in relaxed styles. Stop in Casa Vieja for beautiful women's apparel by Mexican designers, including Pineda-Covalin—you'll find a wide range of styles in fibers such as cotton, silk, linen, and even cactus. **Trópica Calipso Swimwear** carries a wide selection of swimwear for women. Owner Margarita Partridge, a longtime Los Cabos resident, still personally tends to her many clients.

SUNDRIES

La Europea (⊠ *Hwy. 1, Km 6.7* ☎ *624/145–8755*) carries a wide selection of imported wines and deli products.

Trader Dick's (⊠ *Hwy. 1, Km 29.5* ☎ *624/142–2828*), located along the Costa Azul surf coast near the popular Zipper's Restaurant, is a favorite with Americans seeking newspapers from home, along with familiar deli meats and cheeses.

CABO SAN LUCAS

Cabo San Lucas has the widest variety of shopping options in Los Cabos area, with everything from intriguing Mexican folk art and designer clothing to beer holsters and touristy T-shirts. Bargains on typical Mexican tourist items can be found in the dozens of shops between Boulevard Paseo de la Marina and Avenida Lazaro Cárdenas.

Get hungry when you're shopping? Worth trying in this zone are the very inexpensive taco and juice stands tucked into the mini–flea markets that stretch between streets.

Many of the shops in malls like Puerto Paraiso are typical of those you'd find in any mall in the United States—with prices to match. All over the downtown and marina areas, however, are great shops and galleries with unique and compelling items.

ART GALLERIES

Fodor's Choice ★ **Arte de Origen** (⊠ *Madero between Guererro and Blvd. Marina* ☎ *624/105–1965* ⊕ *www.artedeorigen.com* ✛ *2:B4*) is a standout among the shops on the increasingly hip Madero Street. Pan-American cultural traditions inform the original decorative art in this richly colored open space. Painting, ceramics, and inventive, painting-like collages are applied to a wide variety of objects like boxes, tables, and mirror frames.

Small sculptures, jewelry, and some textiles are also part of a collection of art that is clearly meant to be part of your living space.

★ **Galería de Kaki Bassi** (✉ *Puerto Paraíso, Av. Cárdenas* ☎ *624/144–4510* ⊕ *www.kakibassi.com* ✛ *2:C3*) displays art—often textural and inspired by the Baja cave paintings—by Kaki Bassi, who has exhibited all over Europe and has seven pieces of art in the Mexican government's permanent collection. Her gallery exhibits many Mexican artists' work as well, from paintings and handicrafts to sculpture crafted from found objects.

Galería La Grande (✉ *Plaza Nautica* ☎ *624/143–1415* ⊕ *www.galerialagrande.com* ✛ *2:B4*) claims to be "the largest gallery in Baja California" and we won't challenge them. There's truly a huge selection of fine Mexican art—more than 1,500 pieces—and if something catches your eye and you'd like to make a purchase, they'll pack it up and ship it home for you.

★ **Golden Cactus Gallery** (✉ *Guerrero and Madero* ☎ *624/143–6399* ⊕ *www.goldencactusgallery.com* ✛ *2:A4*), run in a second-floor space by painter Chris MacClure and his partner Marilyn Hurst, has been showcasing local artists' work (paintings, lithographs, and many colorful gifts) since 1997. Bill Clinton is among those with MacClure's pieces in their collections.

Tomás Spangler Photographic Gallery (✉ *Tesoro Los Cabos Hotel lobby* ☎ *624/147–7709* ⊕ *www.fotomas.com* ✛ *2:B5*) is owned by an accomplished art photographer who has accumulated a number of stunning images from his travels throughout Mexico and the world; several dozen are matted and mounted and on display here.

BOOKS

Libros Libros, Books Books (✉ *Blvd. Marina at Plaza de la Danza* ☎ *624/143–3173* ✛ *2:B5*) carries a vast number of Spanish- and English-language newspapers, novels, magazines, plus fun souvenirs.

CAMERAS AND FILM

Foto Fuji (✉ *Morelos and Revolucion de 1910* ☎ *624/143–2020* ✛ *2:B2*) has one-hour film developing and sells film, batteries, videotapes, and cameras. Sure, the digital age has lessened the need for film, you never know when you're going to need a backup.

CLOTHING

Chicas Sin Limites (✉ *Hidalgo at Plaza Amelia* ☎ *624/143–1500* ⊕ *www.chicassinlimites.com* ✛ *2:A4*) translates to "girls without limits," which describes the apparel services here. Need your own custom-designed bathing suit—and fast? Select the fabric and cut, and your suit will be ready in 24 hours.

"Cotton" might be in the name, but the **Cotton Club** (✉ *Puerto Paraíso, Av. Cárdenas* ☎ *624/143–2388* ✛ *2:C3*) stocks women's resort wear made from all sorts of natural fibers, crafted by both Mexican and international designers.

Dos Lunas (✉ *Plaza Bonita, Blvd. Marina* ☎ *624/143–1969* ✉ *Puerto Paraíso, Blvd. Marina* ☎ *624/143–1969* ✛ *2:B3*) is full of trendy, colorful sportswear and straw hats.

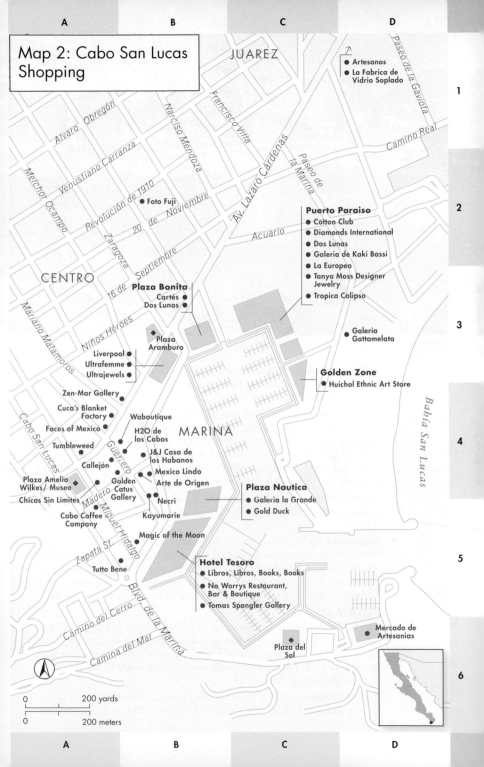

Map 2: Cabo San Lucas Shopping

JUAREZ

CENTRO

MARINA

Artesanos
La Fabrica de Vidrio Soplado

Puerto Paraiso
- Cotton Club
- Diamonds International
- Dos Lunas
- Galeria de Kaki Bassi
- La Europea
- Tanya Moss Designer Jewelry
- Tropica Calipso

Galeria Gattamelata

Golden Zone
- Huichol Ethnic Art Store

Plaza Bonita
Cartés
Dos Lunas

Plaza Aramburo

Liverpool
Ultrafemme
Ultrajewels

Zen-Mar Gallery

Cuca's Blanket Factory
Waboutique

Faces of Mexico

H2O de los Cabos

Tumbleweed

J&J Casa de los Habanos

Callejón

Mexico Lindo

Golden Catus Gallery
Arte de Origen

Plaza Amelia Wilkes/ Musea
Necri

Chicas Sin Limites

Kayumarie

Cabo Coffee Company

Magic of the Moon

Plaza Nautica
- Galeria la Grande
- Gold Duck

Hotel Tesoro
- Libros, Libros, Books, Books
- No Worrys Restaurant, Bar & Boutique
- Tomas Spangler Gallery

Tutto Bene

Mercado de Artesanias

Plaza del Sol

Foto Fuji

Bahia San Lucas

Álvaro Obregón
Venustiano Carranza
Melchor Ocampo
Narciso Mendoza
Revolución de 1910
20 de Noviembre
Zaragoza
16 de Septiembre
Niños Héroes
Mariano Matamoros
Cabo San Lucas
Guerrero
Madero
Miguel Hidalgo
Zapata St.
Camino del Cerro
Camina del Mar
Blvd. de la Marina
Francisco Villa
Av. Lázaro Cárdenas
Acuario
Paseo de la Marina
Paseo de la Gaviota
Camino Real

0 — 200 yards
0 — 200 meters

The inviting Plaza Bonita Shopping Mall in Cabo San Lucas.

H2O de los Cabos (✉ *Madero and Guerrero* ☎ *624/143–1219* ✛ *2:B4*) offer bathing suits ranging from skimpy thongs to modest one-piece suits, all with a Mexican flair.

Magic of the Moon (✉ *Hidalgo off Blvd. Marina* ☎ *624/143–3161* ✛ *2:B5*) is a favorite among locals and Cabo regulars, featuring clothing designed by Pepita Nelson, the owner. If you can't find anything that fits you or your style, she will design an outfit for you and finish it in three days. Also check out the handmade ceramic jewelry, beaded bustiers, and colorful bathing suits.

Tropica Calipso (✉ *Puerto Paraíso, Blvd. Marina* ☎ *624/143–9792* ✛ *2:C3*) sells resort wear for both sexes, and can make an outfit in 24 hours.

★ **Tumbleweed** (✉ *Lazaro Cárdenas at Hidalgo* ☎ *624/143–7677* ⊕ *www.tumbleweedmexico.com* ✛ *2:A4*) is a hip little shop full of the things that amuse its creator, Miranda Fae: T-shirts, pants, dresses, records, accessories, and more, from Mexican and American designers—with an eye toward DJ and DIY cultures. It's not your average resort-town store.

FOLK ART

Faces of Mexico (✉ *Av. Cárdenas beside Mar de Cortéz hotel* ☎ *624/143–2634* ✛ *2:A4*) is one of the oldest folk-art shops in the area; it has a selection of masks from Oaxaca and Guerrero, though the owner's wonderful collection of handmade masks at the back of the tiny shop may be the biggest draw of all.

Huichol Collection (✉ *Blvd. Marina and Ocampo* ☎ *624/143–4055*) carries the Huichol Indian tribe's beautiful beaded crafts, as well as posters,

Vibrant, hand-painted masks make for memorable souvenirs and gifts.

postcards, and T-shirts in the vibrant colors and patterns typical of this ancient culture.

Mercado de Artesanías (⊠ *South end of Blvd. Marina* ☎ *No phone* ✛ *2:D6*) is at the far western end of Marina San Lucas, where the fishing boats drop anchor to weigh and photograph the few fish still brought in. This crafts market sells pottery, blankets, jewelry, and Mexican sombreros.

Necri (⊠ *Blvd. Marina between Madero and Ocampo* ☎ *624/143-0283* ✛ *2:B4*) has an excellent selection of folk art and home furnishings.

Zen-Mar Gallery (⊠ *Cárdenas between Matamoros and Ocampo* ☎ *624/143–0661* ⊕ *www.zen-mar.com* ✛ *2:A4*) is a friendly place that carries hundreds of masks, Day of the Dead figures, rugs, glassware, bark-paper wall hangings from Puebla, and all sorts of other fun and captivating items. This is one of Cabo's more comprehensive folk-art shops.

FOOD

★ **Cabo Coffee Company** (⊠ *Madero and Hidalgo* ☎ *624/105–1130* ✛ *2:A5*) sends forth the aroma of roasting coffee beans and lures java junkies to its shop. The organic green coffee beans are flown fresh from Oaxaca, where they are roasted and bagged for sale. The store sells a number of Starbucks-like flavored coffee drinks, chai tea, as well as ice cream.

La Europea (⊠ *Puerto Paraíso Mall, next to Harley-Davidson Shop* ✛ *2:C3*) has a great deli and selection of wines, champagne, beers, and nibblies for the home, fiesta, or even picnic with box lunches for those on the go.

Continued on page 178

THE ART OF THE HUICHOL

Updated by Georgia de Katona

The intricately woven and beaded designs of the Huichols' art are as vibrant and fascinating as the traditions of its people, best known as the "Peyote People" for their traditional and ceremonial use of the hallucinogenic drug. Peyote-inspired visions are thought to be messages from God and are reflected in the art.

Like the Lacandon Maya, the Huichol resisted assimilation by Spanish invaders, fleeing to inhospitable mountains and remote valleys. There they retained their pantheistic religion in which shamans lead the community in spiritual matters and the use of peyote facilitates communication directly with God.

Roads didn't reach larger Huichol communities until the mid-20th century, bringing electricity and other modern distractions. The collision with the outside world has had pros and cons, but art lovers have only benefited from their increased access to intricately patterned woven and beaded goods. Today the traditional souls that remain on the land—a significant population of perhaps 6,000 to 8,000—still create votive bowls, prayer arrows, jewelry, and bags, and sell them to finance elaborate religious ceremonies. The pieces go for as little as $5 or as much as $5,000, depending on the skill and fame of the artist and quality of materials.

(left) Huichol yarn painting, National Museum of Anthropology, (top) Huichol art, Puerto Vallarta

6

IN FOCUS THE ART OF THE HUICHOL

UNDERSTANDING THE HUICHOL

When Spanish conquistadors arrived in the early 16th century, the Huichol, unwilling to work as slaves on the haciendas of the Spanish or to adopt their religion, fled to the Sierra Madre. They lived there, disconnected from society, for nearly 500 years. Beginning in the1970s, roads and electricity made their way to tiny Huichol towns. Today, about half of the population of perhaps 12,000 continues to live in ancestral villages and *rancheritas* (tiny individual farms).

THE POWER OF PRAYER
They believe that without their prayers and offerings the sun wouldn't rise, the earth would cease spinning. It is hard, then, for them to reconcile their poverty with the relative easy living of "free-riders" (Huichol term for non-spiritual freeloaders) who enjoy fine cars and expensive houses thanks to the Huichols efforts to sustain the planet. But rather than hold our reckless materialism against us, the Huichol add us to their prayers.

THE PEYOTE PEOPLE
Visions inspired by the hallucinogenic peyote plant are considered by the Huichol to be messages from God and to help in solving personal and commu-

Huichol artisans and beadwork

nal problems. Indirectly, they provide inspiration for their almost psychedelic art. Just a generation or two ago, annual peyote-gathering pilgrimages were done on foot. Today the journey is still a man's chief obligation, but they now drive to the holy site at Wiricuta, in San Luis Potosi State. Peyote collected is used by the entire community—men, women, and children—throughout the year.

SHAMANISM
A Huichol man has a lifelong calling as a shaman. There are two shamanic paths: the path of the wolf, which is more aggressive, demanding, and powerful (wolf shamans profess the ability to morph into wolves); and the path of the deer, which is playful—even clownish—and less inclined to prove his power. A shaman chooses his own path.

Huichol bird, Jalisco

HOW TO READ THE SYMBOLS

Spiders that come out at dawn are thought to welcome the rising sun.

The deer is the animal manifestation of the god Kahumari, who intercedes in heaven on earthlings' behalf.

Anything with horns or antlers symbolizes communion and oneness with God.

Yarn painting

■ The trilogy of corn, peyote, and deer represents three aspects of God. According to Huichol mythology, peyote sprang up in the footprints of the deer. Depicted like stylized flowers, peyote represents communication with God. Corn, the Huichol's staple

Peyote

Corn symbol

food, symbolizes health and prosperity. An image drawn inside the root ball depicts the essence of God within it.

■ The double-headed eagle is the emblem of the omnipresent sky god.

■ A nierika is a portal between the spirit world and our own. Often in the form of a yarn painting, a nierika can be round or square.

■ Salamanders and turtles are associated with rain; the former provoke the clouds. Turtles maintain underground springs and purify water.

■ A scorpion is the soldier of the sun.

Scorpion

■ The Huichol depict raindrops as tiny snakes; in yarn paintings they descend to enrich the fields.

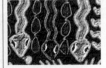

Snakes

Jose Beníctez Sánchez, (1938—) may be the elder statesman of yarn painters and has shown in Japan, Spain, the U.S., and at the Museum of Modern Art in Mexico City. His paintings sell for upward of $3,000 a piece.

TRADITION TRANSFORMED

The art of the Huichol was, for centuries, made from undyed wool, shells, stones, and other natural materials. It was not until the 1970s that the Huichol began incorporating bright, zingy colors, without sacrificing the intricate patterns and symbols used for centuries. The result is strenuously colorful, yet dignified.

YARN PAINTINGS
Dramatic and vivid yarn paintings are highly symbolic, stylized visions of life.

MASKS AND ANIMAL STATUETTES
Bead-covered wooden or ceramic masks and animal statuettes are other adaptations made for outsiders.

PRAYER ARROWS
Made for every ceremony, prayer arrows send petitions winging to God.

VOTIVE BOWLS
Ceremonious votive bowls, made from gourds, are decorated with bright, stylized beadwork.

WOVEN SHOULDER BAGS
Carried by men, the bags are decorated with traditional Huichol icons.

For years, Huichol men as well as women wore BEADED BRACELETS; today earrings and necklaces are also made.

Diamond-shape GOD'S EYES of sticks and yarn protect children from harm.

SMART SHOPPING TIPS

BEADED ITEMS: The smaller the beads, the more delicate and expensive the piece. Beads with larger holes are fine for stringed work, but if used in bowls and statuettes cheapen the piece.

Items made with iridescent beads from Japan are the priciest. Look for good-quality glass beads, definition, symmetry, and artful use of color.

Beads should fit together tightly in straight lines, with no gaps.

Bead-covered
a ram figurine

YARN PAINTINGS: Symmetry is not necessary, although there should be an overall sense of unity. Thinner thread results in finer, more costly work. Look for tightness, with no visible gaps or broken threads. Paintings should have a stamp of authenticity on the back, including artist's name and tribal affiliation.

PRAYER ARROWS: Collectors and purists should look for the traditionally made arrows of brazilwood inserted into a bamboo shaft. The most interesting ones contain embroidery work, or tiny carved icons, or are painted with copal symbols indicative of their original, intended purpose, for example protecting a child or ensuring a successful corn crop.

WHERE TO SHOP

Huichol Ethnic Art Store
(⊠ *Along Marina Cabo San Lucas, in the Golden Zone in Marina Fiesta Shops 23410.* ☎ *624/145–6020*) is a tiny little store that carries a variety of art forms from the Huichol people. If you're lucky they'll have some of the intricately woven bags worn by the men of the tribe; colorful and tightly woven these bags will last for decades even if you carry them everyday.

Kauyumarie (⊠ *Guerrero near Madero 23410.* ☎ *no phone*) is an informal co-op, operated by Huichol people, so tribal members take turns running the shop. You'll find all sorts of Huichol pieces

here, from the familiar carved wood animals covered in colorful beads and designs, to the intricately beaded earrings and necklaces with flowers and hummingbirds and butterflies.

Quality and selection range widely in here, but you know the money is going straight into the pockets of the producers, and it's a fun cultural experience.

The person minding the store might speak almost no Spanish or might have a working knowledge of English as well as Spanish. Regardless, leave any notion of rushing through at the door and enjoy the chance to learn

something about these amazing people.

Silvermoon gallery
(⊠ *Blvd. Mijares No. 10, 23400* ☎ *624/142–6077* ✍ *silvermoon_gallerysjc@ hotmail.com*) is where you'll find museum quality Huichol work, including the magnificent yarn paintings by Mexican Master Juan Silva. Señor Silva manages to create contemporary-feeling Huichol designs that are still deeply rooted in traditional imagery.

Gallery owner Armando Sanchez Icaza is a wealth of information about the Huichol art he carries.

CLOSE UP

People in Glass Houses

A beautiful glass mosaic over the entrance to **Fábrica de Vidrio Soplado** (Blown-Glass Factory) welcomes Los Cabos' most famous artisans every day. Founded in 1988 by engineer Sebastian Romo, the factory uses a glassmaking process close to the one first developed in western Asia 4,000 years ago, later refined into glassblowing during the Roman empire.

At the factory, 35 artisans produce more than 450 pieces a day from hundreds of pounds of locally recycled glass. Visitors watch while crushed recycled glass is liquefied in gas-fired ovens and, seconds later, transformed into exquisite figures. Secrets for making the thick glassware's deep blues,

greens, and reds—the result of special mixtures of metals and gold—are passed from generation to generation.

You are sometimes invited to make your own glassware by blowing through a hollow rod to shape a glob of molten glass at the end. The results are usually not impressive, but it's good fun nonetheless. The factory is in the industrial area of Cabo San Lucas and is usually open to the public Monday through Saturday 8 AM to 2 PM. It's best to take a taxi.

⊠ *Drive toward San José on Av. Cárdenas, which turns into Hwy. 1; the fábrica is 2 blocks northwest of Hwy. 1, near the bypass road to Todos Santos* ☎ *624/143–0255* ✛ *2:D1.*

Locals appreciate the selection of imported wines, cheeses, pâtés, and other gourmet delicacies, including organic foodstuffs, at **Tutto Bene** (⊠ *Blvd. Marina near Av. Cabo San Lucas* ☎ *624/144–3300* ✛ *2:B5*).

GIFTS
Gold Duck (⊠ *Plaza Nautica, Blvd. Marina* ☎ *624/143–2335* ✛ *2:B4*) sells leather products, including handbags, belts, and wallets.

Mama Eli's (⊠ *Av.Cabo San Lucas* ☎ *624/143–1616*) is a three-story gallery with fine furnishings, ceramics, appliquéd clothing, and children's toys.

No Worry's Restaurant, Bar & Boutique (⊠ *Cabo Marina, Tesoro Hotel, in the No Worry's Lighthouse* ☎ *624/143–8575* ✛ *2:B5*) is the spot if you're in the mood to eat, drink, shop, and listen to great rock and roll. This one-stop spot has it all, including a sizable clothing boutique as large, or larger, than many Cabo clothing stores.

Waboutique (⊠ *Calle Guerrero between Madero and Lazaro Cárdenas* ☎ *624/143–1188* ⊕ *www.cabowabo.com* ✛ *2:B4*) is the store associated with the funky Cabo Wabo bar. It sells memorabilia, excellent tequila, and souvenirs.

HOME FURNISHINGS
Cartes dos Lunas(⊠ *Plaza Bonita, Blvd. Marina* ☎ *624/143–1770* ✛ *2:B3*) has hand-painted pottery and tableware, pewter frames, handblown glass, and carved furniture.

★ **El Callejón** (⊠ *Guerrero between Av. Cárdenas and Madero* ☎ *624/143–1139* ✛ *2:A4*) is known for the gorgeous Mexican furniture, lamps, dishes, home decor, tableware, lamps, accessories, and pottery it sells.

★ **Galería Gattamelata** (✉ *Calle Gómez Farias, road to Hotel Hacienda* ☎ *624/143–1166* ✛ *2:D3*) can be reached by walking around the marina to the quiet street east of Puerto Paraiso; the specialties here are Mexican colonial furniture and furnishings. This is a treasure trove.

JEWELRY

Diamonds International (✉ *Puerto Paraíso Mall, Blvd. Marina* ☎ *624/143–3954* ✛ *2:C3*) sells impressive diamonds, designer jewelry, and luxury timepieces, and has certified master jewelers on staff.

Mexico Lindo (✉ *Plaza del Sol* ☎ *No phone* ✛ *2:B4*) has more than a dozen years of experience custom-designing sterling and 14k- and 18k-gold jewelry. Watch its craftsmen work at the store located at Madero and Guerrero streets in downtown Cabo San Lucas.

Tanya Moss Designer Jewelry (✉ *Puerto Paraíso Mall* ☎ *No phone* ✛ *2:C3*) works with freshwater pearls, amber, and precious and semiprecious stones, all with unique flair.

Ultrajewels (✉ *Blvd. Marina* ☎ *No phone* ✛ *2:B3*) offers all the top names in jewelry—Rolex, Cartier, Tiffany & Co. Mikimoto, TAG Heuer, Omega, Mont Blanc—at affordable prices.

LINENS

Cuca's Blanket Factory (✉ *Av. Cárdenas and Matamoros* ☎ *624/143–1913* ✛ *2:A4*) displays many serapes and cotton blankets with which you can design your own and have it ready the next day.

MALLS

As Los Cabos continues on its upscale trajectory, it's safe to declare that this region has arrived and the shopping here has gone palatial. There is no better, or more apt, way to describe **Puerto Paraíso** (✉ *Av. Cárdenas, Marina San Lucas*), the city's thriving, air-conditioned three-story marble- and glass-enclosed mall. With well more than 100 stores, boutiques, restaurants, galleries, and services, it's quickly becoming the social center of San Lucas. Paraíso offers a dizzying selection from "A" as in **Amarone**, an Italian gourmet restaurant, to "Z" as in the **Zingara Swimwear** shop. If you're in the mood for a tasty steak or a big salad, dine at **Senor Greenburg's Mexicatessen**, custom-design your own bikini, check your e-mail at an Internet café, shop for beautiful art glass, or rent (or even buy) a Harley-Davidson motorcycle, then plan on spending substantial time in this shopper's paradise. **Kaki Bassi**, a long-time Cabo resident and well-known artist, has opened a gallery here, as has **Sergio Bustamante**, an acclaimed silversmith and sculptor. Clothing shops include **Cotton Club**, **Tommy Bahama**, and **Quicksilver**, plus a number of beachwear boutiques such as **Allegra**, **Serdio**, **Dos Lunas**,

Arena, Tropica Calipso, and **Nautica.** A bowling alley and a 10-screen movie theater complex will take care of your entertainment needs.

Golden Zone Shopping Center (⊠ *Marina San Lucas23410*) is directly adjacent to Puerto Paraíso and is part of the Marina Fiesta Resort. Here you'll find the Tequila Museum, a Huichol Souvenir Shop, Mi Mexico Lindo Jewelry, the All in One Aqua Market, and Presto Fast and Casual Cuisine, which offers pizzas, wraps, and pastas.

Plaza Aramburo (⊠ *Av. Cárdenas and Zaragoza23410*) is a primarily service-oriented shopping area with a pharmacy, bank, dry cleaner, and grocery store. But it also has clothing and swimwear shops and a nice but small Internet café and inexpensive "phone home" service.

Plaza Bonita (⊠ *Blvd. Marina and Av. Cárdenas23410*) is a pleasant place to stroll; it's located at the western edge of the marina and has restaurants and bars catering to the cruise-ship crowd, with shops featuring Sergio Bustamante, Dos Lunas, Cartes, Hannas Leather House, and the Squid Roe Clothesline collection.

Plaza del Mar (⊠ *Av. Cárdenas*), across from the Plaza Bonita Mall, sells T-shirts, tank tops, sweatshirts, and more, at its souvenir boutiques. fine art, and several eateries.

Plaza del Sol Center (⊠ *Blvd. Marina*) offers a variety of shops such as the CSL Boutique and Tropica, known for its resort wear, and several jewelry stores.

Plaza Nautica (⊠ *Blvd. Marina*) is a mini-mall that borders the Cabo San Lucas marina. It's where you can find Gold Duck, Golf Pro Shop, and the Cabo Sports Center as well as other resort wear, jewelry, and furniture.

TOBACCO AND LIQUOR

J&J Casa de los Habanos (⊠ *Madero and Blvd. Marina* ☎ *624/143–6160* ✛ *2:B4*) sells Cuban and international cigars, lighters, and ashtrays as well as tequila, Cuban coffee, and clothing. You can schedule a tequila tasting while you shop for cigars.

TODOS SANTOS

Todos Santos was designated as one of the country's Pueblos Magicos (Magical Towns) in 2006, joining 23 other towns around the country chosen for their religious or cultural importance. Pueblos Magicos receive important financial support from the federal government for development of tourism and historical preservation. Even before this designation, artists from throughout the U.S. Southwest (and a few from Mexico) found a haven in this small town near the Pacific coast north of Los Cabos. Architects and entrepreneurs have restored early-19th-century adobe-and-brick buildings around the main plaza of this former sugar town. A good number of restaurateurs provide sophisticated, globally inspired food at hip eateries, and the galleries and shops showcase traditional and contemporary work. There is a strong Baja emphasis in the art, and you'll find beautiful jewelry from Taxco and fine crafts from all over Mexico. Break the typical pattern of day-

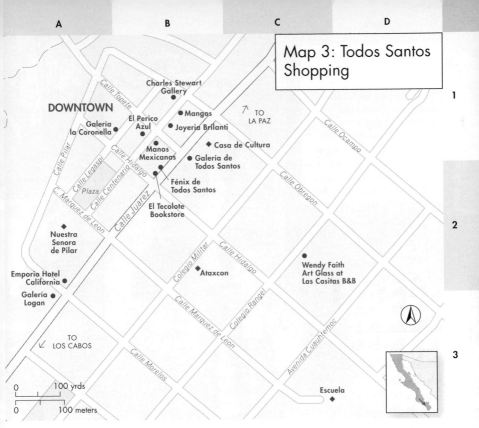

DOWNTOWN

Charles Stewart Gallery

Galeria la Coronella

El Perico Azul

Mangas

Joyeria Brilanti

↗ TO LA PAZ

Manos Mexicanas

◆ Casa de Cultura

Galería de Todos Santos

Fénix de Todos Santos

El Tecolote Bookstore

◆ Nuestra Senora de Pilar

Emporio Hotel California ●

Galería Logan ●

Colegio Militar

● Ataxcon

Calle Hidalgo

Calle Marquez de Leon

Colegio Rangel

Wendy Faith Art Glass at Las Casitas B&B

TO ↙ LOS CABOS

Calle Morelos

Avenida Cuauhtemoc

Escuela ◆

Calle Topete
Calle Pilar
Calle Legaspi
C. Marquez de Leon
Calle Centenario
Plaza
Calle Hidalgo
Calle Juarez
Calle Ocampo
Calle Obregon

0 — 100 yrds
0 — 100 meters

tripping to Todos Santos and spend at least one night here amid the palms, at one of the very nice small inns. En route from Cabo, you'll pass through El Pescadero, the largest settlement between Todos Santos and Cabo—home to farmers who grow herbs and vegetables, and surfers who just can't break away from the waves. If you're not going to spend the night, be sure to head back to Cabo from Todos Santos before dark, because Carretera 19 between the two towns is unlighted, narrow, and prone to high winds and flooding.

There are dirt roads leading to the coast that take you to advertised beaches and hotels; though often full of potholes, they're fine for all types of vehicles if you drive slowly and carefully. Don't be tempted to try the dozens of other dirt roads that intersect the highway unless you're in a four-wheel-drive vehicle. Sands on the beach or in the desert stop conventional vehicles in their tracks.

ART GALLERIES

Charles Stewart Gallery & Studio (✉ *Calle Centenario at Obregón* ☎ *612/145–0265* ⊕ *www.charlescstewart.com* ✦ *3:B1*) is a leader in the art scene here. Stewart moved from Taos, New Mexico, to Todos Santos in 1986, and is credited as one of the founders of the town's artist community. Baja and Mexican themes run through much of his work.

DID YOU KNOW?

Ignore rumors that every-body's favorite Eagles song originated at this Hotel California. It didn't. It hasn't stopped the establishment from playing up the ambigu-ity, and you can now buy T-shirts and tequila embla-zoned with the iconic name.

The gallery is in one of the town's wonderful 19th-century buildings and is surrounded by a wild, jungle-like garden.

Galería de Todos Santos (⊠ *Calle Topete at Calle Juarez* ☎ *612/145–0040* ⊕ *www.galeriadetodossantos.com* ✛ *3:B1*) is owned by Michael and Pat Cope. The gallery displays Michael's modern art and exhibits works by international artists living in Baja. The gallery opened in 1994 and is one of the focal points for the ever-changing local arts scene.

Galería la Coronela (⊠ *Calle Legaspi between Hidalgo and Topete* ☎ *612/149–8294* ✛ *3:B1*) shows the work of prodigious painter Victor Vega, as well as paintings by his daughter, Sophia.

Galería Logan (⊠ *Calle Juarez and Morelos* ☎ *612/145–0151* ⊕ *www. jilllogan.com* ✛ *3:A3*) features the work of Jill Logan, a Southern Californian who has been in Todos Santos since 1998. Jill does bold oil-on-canvas paintings and complexly layered multimedia pieces.

Wendy Faith (⊠ *Calle Rangel between Obregón and Hidalgo* ☎ *612/145– 0255* ⊕ *www.lascasitasbandb.com* ✛ *3:C2*) sells semiprecious gemstone jewelry. The art-glass studio has stained, fused, and slumped glass.

BOOKS

El Tecolote Bookstore (⊠ *Calle Juárez at Calle Hidalgo* ☎ *612/145–0295* ✛ *3:B2*) is the best bookstore in Los Cabos region. Stop here for Latin American literature, poetry, children's books, current fiction and nonfiction, and books on Baja.

CLOTHING AND FOLK ART

El Perico Azul (⊠ *Centenario at Topete* ☎ *612/145–0222* ✛ *3:B1*) has fine handmade Mexican clothing (check out guayaberas from the Yucatán) for men and women, handwoven tablecloths, and a selection of folk art.

Fénix de Todos Santos (⊠ *Calle Juárez at Calle Topete* ☎ *612/145–0666* ✛ *3:B2*) has bowls and plates from Tonalá, handblown glassware, Talavera pottery from the state of Puebla, and cotton clothing by the designer Sucesos.

Galería Santa Fé (⊠ *Calle Centenario 4* ☎ *612/145–0340*) is set in an 1850s adobe building. Paula and Ezio Colombo sell collector-quality folk art, including frames adorned with images of Frida Kahlo and her art, kid-size chairs decorated with bottle caps, Virgin of Guadalupe images, and *milagros* (small tin charms used as offerings to saints).

Fodor's Choice
★ **Mangos** (⊠ *Calle Centenario across from Charles Stewart Gallery* ☎ *612/145–0451* ✛ *3:B1*) is filled with gorgeous Guatemalan textiles, Mexican folk art, belts, purses, wood carvings, and Day of the Dead figurine.

Manos Mexicanas (⊠ *Topete at Centenario* ☎ *612/145–0538* ✛ *3:B1*) is a treasure trove of fine Mexican crafts, jewelry, decorative objects, and work by local potter Rubén Gutiérrez. Owner Alejandra Brilanti Nunez has amassed an incredible collection of affordable pieces. You are not likely to leave empty-handed.

Colorful blankets for sale in a Todos Santos market.

JEWELRY

Fodor's Choice
★

Joyeria Brilanti (✉ *Centenario near Topete* ☎ *612/145–0799* ⊕ *www. brilanti.com* ✛ *3:B1*) is a showcase for the stunning jewelry and design works of famed Taxco silversmith Ana Brilanti, in addition to a number of other contemporary-jewelry artists whose work shares the same dramatic aesthetic. Be sure to look at the silver tea services and other functional pieces. You'll also find selected stone carvings and bronzes from local artists. Prices are very good and the charming proprietor, José, happens to be the deceased Ms. Brilanti's son.

MARKETS

The Todos Santos Arts Fest happens every year, for a whole week at the end of January into early February. The festival celebrates Mexican culture and performing arts as much as the paintings, drawings, and sculpture on display. It is held at the Centro Cultural Prof. Nestor Agundez Martinez on Juárez at Obregón. Visit ⊕ *www.elcalendariodetodossantos.com* for dates and details.

There's an informal farmers' market on Camino Militar near Hidalgo on Friday, where you can find a surprising amount of organic produce. If you get hungry while you're wandering among the stalls, don't hesitate to grab a taco or three at one of the carts by the corner.

Nightlife and the Arts

WORD OF MOUTH

"I just got back from a week in Cabo San Lucas. I was worried it would be too much of a "party town" and was pleasantly surprised to find that it was not. Certainly some bars were party-hardy, but plenty of places are family-friendly."

—Suze

NIGHTLIFE AND THE ARTS PLANNER

What It Costs

Want to drink inexpensively? Think beer, especially Baja's very own Tecate. Many places compete for the best happy-hour prices, often about $2 for a cerveza. Margaritas, the other keep-'em-coming drink, cost around $5. A glass of wine in an upscale venue should run $5 and up. Many places add a 10%–15% tip to your tab; others do not. (Look for the word "servicio" on your bill.) A big musical event means a nominal cover charge of a few dollars; those are rare.

What to Wear

"Informal" is the word, although there's some wiggle room in that label. The more authentic a place is, the more likely patrons dress to impress. (Think casual-classy when taking in dance clubs such as Mambo Café.) "Gringo" means less formal. (Shorts and T-shirts are acceptable at the Giggling Marlin.) But do keep those signs you see back home in mind: NO SHOES, NO SHIRT, NO SERVICE is always followed here.

Location Rundown

San José del Cabo: Proprietors here say that you "graduate" to San José del Cabo after you sow the wild oats of your youth in Cabo San Lucas. It's quieter and more intimate here, and for a cozy, romantic evening, nothing beats San José's nightlife.

The Corridor: This sprawling strip between the two cities is the province of big resorts and their in-house bars. Expect upscale venues (and patrons). A few nightspots not affiliated with any hotel do exist here and are quite popular.

Cabo San Lucas: Had the phrase "What happens in Vegas, stays in Vegas" not already been taken, Cabo San Lucas might have snapped it up. You can experience spring break here, even if you went to college 30 years ago. Quiet Cabo nightlife does exist; you just need to look a bit harder.

Finding Out What's Going On

One Los Cabos publication that's all about the nightlife scene is *Noche Magazine* (⊕ *www.hautter.com*): it's full of useful party tips; up-to-the-minute club, restaurant, and bar information; and the obligatory photo pages of beautiful, stylish people enjoying the Cabo scene. You'll find copies in hotels, restaurants, and bars all over the city. There are several other local publications to choose from with less of a nightlife focus. The most helpful are *Los Cabos Visitors Guide* and *Los Cabos Magazine*. Both provide a wealth of information on everything Los Cabos, from the restaurant, hotel, bar, and shopping scenes, to the many activities. The free English-language newspapers *Gringo Gazette* (⊕ *www.gringogazette.com*) and *Destino: Los Cabos* (⊕ *www.destinomagazines.com*) offer timely and cultural articles on the ever-changing scene. (We especially like the *Gringo Gazette* for its fun-loving, humorous look at expatriate life in Los Cabos.) The English-Spanish *Los Cabos News* (⊕ *www.loscabosnews.com.mx*) is also a good source for local event listings. These publications are available free at many hotels and stores or at racks on the sidewalk.

Updated by
Jeffrey Van
Fleet

Party-minded crowds roam the main strip of Cabo San Lucas every night from happy hour through last call, often staggering home or to hotel rooms just before dawn. It's not hard to see why this is *the* nightlife capital of southern Baja. Indeed, Cabo is internationally famous (or infamous, depending on your view) for being a raucous party town, especially during spring break. On the other hand, nightlife in San José del Cabo is much more low-key: it's more about a good drink and conversation as opposed to the table-dancing chaos you'll find in some Cabo hot spots.

7

Between the two towns, the self-contained resorts along the Corridor have some nightlife, mainly in ever-improving restaurants and bars, which can mix up some fabulous cocktails themselves.

The lines between "bar," "nightclub," and "restaurant" are blurry here. Never forget that enjoying a fine dinner is a time-honored way to spend a Los Cabos evening. Also, don't forget that things shift into lower gear during the lowest of the low season—those slow, sweltering months of August and September when some places curtail their offerings, or may close for a few weeks altogether. Never fear though: you'll find night-time fun here no matter what season you visit.

SAN JOSÉ DEL CABO

After-dark action in San José del Cabo caters mostly to locals and tourists seeking tranquillity and seclusion. There are no big dance clubs or discos in San José. What little nightlife there is revolves around restaurants, casual bars, and large hotels. A pre- or post-dinner stroll makes a wonderful addition to any San José evening. When night falls, people begin to fill the streets, many of them hurrying off to evening mass when they hear the church bells peal from the central plaza.

A number of galleries hold court in central San José del Cabo, creating the **San José del Cabo Art District**. It's just north and east of the town's cathedral, primarily along Obregón, Morelos, and Guerrero streets. On Thursday nights from November through June, visit the **Art Walk,** where you can meander around about 15 galleries, sampling wine and cheese as you go.

BARS

The **Baja Brewing Co.** (✉ *Morelos 1277 and Obregón* ☎ *624/146–9995* ⊕ *www.bajabrewingcompany. com* ✛ *1:C1*) serves cold, on-site-microbrewed cerveza and international pub fare "with a touch of elegance." You'll find entrées ranging from ahi tuna quesadillas to shepherd's pie, plus more basic pub food such as basil-and-blue-cheese burgers and pizzas. As for the seven beers, we recommend the India Pale Ale; the BBC also brews Cactus Wheat, Raspberry Lager, and a dark, smooth Black Scorpion.

If you feel the need to belt out *Love Shack* or *My Way,* grab the karaoke mike at **Cactus Jack's** (✉ *Blvd. Mijares 88* ☎ *624/142–5601* ✛ *1:D2*) a modest, fun, open-air gringo hangout that's open until the wee hours on weekends. It has more TV screens than you normally see in a small pub, but that's why the largely American crowd comes here (football, football, and more NFL football). That, and the free pool.

If you know your colors, you'll easily spot the big, red, square lounge appropriately named **Red Lounge** (✉ *Paseo de los Cabos* ☎ *624/142–3099* ✛ *1:B5*) down near the beach, across from Desire Resort. At night it's a stylish martini bar popular with the younger set, locals, and visitors alike. Tasty international food is served.

The 18-hole miniature golf course is the best feature at the **Rusty Putter** (✉ *Plaza Los Cabos across from Desire Resort on San José del Cabo's beachfront drive* ☎ *624/142–4546* ✛ *1:B5*), an open-air sports bar that's getting more than a little tired from extended neglect. Grab a beer and proceed immediately to the links, where long holes, creative obstacles, and variations in the carpet make for a particularly good course. The bar and course are open daily 8 AM–1 AM, except Monday.

For a gringo-friendly atmosphere where you're fine ordering your Bud in English, and sports blast on big-screen TVs, head to **Shooters** (✉ *Manuel Doblado at Blvd. Mijares* ☎ *624/146–9900* ✛ *1:C2*), on the rooftop at the Tulip Tree restaurant. It's open until everyone leaves. Days are busy here, too, with breakfast and lunch served as well as Shooters's heavily promoted 10-peso (less than $1) beers from 9 to 4.

★ The bar at the **Tropicana Inn** (✉ *Blvd. Mijares 30* ☎ *624/142–1580* ✛ *1:C2*) is a great place to mingle and enjoy live music. Conversation

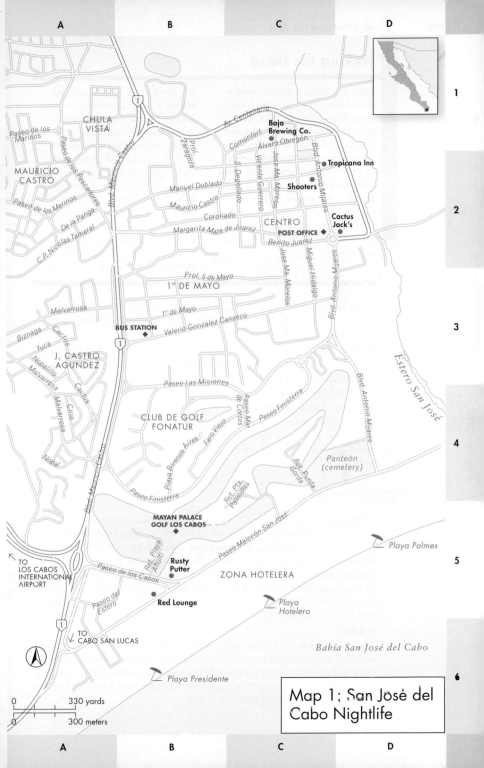

Map 1: San José del Cabo Nightlife

CLOSE UP

Waking the Dead

Celebrated throughout Mexico, the most important religious and indigenous festival in Los Cabos takes place November 1 and 2: All Saints' and All Souls' Day, more commonly referred to as **Día de los Muertos** (Day of the Dead). Long before Spain conquered Mexico, the festival was part of Indian culture and held during the winter equinox. In true colonial spirit, Spain changed the timing to coincide with its religious All Saints' and All Souls' Day.

Not as macabre as it sounds, the festival is a joyous celebration to welcome a visit from the souls of deceased loved ones. Family and friends prepare favorite foods and drink of the dearly departed, burn candles and incense, and place flowers in cemeteries and at memorials along the road. Shops carry candy shaped like skulls and coffins, and bread is baked to look like ghosts. No tears are to be shed, as it is said that the path back to the living world must not be made slippery by tears.

is usually possible on the balcony overlooking the bar and stage, though when a really hot band gets going you'll be too busy dancing to talk.

MOVIES
Cinema Versailles (⊠ *Hwy. 1, Plaza Cabo Ley* ☎ 624/142–3333 💺 $4) has a selection of American movies, generally a few weeks behind what's showing in the United States. There are two theaters, with the last feature starting around 11 PM.

MUSIC AND DANCE
Classical music and dance performances take place two or three nights a week at the city's **Teatro de la Ciudad** at the corner of Zaragoza and Guerrero. Offerings are quite varied and high quality, and all are in Spanish.

THE CORRIDOR

Nightlife along Highway 1 between San José del Cabo and Cabos San Lucas historically consists of hotel bars in big resorts, most of which are frequented only by their guests. A few stand-alone places have sprung up in recent years. A taxi or car is the best way to reach these places. Because walking home is generally not an option, unless you're staying in-house or next door, nightlife ends early out here, with most places turning off the lights around 10 or 11 PM. Head to Cabo San Lucas if you want to party later.

BARS
The name **El Bar** (⊠ *At Esperanza Resort, Hwy. 1, Km 3.5* ☎ 624/145–6400 ⊕ *www.esperanzaresort.com* ✛ *2:C2*) sounds pretty utilitarian, but the dim lighting and intimacy here are anything but. Enjoy stunning views of El Arco—you are, after all, on the Cabo San Lucas end of the Corridor—over quiet drinks.

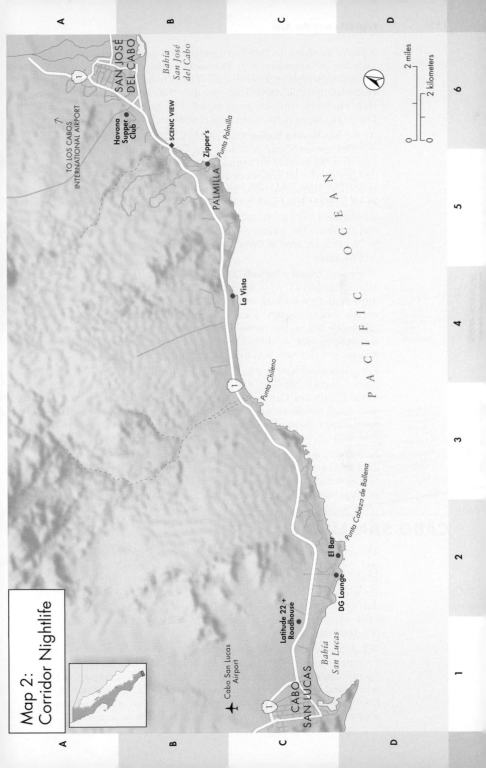

Map 2:
Corridor Nightlife

TO LOS CABOS
INTERNATIONAL AIRPORT

SAN JOSÉ
DEL CABO

Havana Supper
Club

SCENIC VIEW

Bahía
San José
del Cabo

Zipper's

PALMILLA

Punta Palmilla

La Vista

Cabo San Lucas Airport

Punta Chileno

El Bar

Latitude 22 +
Roadhouse

DG Lounge

Punta Cabeza de Ballena

Bahía
San Lucas

CABO
SAN LUCAS

PACIFIC OCEAN

0   2 miles
0   2 kilometers

If you're searching for "intellectual nightlife," the **DG Lounge** (⊠ *At Mona Lisa Sunset Restaurant, near Misiones Condos and Hotel* ☎ *624/145–8166* ⊕ *www.dglounge.net* ⊕ *2:C2*) claims to have it. We're not exactly sure what makes it intellectual—we didn't see books at this open-early club. However, there are great views of El Arco. DG features eclectic live music, tapas, wine, champagne, and special events.

At the hip **Havana Supper Club** (⊠ *Hwy. 1, Km 29* ☎ *624/172–6269* ⊕ *2:B6*), owner Sheila Reséndiz sings in an excellent jazz band that performs Wednesday through Friday. On weekends, a six-piece band delights locals and visitors of all ages with a fun selection of live jazz, bossa nova, salsa, and other tropical rhythms. Though the crowd tends to be upscale, food and drink prices are reasonable. The bar on the second floor has a great open-air overlook of the Costa Azul coastline, and is filled with antiques from Cuba and some from an old saloon in Nevada. Havana is open until about midnight; it's closed Sunday and Monday.

The noisy, friendly **Latitude 22+ Roadhouse** (⊠ *Hwy. 1, Km 4.5, near Costco* ☎ *624/143–1516* ⊕ *www.lat22nobaddays.com* ⊕ *2:C1*) always attracts gringos looking to sip cold beer, down a shot of tequila, and mingle with old or new friends. There's good, dependable, and mostly American fare on the menu. For musical entertainment, pianist Peter Bacon sings popular oldies Thursday through Saturday. While Latitude 22+ is close to town, it is still not walkable.

For classy hotel bars, it's hard to top **La Vista** (⊠ *At Hilton Los Cabos, Hwy. 1, Km 19.5* ☎ *624/145–6500* ⊕ *www.hiltonloscabos.com* ⊕ *2:C4*) in the Hilton Los Cabos. The terrace bar overlooks the Sea of Cortez and claims terrific views. There's nothing raucous here; just quiet, intimate conversation over wine and drinks with free hors d'oeuvres from 7 to 8 PM.

Named for the nearby surf break, beachfront **Zipper's** (⊠ *Hwy. 1, Km 28.5* ☎ *624/172–6162* ⊕ *2:B5*) attracts a mixed crowd of surfers and nonsurfers alike. A good selection of beer, as well as ribs and burgers, is always on hand, with live music every Friday night.

CABO SAN LUCAS

The epicenter of Cabo San Lucas nightlife is along the Marina San Lucas and the two streets that run parallel beyond it. You'll walk a gauntlet of servers waving menus in your face, but the many fun sidewalk bars along the marina between Plaza Bonita and Puerto Paraíso are great during happy hour and late into the night. Many nightlife places do a brisk daytime business, too, esp when cruise ships are in port, which is several days a week.

Watch out for the tequila shooters and Jell-O shots forced upon revelers by merry waiters—they usually cost at least $5 each. Topless bars and "gentlemen's" clubs are abundant, too. (Their SHOWGIRLS signs give away what—and where—they are.) Single men are often accosted outside San Lucas bars with offers for drugs and sex. Be careful in this area, and be aware that the police may be behind some of these solicitations.

The bars, cantinas, clubs, and restaurants of Cabo San Lucas come alive when the sun sets.

BARS

If you're in the mood for jazz, the bar at the Italian **Amarone Ristorante** (✉ *In the Puerto Paraíso Mall, lower-level marina* ☎ *624/105–1035* ⊕ *www.ristoranteamarone.com* ✛ *3:C4*) will provide a cool, relaxed, international atmosphere. It has windows in every direction with views of the marina, plus plush decor with wood floors, starched tablecloths, candelabras, and soft, warm lighting that is as classy as anything you'll see in Los Angeles, New York, or Rome. Enjoy music on Tuesday and Thursday through Saturday, from 8 PM to 11 PM. You'll find the best Italian wines available in Cabo, and dinner as well.

Brand-spanking new in late 2009, the **Baja Brewing Co.** (✉ *Rooftop of Cabo Villas, Médano Beach* ☎ *624/143–9199* ⊕ *www.bajabrewingcompany.com* ✛ *3:C4*) is the Cabo San Lucas branch of the microbrewery in San José del Cabo. The menu is the same. The beers are the same. But the partly open site here on the rooftop of a beach hotel means the vibe could not be more different. It's the type of place you roll into—well, up to on an elevator—after a day at the beach. Thursday is classic rock night; Friday means salsa, with a free mini-lesson in the afternoon; and Saturday presents reggae and soul.

Classy, tranquil, and comfortable **Barómetro** (✉ *On Marina boardwalk, near Puerto Paraíso Mall* ☎ *624/143–1466* ⊕ *www.barometro.com.mx* ✛ *3:B4*) gives you a peaceful panoramic view of the fishing yachts in the Marina San Lucas. Inside, a giant screen shows sports, and tasty seafood is served. You can also relax outside on the couches, or across the sidewalk at a table overlooking the marina pier.

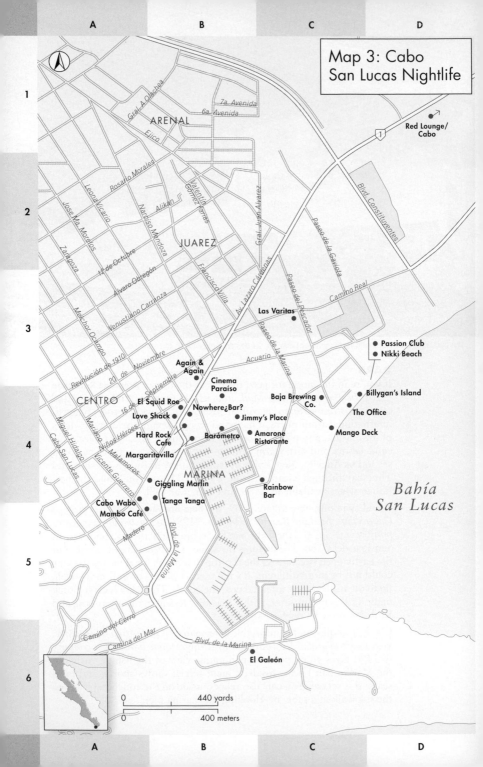

Map 3: Cabo
San Lucas Nightlife

7a. Avenida
6a. Avenida

ARENAL

JUAREZ

CENTRO

Red Lounge/
Cabo

Las Varitas

Passion Club
Nikki Beach

Again &
Again

Cinema
Paraíso

Baja Brewing
Co.

Billygan's Island

El Squid Roe

Nowhere¿Bar?

The Office

Love Shack

Jimmy's Place

Hard Rock
Cafe

Barómetro

Amarone
Ristorante

Mango Deck

Margaritavilla

MARINA

Giggling Marlin

Rainbow
Bar

Cabo Wabo

Tanga Tanga

Mambo Café

Bahía
San Lucas

El Galeón

0   440 yards
0   400 meters

If you're past 30 and don't feel comfortable in moderately revealing swimwear, you'll probably want to give **Billygan's Island** (✉ *Médano Beach* ☎ *624/143–4830* ⊕ *www.billygans.com* ✛ *3:C4*) a pass. Spring break seems to take place year-round at this boisterous place on Médano Beach. Beer and margaritas flow to the accompaniment of bikini and dance contests.

Ronald Valentino plays everything from *My Way* to *Bésame Mucho* at the piano at **El Galeón** (✉ *Blvd. Marina* ☎ *624/143–0443* ✛ *3:B6*). The crowd is generally restaurant patrons wishing to extend their nights a little longer, and you'll find it to be a very comfortable scene, with a nice, elevated view of the Marina San Lucas. (Check out the Web site—it'll give you a nice audio preview of what you'll hear from Ronald.)

Jimmy's Place (✉ *Puerto Paraíso, next to Señor Greenberg's* ☎ *624/144–3805* ✛ *3:B4*) keeps more than 60 varieties of wine in stock and serves a good selection of Spanish-style tapas. It's nice and all, and it could be a quiet, intimate place to go for drinks, but there's usually a sporting event showing on multiple TV screens. That detracts a bit.

Las Varitas (✉ *About 1 block north of the entrance to the ME Cabos Hotel by Meliá, on Calle Gomez behind Puerto Paraíso* ☎ *624/143–9999* ⊕ *www.lasvaritas.com* ✛ *3:C3*) is a branch of a La Paz rock club favored by young Mexicans. One of Cabo's most popular clubs, it hosts live music almost every night, and even boasts a house label Las Varitas tequila.

If you're in the mood to spend some time in a relaxed bar just like at home, watch some American sports, shoot a couple of games of pool, or have a burger and listen to some tunes, the **Love Shack** (✉ *Morelos and Niños Héroes* ☎ *624/143–5010* ✛ *3:B4*) is your type of casual locale.

Feel like dancing in the sand? **Mango Deck** (✉ *At the western end of El Médano Beach, near the Casa Dorada resort* ☎ *624/143–0901* ⊕ *www. mangodeckcabo.com* ✛ *3:C4*) is open just about every night of the week, with DJs spinning late.

Facing Boulevard Marina and the boats in the water, the aptly named **Margaritavilla** (✉ *Blvd. Marina* ☎ *624/143–0010* ✛ *3:B4*) serves scads of frozen margaritas in fishbowl-size glasses at outdoor tables. It's also a restaurant, but there's better food elsewhere. It's best to enjoy the view of the boats, the mariachis as they stroll the marina walk, and the great people-watching from here.

Miami meets Cabo at **Nikki Beach** (✉ *ME Cabo Hotel by Meliá, Playa Médano* ☎ *624/145–7800* ⊕ *www.me-cabo.com* ✛ *3:D3*). This restaurant, bar, and club has an over-the-top luxury feeling. If you've ever wanted to feel like you're in a music video this is your chance. White gauze canopies shade plush white sun beds and lounge chairs around swimming pools, while DJs spin all day long. Try the salmon and scallop carpaccio or cornmeal-crusted calamari.

Local professionals loosen up over beers while crazed tourists have too much fun at the **Nowhere ¿Bar?** (✉ *Plaza Bonita, Blvd. Marina 17* ☎ *624/143–4493* ⊕ *www.nowherebar.com* ✛ *3:B4*), where two-for-one drinks and a large dance floor are the main draw. (You haven't lost your

CLOSE UP

Hagar's Hangout: Cabo Wabo

According to local lore, in the mid-1980s former Van Halen lead singer Sammy Hagar and a friend were walking along the beach in Cabo San Lucas when they passed a drunk man stumbling. Hagar remarked, "Hey, he's doing the Cabo Wabo." A few years later, in 1990, Hagar and the rest of Van Halen opened the bar called Cabo Wabo—establishing one of the premier stops on the Cabo party circuit. When the group broke up in 1996, all but Hagar sold their shares in the bar.

Mexican and American rock bands perform every night. Almost always packed, the place erupts when Hagar comes to play. When he's on tour, he may only make it to the club four or five times a year. Three of those visits fall on April 22 (the bar's anniversary), October 3–4 for the bar's MELT DOWN celebration, and the week around October 13 (for Hagar's birthday celebration). When not on tour, Hagar hits Cabo Wabo up to 12 times a year. The

dates are usually announced on the club's Web site, ⊕ *www.cabowabo. com*.

Often accompanying Hagar are some of his rock-and-roll friends, who come to perform with him. These have included Chris Isaak, Kirk Hammett of Metallica, David Crosby, Slash, Rob Zombie, the Cult, and the Sex Pistols.

Easily seen from afar due to a lighthouse replica at the main entrance, the bar was designed by architect Marco Monroy. He built high, cavernous ceilings and painted the walls with zebra stripes and psychedelic neon patterns. Hagar liked Monroy's work so much that the design of the bar was replicated for his set on the "Red Voodoo" tour. The club has four pool tables and numerous bars, one strung with bras and panties donated over the years by doting female patrons.

⇨ *Rock Clubs, below.*

bearings; the word BAR on the sign is inverted.) Reckless gyrating isn't strictly limited to the dance floor, though—don't be at all surprised to see people busting a move on the tables from early evening on. On weekend nights, especially over holidays and spring break, it's a madhouse scene. Sushi and tacos are served from adjacent businesses, and bartenders hand out baskets of popcorn to keep people thirsty.

The oddly named **The Office** (⊠ *Médano Beach* ☎ *624/143–3464* ✢ *3:C4*) began life as a place to rent windsurfing equipment, but expanded into a bar-slash-eatery now famous for its seafood and pint-size margaritas. Despite the fact that the floor here is the sand, this place is a tad more upscale than the other venues on Médano Beach. Sunday and Thursday nights mean a music show with traditional Mexican folk dances—a little cheesy, but always a crowd pleaser.

If you like martinis, the **Red Lounge/Cabo** (⊠ *On Zaragoza near El Squid Roe* ☎ *624/143–5644* ✢ *3:D1*) is your kind of place. It's a classy spot where younger clientele enjoy a dizzying array of specialties.

A hot and popular spot for listening to live music, playing pool or darts, and watching sports on big-screen TVs, the sidewalk bar **Tanga Tanga,** (⊠ *Blvd. Marina outside Tesoro Hotel* ☎ *624/144–4501* ✢ *3:B4*) has a bar outdoors and another (air-conditioned) one inside. Local reggae and rock groups play here most afternoons and nights.

DANCE CLUBS

Again & Again (✉ *Av. Cárdenas between Leona Vicario and Morelos* ☎ *624/143–6323* ✛ *3:B3*) is one of the most popular dance clubs for locals in town. Two levels with pillared balconies overlook the stage and dance floor. On Thursday, the live *banda* (band) music draws a large crowd. The music, born in the 19th century in the northern state of Sinaloa, is traditional and often slow, for dancing in pairs, but very brassy. On other nights—the place is open only Thursday through Sunday—the music is a mix of dance styles, including salsa and merengue.

★ If you have any religious sensitivity, moral convictions, a hard time letting loose, or a heart condition, you may want to think twice before entering **El Squid Roe** (✉ *Av. Cárdenas s/n* ☎ *624/143–0655* ✛ *3:B4*). Just about anything goes here: waiters dance and gyrate with female patrons, roaming waitresses shove Jell-O shots down your throat, frat-boy wannabes attempt beer-chugging contests, scantily clad dancers undulate in a makeshift penitentiary. Be prepared for a scene. During spring break or high season, more than 5,000 revelers come here on any given night—and many stay until 3 AM, 4 AM, 5 AM, or even sunrise. Feeling out of place? Head for one of the balconies—third and fourth floors were added in 2009 and are reached by elevator—where the scene is a bit less lurid. Around the corner stands the bar's souvenir shop with T-shirts proclaiming such pearls of wisdom as: I SPENT MOST OF MY LIFE DRINKING BEER AND CHASING WOMEN. THE REST OF IT, I WASTED. You get the general idea.

Giggling Marlin (✉ *Blvd. Marina and Matamoros* ☎ *624/143–1182* ⊕ *www.gigglingmarlin.com* ✛ *3:B4*) has been around forever and actually predates Cabo's tourism explosion, but its gimmicks remain popular. Watch brave (and inebriated) souls be hoisted upside down at the mock fish-weighing scale, or join in an impromptu moonwalk between tables. Many fun (if a bit risqué) floor shows seem to relax people's inhibitions. The age of the clientele varies, as does the music, but the dance floor is usually jammed. A nightly two-for-one drinks special packs 'em in from 11 PM until 1 AM. The bartender may place a shot of tequila in front of you the minute you sit down—you'll pay at least $5 if you drink it.

Part of a chain of 11 clubs throughout the country (with one branch in Dallas, Texas, too), **Mambo Café** (✉ *On the marina* ☎ *624/143–1484* ⊕ *www.mambocafe.com.mx* ✛ *3:B5*) is a high-energy place that plays music ranging from Caribbean salsa and merengue to the best of Latin pop. There are live performances by top international musical groups from Cuba, the Dominican Republic, Puerto Rico, and Colombia.

7

There is no doubt that the hippest (and most expensive) spot in Los Cabos is the **Passion Club** (⊠ *At ME by Meliá Hotel, on El Médano Beach* ☎ *624/145–7800 Ext. 745* ⊕ *www.me-cabo.com* ✛ *3:D3*). Top DJs from around the world come to spin the vinyl and light up the neon-cozy club. It has a great dance floor and there are various VIP events throughout the year.

MOVIES

Cinema Paraíso (⊠ *Av. Cárdenas at Puerto Paraíso* ☎ *624/143–1515* ⊕ *www.cinemaparaiso.com.mx* ✛ *3:B4*) has 10 screens, including a VIP screening room with reclining leather seats. First-run Hollywood movies are shown usually in English with Spanish subtitles (*subtitulada* or *versión original*), just a few weeks behind premieres in the States. Kids' movies are the exception: they will be dubbed (*doblada* or versión español) into Spanish since their very young fans don't read subtitles.

ROCK CLUBS

The latest American rock plays over an excellent sound system at **Cabo Wabo** (⊠ *Calle Guerrero* ☎ *624/143–1188* ⊕ *www.cabowabo.com* ✛ *3:B4*), but the jam sessions with owner Sammy Hagar and his many music-business friends are the real highlight. Plan way in advance to attend Hagar's Birthday Bash Week—usually the second week in October—as tickets sell out. It's a large venue, with a raised stage, a tall ceiling resembling an auditorium, the longest bar in town, and, for VIPs, a lounge upstairs. Strong air-conditioning scores lots of points in the heat of summer. Here's a tip: make dinner reservations—then you'll avoid the long lines to get in the club. Breakfast, lunch, and dinner are served with extensive menus. A taco grill cooks up tasty munchies outside if you wish to cool off after dancing. Shops on-site or at the international airport sell Cabo Wabo souvenir clothing.

With a '59 pink Cadillac jutting through the window and dozens of rock-and-roll albums and memorabilia on the walls, this **Hard Rock Cafe** (⊠ *Blvd. Marina across from El Squid Roe* ☎ *624/143–3779* ⊕ *www.hardrock.com* ✛ *3:B4*) might be in Mexico, but is a typical member of the chain. Live rock music starts at 10 PM every night. Thursday is ladies' night, when women drink free from 9 PM to 11 PM. On the first floor is the requisite shop where you can purchase your HARD ROCK CAFE CABO SAN LUCAS caps and T-shirts.

DRINKING AND SMOKING

Mexico's nationwide drinking age is 18. Bars here check IDs at the door if they have any doubts about your age. Consumption of alcohol or the possession of an open beverage container is not permitted on public sidewalks, streets, or beaches (outside of licensed establishments), or in motor vehicles, whether moving or stationary.

Smoking is prohibited in all enclosed businesses, including bars and restaurants. Lighting up is allowed at outdoor-seating areas provided by such venues, but not indoors.

7

SUNSET CRUISES
Several companies run nightly cruises for dinner and/or drinks that capture stunning sunsets as their vessels rounds the cape. Stands around the marina act as agents and can book excursions for you, but some manage to rope you into a time-share visit in the process. Better to book through your hotel's front desk or directly through the company.

Caborey (☎ 624/143–8060, 866/460–4105 *in North America* ⊕ *www. caborey.com*) offers a nightly 2½-hour sunset-dinner cruise on a three-deck catamaran. Cost is $89 and includes a full prix-fixe dinner with your choice of one of six main courses, an open bar for domestic beverages, and a Las Vegas–style show of Mexican music. Departure time is 6 PM September–April, and 5 PM the rest of the year.

Fiesta Cabaret (☎ 624/146–3563 ⊕ *www.yatefiestacabaret.com*) offers two options for the nightly three-hour sunset-dinner cruise departing 6 PM September–April, and 5 PM the rest of the year: the $82 cost includes an all-you-can-eat buffet, an open bar with domestic drinks, and a tropical-music show. If just the bar interests you, you'll pay $50 for the excursion.

It's jazz each evening in time for the sunset on the **Tropicat** (☎ 624/143–3797 ⊕ *www.tropicatcabo.com*), a 65-foot catamaran, that departs 6 PM September–April, and 4:30 PM the rest of the year. The two-hour excursion includes premium wines and hors d'oeuvres.

Baja Peninsula

WORD OF MOUTH

"We stayed at Las Rosas Hotel, which is 3 miles from Ensenada. It is charming and well appointed. Every room has an ocean view. We never felt unsafe and have not heard of any tourists having any difficulty."

— mflickermd

WELCOME TO BAJA PENINSULA

TOP REASONS TO GO

★ **Water Sports:** Surfers, sailors, divers, and fisherfolk flock to both sides of the peninsula to get their adrenaline fixes in the Pacific and the Sea of Cortez.

★ **Beaches and More:** Year-round sunshine, pampering spas, and miles of sandy beach make Baja the perfect winter escape.

★ **Epic Migrations:** Gray whales mate and calve in three lagoons on the peninsula's west coast. Migratory birds return to Baja California from December through April.

★ **The Open Road:** Explore Baja Norte's starkly beautiful landscapes and remote beaches, and meander through tiny villages along the southern part of the peninsula.

★ **The** *other* **California's finest wines:** The Valle de Guadalupe, near Ensenada, is a gorgeous valley filled with vineyards and inns with unpretentious hosts.

1 East Cape to Guerrero Negro. On this long and fascinating stretch of land crossing the bulk of Baja Sur, you'll find the dear capital of Baja California Sur, La Paz, which has maintained its authentic Mexican feel even though it's frequented by docking cruise ships. Loreto is a charming town with refined airs, a few lovely boutique hotels, precious restaurants, and upscale art galleries. Mid-peninsula is home to long stretches of highway and desolate landscapes, making this section of Baja a sight to be seen, if not a destination in its own right.

2 Baja Norte: Beach Towns. Ensenada is a seaport sandwiched by beaches; head inland from here for a day trip to experience a burgeoning wine region in the Valle de Guadalupe. Rosarito's lovely beach abuts a less-than-beautiful town full of cheesy bars targeting college students in search of a "what

happens in Mexico, stays in Mexico" kind of weekend. And Puerto Nuevo is a picturesque seaport bursting with buttery lobster.

3 Baja Norte: Border Towns. Within the grit of Tijuana, Baja's largest urban sprawl, brave day-trippers mingle with residents from throughout Latin America struggling to better their lives. Tecate has small-town attitude and big-scale beer production. Baja California's capital, Mexicali, is a town of big-box stores without much for tourists, save the dying embers of a Chinatown, bull-fighting stadium, and lovely cathedral.

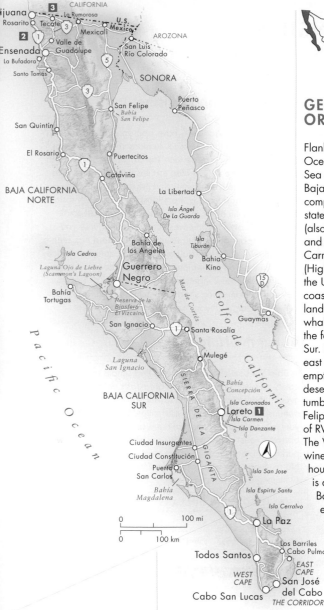

GETTING ORIENTED

Flanked by the Pacific Ocean to the west and the Sea of Cortez to the east, Baja California is actually comprised of two separate states: Baja California (also called Baja Norte) and Baja California Sur. Carretera Transpeninsular (Highway 1) meanders from the U.S. border through coastal regions, mountain landscapes, and gray whale mating grounds to the fancy resorts of Baja Sur. In Baja Norte, traveling east of Highway 1 offers empty and starkly beautiful desert landscape, until it tumbles into the sea at San Felipe, a snowbird village of RVs and sports fisherman. The Valle de Guadulupe wine region, less than two hours from San Diego, is a northern highlight. Baja Sur's remote northern areas are riddled with cave paintings, while Loreto and La Paz have beautiful beaches, missions, and museums. The lush capes are meccas for water-sport enthusiasts of every ilk, while Todos Santos, renowned among surfers, has a booming art scene.

8

ᴐAJA PENINSULA PLANNER

When to Go

Like the American southwest, Baja California's weather is conducive to year-round travel, though "peak season" will have a different meaning for beach bums and marine-life enthusiasts. Lower altitudes tend to have higher temperatures. The deserts and sections of Baja Sur can be sweltering between May and October (most locals say that conditions start to improve around mid-October), and parts of the Pacific coast can necessitate sweaters or windbreakers between November and February. Cabo San Lucas and San José del Cabo are famous for nearly perfect year-round weather, but rainfall is highest in September.

■TIP→ Remember these annual events as you plan your trip:

Gray whales and migratory birds tend to travel to Baja California from December through April.

Most surfers recommend traveling in central and southern Baja during the summer months.

The best scuba and snorkeling conditions are reported in September and October.

Although fishing is possible all year-round, local experts consider the summer months the best time to hook a big one.

Restaurants and Cuisine

Most Baja California towns have appropriated their local cuisine from mainland Mexico. In many regions, the best meals are had at curbside taco stands, where grilled meat and fried fish are served atop tortillas with shredded cabbage and hot sauce. It seems that the farther south you go, the more seafood there is, from lobster tacos to fish tostadas. Eat your fill at the inexpensive (but delicious) small street stands or in the finer restaurants—either way you won't be disappointed. In recent decades, Baja has seen a slow influx of upscale restaurants and international cuisine, often centered on the region's excellent seafood and incorporating other local ingredients. Although the peninsula may still fall something short of a culinary destination, eating well no longer means only taco stands and beer.

About the Hotels

In Baja Sur's smaller towns, you'll find simple roadside hotels and welcoming bed-and-breakfasts with basic accommodations (most small towns don't have luxury options). In the large towns and cities, you can pamper yourself in elegant hotels that have spas and gourmet bistros. Expect your own bathroom, daily maid service, a parking lot, and clean quarters most establishments in Baja Norte. Many hotels offer breakfast for an extra fee, and swimming pools are prevalent.

WHAT IT COSTS IN DOLLARS

	¢	$	$$	$$$	$$$$
Hotels	under $50	$50–$74	$75–$149	$150–$250	over $250
Restaurants	under $8	$8–$12	$13–$19	$20–$30	over $30

Hotel prices are for two people in a standard double room in high season, excluding tax. Restaurant prices are per person for a main course at dinner, excluding service charges or taxes.

Getting Here and Around

The cities with major airports that receive commercial flights into Baja are Tijuana, Loreto, La Paz, and Los Cabos. Small planes fly less regularly into Ensenada, Guerrero Negro, and Isla Cedros.

The 1,609 km (1,000 mi) of winding road of Highway 1 connects northern and southern Baja from one end to the other. Although finding your way might be simple, the actual act of driving it is a little trickier. Narrow lanes, dips, speed bumps, and military stops (where you will usually be waved on with little more than a quick question) force you to drive carefully.

Beware the long stretches of desert road with no cell-phone reception or gas stations. Road hazards aside, the scenery and the stops are a treat.

If you're driving into Baja California from San Diego during peak hours, you might try heading 35 km (19 mi) east to the much less congested border crossing at Tecate. From there, Highway 3 takes you south through the Valle de Guadalupe to Ensenada.

Highway 3 continues southeast from Ensenada over the San Martír pass, where it meets Highway 5. From here, you can head north to Mexicali or south to San Felipe, where the road ends.

You'll almost certainly need a car to see Baja Norte: public transportation is infrequent and only serves the major hubs. If you're driving in from the United States, purchase Mexican insurance (required) from any of the brokers near the border.

Pack plenty of water and make sure your tires are in good shape: although the major highways are well maintained, a number of smaller roads are unpaved.

Planning Ahead

Making reservations ahead time, especially during high season (November through May), is essential in Baja Sur and can save you time and money, and ensure that your experience is that much more pleasant. Hotels fill up quickly around whale-watching season (December through April), spring break, and the Baja 1000 race in November. Small hotels often give better rooms and rates to advance bookings.

Outside of Tijuana and Ensenada, Baja California Norte has little to offer by way of nightlife and big-city culture, but instead attracts travelers who crave adventure and appreciate both seascapes and desert scenes. Here, you can fish the warm, tranquil Sea of Cortez at sunrise and still make it to the Pacific in time to surf the afternoon waves. Diving in the Bay of Los Angeles rivals the best of Mexico; the Central Desert of Baja California lavishes hikers with one-of-a-kind flora and fascinating cave paintings by prehistoric artists; and wine lovers who tire of their usual Napa haunts congregate in the Valle de Guadalupe.

Baja California isn't a place for city slickers, and that's exactly what many people love about it; being here is an adventure in and of itself.

8

A PENINSULA
ANNER

Emergencies

The state of Baja California Sur has instituted an emergency number for police and fire: 060.

A second number, 065, is available to summon medical assistance.

Both numbers can be used throughout the state, and there are English-speaking operators. For medical emergencies, Tourist Medical Assist has English-speaking physicians who make emergency calls around the clock.

In an emergency anywhere in Baja Norte, dial 066.

Operators speak at least a bit of English. For tourist assistance with legal problems or accidents dial the Tourist Information and Assistance hotline at 078.

A Quick History Lesson

Historically, Baja California has always been the bad boy on Mexico's block. Rugged terrain, tough-as-nails natives, and its relative isolation from the rest of the country kept the Spanish at bay for 100 years after they had colonized the rest of the country.

When the Spanish finally managed to establish missions, European diseases decimated the native population. Finally, the native population decided to fight back against Spanish colonial powers. The war—fought mostly guerrilla-style on the Mexican side—started on September 16, 1810, and lasted for 10 years, when their efforts, along with a military coup in Spain (with many repercussions) finally paid off.

In 1853, during the land-hungry era of Manifest Destiny, American adventurer William Walker captured La Paz, on the east coast, and declared himself president of the new Republic of Lower California. Within months, the Mexican government flexed its muscles and forced Walker to flee (though he later went on to invade Nicaragua and install himself as president).

Baja California Sur remained remote, sparsely populated, and rarely visited until the construction of the Carretera Transpeninsular, or Highway 1, in 1973. In spite of an increase in population and tourism, the region has kept its individuality—the mission architecture, cave paintings, Sahara-like heat, and rugged terrain are unlike anywhere else in the country.

Today, the luxury resorts of Baja Sur have brought a new population to the region: visitors from around the globe looking for sunny escapes and warm, turquoise waters.

$$$ ⌂ **Hotel Palmas de Cortez.** The Palmas is the East Cape's social center. Often featured on sportfishing shows, the hotel is near the famed Cortez Banks—a submerged island that is famous for its fishing, diving, and big-wave surfing. Palma's enormous pool has a swim-up bar, and there's also a 9-hole golf course and driving range where you can dedicate an afternoon or two. Some

WINDSURFING

From mid-October through March, Cabo Pulmo, La Ribera, and Los Barriles have excellent windsurfing conditions with breaks up to 10 to 12 feet high. This is recommended only for experienced windsurfers.

guest rooms have fireplaces and/or kitchens. Special events, including an arts festival in March and several fishing tournaments, are big draws. **Pros:** good food; lots of activities. **Cons:** can be difficult to find; not a good choice if you want solitude. ✉ *On the beach; take road north through Los Barriles and continue to beach* ☎ *624/141–0050, 888/241–1543 in U.S.* ⊕ *www.palmasdecortez.com* ⤴ *22 rooms, 24 suites, 10 condos* ⟳ *In-room: refrigerator, no TV (some). In-hotel: Restaurant, bar, golf course, tennis court, pool, gym, spa, water sports, Internet terminal* ⊟ *MC, V* ¶◯¶ *FAP.*

$ ⌂ **Los Barriles Hotel.** Across the street from beachside businesses, this motel-like inn offers large, comfy, if somewhat basic, rooms. The two-story building wraps around a nicely landscaped central pool and lounging area with a palapa bar and hot tub; water and cold drinks are available at the front desk, as are tours and fishing trips. Reservations are highly recommended since the hotel fills up fast. **Pros:** terrific value; spotless rooms. **Cons:** plain decor; fills up quickly; can be difficult to find. ✉ *Take road off Hwy. 1 north through Los Barriles and turn left when it ends at beach* ☎ *624/141–0024* ⊕ *www.losbarrileshotel.com* ⤴ *20 rooms* ⟳ *In-room: no TV, refrigerator. In-hotel: pool, water sports* ⊟ *MC, V* ¶◯¶ *EP.*

SHOPPING

The **Plaza Del Pueblo** (✉ *Carretera 1*) is the area's most complete shopping opportunity. The small center includes a friendly restaurant-bar, an Internet café, a gym, a realty office (of course), and an excellent shop with postcards, Baja books, and desirable souvenirs.

SPORTS AND THE OUTDOORS

Water-sports equipment and boat trips are available through area hotels, although veterans tend to bring their own gear and rent cars to reach isolated spots. Windsurfers take over the East Cape during winter months, when stiff breezes provide ideal conditions. Catch them flying over the waves at Playa Norte in Los Barriles. **VelaWindsurf** (☎ *800/223–5443 in U.S.* ⊕ *www.velawindsurf.com*), with branches here and in several locales around the world, offers windsurfing and kite-boarding lessons and trips to Los Barriles in winter and fall; its center is located in front of the Hotel Playa del Sol.

EN ROUTE A large white sphere and a shrine to the Virgin of Guadalupe on Highway 1 at Km 93 mark 23.27° latitude north, or the Tropic of Cancer. You cross the line between Earth's temperate zone and the tropics here. Of course, Baja is Baja, and you won't detect any difference in climate no matter on which side of the line you find yourself. Many stop for a photo posing in front of the marker, which is 2 km (1¼ mi) south of the turnoff to Santiago. You can decide how obligatory that seems.

The Tropic of Cancer also crosses Highway 19 on the West Cape, just outside Todos Santos on the road to La Paz. There is no marker there.

LA PAZ

195 km (121 mi) north of San José del Cabo.

Tidy, prosperous La Paz may be the capital of Baja Sur and home to about 250,000 residents, but it still feels like a small town in a time warp. This east-coast development could easily be the most traditional Mexican city in Baja Sur, the antithesis of the "gringolandia" developments to the south. Granted, there are plenty of foreigners in La Paz, particularly during snowbird season. But in the slowest part of the off-season, during the oppressive late-summer heat, you can easily see how La Paz aptly translates to "the peace," and how its residents can be called *paceños* (peaceful ones).

Travelers use La Paz as both a destination in itself and a stopping-off point en route to Los Cabos. There's always excellent scuba diving and sportfishing in the Sea of Cortez. La Paz is the base for divers and fishermen headed for Cerralvo, La Partida, and the Espíritu Santo islands, where parrot fish, manta rays, neons, and angels blur the clear waters by the shore, and marlin, dorado, and yellowtail leap from the sea. Cruise ships are more and more often spotted sailing toward the bay as La Paz emerges as an attractive port. (Only small ships can berth at La Paz itself; most cruise liners dock at its port of Pichilingue, about 16 km [10 mi] north of town.)

La Paz officially became the capital of Baja California Sur in 1974, and is the state's largest settlement (though the combined Los Cabos agglomeration is quickly catching up). It's the site of the state's bureaucracy, jail, and power plant, as well as the ferry port to Mazatlán and Topolobampo, the port of Los Mochis, on the mainland. There are few chain hotels or restaurants, but that's sure to change as resort developments come to fruition around the area.

La Paz region, including parts of the coastline south of the city, is slated as the future building site of several large-scale, high-end resort developments with golf courses, marinas, and vacation homes, but economic doldrums have put brakes on some of those plans.

| 1810, Declaration independence from Spain | Independence from Spain, 1821 | 1825, Lands returned to indigenous people. | 1855, The Baja Peninsula's last mission closed |

— Franciscans (1767–1855)

| 1800 | 1825 | 1850 | 1875 |

— Dominicans (1773–1834)

At first, the Spanish were no match for Baja. Arid, inhospitable terrain and even less hospitable inhabitants made governing the peninsula impossible. The conquistadors failed, but the Catholic church did not. Its mission system ultimately allowed Spain to rule.

First came the Jesuits, then the Franciscans and Dominicans. The priests struggled under harsh conditions to create flourishing rural communities where hunting-and-gathering tribes had merely subsisted. They offered the indigenous peoples protection from Spain's military, gave them religious training (or, as the Church saw it, transformed "heathens" into Christians), and taught them trades—ones that were useful to the Crown, of course.

Many indigenous people became assimilated; some even came to care a great deal for mission life. Enough rebellion remained on the part of the local population, however, that a militia was needed to protect the missions up until independence from Spain.

The litany of Baja's 30 missions (only 26 remain) reads like entries in a book of saints. They were set about 30 miles apart along the Camino Real (Royal Road), and it took a day's journey by horse—three days on foot—to travel between them. The math shows how successful the Spanish plan for control of Baja was via this system: 30 missions x 30 miles = 900 miles, just shy of the peninsula's 1,000-mile length.

Despite the priests' efforts European diseases hastened the decline of the missions. An estimated 50,000 indigenous people lived here when Spanish explorers arrived in 1534; by 1800, some 90% of that population had died. In 1834, a secularization order returned land to the indigenous peoples, signaling the end of the mission system. The Baja Peninsula's last mission closed in 1855, although a few structures live on to this day as parish churches.

IN FOCUS ON A MISSION

8

GIVING PROPER CREDIT

The iconic Father Junípero Serra frequently gets credit for spearheading the construction of the first California (Baja or Alta) mission. Any Mexican schoolchild knows that the honor belongs to Italian-born **Father Juan María de Salvatierra** (1648–1717). After stumbling on a book about indigenous peoples he sailed to Mexico, establishing the mission at Loreto in 1697, and naming the settlement for the town in his native Italy.

Under Father Salvatierra Nuestra Señora de Loreto became the mother church from which all power flowed to missions in Baja and Alta California. But Charles III expelled the Jesuits in 1767 because he believed that they held too much wealth and control. That same year, the Franciscans arrived in Loreto, took over, and expanded the mission system. In 1773, the Dominicans began to aid the Franciscans.

Above: Juan María de Salvatierra

ON THE TRAIL

The Baja Peninsula doesn't have a well-marked Mission Trail like the one in the U.S. state of California. That said, the structures sit on or just off Highway 1. Those worth a stop are far flung, so you need to pick and choose visits based on where you're staying. The current condition of the missions ranges from active parish church to intact edifice (for which you have to hunt around town for a caretaker to let you in) to stones incorporated into another building to just stones.

BAJA CALIFORNIA NORTE

Santo Tomás de Aquino Guadalupe Valley (1791). Baja's wine industry was born here over two centuries ago, and the mission ruins sit on the grounds of today's Santo Tomás winery.

San Fernando de Velicatá El Rosario (1769). The Franciscan mission is in ruins, but the stark, beautiful desert surroundings are a draw.

San Francisco de Borja Santa Rosallita (1769). A family descended from original parishioners still looks after this impressive church. Area residents tend to the mission's farms, just as their ancestors did.

OTHER MISSIONS

El Descanso, Rosarito (1817).

Nuestra Señora de Guadalupe, Guadalupe (1834).

San Miguel Arcángel, Ensenada (1797).

Santa Catarina Mártir, Ensenada (1797).

San Vicente Ferrer, San Vicente (1780).

Santo Domingo de la Frontera, Vicente Guerrero (1775).

San Pedro Mártir, Parque Nacional San Pedro Mártir (1794).

Nuesta Señora del Santísimo Rosario, El Rosario (1774).

Santa María de Los Ángeles, Cataviña (1767).

Santa Gertrudis, north of San Ignacio (1752).

Statues at Mision Santa Gertrudis

San Ignacio Kadakaamàn

San Francisco de Borja

Santa Rosalia de Mulegé

BAJA CALIFORNIA SUR

San Ignacio Kadakaamán San Ignacio (1728). The peninsula's largest, most ornate mission was lovingly restored three decades ago and today serves as an active parish church.

Nuestra Señora de Loreto Loreto (1697). This church's bell tower has become Loreto's symbol. A visit to Baja's mother mission and its next-door museum is essential to understanding the whole system.

San Javier San Javier (1699). The bells, stained glass, and ornate statuary typify the Jesuit missions of the era. This one is in the midst of a still-functioning orchard. Count on a rough trip to get here, though.

Nuestra Señora del Pilar La Paz (1720). A few of the original mission's stones are today part of La Paz's central cathedral.

Santa Rosa de las Palmas Todos Santos (1733). This Jesuit mission today serves as the parish church in the West Cape's best known community.

San José del Cabo San José del Cabo (1730). Baja's southernmost mission is San José's parish church, and it buzzes with well-attended masses all week.

OTHER MISSIONS

Nuestra Señora de Guadalupe, Guadalupe (1720).

San José de Magdalena, Santa Rosalía (1774).

Santa Rosalía de Mulegé, Mulegé (1705).

La Purísima Concepción de Cadegomó, La Purísima (1720).

San José de Comondú, north of Loreto (1708).

San Juan Bautista, Liguí (1705).

San Luis Gonzaga Chiriyaquí, north of La Paz (1740).

If you're only going to be in Los Cabos at the peninsula's southern tip, you can easily see **Santa Rosa de la Palmas** in Todos Santos or **San José del Cabo** in the town of the same name.

THE ROLE OF THE MISSION

Francisco Pareja, Spanish Franciscan missionary sent to Florida in 1593 or 1594.

The church dominated the mission site and its village and farm, and its architecture reflected the order responsible for the construction. The Jesuits built more elaborate—well, as elaborate as possible in such a remote locale—stone-and-mortar churches with ornate altars and statuary. Unadorned adobe walls reflected the simpler lifestyles of their Franciscan and Dominican successors.

Each compound was designed to be self-supporting, with parishioners raising crops and livestock as provisions for the community. They also, however, provided goods for Spain's colony, and proceeds from the sales of those goods enriched the Crown.

The priests were often wealthy, educated men who relished the adventure and challenge of their work. But the onetime portrait of the altruistic, benevolent missionary concerned only with converting the souls of indigenous peoples has given way to a grayer picture of men complicit in the force to subdue subjects for Spain; men who stamped out all traces of existing culture. Historians continue to debate the role of the priests.

THE LOST MISSION

Stories abound of one final mission site the Jesuits established upon receiving the news of their expulsion from Spain's empire in 1767. Reluctant to give up their massive wealth, they're reputed to have transported most of it to the legendary Misión Santa Isabela built somewhere in Baja. Who knows where?

Early 20th century French archaeologist Gaston Flourie devoted much effort—some suggest he was obsessed—with finding Baja's famed lost mission but to no avail. So what do you do when your mission expedition is unsuccessful? You build a hotel in its honor. Indeed the Misión Santa Isabela, built in Spanish-mission style, makes for a great place to stay in the center of Ensenada. We wish you well if you decide to hunt for the original Santa Isabela and its reputed wealth, assuming it ever existed.

exterior, but the beige-and-gray interiors are agreeable. The service, which mainly caters to business travelers, is excellent. **Pros:** friendly staff; spacious rooms; stunning exterior. **Cons:** you'll need a car to stay here; ho-hum food in restaurant; plain rooms. ⌧ *Hwy. to Pichilingue, Km 5, in Marina Costa* ☏ *612/123–6000* ⊕ *www.fiestamericana.com* ↬ *114 rooms, 6 suites* ♿ *In room: Wi-Fi, safe, refrigerator. In hotel: Restaurant, room service, bar, pools, gym, beachfront, Internet terminal, laundry service, parking (free)* ⊟ *D, MC, V* ⌾ *EP.*

$$-$$$ ⊡ **Hotel Marina.** The full-service marina offers fishing, scuba diving, and kayaking. Private charters are available. Most rooms have terraces or balconies with water views, gardens surround the pool and hot tub, and a seaside promenade lines the property. Naturally, it's popular with boaters sailing the Sea of Cortez; they share tall tales and tips at the Dinghy Dock restaurant right on the harbor. **Pros:** good value and amenities for fishing vacations. **Cons:** you may feel out of place if you're not here on a fishing vacation. ⌧ *Hwy. to Pichilingue, Km 2.5* ☏ *612/121–6254, 866/262–1787 in U.S.* ⊕ *www.hotelmarina.com.mx* ↬ *85 rooms, 5 suites* ♿ *In room: Safe, refrigerator (some), Wi-Fi. In-hotel: Restaurant, room service, bar, tennis court, pool, spa, Internet terminal, parking (free)* ⊟ *AE, MC, V* ⌾ *EP.*

$$ ⊡ **Hotel Perla.** The brown low-rise faces the malecón and has seen a flurry of activity since 1940, due largely to its nightclub, La Cabaña. Rooms are a little kitschy, with light-wood furnishings with pink-and-teal accents; some have king-size beds. The pool is on a second-story sundeck, away from the traffic of the main street. Noise is a factor in the oceanfront rooms, the trade-off being wonderful sunset views, so take your pick. **Pros:** central location; friendly staff; decent value for the price. **Cons:** room facing street can be noisy; dated decor. ⌧ *Paseo Alvaro Obregón 1570, Malecón* ☏ *612/122–0777 or 888/242–3757* ⊕ *www.hotelperlabaja.com* ↬ *110 rooms* ♿ *In-room: Refrigerator, Internet. In-hotel: restaurant, bar, pool, Wi-Fi hotspot, parking (free)* ⊟ *AE, MC, V* ⌾ *EP.*

$$ ⊡ **Hotel Seven Crown.** This very reasonable, modern, minimalist hotel is perfectly situated to one side of the malecón's action. Take off from your hotel room for nearby cafés and restaurants, and prime people-watching. Other hotels are a little farther off. Hotel Seven Crown's rooms are comfortable, if a little plain, and come complete with a small refrigerator and extra sink. Other advantages here: there's a small bar on the roof from which you can enjoy a view of the bay; no one ever seems to use the small hot tub next to the bar; and rooms have petite, private balconies. Book your excursions with the travel agency representative in the lobby. **Pros:** central location; affordable. **Cons:** very simple rooms; some rooms facing street can be noisy. ⌧ *Paseo Alvaro Obregón 1710, Centro* ☏ *612/128–7788* ⊕ *www.sevencrownhotels.com* ↬ *55 rooms, 9 suites* ♿ *In-room: Kitchen (some), refrigerator, Wi-Fi. In-hotel: Restaurant, room service, bar, parking (free)* ⊟ *MC, V* ⌾ *EP.*

$$ ⊡ **La Casa Mexicana Inn.** Arlaine Cervantes has created a lovely home-like ambience in her small bed-and-breakfast just one block from the malecón. The rooms are exquisite in calming pastels with niches and shelves full of folk art, beds with hand-carved headboards, wrought-

8

iron work, Guatemalan textiles, and custom ceiling and door moldings. Some rooms overlook the bay, while others face the peaceful garden. Guests rave about the breakfasts (for an extra cost) with local fruit, Mexican pastries, crepes, frittatas, and home-baked breads. **Pros:** central location; friendly owner; attentive service. **Cons:** not right on malecón. ✉ *Calle Nicolas Bravo 106, Centro* ☎ *612/125–2748* ⊕ *www. casamex.com* 🔖 *6 rooms* ☖ *In-room: No phone, no TV, kitchen (some), Wi-Fi, refrigerator. In-hotel: No kids under 10, parking (free)* ⊟ *MC, V* ⑴◎⑴ *EP.*

$$–$$$ 🔅 **La Concha Beach Resort.** On a long beach with calm water, this older
⟲ resort has a water-sports center and a notable restaurant. Rooms can be dark and uninviting, but are gradually being renovated with white walls and cheery yellow-and-blue textiles. If you can, splurge on a condo unit with a separate bedroom and kitchen. These are in a separate apartment-style building with an elevator, within walking distance to the beach. There's also an infrequent shuttle to town. **Pros:** renovated rooms in good shape; lower priced rooms are good value. **Cons:** you'll need a car to stay here; some dark rooms. ✉ *Hwy. to Pichilingue, Km 5* ☎ *612/121–6161, 800/999–2252 in U.S.* ⊕ *www.laconcha.com* 🔖 *107 rooms* ☖ *In-room: Refrigerator. In-hotel: Restaurant, room service, bar, pool, beachfront, diving, water sports, laundry service, Internet terminal, Wi-Fi hotspot, parking (free)* ⊟ *AE, MC, V* ⑴◎⑴ *EP.*

NIGHTLIFE AND THE ARTS

El Teatro de la Ciudad (✉ *Av. Navarro 700, Centro* ☎ *612/125–0486*) is La Paz's cultural center.

The theater seats 1,500 and stages shows by visiting and local performers. **La Terraza** (✉ *Hotel Perla, Paseo Alvaro Obregón 1570, Malecón* ☎ *612/122–0777*) is the best spot for both sunset- and people-watching along the malecón. The hotel also has a disco called **La Cabaña** where you can dance to Latin music on weekends.

★ **Las Varitas** (✉ *Av. Independencia 111, Centro* ☎ *612/123–1590* ⊕ *www. lasvaritas.com*), a Mexican rock club, heats up after midnight.

SHOPPING

Allende Books (✉ *Independencia 518, between Serdán and Guillermo Prieto, Centro* ☎ *612/125–9114*) stocks La Paz's best selection of English-language books, mainly about Baja and Mexico, as well as laminated nature field guides. You'll also find a terrific selection of gifts here, including handcrafted jewelry, table runners, and wall hangings. **Antigua California** (✉ *Paseo Alvaro Obregón 220, Malecón* ☎ *612/125–5230*) has the nicest selection of Mexican folk art in La Paz, including wooden masks and lacquered boxes from the mainland state of Guerrero.

Artesanía Cuauhtémoc (✉ *Av. Abasolo between Calles Nayarit and Oaxaca, south of downtown, Centro* ☎ *612/122–4575*) is the workshop of weaver Fortunado Silva, who creates and sells cotton place mats, rugs, and tapestries.

★ Julio Ibarra oversees the potters and painters at **Ibarra's Pottery** (✉ *Guillermo Prieto 625, Centro* ☎ *612/122–0404*). His geometric designs and glazing technique result in gorgeous mirrors, bowls, platters, and cups.

La Tiendita (⊠ *Malecón, Centro* ☎ *612/125–2744*) has embroidered guayabera shirts and dresses, tin ornaments and picture frames, and black pottery from Oaxaca in southern Mexico. There's unusual pottery at **Mexican Designs** (⊠ *Calle Arreola 41, at Av. Zaragoza, Centro* ☎ *612/123–2231*). The boxes with cactus designs are particularly good souvenirs.

SPORTS AND THE OUTDOORS
BOATING AND FISHING
The considerable fleet of private boats in La Paz now has room for docking at three marinas: Fidepaz Marina at the north end of town, and the Marina Palmira and Marina La Paz south of town. Most hotels can arrange trips. Fishing tournaments are held in August, September, and October. The **Fishermen's Fleet** (☎ *612/122–1313, 408/884–3932 in U.S.* ⊕ *www.fishermensfleet.com*) has daylong fishing on pangas (skiffs).

The **Mosquito Fleet** (☎ *612/121–6120, 877/408–6769 in U.S.* ⊕ *www.bajamosquitofleet.com*) has cabin cruisers with charters starting around $550 per person for up to four people, and superpangas at $399 per person for two people.

DIVING AND SNORKELING
Popular diving and snorkeling spots include the coral banks off Isla Espíritu Santo, the sea-lion colony off Isla Partida, and the seamount 14 km (9 mi) farther north (best for serious divers).

Baja Expeditions (⊠ *2625 Garnet Ave., San Diego, CA* ☎ *612/125–3828, 800/843–6967 in U.S.* ⊕ *www.bajaex.com*) runs multiday dive packages in the Sea of Cortez. Seven-day excursions aboard the 80-foot *Don José* dedicated dive boat start at $1,595 for cabin, food, and nearly unlimited diving. Live-aboard trips run from June into November. You may spot whale sharks in June.

★ The **Cortez Club** (⊠ *La Concha Beach Resort, Hwy. to Pichilingue, Km 5, between downtown and Pichilingue* ☎ *612/121–6120* ⊕ *www.cortezclub.com*) is a full-scale water-sports center with equipment rental and scuba, snorkeling, kayaking, and sportfishing tours. A two-tank dive costs about $125.

Fun Baja (⊠ *Hwy. to Pichilingue, Km 2* ☎ *612/121–5884, 800/667–5362 in U.S.* ⊕ *www.funbaja.com*) offers scuba and snorkel trips with the sea lions. Two-tank scuba trips start at $135.

KAYAKING
The calm waters off La Paz are perfect for kayaking, and you can take
★ multiday trips along the coast to Loreto or out to the nearby islands.
Baja Expeditions (⊠ *2625 Garnet Ave., San Diego, CA* ☎ *612/125–3828, 800/843–6967 in U.S.* ⊕ *www.bajaex.com*), one of the oldest outfitters working in Baja (since 1974), offers several kayak tours, including multinight trips between Loreto and La Paz. A support boat carries all the gear, including ingredients for great meals. The seven-day trip in the Sea of Cortez with camping on remote island beaches starts at $1,395 per person, based on double occupancy.

Baja Quest (⊠ *Sonora 174, Centro* ☎ *612/123–5320* ⊕ *www.bajaquest.com.mx*) has day and overnight kayak trips. Day trips cost $90

8

A diver gets up close and personal with a sea lion in the waters of the Sea of Cortez.

per person. **Fun Baja** (✉ *Hwy. to Pichilingue, Km 2* ☎ *612/121–5884, 800/667–5362 in U.S.* ⊕ *www.funbaja.com*) offers kayak trips around the islands, scuba and snorkel excursions, and land tours. A day of kayaking and snorkeling will run about $125. **Nichols Expeditions** (✉ *497 N. Main, Moab, UT* ☎ *800/648–8488 in U.S.* ⊕ *www.nicholsexpeditions. com*) arranges kayaking tours to Isla Espíritu Santo and between Loreto and La Paz, with camping along the way. A nine-day trip costs $1,350. It also offers a combination of sea kayaking in the Sea of Cortez with whale-watching in Magdalena Bay. A nine-day trip costs $1,400.

WHALE-WATCHING

La Paz is a good entry point for whale-watching expeditions to **Bahía Magdalena**, 266 km (165 mi) northwest of La Paz on the Pacific coast. Note, however, that such trips entail about six hours of travel from La Paz and back for two to three hours on the water. Only a few tour companies offer this as a daylong excursion, however, because of the time and distance constraints.

Many devoted whale-watchers opt to stay overnight in San Carlos, the small town by the bay. Most La Paz hotels can make arrangements for excursions, or you can head out on your own by renting a car or taking a public bus from La Paz to San Carlos, and then hire a boat captain to take you into the bay. The air and water are cold during whale season from December to April, so you'll need to bring a warm windbreaker and gloves. Captains are not allowed to "chase" whales, but that doesn't keep the whale mamas and their babies from approaching your panga so closely you can reach out and touch them.

An easier expedition is a whale-watching trip in the Sea of Cortez from La Paz, which involves boarding a boat in La Paz and motoring around until whales are spotted. They most likely won't come as close to the boats and you won't see the mothers and newborn calves at play, but it's still fabulous watching the whales breeching and spouting nearby. **Baja Expeditions** (✉ *2625 Garnet Ave., San Diego, CA* ☎ *612/125–3828, 800/843–6967 in U.S.* ⊕ *www.bajaex.com*) runs adventure cruises around the tip of Baja between La Paz and Magdalena Bay. The eight-day cruises start at $1,995 per person, based on double occupancy.

Shorter trips including camping at Magdalena Bay are available through **Baja Quest** (✉ *Sonora 174, Centro* ☎ *612/123–5320* ⊕ *www.bajaquest. com.mx*). The two-night camping trip starts at $695 per person; the four-night trip starts at $1,050 per person. The water-sports center **Cortez Club** (✉ *La Concha Beach Resort, Hwy. to Pichilingue, Km 5, between downtown and Pichilingue* ☎ *612/121–6120* ⊕ *www.cortez-club.com*) runs extremely popular whale-watching trips in winter. The one-day excursion costs $150 per person.

LORETO

354 km (220 mi) north of La Paz.

There's not too much going on between La Paz and Loreto. Once you've passed through Ciudad Constitución and Ciudad Insurgentes, north of La Paz, the highway becomes much quieter. It is well marked and easy to navigate as it veers west through Ciudad Constitución and Ciudad Insurgentes (which really don't merit any exploration, other than a stop for gas), and then east again through the flat, dusty desert up to Loreto.

Loreto's setting on the Sea of Cortez is spectacular: the gold and green hills of the Sierra de la Giganta seem to tumble into cobalt water. The desert climate harbors few bothersome insects, and according to local promoters, the skies are clear 360 days of the year.

The indigenous Kikiwa, Cochimí, Cucapa, and Kumiai peoples first inhabited the barren lands of Baja. Jesuit priest Juan María Salvatierra founded the first California mission at Loreto in 1697 and, not long after, the indigenous populations were nearly obliterated by disease and war. Seventy-two years later, a Franciscan monk from Mallorca, Spain—Father Junípero Serra—set out from here to establish a chain of missions from San Diego to San Francisco, in the land then known as Alta California.

In 1821 Mexico achieved independence from Spain, which ordered all missionaries home. Loreto's mission was abandoned and fell into disrepair. Then in 1829 a hurricane virtually destroyed the settlement, capital of the Californias at the time. The capital was moved to La Paz, and Loreto languished for a century. In the late 1970s, when oil revenue filled government coffers, the area was tapped for development. An international airport was built and a luxury hotel and tennis center opened, followed a few years later by a seaside 18-hole golf course. The infrastructure for a resort area south of town at Nopoló was set up. But the pace of development has slowed as the money has dried

CIUDAD CONSTITUCIÓN

Though Ciudad Constitución is the largest city on Highway 1 between Loreto and La Paz, not many tourists stop off for much more than gas (there are two gas stations). A small airstrip here (CUA) receives daily flights from Los Cabos, and would be the closest airport if you were visiting Magdalena Bay on your own; it's far easier to take in the bay with an organized tour out of La Paz or Loreto.

In fact, Ciudad Constitución is the second-largest city in Baja California Sur, after La Paz. But, this is an agricultural town, and there is not much to see if you do decide to stay at one of the unremarkable small hotels or trailer parks for the night; however, it is a convenient place to take a break from driving. There are a few places to grab a taco at one of the many small restaurants on the main street, which itself is part of Highway 1.

up in the worldwide economic turndown. Visions of Loreto becoming another Los Cabos are in "stay tuned" mode right now, and some here say that's a good thing.

Loreto has a population of around 13,000 full-time residents and an increasing number of part-timers who winter at hotels, homes, and trailer parks. It's still a good place to escape the crowds, relax, and go fishing or whale-watching. The Parque Marítimo Nacional Bahía de Loreto protects much of the Sea of Cortez in this area, but there are a few cruise ships that use Loreto as a port of call, and the marina at Puerto Escondido is central to the government's plans for a series of marinas.

GETTING HERE AND AROUND

The Aeropuerto Internacional Loreto (LTO) is 7 km (4½ mi) southwest of town. Alaska Airlines flies from Los Angeles to Loreto on Thursday and Sunday; its affiliate Horizon Air does the route on Tuesday and Friday. Aereo Calafia connects Loreto with Los Cabos daily. Several airlines connect Loreto with Mexico City and other domestic airports in Mexico. Taxis from the airport into town are inexpensive (about $5) and convenient. Loreto's Terminal de Autobus sits at the entrance to town and has service from La Paz, Los Cabos, and points north. In Loreto taxis are in good supply and fares are inexpensive; it costs $5 or less to get anywhere in town and about $10 from downtown Loreto to Nopoló. Illegitimate taxis aren't a problem in this region.

■TIP→ Don't go north from here without a full tank of gas; Pemex stations between Loreto and Guerrero Negro have been known to run out of gas on occasion.

ESSENTIALS

Airlines **Aereo Calafia** (☎ 613/135–2503 ⊕ www.aereocalafia.com.mx). **Alaska Airlines/Horizon Air** (☎ 800/252–7522 ⊕ www.alaskaair.com).

Bus Contacts **Loreto Terminal de Autobus** (✉ Calle Salvatierra at Calle Tamaral ☎ 613/135–0767). **SuburBaja** (☎ 624/146–0888).

Mail and Shipping **Loreto Oficina de Correo** (✉ Palacio Municipal ☎ No phone).

Visitor and Tour Info Loreto Tourist Information Office (✉ *Municipal Bldg. on Plaza Principal, Loreto* ☎ *613/135–0411* ⊕ *www.gotoloreto.com*).

EXPLORING

❸ **El Museo de las Misiónes,** also called the Museo de Historia y Antropología
★ (Missions Museum or Museum of History and Anthropology), contains religious relics, 19th-century leather saddles, and displays on Baja's history. A permit to take photos is an extra $2.50 beyond the admission price. ✉ *Calle Salvatierra s/n, next to La Misión de Nuestra Señora de Loreto* ☎ *613/135–0441* 🎫 *$2.50* ⊙ *Tues.–Sun. 9–noon and 2–6.*

❷ Loreto's main historic sight is **La Misión de Nuestra Señora de Loreto** (✉ *Calle Salvatierra at Calle Misioneros* ☎ *613/135–0005*). The stone church's bell tower is the town's main landmark, rising above the main plaza and reconstructed pedestrian walkway along Salvatierra.

❶ The **malecón** along Calle de la Playa (also called Paseo Lopez Mateos) is
☯ a pleasant place to walk, jog, or sit on a cast-iron bench watching the sunset. A small marina shelters yachts and the panga fleet; the adjoining beach is popular with locals, especially on Sunday afternoons, when kids hit the playground.

❺ **Puerto Escondido,** 25 km (15½ mi) down Highway 1 from Loreto, has an RV park, **Tripui** (☎ *613/133–0814* ⊕ *www.tripui.com*), with a good restaurant, a few motel rooms, a snack shop, a bar, stores, showers, a laundry, a pool, and tennis courts. There's a boat ramp at the small Puerto Escondido marina close to Tripui; you pay the fee required to launch here to the attendant at the parking lot. The **port captain's office** (☎ *613/135–0656*) is just south of the ramp, but it's rarely open.

❻ **Isla Danzante,** 5 km (3 mi) southeast of Puerto Escondido, has good reefs and diving opportunities.

8

❼ You can arrange picnic trips to **Isla Coronados,** inhabited only by seals, sea lions, and seabirds, from Loreto or Puerto Escondido. The snorkeling and scuba diving off the island are excellent. Danzante and other islands off Loreto are part of the Parque Maritímo Nacional Bahía de Loreto. Commercial fishing boats aren't allowed within the 60-square-km (23-square-mi) park.

❹ A trip to **Misión San Javier,** 32 km (20 mi) southwest of Loreto, shows
☯ Baja at its best. A high-clearance vehicle is useful for the two-hour
★ drive to the mission—don't try getting here if the dirt-and-gravel road is muddy. The road climbs past small ranches, palm groves, and the steep cliffs of the Cerro de la Giganta. Marked trails lead off the road to remnants of a small cluster of indigenous cave paintings. The mission village is a remote community of some 50 full-time residents, many of whom come outdoors when visitors arrive.

The mission church (circa 1699), which is set in the middle of orchards, is built of blocks of gray volcanic rock and topped with domes and bell towers containing three bells from the 18th and 19th centuries. The side stained-glass windows are framed with wood. Inside, a gilded central altar contains a statue of Saint Javier; side altars have statues of Saint Ignacio and the Virgen de los Dolores. Vestments from the 1700s are displayed in a glass cabinet. The church is often locked; ask anyone

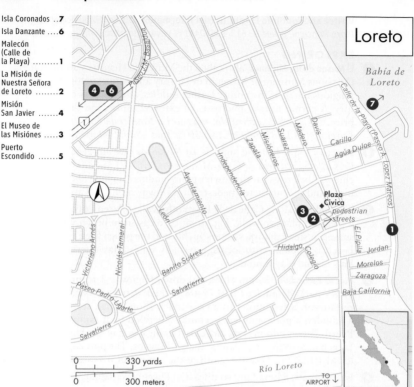

hanging about to find the person with the keys. Slip a few pesos into the contribution box as a courtesy to the village's inhabitants, who need all the help they can get to keep the church well maintained. Loreto residents make pilgrimages to the mission for the patron saint's festival, celebrated December 1–3. Although you can drive to San Javier on your own, it helps to have a guide along to lead you to the caves and indigenous paintings. Many hotels and tour companies can arrange trips. In San Javier you can spend the night **Casa Ana** (☎ *613/135–1552*) in a little bungalow near the mission to get a rare view into a small Baja community ($35 per night).

WHERE TO EAT

¢   ✕ **Café Olé.** Locals and gringos alike hang out at this casual spot for

ECLECTIC   terrific breakfasts of scrambled eggs with chorizo (sausage), huevos rancheros, and other typical, delicious Mexican breakfasts. Later in the day (it's open until 10 PM most nights) it steers away from Mexican specialties and also serves good burgers, french fries, and ice cream. If you come on Sunday, make it breakfast or a very early lunch; it closes at 1 PM. ⊠ *Calle Francisco Madero 14* ☎ *613/135–0496* ▭ *No credit cards* ☯ *No dinner Sun.*

¢ MEXICAN ★ **Canipole.** Sofia Rodriguez reigns over the open kitchen of this down-home, open-air Mexican restaurant. The 34 ingredients she uses in her savory mole are displayed in tiny bowls on one table, the ingredients for her homemade Mexican hot chocolate are in bowls on another. Pots of *pozole* (a hominy stew) and tortilla soup simmer over a gas fire on the patio while Sofia pats out fresh tortillas for each order. Specialties include *conejo* (rabbit), quesadillas with *flor de calabaza* (squash blossoms), and unusual carnitas made with lamb. Check out the view of the mission's dome from the restaurant's backyard. ✉ *Pino Suárez s/n beside mission* ☎ *613/133–0282* ▭ *No credit cards* ⏲ *Closed Sun.*

$ STEAKHOUSE **El Nido.** If you're hungry for steak, chicken, and hearty Mexican combo plates, then this is your place. It's as close as you'll get to a steak house in these parts. The brass and woodwork and the courteous waiters make this a good place for a special night out or a big, satisfying meal after a hard day's fishing or kayaking. If you come for lunch, make it a late one; the restaurant opens at 1 PM. ✉ *Calle Salvatierra 154* ☎ *613/135–2445* ▭ *No credit cards.*

$ ECLECTIC Fodor's Choice ★ **Pachamama.** The owners—she's from Argentina, he's from Mexico City—have combined their cultures and cuisines to create a restaurant worth repeat visits. Nibble on regional cheeses or empanadas, then move on to a salad of goat cheese and sliced homegrown tomatoes or a marinated *arrachera* (flank steak). Sandwiches on homemade bread make you wish the place were open for lunch. ✉ *Calle Zapata between Calles Salvatierra and Juárez* ☎ *613/135–2219* ▭ *MC, V* ⏲ *Closed Tues. No lunch.*

¢ MEXICAN **Restaurante Santa Lucía.** This second-story café with unbeatable ocean views is the hot spot for breakfast in town. It offers well-done, typical Mexican breakfasts, like *chilaquiles* (fried tortillas served in red or green sauce, the way it should be), and home-baked breads daily. Dishes are served with fabulous fresh-baked goods like cinnamon rolls, wheat rolls, and freshly squeezed juices. ✉ *Blvd. Mateos s/n, at Jordón* ☎ *613/100–1332* ▭ *No credit cards* ⏲ *Closed Wed. No dinner.*

8

WHERE TO STAY

$ **Hotel Luna.** This Swiss-owned, modern hotel is clean and minimalist. There are only three rooms, and no lobby to speak of, only a small office. The rooms are air-conditioned and comfortable with a small sofa and shelves to put away your things; the palette is mostly a stark white, decorated with beige, browns, and grays. Prices are reasonable. **Pros:** good value; comfortable, if spartan, rooms. **Cons:** few amenities; rooms can feel a bit claustrophobic. ✉ *Benito Juárez s/n* ☎ *613/135–2288* 🌐 *www.hotellunaloreto.com* *3 rooms* *In room: Wi-Fi. In hotel: Bar, parking (free)* ▭ *MC, V* *EP.*

$$ **Hotel Oasis.** One of the original in-town hostelries, the Oasis remains an ideal base for those who want to be in town and spend plenty of time on the water. Rooms vary greatly in size and comfort; the best have coffeemakers, water views, and hammocks on the front terraces. Guests gather in the large bar to wish each other luck over breakfast or exchange fishing tales in the evening. Meal plans vary with the season and with packages. The hotel has its own fleet of skiffs. **Pros:** central location; friendly staff, knowledgeable about the fishing scene. **Cons:**

some plain rooms; room quality varies greatly; you'll feel out of place if you're not here to fish. ⊠ *Calle de la Playa, Apdo. 17* ☎ *613/135–0211, 866/482–0247 in U.S.* ⊕ *www.hoteloasis.com* ⤳ *27 rooms, 12 suites* ⚒ *In-room: No phone (some), refrigerator, Wi-Fi. In-hotel: Restaurant, room service, bar, pool, Internet terminal, parking (free)* ☰ *MC, V* ❖ *BP, EP, FAP.*

$$$ ⊡ **Hotel Posada de las Flores.** The rose-color walls of this surprisingly chic hotel rise beside downtown's plaza. The public areas are its forte. A glass-bottom pool doubles as a skylight above the atrium lobby, and the rooftop sundeck and restaurant have huge planters of bougainvillea. Exposed beams and locally crafted tile adorn the lobby and hallways. Guest rooms, however, can be very dark and noisy, though they are also beautifully decorated. Have a drink at the rooftop bar for a good view of town and the mountains. There is also a tapas bar that is open in the evenings on the ground level. Sit outside and you can people-watch while you munch. **Pros:** beautiful public spaces; pool above lobby ceiling is novel to watch. **Cons:** some dark, noisy rooms. ⊠ *Calle Salvatierra at Calle Francisco Madero* ☎ *613/135–1162* ⊕ *www.posadadelasflores. com* ⤳ *10 rooms, 5 suites* ⚒ *In-room: Safe, refrigerator, Wi-Fi. In-hotel: Restaurant, bar, pool, laundry service, no kids under 12, parking (free)* ☰ *MC, V* ❖ *CP.*

$ ⊡ **Motel el Dorado.** Low rates, accessible parking, and a congenial bar are available at this spanking-clean motel. All that's missing is a pool, but the waterfront is a block away. Rooms are classic Baja basic, with thin mattresses, TVs anchored to the walls, and inexpensive dark-wood furnishings. The motel also offers rents motorbikes and fishing charters. A seven-hour trip on a 23-foot boat goes for $175. **Pros:** good value; immaculate rooms. **Cons:** no-frills rooms; a pool would be a nice addition in the heat. ⊠ *Paseo Hidalgo at Calle Pipila* ☎ *613/135–1500 or 888/314–9023* ⊕ *www.moteleldorado.com* ⤳ *11 rooms* ⚒ *In-room: No phone, Wi-Fi. In-hotel: Bar, laundry service, parking (free)* ☰ *MC, V* ❖ *EP.*

$–$$ ⊡ **Sukasa.** Roomy air-conditioned bungalows with brick-and-stucco walls, palapa ceilings, and separate bedrooms are clustered in a compound just steps from the malecón. One sturdy, canvas-sided yurt is another affordable and definitely unique option. It's easy to imagine you've moved to Loreto, at least for a while, as you set up housekeeping in the kitchen and wander across the street, coffee in hand, to watch the sun rise and set. The manager is a delight, quick to make guests feel totally at home and set up excursions. Kayaks and bikes are also on hand for guest use. **Pros:** lovely owner; friendly service; yurt is a kick to stay in. **Cons:** some street noise. ⊠ *Calle de la Playa at Calle Jordan* ☎ *613/135–0490* ⊕ *www.loreto.com/sukasa* ⤳ *3 bungalows, 1 yurt* ⚒ *In-room: Kitchen, Wi-Fi. In hotel: Water sports, parking (free)* ☰ *MC, V* ❖ *EP.*

SHOPPING

Loreto's shopping district is along the pedestrian zone on Calle Salvatierra, where there are several souvenir shops and stands, plus the town's

★ only supermarket. **El Alacrán** (⊠ *Calle Salvatierra 47* ☎ *613/135–0029*) has remarkable folk art, jewelry, and sportswear.

SPORTS AND THE OUTDOORS
FISHING

Fishing put Loreto on the map. You can catch cabrilla and snapper year-round; yellowtail in spring; and dorado, marlin, and sailfish in summer. If you're a serious angler, bring tackle. Some sportfishing fleets do update their equipment regularly. All Loreto-area hotels can arrange fishing, and many own skiffs. Local anglers congregate with their small boats on the beach at the north and south ends of town.

Arturo's Fishing Fleet (⊠ *Paseo Hidalgo between plaza and marina* ☎ *613/135–0766* ⊕ *www.arturosport.com*) has several types of boats and fishing packages. The **Baja Big Fish Company** (⊠ *Paseo Hidalgo 19, by plaza* ☎ *613/135–1603* ⊕ *www.bajabigfish.com*), which specializes in light tackle and fly-fishing, has packages from the United States that sometimes include free hotel nights and fishing trips from Loreto. Half-day fishing rates start at $270.

WATER SPORTS

Arrange kayaking excursions, whale-watching tours, scuba-certification courses, and dive and snorkeling trips through the **Baja Outpost** (⊠ *Blvd. Mateos near Oasis Hotel* ☎ *613/135–1134, 888/649–5951 in U.S.* ⊕ *www.bajaoutpost.com*). The company specializes in sports packages. A three-day, two-night snorkeling package starts at $223 per person based on double occupancy in its hotels; with kayaking, the package starts at $307. The company also offers day tours to Misión San Javier.

Club Cantamar (⊠ *Paseo Alvaro Obregón 1665-2* ☎ *612/122–1826* ⊕ *www.clubcantamar.com*) offers kayak rentals and guided tours. A half-day tour of Pichilingue Bay including transport, kayak, breakfast, and guide goes for $45 per person.

Dolphin Dive Center (⊠ *Calle Juárez between Calles Davis and Playa* ☎ *613/135–1914* ⊕ *www.dolphindivebaja.com*) is a PADI shop offering dives around the islands off Loreto and instruction. A two-tank trip costs $99–$120 depending on location; snorkeling excursions run $65. The company also has whale-watching and Misión San Javier tours.

Loreto outdoor specialists **Las Parras Tours** (⊠ *Calle Salvatierra at Calle Francisco Madero* ☎ *613/135–1010*) provides day trips with kayaking, island skiff trips, as well as whale-watching, scuba diving and certification, and visiting San Javier village in the mountains. Day trips in the desert cost $35 and up, and tours to San Javier run $50.

Paddling South (⊠ *Box 827, Calistoga, CA 94515* ☎ *800/398–6200 in U.S.* ⊕ *www.tourbaja.com*) runs guided kayaking trips starting at $1,045, including meals. The company also offers mountain-biking trips, and multiday mule pack trips with a historic focus.

The U.S.–based company **Sea Quest Expeditions** (☎ *888/589–4253 in U.S.* ⊕ *www.sea-quest-kayak.com*) has several trips that begin in Loreto. Options include kayaking with gray whales in Magdalena Bay or in the San Ignacio Lagoon. Weeklong trips start at $1,299.

A bottlenose dolphin (*Tursiops truncatus*) makes a leap for it in azure Baja waters.

MULEGÉ

134 km (83 mi) north of Loreto.

Mulegé (pronounced moo-lay-HAY) is a popular base for exploring the Sierra de Guadalupe mountains, the site of several prehistoric rock paintings of human and animal figures. Kayaking in Bahía Concepción, Baja's largest protected bay, is spectacular.

Once a mission settlement, this charming town of some 3,500 residents swells in winter, when Americans and Canadians fleeing the cold arrive in droves of motor homes. Amid an oasis of date palms on the banks of the Río Santa Rosalía, Mulegé looks and feels more tropical than other Baja Sur communities. Several narrow streets make up the business district, and dirt roads run from the highway to RV parks south of town.

Access to the rock paintings is good, though you must have a permit and be accompanied by a licensed guide. Tours typically involve a bumpy ride followed by an even bumpier climb on the backs of burros.

GETTING HERE AND AROUND

Mulegé's bus terminal sits 4 km (2½ mi) north of town. Informal taxis wait for each arriving bus and take you where you need to go. Services come and got from Loreto, Santa Rosalía, San Ignacio, and Guerrero Negro several times daily. ■TIP→ The one Pemex gas station in town periodically runs out of fuel.

HURRICANE JIMENA

A fortunately rare occurrence in Baja California unfortunately came to pass in September 2009 with the roaring ashore of Hurricane Jimena in this sector of the peninsula.

Original projections put the storm on target to hit highly populated Los Cabos on the tip of Baja, but Jimena veered north by several hundred miles, inflicting damage on Mulegé and Santa Rosalía.

News reports at the time expressed "Thank goodness the hurricane hit an unpopulated region" sentiments, leaving residents here to say, "Excuse us, but we're plenty populated here, too."

Repairs were ongoing and progressing well at this writing, with eventual full cleanup and restoration of services expected to take a few months.

EXPLORING

Mulegé Tours (*Madero 50* ☎ *615/161–4987* ⊕ *www.mulegetours.com*) is run by Salvador Castro, a Mulegé native who peppers his tours with informational tidbits on the medicinal uses of local plants and on the history of the indigenous Chochimí people who used to make their homes in this area. He leads treks to the cave paintings and to working ranches in the mountains. Cave excursions start at around $40 per person, but there are discounts for groups of four or more. Excursions can be arranged by phone or e-mail through the Web site.

WHERE TO STAY

$$ 🛏 **Hotel Serenidad.** A Mulegé mainstay for Baja aficionados since the late
★ 1960s, this delightful escape is owned by the Johnson family, longtime residents. The Serenidad's simple rooms in brick-and-stucco buildings are scattered under bougainvillea vines and fruit trees. Some suites have fireplaces and separate bedrooms. An expansive riverfront villa is set off from the complex and is fully furnished. (There's a minimum five-night stay in the villa.) The Saturday-night pig roast is a tradition. **Pros:** owners are a wealth of information about Baja; weekly pig roast is fun. **Cons:** lots of activity, so not a good option if you seek solitude. ✛ *2½ km (1½ mi) north of Mulegé, Hwy. 1* ☎ *615/153–0530* ⊕ *www.serenidad.com* ➳ *40 rooms 10 suites, 1 villa* ♿ *In-room: No phone, kitchen (some) Wi-Fi. In-hotel: Restaurant, bar, pool* ▭ *MC, V* ❑ *EP.*

SANTA ROSALÍA

64 km (40 mi) north of Mulegé.

The architecture in this dusty mining town, the last desert town north of Baja's subtropical region, is a fascinating mix of French, Mexican, and American Old West styles. It is so different from other architecture in the area that you can easily forget that you are in Baja California.

GETTING HERE AND AROUND

The Ferry Santa Rosalía makes four-times-weekly crossings between Santa Rosalía and Guaymas on the mainland, departing Tuesday and Wednesday at 9 AM and Friday and Sunday at 8 AM. The cost is $65 per person. The ferry terminal at the harbor also serves as Santa Rosalía's bus terminal, with services to Loreto, La Paz, San Ignacio, and Mulegé several times daily. The Pemex gas station in town has a reputation for overcharging and/or shortchanging tourists; fill up elsewhere if you can, although the spottiness of stations between Loreto and Guerrero Negro means you might need to do it here.

ESSENTIALS

Ferry Contacts Ferry Santa Rosalía (⊠ *Marina Santa Rosalía* ☎ *615/152–0013* ⊕ *www.ferrysantarosalia.com*).

EXPLORING

Santa Rosalía is known for its **Iglesia Santa Bárbara** (⊠ *Av. Obregón at Calle Altamirano*), a prefabricated iron church designed by Alexandre-Gustave Eiffel, creator of the Eiffel Tower. The iron panels of the little church are brightened by stained-glass windows.

WHERE TO EAT AND STAY

¢ ✗ **El Boleo.** Be sure to stop by this small shop where fresh breads tempt
CAFÉ customers weekday mornings at 10 AM. The name, El Boleo, is taken from the French mining company that moved into town to exploit the mineral riches of the land here in the late 1800s. Try the *pitahaya,* an unexpected and very tasty combination of a sort of sugar cookie and bread roll in one. You won't find it anywhere else. ⊠ *Av. Obregón at Calle 4* ☎ *615/152–0310* ▭ *No credit cards.*

$ ⛺ **Hotel Francés.** The glory days of this well-kept 1886 French hillside mansion shine through. The lobby is decorated with framed embroidered flowers, old black-and-white photos of the town, and lace curtains. Many rooms open onto a second-story porch with views of town and the sea. There's a small pool and a classy restaurant in the courtyard. **Pros:** historic building; friendly staff. **Cons:** can be difficult to find (double-check your directions). ⊠ *Av. 11 de Julio at Calle Jean M. Cousteau* ☎ *615/152–2052* ↝ *16 rooms* ⚐ *In-room: Wi-Fi. In-hotel: Restaurant, pool, laundry service, Internet terminal, parking (free)* ▭ *No credit cards* ⦿ *EP.*

SAN IGNACIO

77 km (48 mi) west of Santa Rosalía.

The gently swaying date palms of San Ignacio, in the Desierto de Vizcaíno, first planted here by Jesuit missionaries in the late 1700s, seem to keep time with the small town's laid-back rhythms. This town is primarily a point to sign on for one of the organized tours that take visitors to see the paintings in the caves in the nearby Sierra de San Francisco. The caves were declared a UNESCO World Heritage site in 1993.

The town is home to arguably the most stunning (and at the time, most expensive) of Baja's mission churches, the **Misión San Ignacio Kadakaamán.** (Kadakaamán means "reeds" in the indigenous Cochimí language.) Built by the Jesuits in 1728, the mission was estimated to have served a community of 5,000 in this fertile agricultural region. The Dominicans took over following the Jesuits' expulsion and in 1786 built an even more elaborate church with thick volcanic stone and ornate wooden doors. Unlike some of Baja's mission churches, which now sit starkly, beguilingly forlorn, San Ignacio is a living, breathing, extremely active parish church these days. A small museum next door documents the history of the mission, with exhibits in Spanish only. ⊠ *Plaza Ecoturismo* 🕾 *No phone* 🖃 *Donation requested* ⊙ *Mon.–Sat. 9–6.*

San Ignacio is also known as home to some of the world's friendliest gray whales and a statue of a whale skeleton stands at the town's entrance. Between December and April, the gray whales that come here to breed often swim close enough to allow visitors to touch them.

Locals insist that the calm waters in the lagoon here make whale-watching more pleasant than in nearby towns where they report choppier, unprotected sea water. Some tourism promoters go as far as to insist that this makes the whales more comfortable and more likely to approach visitors. You'll have to decide for yourself.

GETTING HERE AND AROUND

San Ignacio has no bus terminal per se. Coaches head north to Guerrero Negro and south to Santa Rosalía and beyond several times a day and stop next to the Pemex station here. Buy your tickets when you board the bus. ■TIP➜ The Pemex gas station here occasionally runs out of fuel. Fill up elsewhere to be on the safe side.

WHERE TO STAY

¢–$ 🏨 **Casa Lereé.** This historic adobe building just off the zócalo was the first guesthouse in San Ignacio. Today it is once again a small hotel, run by San Francisco native Jane Beard Ames, known as "Juanita" in these parts. Juanita painted the place with bright colors, decorated the simple rooms with local crafts, and cultivated a shady central garden and a large living room area full of rocking chairs where guests can swap stories. In addition to the two rooms that sit just off the garden, there is a larger room with a kitchen and a full private bathroom. She also has a small bookstore with books on Mexican history, Spanish language, and Baja California. Juanita, who first became interested exploring Baja California as a marine biologist, is so knowledgeable that you could not find a better source of information on San Ignacio. She has compiled an oral history of the town (a copy is in every guest room and is also available for sale) and maintains a collection of historic photos of San Ignacio that locals stop by to consult when they are looking for long-lost images of their own families. A stay with Juanita, a glimpse at her collection, and a flip through her book could easily turn you on to the charm and the magic of this small town. **Pros:** the lovely owner is a wealth of knowledge; attentive service. **Cons:** shared bath. ⊠ *Calle Madero s/n, 1 block northeast of the zócalo, Col. Centro* 🕾 *615/154–0158* ⊕ *www.casaleree.com* ⇶ *3 rooms without bath* ⚼ *In-room: No phone, Wi-Fi. In-hotel: parking (free)* 🚭 *No credit cards.*

$$ 🏨 **Desert Inn.** This simple, functional hotel is a pleasant place to stay on your trans-peninsular journey—it's part of a six-hotel Baja-wide chain that has no connection to the famous, onetime Las Vegas lodging—although you may wish for a bit more for the money. White arches frame the courtyard and pool, and the rooms are decorated with folk art and wood furnishings. Both the river and town are within walking distance. **Pros:** good value; makes an effort to be more homey than other

hotels in this chain. **Cons:** no-frills service; grounds are drab. ⊹ *2 km (1 mi) west of Hwy. 1 on unnamed road into San Ignacio* ☎ *615/157–1305, 619/275–4500, 800/542–3283 in U.S.* ⊕ *www.desertinns.com* ⟲ *28 rooms* ⚹ *In-room: No phone, Wi-Fi. In-hotel: Restaurant, room service, bar, pool, laundry service, parking (free)* ☰ *MC, V* ¶◎¶ *EP.*

$ ⊞ **Ignacio Springs Bed & Breakfast.** At this unique bed-and-breakfast you won't be able to ignore that you're in an oasis-like setting. As you drive in, the first thing that you'll see is the river ahead. In the middle of the desert, crushed clamshells line the paths that take you to small yurts (comfortably furnished circular tents in the Mongolian tradition), hidden away among the palm trees. Some yurts have private bathrooms, and others share a clean and comfortable bathroom. Other options include three small casitas and a single tent. Terry and Gary Marcer, the Canadian expat owners, enjoy conversations with their guests every morning over a tasty breakfast (which is included in the price of an overnight stay) and a home-style dinner (available by reservation only). After breakfast, you might want to swim in the spring-fed river, or take out the kayak that's on hand for guest use. Plans to arrange transport to see cave paintings are also in the works. **Pros:** friendly owners are longtime Baja experts; yurts are surprisingly comfortable. **Cons:** some shared baths. ⊠ *At San Ignacio main entrance* ☎ *615/154–0333* ⊕ *www.ignaciosprings.com* ⟲ *6 yurts, 3 houses* ⚹ *In-room: Wi-Fi. In-hotel: Water sports, restaurant, parking (free)* ☰ *MC, V* ¶◎¶ *BP.*

$$ ⊞ **Rice and Beans Oasis.** This is not the most comfortable hotel in town, but it's where you'll likely find the biggest crowd. Expect to meet drivers involved in the Baja 1000 and other enthusiasts at the bar. The bar itself is covered in stickers—mostly paraphernalia related to the race. Rooms are large and simple. Most have tile floors and are sparsely decorated with bright colors. RV hookups are also available for $20 per night. Transport to the lagoon can be arranged from the hotel for those interested in whale-watching. **Pros:** pretty good value; convenient for RV drivers. **Cons:** spartan rooms; you might feel out of place if you're not a race enthusiast. ⊠ *Carretera Transpeninsular Aceso at San Lino* ☎ *615/154–0283* ⊕ *ricardoriceandbeans.googlepages.com/home* ⟲ *30 rooms* ⚹ *In room: Wi-Fi. In hotel: Bar, restaurant, parking (free)* ☰ *MC, V* ¶◎¶ *EP.*

SPORTS AND THE OUTDOORS

San Ignacio is the base for trips to San Ignacio Lagoon, 59 km (35 mi) from San Ignacio on the Pacific coast. The lagoon is one of the best places to watch the winter gray-whale migration, and local boat captains will usually take you close enough to pet the baby whales. Tours

★   arranged through **Baja Discovery** (⌂ *Box 152527, San Diego, CA 92195* ☎ *619/262–0700, 800/829–2252 in U.S.* ⊕ *www.bajadiscovery.com*) include round-trip transport from San Diego to San Ignacio Lagoon, by van to Tijuana and by private plane to the company's comfortable camp at the lagoon. Accommodations are in private tents facing the water, and there are solar-heated showers. The cost of a five-day package—including transportation, tours, and meals—is $2,375.

★   **Baja Expeditions** (⊠ *2625 Garnet Ave., San Diego, CA* ☎ *612/125–3828 in La Paz, 800/843–6967 in U.S.* ⊕ *www.bajaex.com*) operates a camp at San Ignacio Lagoon and offers five-day tours including air transportation from San Diego. The fee is $2,295 including transport, meals, and tours.

Ecoturismo Kuyimá (✉ *Av. Morelos 23* ☎ *615/154–0070* ⊕ *www. kuyima.com*) in San Ignacio offers transportation between the town and San Ignacio Lagoon, operates a campground at an isolated area of the lagoon, and has adventure tours to caves with prehistoric paintings that include overnights in San Ignacio and at the lagoon. Whale-watching tours with camping and transportation from San Ignacio cost $165 per person per day. Day tours to area cave paintings from San Ignacio cost $50–$70 per person.

GUERRERO NEGRO

143 km (89 mi) northwest of San Ignacio.

At the end of the dirt road, you look across Scammon's Lagoon—past the rusting remains of an old salt compound, where pelicans land and take off ad infinitum—to the geometrically perfect sand dunes. The juxtaposition of the dunes with the lagoon seems like something out of a science fiction film.

Situated just south of the 28th parallel, which separates Baja California Norte from Baja California Sur, Guerrero Negro is a town of 12,000 whose population grew out of the success of Exportadora de Sal, a salt exportation company that is now the largest business of its kind in the world. Guerrero Negro itself is a working-class town without much in the way of restaurants or nightlife, but it attracts thousands of tourists every winter for its proximity to Scammon's Lagoon, to which gray whales migrate year after year.

Notably, the town and the lagoon sit on El Vizcaíno, the largest nature preserve in all of Latin America. A visit to this region promises exposure not only to the 39 regionally endemic species of flora, but also to diverse man-made treasures like the salt flats and the UNESCO-recognized cave paintings, the latter of which date to prehistoric times. The salt company's chemically tinted "pools" are bordered by crystallized salt, which looks strangely like snow in the middle of the desert, and it's difficult not to ogle the giant, futuristic machines that navigate the compound harvesting the crystals. The company's relationship with its employees is one of the best in Baja, providing quality housing for them and their families and even paying their utilities. According to many locals, the company won't even consider a new applicant unless his father or mother worked there, a fact that helps to explain the close-knit, even cliquey, feel of the community.

Gray-whale season in Guerrero Negro begins around December and typically runs through April. Laguna Ojo de Liebre, also known as Scammon's Lagoon (after the America whaler Captain Charles Melville Scammon who frequented the lagoon in the 1800s), is just on the edge of town. The whales, having begun their migration in the arctic waters of Alaska, typically arrive at Laguna in the early weeks of winter, at which time some will give birth and others will commence their

mating ritual. Come January, many local fishermen transition into second careers as tour boat captains, treating their passengers to up-close encounters with the marine mammals, an experience that can be had in very few places around the world.

GETTING HERE AND AROUND

Guerrero Negro sits along the Carretera Transpeninsular (Highway 1) just south of the 28th parallel. That single highway provides the only access to and from the town, whether you're continuing on to Cataviña to the north or La Paz to the south. If you drive in from the north, you cross the state line into Baja California Sur as you enter Guerrero Negro. Officials at a police checkpoint at the edge of town will fumigate your vehicle's tires to protect the state from the entrance of pests that might have hitched a ride—one quick spray and you're on your way—and ask to see your passport, Mexican tourist card, and car-insurance papers. ■TIP➔ Don't head south from here without a full tank of gas; Pemex stations between Guerrero Negro and Loreto have been known to run out of gas on occasion. The small Aeropuerto Nacional de Guerrero Negro (GUB) sits 6 km (4 mi) north of town and offers reliable commercial flights provided by Aereoservicio Guerrero to Ensenada and Isla de Cedros.

Airlines Aereoservicio Guerrero (🕾 *615/157–0137* ⊕ *www.aereoservicioguerrero.com.mx*).

EXPLORING

Ⓒ A trip to the nearby **Isla de Cedros,** approximately 72 km (43 mi) north-
★ west of Guerrero Negro, will take you to an even more isolated community with even fewer obvious attractions for visitors. In fact, many travel agents and tour guides in Guerrero Negro have never even ventured to Isla de Cedros themselves. They say it's an island that is only of interest to the Exportadora de Sal workers who are stationed there. Adventure travelers enjoy the mountains of this desert island, taking in the local fauna—including sea lions—and spending time on the beach. There are a few guesthouses on the island, where rooms go for $10 to $15 a night, but note that electricity and hot water on the island are inconsistent, and at times you might go without both. Planes with **Aereoservicio Guerrero** (🕾 *615/157–0137)* fly to the small airstrip here (CDI) from Guerrero Negro every Monday, Wednesday, Friday, and Saturday. A taxi ride from town costs about $5, and the flight itself is $55, which is paid at the time of boarding. Note that these flights are not always on time. It is best to arrive early to make sure that the plane doesn't leave without you, but also be prepared for the plane to arrive a bit late.

Gray-whale-watching is hands down the principal reason to visit Guerrero Negro. Distinct among other families of marine mammals, gray whales flock to the shallow waters of Baja's lagoons for mating and calving. During **whale-watching season** (December through April), individual sightings are common as far north as Ensenada. Still, nothing rivals the experience of whale-watching from a panga (small, motorized skiff) on Scammon's Lagoon, where tourists can observe the friendly, even ostentatious, giants up close and in great numbers.

8

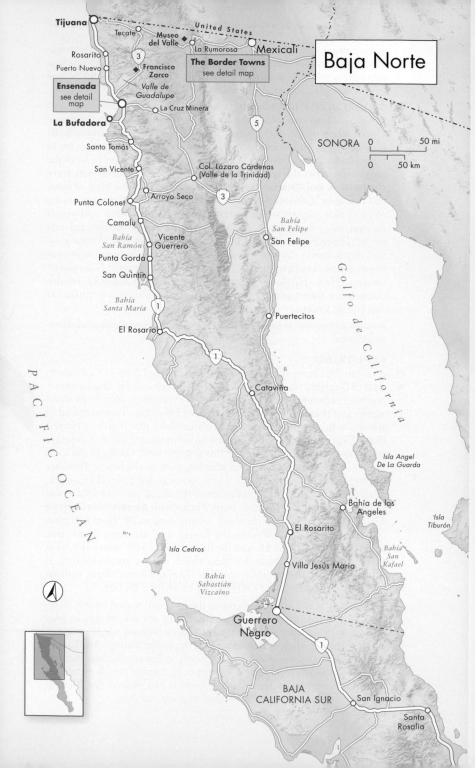

Baja Norte

United States

Tijuana

Tecate
Museo
del Valle
La Rumorosa
Mexicali

Rosarito
Puerto Nuevo

Francisco
Zarco
The Border Towns
see detail map

Ensenada
see detail
map

Valle de
Guadalupe

La Cruz Minera

SONORA

La Bufadora

5

0   50 mi

0   50 km

Santo Tomás

San Vicente

Col. Lázaro Cárdenas
(Valle de la Trinidad)

Arroyo Seco

Punta Colonet

3

Bahía
San Felipe

Camalu

San Felipe

Bahía
San Ramón

Vicente
Guerrero

Punta Gorda

San Quintín

Bahía
Santa María

1

Puertecitos

Golfo de California

El Rosario

1

Cataviña

Isla Angel
De La Guarda

PACIFIC OCEAN

Bahía de los
Ángeles

Isla
Tiburón

Isla Cedros

El Rosarito

Bahía
San
Rafael

Villa Jesús Maria

Bahía
Sabastián
Vizcaíno

Guerrero
Negro

BAJA
CALIFORNIA SUR

1

San Ignacio

Santa
Rosalía

Exportadora de Sal (✉ *Blvd. Zapata s/n* ☎ *615/157–5100* ⊕ *www.essa. com.mx*) tours, which can be surprisingly interesting, offer a good way to spend a couple of free hours while you are not whale-watching. Tours should be arranged at least two days in advance and are in Spanish only. Tour guides, Exportadora employees, give you a guided tour of the salt production facilities and explain the processes to you from the seat of your car. Also, there are no established fees for the tour, but guides ask for around $20. The scale of the plant is impressive. First, you will be taken through huge "cups" of salt, large pool-like areas, where salt is cultivated over the course of a few months. The water in these cups is evaporated, and the salt is then harvested, cleaned, and stored. Although the tour is only about an hour and a half, it may have you remembering it for years, every time that you reach for the salt shaker.

A short drive out to the lagoons at sunset affords travelers one of the most impressive views in the area. The *barchan,* or arc-shape, **sand dunes** look out upon the biologically diverse and incomparably beautiful Scammon's Lagoon (known locally as the Laguna del Ojo de Liebre, or "Eye of the Jackrabbit Lagoon"). Heading north on Highway 1, take a left at the first dirt road after the agricultural inspection station and follow it straight down to the water.

WHERE TO EAT AND STAY

¢ ✕ **Don Gus.** Ask locals where to have a good meal and they'll likely point

MEXICAN you in the direction of this simple restaurant. Although the atmosphere could be more inviting—the place is decorated with fabric plants and plastic tables—the great service makes you feel right at home. The food is delicious and the portions are generous. Try the garlic soup (the serving size is enough for two) and the delicious, buttery shrimp fried in garlic served alongside flavorful rice and vegetables. Don Gus also rents out 10 simple rooms with cable TV and HBO. ✉ *Blvd. Zapata s/n* ☎ *615/159–1115 or 615/257–1611* ▭ *No credit cards.*

$ ✕ **Mario's.** This Mexican-style restaurant under a huge palapa offers

MEXICAN simple food in a simple atmosphere. Tables and chairs are made of plastic and beneath your feet is a plain dirt floor. The service is as laid-back as the atmosphere. If the restaurant is full and you order anything more elaborate than a beer, expect a decent wait. Mario's also offers three-hour whale-watching tours, leaving at 8 AM and at 11 AM daily during whale season. These tours don't fill up as fast as others in town, and they are a great option if you didn't reserve in advance elsewhere for your tour. ✉ *Hwy. 1, Km 217.3* ☎ *615/157–1940* ▭ *No credit cards.*

$ ⊟ **Desert Inn.** Despite uninspiring views and the inconvenient distance from town (about five minutes by car), the Desert Inn is still the most comfortable place to stay in or around Guerrero Negro. Situated on a drab strip of desert near a military base, the hotel has 28 rooms—which are quiet and pleasant—and excellent service. Consider it a place to rest up before your whale-watching expeditions. Las Cazuelas Restaurant serves breakfasts, lunches, and dinners that are well above the local standard. Your best bet is to stick with Mexican classics though—the chef's interpretation of Italian isn't very convincing. The entire hotel chain recently changed ownership and the rooms here are being completely renovated. They promise to be large and cool rooms, and open on to a

8

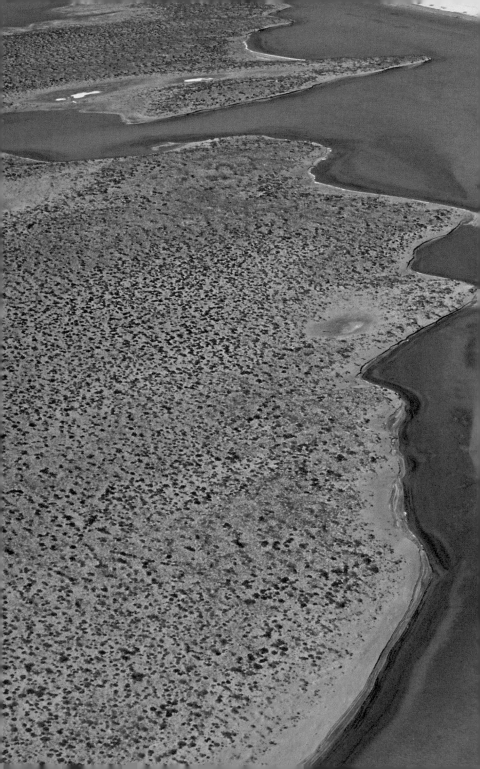

charming interior patio. **Pros:** satellite television; large bathrooms; great staff. **Cons:** ugly courtyard; drab surroundings; can't walk to town. ✉ *Parallelo 28, Guerrero Negro* ☎ *619/422–0084, 800/542–3283 in U.S.* ⊕ *www.desertinns. com* ⬅ *28 rooms* ⬠ *In-room: No phone. In hotel: Restaurant, room service, bar, laundry service, parking (free), some pets allowed* ⊟ *AE, D, MC, V* ⍾ *EP.*

¢–$ ⬚ **Hotel Los Caracoles.** Conveniently located within walking distance of all the town's supermarkets, souvenir shops, and restaurants, this hotel, decorated in several shades of orange, is easy to spot, because seashells are the motif that runs throughout this comfortable little place. Like an old-style motel, many of the simple rooms face the park-

WHAT TIME IS IT AGAIN?

The Baja Peninsula bends slightly eastward as it runs north to south. Consequently, northern Baja California and Baja California Sur are on different time zones, Pacific Standard Time and Mountain Standard Time, respectively. When you leave Guerrero Negro heading north, you cross the 28th parallel and the state boundary. Remember to set your watch back one hour. Though Isla de Cedros belongs to Baja California Sur, it lies far enough west that it observes Pacific time. Like most of the rest of Mexico, both states switch to Daylight Saving Time.

ing lot, but they are modern, clean, and very affordable, which makes up for the lack of views. The lobby has a small gift shop with local art and computers with Internet access, and the staff is very helpful and friendly. The Casa Caracoles, a comfortable three-bedroom house for rent, is another option for large parties. **Pros:** cheery and clean; good prices; convenient location. **Cons:** no restaurant; thin walls. ✉ *Calz. de la República s/n* ☎ *615/157–1088* ⊕ *www.hotelloscaracoles.com. mx* ⬅ *13 rooms, 6 cabanas* ⬠ *In-room: refrigerator (some), Wi-Fi. In hotel: Internet terminal, parking (free)* ⊟ *MC, V* ⍾ *EP.*

¢ ⬚ **Malarrimo Motel.** If you're looking for one-stop shopping, the staff at
★ Malarrimo can wine and dine you, and arrange your whale-watching expedition. The most comfortable place to stay along Boulevard Zapata, the main drag in Guerrero Negro, this motel has 18 rooms and 6 "Mex" rooms sometimes called cabañas though they're not freestanding. The Mex rooms are a little larger, so they tend to stay cooler when the weather is warm, while the smaller rooms are better in winter. Rooms are spartan, although the hotel's miniature courtyard manages to enliven the ambience a bit. The hotel staff suggests making reservations around six months in advance if you are planning on visiting during whale-watching season. This is the largest, best-established hotel in the area, so rooms go quickly. The restaurant and bar, widely considered the best in town, are a great place to enjoy well-prepared seafood and delicious meats. The walls are covered in bric-a-brac including newspaper articles about the area, and found items like whale bones; buoys hang from the ceilings. The gift shop next door, Casa El Viejo Cactus, offers arts and crafts and a small selection of books. **Pros:** chilaquiles; fresh oysters; convenient tour operator. **Cons:** slow wait service; plain hotel rooms. ✉ *Blvd. Zapata s/n 23940* ☎ *615/157–0250* ⊕ *www.*

malarrimo.com ⏎*10 rooms, 6 Mex rooms* ♿*In room: No phone, Wi-Fi. In hotel: Restaurant, parking (free)* ⊟*AE, MC, V* ⏏⌾*EP.*

SHOPPING

Mar y Mar. Outside of the gift shops at Los Caracoles and Malarrimo hotels, even touristy trinkets are hard to come by in this bare-bones town. The handicrafts at Mar y Mar, all handmade out of salt crystals from the area, are arguably the only souvenirs you can find that are truly unique to the region. Unfortunately, these sculptures can be rather pricey for the quirky novelties they really are. But if you're committed to bringing a piece of your trip home with you, this might be your only option. ⊠ *Calz. de la República s/n, 3 blocks from main road* ☎ *615/157–1371.*

SPORTS AND THE OUTDOORS

Malarrimo Eco-Tours (⊠ *Blvd. Zapata s/n* ☎ *615/157–0100* ⊕ *www.malarrimo.com* ⊟ *AE, MC, V*) offers the original whale-watching tour in Guerrero Negro. You can arrange for a tour at the Malarrimo Restaurant, but to make sure that you can get a spot, reserve in advance, especially if you want to go out on a weekend. (A 50% deposit is necessary to make the reservation.) Excursions run late December through early April. Owner Luis Enrique Achoy and his crew offer two tours daily. One leaves at 8 AM and the other at 11 AM. Both tours last about four hours and are a reasonable $49 per person. If the weather won't allow you to see the whales, Malarrimo will reschedule.

> ## SCAMMON'S TERRIBLE LEGACY
>
> Guerrero Negro is Spanish for "black warrior." The town takes its name from an American whaling ship by that name sunk in the area in the 1850s. The ship's captain, Charles Melville Scammon, discovered an entrance into the Laguna Ojo de Liebre. For this reason, the lagoon is also known as Scammon's Lagoon. Whaling here became so popular that Scammon and other whalers nearly wiped out the gray whale population entirely.

8

BAJA NORTE: BEACH TOWNS

The beaches of the northern peninsula are the stuff of dreams: fine sand, water that's refreshing but not too cold, excellent sunshine and, for the surfer, some of the west coast's top waves. Part of that dream can evaporate, however, when you venture into the beach towns themselves.

More than a few of the stops along Highway 1 have been run down by years of American spring-breakers looking for a good time, and then leaving that good time's remnants behind. Ensenada is an exception: a charming fisherman's enclave, something-larger-than-a-village with a village's sleepy feel, complete with beachside trinket stores and fish taco stands (the town's beaches, conversely, are nothing special at all). Along this part of the peninsula, towns are close together, and the essentials (gas, food, lodging) are never far.

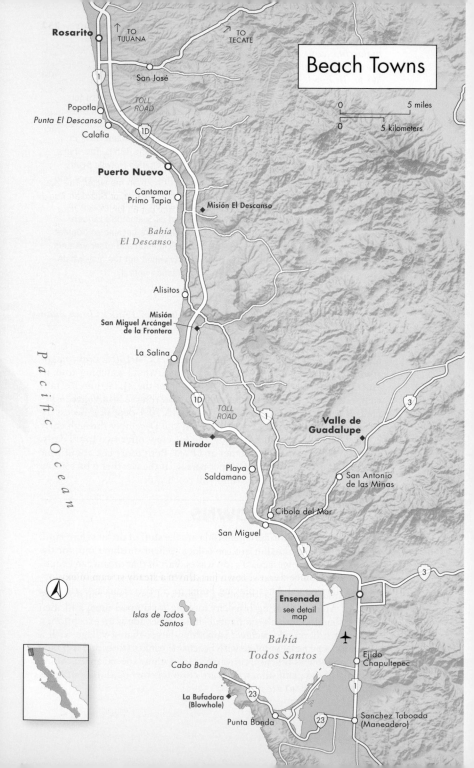

Beach Towns

Rosarito

TO TIJUANA

TO TECATE

San José

Popotla

Punta El Descanso

Calafia

TOLL ROAD

1D

Puerto Nuevo

Cantamar

Primo Tapia

◆ Misión El Descanso

Bahía El Descanso

Alisitos

Misión San Miguel Arcángel de la Frontera ◆

La Salina

1D

TOLL ROAD

1

Valle de Guadalupe ◆

El Mirador ◆

Playa Saldamano

San Antonio de las Minas

Cibola del Mar

San Miguel

1

3

Pacific Ocean

3

Islas de Todos Santos

Ensenada see detail map

Bahía Todos Santos

Ejido Chapultepec

Cabo Banda

La Bufadora ◆ (Blowhole)

23

Punta Banda

23

Sanchez Taboada (Maneadero)

1

0   5 miles

0   5 kilometers

CLOSE UP

Detour to the Bahía de los Angeles

It would be a farce to claim that Bahía de los Angeles is representative of Baja culture; the vast majority of its 600 residents work in the local tourism industry. And yet, it's not a "touristy" place—at least not in the dirty sense of the word. For decades, outdoorsman have come to Bahía de los Angeles for fishing, boating, and diving in the warm and placid bay, which owes its tranquillity to the islands that separate it from the Sea of Cortez. And although there are now as many hotels as campgrounds in the region, Bahía de los Angeles continues to attract the adventurous set, giving the entire town a cool and distinct vibe, even if it's not Mexican vibe, per se.

■TIP→ Traveling north on the Carretera Transpeninsular from Guererro Negro, the turnoff for the Bay of Los Angeles (Parador Punta Prieta) is about 3 km (2 mi) after Punta Prieta proper, around Km 480. This side highway is about 64 km (40 mi) long and dead-ends at the town.

The islands of the Bay of Los Angeles provide some of the best opportunities in Baja for observing seabirds and marine life. Boat rentals are available in town. Many of the islands are also accessible by kayak, though most such trips require careful planning and experience on the water. The Isla Angel de la Guarda, or Guardian Angel Island, is about 68 km (42 mi) long, and is credited with maintaining the placidity of the Bay of Los Angeles. At 19 km (12 mi) from shore, Isla Angel de la Guarda seems like an easy trip, but the safest anchorages can take a full day to reach.

Between August and November, experience the whale sharks in the Bay of Los Angeles which come to this coastal region to feed (primarily on plankton). Snorkelers have the unique opportunity to swim alongside and even touch these gentle behemoths, the largest species of fish on the planet. Guided snorkeling trips in the Bay of Los Angeles may well also yield sea lion and sea turtle sightings; all this in a body of water that can feel like a heated swimming pool.

8

ENSENADA

190 km (120 mi) north of San Quintín.

In 1542 Juan Rodríguez Cabrillo first discovered the seaport that Sebastián Vizcaíno named Ensenada-Bahía de Todos Santos (All Saints' Bay) in 1602. Since then the town has drawn a steady stream of explorers and developers. After playing home to ranchers and gold miners, the harbor gradually grew into a major port for shipping agricultural goods, and today Baja's third-largest city (population 369,000) is one of Mexico's largest sea and fishing ports.

There are no beaches in Ensenada proper, but sandy stretches north and south of town are satisfactory for swimming, sunning, surfing, and camping. Estero Beach is long and clean, with mild waves; the Estero Beach Resort takes up much of the oceanfront, but the beach is public. Surfers populate the strands off Highway 1 north and south of Ensenada, particularly San Miguel, Tres Marías, and Salsipuedes, while scuba divers prefer Punta Banda, by La Bufadora. Lifeguards are rare, so be cautious. The tourist office in Ensenada has a map that shows safe diving and surfing beaches.

Both the waterfront and the main downtown street are pleasant places to stroll. If you're driving, be sure to take the Centro exit from the highway, since it bypasses the commercial port area.

GETTING HERE AND AROUND

If you're flying into Tijuana, from Aeropuerto Alberado Rodriguez (TIJ) you can find buses that also serve Rosarito and Ensenada. Or you can hop on a bus at Tijuana Camionera de la Línea station, just inside the border, with service to Rosarito and Ensenada along with city buses to downtown. To head south from Tijuana by car, follow the signs for Ensenada Cuota, the toll road (i.e., Carretera Transpeninsular or Highway 1) along the coast. Tollbooths accept U.S. and Mexican currency; there are three tolls of about $2.50 each between Tijuana and Ensenada. Restrooms are available near toll stations. Ensenada is an hour south of Tijuana on this road. The alternative free road—Carretera 1D or Ensenada Libre—is curvy and not as well maintained. (Entry to it is on a side street in a congested area of downtown Tijuana.)

Highway 1 continues south of Ensenada to Guerrero Negro, at the border between Baja Norte and Baja Sur, and on to Baja's southernmost resorts; there are no tolls past Ensenada. Highway 1 is fairly well maintained and signposted.

Taxis are a reliable means of getting around Ensenada, and you can flag them down on the street.

ESSENTIALS

Internet Equinoxio Internet Café (✉ *Cárdenas 26722800* ☎ *646/174–0455*).

Medical Assistance Emergencies (☎ *Dial 066*) . **Tourist Information and Assistance Hotline** (☎ *Dial 078*).

Visitor and Tour Info Ensenada Tourist Information Office (✉ *Lázaro Cárdenas 609, Centro* ☎ *01800/025–3991 toll-free in Mexico, 800/310–9687* ⊕ *www.enjoyensenada.com*).

EXPLORING

❶ **Las Bodegas de Santo Tomás.** One of Baja's oldest wine producers gives tours and tastings at its downtown winery and bottling plant. Take a moment to see the satirical paintings in the main building, depicting the early days of the winery. Santo Tomás's best wines are the Alisio chardonnay, the cabernet, and the Sirocco syrah; avoid the overpriced Unico. The restaurant, La Embotelladora Vieja, is a marvel of modern design, and pairs dishes with the winery's picks. The winery also operates La Esquina de Bodegas, a café, shop, and gallery in a bright-blue building across the avenue. ■TIP→ The Santo Tomás Vineyards can be found on the eastern side of Highway 1 about 50 km (31 mi) south of Ensenada, fairly near the ruins of the Misión Santo Tomás de Aquino, which was founded by Dominican priests in 1791: only a few pieces of adobe remain of the old church. ✉ *Av. Miramar 666, Centro* ☎ *646/174–0836 or 646/174–0829* ⊕ *www.santo-tomas.com* ▤ *$5–$10, depending on wines* ☼ *Tours, tastings daily 9–5; it's best to call first.*

2 Mercado de Mariscos. At the northernmost point of Boulevard Costero,
★ the main street along the waterfront, is an indoor-outdoor fish market
where row after row of counters display piles of shrimp, tuna, dorado,
and other fish caught off Baja's coasts. Outside, stands sell grilled or
smoked fish, seafood cocktails, and fish tacos. The smoked salmon
is excellent. You can pick up a few souvenirs, eat well for very little
money, and take some great photographs. The original fish taco stands
line the dirt path to the fish market; around lunchtime, cooks will stand
outside to vie for your attention (and your pesos). If your stomach is
delicate, try the fish tacos at the cleaner, quieter Plaza de Mariscos in
the shadow of the giant beige Plaza de Marina that blocks the view of
the traditional fish market from the street.

3 Paseo Calle Primera. The renamed Avenida López Mateos is the center
of Ensenada's traditional tourist zone. High-rise hotels, souvenir shops,
restaurants, and bars line the avenue for eight blocks, from its beginning
at the foot of the Chapultepec Hills to the dry channel of the Arroyo
de Ensenada. The avenue also has cafés, American-style coffee shops,
and most of the town's souvenir stores.

4 Riviera del Pacífico. Officially called the Centro Social, Cívico y Cultural
de Ensenada, the Riviera is a rambling, white, hacienda-style mansion
built in the 1920s. An enormous gambling palace, hotel, restaurant,

and bar, the glamorous Riviera was frequented by wealthy U.S. citizens and Mexicans, particularly during Prohibition. You can tour some of the elegant ballrooms and halls, which occasionally host art shows and civic events. Many of the rooms are locked; check at the main office to see if someone is available to show you around. ⊠ *Blvd. Costero at Av. Riviera, Centro* ☎ *646/177–0594* 🏛 *Building and gardens free; museum entry $1* ⊙ *Mon.–Sat. 9–5, Sun. 10–5.*

WHERE TO EAT

$$$
FRENCH

✗ **El Rey Sol.** From its chateaubriand *bouquetière* (garnished with a bouquet of vegetables) to the savory chicken chipotle cooked with brandy, port wine, and cream, this French restaurant, family owned since 1947, sets a high standard. Louis XIV–style furnishings and an attentive staff make it both comfortable and elegant. The sidewalk tables are a perfect place to dine and people-watch. The small café in the front sells pastries that are made on the premises. ⊠ *Av. López Mateos 1000, Centro* ☎ *646/178–2351* 🗖 *AE, MC, V.*

¢–$
MEXICAN
Fodor's Choice
★

✗ **Hacienda Del Charro.** Hungry patrons hover over platters of chiles rellenos, enchiladas, and fresh chips and guacamole at heavy wooden picnic tables. Plump chickens slowly turn over a wood-fueled fire by the front window, and the aroma of simmering beans fills the air. ⊠ *Av. López Mateos 454, Centro* ☎ *646/178–2351* 🗖 *No credit cards.*

$–$$$
SEAFOOD

✗ **Manzanilla.** Two of the most exciting chef-owners in Baja Norte, Benito Molina and Solange Muris, are taking a truly modern approach to Mexican cuisine at Manzanilla, integrating the freshest catches from the local waters—oysters, mussels, and clams, for instance—and integrating ingredients like ginger, saffron, smoked tomato marmalade, and *huitlacoche* (corn fungus). The atmosphere is simple and pleasant, if a bit trendy. ⊠ *Teniente Azueta 139 Centro* ☎ *646/175–7073* ⊕ *www. rmanzanilla.com* 🗖 *AE, DC, MC, V* ⊙ *Closed Sun.*

$–$$$
ASIAN

✗ **Ophelia.** For a bit of Asian flair along Carretera 1, check out Ophelia, opened by Rosindo Ramos and already a favorite among the Ensenada foodie crowd. Shiitake mushrooms, pork, and ginger glazes make somewhat unexpected appearances for this seaside town, but at the root of all that's good about Ophelia are a handful of tried, trusted flavors and ingredients: fresh fish, tomatoes, chilies, and cilantro. ⊠ *Carretera Tijuana–Ensenada, Km 103* ☎ *646/175–8365* 🗖 *MC, V* ⊙ *Closed Mon.*

$$–$$$
STEAKHOUSE
★

✗ **Sano's.** This elegant restaurant, along the highway heading out from Ensenada toward Tijuana, is the latest extension of the Hussong empire. It's also the best steak house in Baja California. The Sonora beef is juicy, flavorful, and tender, cooked just as beautifully rare (or done) as you order it, and it can be enjoyed on a wonderful outdoor patio. Throw in impeccable service and a wine list that rivals the best in the country, and you can justify the sky-high prices. ⊠ *Carretera Tijuana–Ensenada, Km 108, just after Playitas Club del Mar if you're heading south to Ensenada* ☎ *646/174–4061* ⊕ *www.sanosrestaurant.com* 🗖 *AE, DC, MC, V.*

WHERE TO STAY

$$ ☺ **Estero Beach Resort.** Families love this long-standing resort on Ensenada's top beach. The best rooms (some with kitchenettes) are by the sand. Be sure to check out the outstanding collection of folk art and artifacts in the resort's small museum. Midweek winter rates are a real bargain, and there are other frequent specials on the Web site. There's also an on-site RV park; its 38 sites have hookups for water, sewer, and electricity. **Pros:** wonderful breakfasts; right on the beach. **Cons:** rooms by parking lot aren't great; needs some updating. ✉ *Carretera Tijuana–Ensenada, 10 km (6 mi) south of Ensenada, Estero Beach* ☎ *646/176–6235* ⊕ *www.hotelesterobeach.com* ⟿ *94 rooms, 2 suites* ⚏ *In-room: Kitchen (some). In-hotel: Restaurant, bar, tennis courts, pool* ▭ *MC, V.*

$$$ ☺ **Hotel Coral & Marina.** This all-suites resort is enormous. It has a spa, tennis courts, a water-sports center, and a marina with slips for 350 boats and customs-clearing facilities. All guest quarters have refrigerators and coffeemakers. Suites in the two eight-story towers are done in burgundy and dark green; most have waterfront balconies, seating areas, and international phone service. **Pros:** affordable; spacious rooms. **Cons:** pool can get noisy with kids; can feel large and impersonal. ✉ *Carretera Tijuana-Ensenada, Km 103, Zona Playitas* ☎ *646/175–0000 or 800/862–9020* ⊕ *www.hotelcoral.com* ⟿ *147 suites* ⚏ *In-room: Refrigerator. In-hotel: Restaurant, room service, bar, tennis courts, pools, gym, spa, laundry service* ▭ *MC, V.*

$$$ ☺ **Las Rosas Hotel & Spa.** All rooms in this intimate hotel north of Ensenada face the ocean and pool; some have fireplaces and hot tubs, **Fodor'sChoice** and even the least expensive are lovely. The atrium lobby has marble ★ floors, mint-green-and-pink couches that look out at the sea, and a glass ceiling that glows at night. **Pros:** boutique; laid-back; great ocean views from hot tub. **Cons:** no restaurants within walking distance. ✉ *Carretera Tijuana-Ensenada, just north of Ensenada, Zona Playitas* ☎ *646/174–4320 or 646/174–4360* ⊕ *www.lasrosas.com* ⟿ *48 rooms* ⚏ *In-hotel: Restaurant, bar, tennis courts, pool, gym, spa, laundry service* ▭ *MC, V.*

$ ☺ **Misión Santa Isabela.** If you prefer to stay in downtown Ensenada, the Misión Santa Isabela is a solid option. Gastón Flourie, a French archaeologist obsessed with (but unable to find) the lost mission of Saint Isabelle in Baja, did the next best thing: he built a hotel in mission style. All of the rooms—which are spotless—face a quiet interior courtyard and pool. **Pros:** interesting architecture; sunny pool. **Cons:** rooms are a little tired. ✉ *Blvd. Lázaro Cárdenas and Av. Costillo* ☎ *646/178–3616* ⟿ *57 rooms* ⚏ *In-hotel: Restaurant, pool* ▭ *MC, V.*

NIGHTLIFE

★ **Hussong's Cantina** (✉ *Av. Ruíz 113, Centro* ☎ *646/178–3210*) has been an Ensenada landmark since 1892, and has changed little since then. A security guard stands by the front door to handle the often-rowdy crowd—mostly local men. The floor is covered with sawdust, and the noise—is usually deafening, pierced by mariachi and ranchera musicians and the whoops and hollers of the pie-eyed. **Papas and Beer** (✉ *Av. Ruíz 102, Centro* ☎ *646/174–0145*) attracts a collegiate crowd.

8

Tourism helps to keep the local economy afloat in Ensenada.

SHOPPING

Most of the tourist shops hold court along Avenida López Mateos beside the hotels and restaurants. There are several two-story shopping arcades, some with empty spaces for rent. Dozens of curio shops line the street, all selling similar selections of pottery, serapes, and the tackier trinkets and T-shirts.

Bazar Casa Ramirez (⊠ *Av. López Mateos 496, Centro* ☎ *646/178–8209*) sells high-quality Talavera pottery and other ceramics, wrought-iron pieces, and papier-mâché figurines. Be sure to check out the displays upstairs.

★ The **Centro Artesenal de Ensenada** (⊠ *Blvd. Costero 1094–39, Centro* ☎ *No phone*) has a smattering of galleries and shops.

Fausto Polanco (⊠ *Av. López Mateos 1100, Centro* ☎ *646/174–0336*) features lovely handcrafted wood furniture and other home accessories.

La Esquina de Bodegas (⊠ *Av. Miramar at Calle 6, Centro* ☎ *646/178–3557*) is an innovative gallery, shop, and café in a century-old winery building.

Los Globos (⊠ *Calle 9, 3 blocks east of Av. Reforma, Centro* ☎ *No phone*) is a daily open-air swap meet. Vendors and shoppers are most abundant on weekends.

SPORTS AND THE OUTDOORS
SPORTFISHING

The best angling takes place from April through November, with bottom fishing the best in winter. Charter vessels and party boats are available from several outfitters along Avenida López Mateos and Boulevard

Costero and off the sportfishing pier. Mexican fishing licenses for the day or year are available at the tourist office or from charter companies.

Sergio's Sportfishing (✉ *Sportfishing Pier, Blvd. Costero at Av. Alvarado, Centro* ☎ *646/178–2185* ⊕ *www.sergios-sportfishing.com*), one of the best sportfishing companies in Ensenada, has charter and group boats as well as boat slips for rent. The fee for a day's fishing is $50 per person on a group boat, including the cost of a license.

WATER SPORTS

Estero Beach and Punta Banda (en route to La Bufadora, south of Ensenada) are both good kayaking areas, although facilities are limited. A limited selection of water-sports equipment is available at the Estero Beach Resort. Some of the best surf on the coast is found off Islas de Todos Santos, two islands about 19 km (12 mi) west of Ensenada. Only the boldest challenge the waves here, which can reach 30 feet in winter. Surfers must hire a boat to take them to the waves. For calmer waves that can still pack a punch (good for those who've got a grom—kiddie surfer—in tow) head to the beaches at San Miguel, Tres Marías, and Salsipuedes. **San Miguel Surf Shop** (✉ *Av. López Mateos at Av. Ruíz, Centro* ☎ *646/178–1007*) is the unofficial local surfing headquarters. Staff can guide you toward the best areas and to gear rental.

WHALE-WATCHING

Boats leave the Ensenada sportfishing pier for whale-watching trips from December through March. The gray whales migrating from the north to bays and lagoons in southern Baja pass through Todos Santos Bay, often close to shore. Binoculars and cameras with telephoto capabilities come in handy. The trips last about three hours. Vessels are available from several outfitters at the sportfishing pier. Expect to pay about $30 for a three-hour tour.

VALLE DE GUADALUPE

The Valle de Guadalupe, northeast of Ensenada on Carretera 3, is filled with vineyards, wineries, and rambling hacienda-style estates. Although Mexican wines are still relatively unknown in the United States, the industry is exploding in Mexico, and the Valle de Gaudalupe is responsible for some 90% of the country's production.

With a region that combines the right heat, soil, and a thin morning fog, some truly world-class boutique wineries have developed in the Valle de Guadalupe, most in the past decade. Several of these are open to the public; most require appointments. Several tour companies, including Bajarama (☎ *646/178–3252)*, leave from Ensenada on tours that include visits to wineries, a historical overview, transportation, and lunch. Better yet is visiting the wineries yourself by car, as they all cluster in a relatively small area. Also worth a look is winemaker Hugo D'Acosta's new school, which brings in some 100 young winemakers to use common facilities to make their own blends. The facilities are on the site of an old olive oil press (a few antique presses remain in the outlying buildings), and the grounds are augmented with artwork made from recycled wine bottles and other materials.

Continued on page 265

VIVA VINO

About an hour south of San Diego, just inland from Ensenada, lies a region that's everything Ensenada is not. The 14-mile-long Valle de Guadalupe is charming, serene, and urbane, and—you might find this hard to believe if you're a wine buff—is a robust producer of quality vino.

There'll be no watered-down tequila drunk here. Red grapes grown include Cabernet Sauvignon, Merlot, Tempranillo, and Syrah, while whites include Chardonnay, Sauvignon Blanc, and Viognier. Drive down and spend a day at the vineyards and wineries that line la Ruta del Vino, the road that stretches across the valley, or better yet (and to avoid talking to border guards when slightly intoxicated on your way back into the States), base yourself here. The inns and restaurants in the Valle de Guadalupe welcome guests with refined material comforts, which complement the region's natural desert-mountain beauty and lovely libations.

(top) Adobe Guadalupe, (bottom left) Grapes from the Guadalupe Valley, Ensenada, (bottom right) Adobe Guadalupe

WINERY-HOPPING

Some wineries along la Ruta del Vino are sizeable enterprises, while others are boutique affairs (⇨ reviews in Valle de Guadalupe section). Here are a few choice picks.

THE FULL-BODIED EXPERIENCE

Serious oenophiles should visit the midsize **Monte Xanic,** which, with a brand-new cellar, is a serious contender for Mexico's finest winery. Tastings are by appointment; don't miss the Gran Ricardo, a high-end Bordeaux-style blend. **L. A. Cetto** is even bigger than Monte Xanic, but it offers a well-orchestrated experience, with free tastings and tours daily 10–5. Look for celebrity winemaker Camillo Magoni's wonderful Nebbiolo. A spectacular terrazza overlooks Cetto's own bullring and a sweeping expanse of wine country.

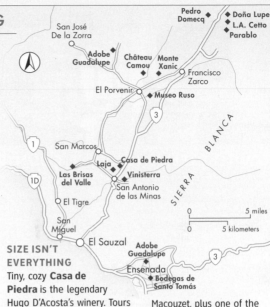

SIZE ISN'T EVERYTHING

Tiny, cozy **Casa de Piedra** is the legendary Hugo D'Acosta's winery. Tours and tastings of D'Acosta's high-end wines are by reservation only. Call ahead to visit the even smaller, but equally impressive, **Vinisterra,** where eccentric Swiss winemaker Christoph Gärtner turns out a small-production line of showstoppers called

Macouzet, plus one of the only wines in the world made from mission grapes; these grapes come from vines descended from those planted by the Spanish in the 1500s for ceremonial services.

BACK TO THE BEGINNING

The imbibing of fermented fruit dates from the Stone Age (or Neolithic period; 8,500–4,000 BC), but the production of wine in the Americas is comparatively adolescent. Mexico actually has the New World's oldest wine industry, dating from 1574, when conquistadors and priests set off north from Zacatecas in search of gold; when none turned up, they decided to grow grapes instead. In 1597, they founded the Hacienda de San Lorenzo,

the first winery in the Americas, in the modern-day state of Coahuila. By the late 1600s, Mexican wine production was so prolific, the Spaniards shut it down so it wouldn't compete with Spanish wine—sending Mexico's wine industry into a three-century hibernation from which it's just beginning to awaken. Now, most Mexican wine producers have moved to the Valle de Guadalupe a cooler, more favorable climate for vineyards.

L.A. Cetto sparkling wines, Valle de Guadalupe

HOW TO EXPERIENCE WINE COUNTRY

LIVE THE VALLEY If you fancy tranquility and a perfectly starry sky, and don't mind an early bedtime, you're best off staying at one of the intimate, romantic haciendas in the middle of the valley itself, where you'll also benefit from your hosts' knowledge of the area. One of the most up-and-coming small wineries in Baja, **Adobe Guadalupe** is also a gracious bed-and-breakfast run by Don and Tru Miller, an American-Dutch couple. They're delightful and passionate hosts—Tru might take you to neighboring wineries on horseback—and Don's wines, made in conjunction with Hugo d'Acosta, are excellent. **La Villa del Valle**, a newer American-run hotel-hacienda, is larger but just as nice, with spectacular countryside views and amenities like massage, a hot tub, and a restaurant with its own market garden.

DO IT BY DAY If you can't live without city buzz and nightlife, Ensenada has tons of it, and staying here is another viable option. In downtown Ensenada you can also visit **Bodegas de Santo Tomás**, one of Baja's oldest wineries. The city is less than an hour's drive to most of the wineries. It's also possible to visit the valley on a long day trip from Tijuana or San Diego.

WINOS UNITE You can expect clear, sunny days in the valley for virtually the whole year, although evening temperatures dip into the 40s F (single digits Celsius) from December through March. A good time to visit is during the first two weeks of August, when the region comes alive for the **Fiestas de la Vendimia** (646/178–3136, www.fiestasdelavendimia.com), a harvest festival that's full of special wine tastings, dinners, and parties—both at the wineries and in Ensenada proper.

(pictured top and bottom) Adobe Guadalupe

Detour to La Bufadora

Legend has it that **La Bufadora** (✉ *Carretera 23, 31 km [19 mi] south of Ensenada, Punta Banda*), an impressive tidal blowhole (*la bufadora* means the buffalo snort) in the coastal cliffs at Punta Banda, was created by a whale or sea serpent trapped in an undersea cave; both these stories, and the less romantic scientific facts, are posted on a roadside plaque.

The road to La Bufadora along Punta Banda—an isolated, mountainous point that juts into the sea—is lined with olive, craft, and tamale stands; the drive gives you a sampling of

Baja's wilderness. If you're in need of some cooling off, turn off the highway at the sign for La Jolla Beach Camp. The camp charges a small admission fee for day use of the beachside facilities, but it's a great place to do a few "laps" of lazy freestyle or breaststroke at La Jolla Beach.

At La Bufadora, expect a small fee to park, and then a half-mile walk past T-shirt hawkers and souvenir stands to the water hole itself. A public bus runs from the downtown Ensenada station to Maneadero, from which you can catch a minibus labeled Punta Banda that goes to La Bufadora.

Several changes are in store, which may alter the isolation of the valley, and in five years the place may have a different, more upscale, feel. The Monte Xanic winery has announced an agreement with the international Banyan tree chain to build a 42-room resort and spa on its property overlooking the vineyards, and the Baja state government has already begun paving some of the region's side roads. It seems that it's not only Mexican wine that's being discovered, but the potential of Guadalupe as a "wine destination," along with the mixed blessings that accompany such discovery.

GETTING HERE AND AROUND

If you're not on a tour, a private car (or hired taxi) is essential for touring the wine country. West of the town of Francisco Zarco (also called Guadalupe), the road is paved past Monte Xanic and the small village of Porvenir; after that, it is mainly gravel. The turnoffs for the major wineries are well marked; if you're looking for a smaller destination, you may end up doing a few loops or asking a friendly bystander. The general area is not too spread out; still, you will need to drive from one winery to the other. You can arrange a half- or full-day tour with many of the taxi drivers in Ensenada, and some drivers in Tecate may also be willing to take you.

ESSENTIALS

Banks are few and far between in this area, so get cash before arriving if you think you'll need it. There is a Pemex station in the town of Francisco Zarco, at the turnoff from Highway 3.

EXPLORING

Fodor's Choice One of the most up-and-coming small wineries in Baja, **Adobe Guada-**
★ **lupe** (✉ *Off Carretera Tecate–Ensenada, turn at sign and drive 6 km [4 mi], Guadalupe* ☎ *646/155–2094, 949/733–2744 in U.S.* ⊕ *www.*

8

adobeguadalupe.com) is making an array of fascinating high-end blends named after angels. Don't miss the Kerubiel, which is a blockbuster blend; the Serafiel, Gabriel, and Miguel are also excellent. Don and his wife Tru also run a bed-and-breakfast, and Tru's beautiful horses are available for riding tours of up to three days.

Casa de Piedra (⊠ *Carretera Tecate–Ensenada, Km 93.5, San Antonio de las Minas* ☎ *646/155–3097 or 646/155–5267* ⊕ *www.vinoscasadepiedra.com*) is the brainchild of Hugo D'Acosta, who also consults for Adobe Guadalupe. The space is interesting and modern, designed by the winemaker's architect brother.

One of the larger and less personal wineries is **Domecq** (⊠ *Carretera Tecate–Ensenada, Km 73.5* ☎ *646/165–2264 or 646/155–2254* ⊕ *www.vinosdomecq.com.mx*), which offers free wine tastings and tours weekdays 10–4 and Saturday 10–3. The operation is one of the most corporate of the Baja wineries—but it's estranged from the Allied Domecq worldwide liquor empire; don't expect to taste its top wines.

Near L.A. Cetto, **Dona Lupe's** (⊠ *Off Carretera 3, turn left and follow road past L.A. Cetto to small yellow building*) boutique sells berry jams, chili marmalades, olive spreads, cheeses, and other local delicacies.

L.A. Cetto (⊠ *Carretera Tecate–Ensenada, Km 73.5* ☎ *646/155–2179* ⊕ *www.cettowines.com*) is another giant, but this is the closest thing to a California wine country experience south of the border. When tasting or buying, avoid the cheaper wines, and go straight for the premiums. There are free wine tastings and tours daily 10–5.

Liceaga (⊠ *Carretera Tecate–Ensenada, Km 93, San Antonio de las Minas* ☎ *646/178–2922* ⊕ *www.vinosliceaga.com*) just across the street from Casa de Piedra, produces a variety of merlot- and cabernet-heavy blends, as well as a new line of grappa. The tasting room is open most days until 5 PM.

★ Call ahead if you want to get into **Monte Xanic** (⊠ *Carretera 3, Km 70* ☎ *646/174–6155 or 646/155–2080* ⊕ *www.montexanic.com.mx*). Most impressive is their consistency, right down to the cheapest table wines. Tastings and tours are available by appointment, and be sure to check out the impressively styled cellar.

Paralelo (⊠ *Carretera Tecate–Ensenada, Km 73.5* ☎ *646/156–5268*) is one of the valley's most recent additions, built by the Hugo d'Acosta clan as "parallel" to Casa de Piedra. Turn off Highway 3 at L.A. Cetto and follow the signs for Paralelo. The winery makes two red blends—the excellent and balanced Arenal and the heavier, mineraly Colina—as well as a sauvignon blanc. A reservation is necessary (ask for Gloria in the office), and there are only faint plans for a formal tasting room. For now, tastings remain a casual and friendly affair, conducted around a big table with the Chilean winemaker Daniel, but a visit to Paralelo offers a hint of a Valle de Guadulupe of a decade pas

★ Within **Vinisterra** (⊠ *Carretera Tecate–Ensenada, Km 94.5, San Antonio de las Minas* ☎ *646/178–3350 or 646/178–3310* ⊕ *www.vinisterra.com*), expect to find Tempranillo and cabernet-merlot blends which are big and juicy. Call well ahead.

WHERE TO EAT AND STAY

$$$$

MEXICAN

Fodor'sChoice

★

✕ **Laja.** One sign that the Valle de Guadalupe has its sights on Napa is this extraordinary restaurant set inside a cozy little house. Celebrity chef Jair Téllez's ambitious prix-fixe menus (there are four-course and seven-course versions) change frequently, but may include cucumber gazpacho, yellowtail tartare, and panna cotta with cold mango soup, all served with excellent regional wines. Polished woods and windows overlooking the valley make the dining room and outdoor plaza as sleek as the menu. A meal here is well worth the drive. ⊠ *Carretera 3, Km 83* ☎ *646/155–2556* ⊕ *www.lajamexico.com* ⤸ *Reservations essential* ⊟ *MC, V* ☉ *Closed Sun.–Tues. and late Nov.–early Jan. No dinner Wed. Last orders taken at 8:30* PM *Thurs.–Sat.*

¢–$$

MEXICAN

✕ **Los Naranjos.** This pleasant restaurant may be overshadowed by the renowned Laja a few steps away, but it holds to more regular hours. Well respected for its homemade salsas and its *codorniz Guadalupe* (quail in red wine sauce), it has pleasant seating both indoors and out on a patio in a little orange grove. Prices are reasonable, too. ⊠ *Carretera 3, Km 82.5* ☎ *646/155–2522* ⊟ *No credit cards.*

$$$

Fodor'sChoice

★

🛏 **Adobe Guadalupe.** Brick archways, white-stucco walls, and fountains set a tone of endless pleasure and relaxation at Don and Tru Miller's magnificent country inn surrounded by vineyards. Don has won several awards for his interestingly blended wines, helping to bring outside attention to the valley. The inn's talented chefs do an admirable dinner in the romantic dining room, generously paired with Adobe Guadalupe wines, for $50 per person. Tru's stable of beautiful horses—she'll take you around the valley and to nearby wineries—is yet another draw. **Pros:** lovely setting; engaging owners; delicious huevos rancheros breakfasts. **Cons:** a drive inland from the coast. ⊠ *Off Carretera 3 through Guadalupe village, 6 km (4 mi) along same road, right turn at small town of Porvenir, Guadalupe* ☎ *646/155–2094, 949/733–2744 in U.S.* ⊕ *www.adobeguadalupe.com* ⤏ *6 rooms* ⚴ *In-room: No phone, no TV. In-hotel: Restaurant, pool* ⊟ *MC, V* ❚❶❚ *CP.*

$$$

🛏 **La Villa del Valle.** At this luxury inn in Valle de Guadalupe, the bright, modern rooms have king-size beds and rustic-chic furnishings; some have balconies. The dining room, where you eat breakfast, has been lovingly done up. It's yet another sign of the emergence of the Baja wine region as a legitimate tourist destination. **Pros:** attention to detail; charming. **Cons:** a drive to town. ⊠ *Off Carretera 3, Km 88, between San Antonio de las Minas and Francisco Zarco; exit at Rancho Sicomoro and follow signs* ☎ *646/183–9249, 818/207–7130 in U.S.* ⊕ *www.lavilladelvalle.com* ⤏ *6 rooms* ⚴ *In-hotel: Restaurant, pool, spa* ⊟ *MC, V* ❚❶❚ *CP.*

8

PUERTO NUEVO

60 km (37 mi) north of Ensenada, 12 km (7½ mi) south of Rosarito.

Southern Californians regularly cross the border to indulge in the classic Puerto Nuevo meal: lobster fried in hot oil and served with refried beans, rice, homemade tortillas, salsa, and lime. At least 30 restaurants are packed into this village; nearly all offer the same menu, but the quality varies drastically; some establishments cook up live lobsters, while others swap in frozen critters. In most places prices are based on size; a medium lobster with all the fixings will cost you about $15.

Though the fried version is the Puerto Nuevo classic, some restaurants also offer steamed or grilled lobsters—why not try one of each and pass 'em around? Each October, to mark the start of the season (which ends in March), the town holds a wine-and-lobster festival.

Artisans' markets and stands throughout the village sell serapes and T-shirts; the shops closest to the cliffs have the best selection.

GETTING HERE AND AROUND
Puerto Nuevo sits just beside Highway 1. When you pull off the highway and enter the town, find a parking spot (free unless otherwise marked) and hop out. There's no other transport to speak of (or needed) in this five-block hamlet.

WHERE TO EAT AND STAY

$–$$$
SEAFOOD
✕ **La Casa de la Langosta.** Seafood soup and grilled fish are options, but lobster is the star. It's served in omelets and burritos or steamed with a wine sauce. Most tables in the large, noisy dining room are covered with platters of fried or grilled lobster and all the standard accompaniments. There's an actual wine list here, and it has several Baja wines. ✉ *Tiburon at Calle Anzuelo* ☎ *661/664–4102* ▭ *MC, V.*

¢–$$
SEAFOOD
✕ **Ortega's Ocean View.** This is one of the cheapest and most unassuming spots on the lobster strip. It's also one of the better ones, serving up lobsters that are fresh, not frozen like many you'll find at the competition. Try the lobster *al ajo* (with garlic), and enjoy it on a rooftop with spectacular sunset views of the Pacific. The quesadillas are also excellent, and the staff is among the friendliest in town. ✉ *Calle Anzuelo 15-A* ☎ *661/112–5322* ▭ *No credit cards.*

¢–$$
SEAFOOD
Fodor's Choice
★
✕ **Rosamar.** This two-story establishment is well patronized by locals, but not so much by tourists. Perhaps it's because of the bright, unromantic lighting. But amble up to the open-air second floor, and you'll be treated to ocean views and fresh lobster at some of the best prices in town. The live lobsters here are so fresh (they come in off the fishing boats each morning) that the restaurant sells its B-list lobsters to other places around town. ✉ *Calle Anzuelo and Barracuda* ☎ *661/614–1210* ▭ *No credit cards.*

$$
🛏 **Grand Baja Resort.** If you're a lobster fanatic, consider spending a relaxing night just steps away from Puerto Nuevo after your enormous dinner and pitchers of margaritas. This resort offers charmingly airy, well-kept "junior suites," which have little living rooms with couches and tables, plus water views; the more impressive "villas," like little apartments with two floors and kitchenettes, boast even better views. Ground-floor rooms have patios, too. **Pros:** nice-size rooms; convenient location. **Cons:** rooms a little spartan. ✉ *Carretera Tijuana–Ensenada, Km 44.5, just past Puerto Nuevo in Ensenada direction* ☎ *661/614–1488, 661/614–1493, or 877/315–1002* ⊕ *www.grandbaja.com* ⬅ *60 villas, 40 suites* ⬧ *In-hotel: Bars, tennis courts, pool, spa* ▭ *AE, DC, MC, V.*

ROSARITO

70 km (44 mi) north of Ensenada, 29 km (18 mi) south of Tijuana.

Southern Californians use **Rosarito** (population 100,000) as a weekend getaway, and during school vacations, especially spring break, the crowd becomes one big raucous party. Off-season, the place becomes a ghost town, which is arguably even less appealing than the frat scene. The beach, which stretches from the power plant at the north end of town about 8 km (5 mi) south, is long with beautiful sand and sunsets, but it's less romantic for the amateur explosives that boom every few minutes.

If you do wind up here for a night, head out to the wooden pier that stretches over the ocean in front of the Rosarito Beach Hotel, or hire a horse at the north or south end of Boulevard Benito Juárez for $10 per hour.

GETTING HERE AND AROUND
Rosarito is off of Highway 1 about 45 minutes south of the border. Follow the exit road directly into town.

EXPLORING
🔅 **Xploration.** Fox Studios has expanded its operation to include a film-oriented theme park. You learn how films are made by visiting one set that resembles a New York street scene and another filled with props from *Titanic*. Fox's most famous films are shown in the large state-of-the-art theater. The park includes a children's playroom where kids can shoot thousands of foam balls out of air cannons. ⊠ *Old Ensenada Hwy., Km 32.8* ☎ *661/614–9444 or 866/369–2252* ⊕ *www.xploration. com.mx* ▣ *$12 adults* ⊗ *Wed.–Fri. 9–4:30, weekends 10–5:30*

8

WHERE TO EAT AND STAY
$–$$$
STEAKHOUSE
✗ **El Nido Steakhouse.** A dark, wood-paneled restaurant with leather booths and a large central fireplace, this is one of Rosarito's oldest eateries, and the best in town for atmosphere. Diners unimpressed with newer, fancier places come here for mesquite-grilled steaks and grilled quail from the owner's farm in the Baja wine country; just skip the underwhelming frozen lobsters. ⊠ *Benito Juárez 67* ☎ *661/612–1430* ▤ *No credit cards.*

$$
🏨 **Rosarito Beach Hotel and Spa.** Charm rather than comfort is the main reason for staying here. The rooms in the oldest section have hand-painted wooden beams and heavy dark furnishings. The more modern rooms in the tower have air-conditioning and pastel color schemes. Every room comes at a ridiculously marked-up price. **Pros:** close to the beach; antique charm. **Cons:** older furnishings; overpriced. ⊠ *Blvd. Benito Juárez 1207, south end of town* ☎ *661/612–0144 or 800/343–8582* ⊕ *www.rosaritobeachhotel.com* 🛏 *203 rooms, 100 suites* 🖨 *In-room: Safe. In-hotel: 2 restaurants, bar, tennis court, pools, gym, spa, beachfront, laundry service* ▤ *MC, V.*

NIGHTLIFE
Papas and Beer (⊠ *On beach off Blvd. Benito Juárez near Rosarito Beach Hotel* ☎ *661/612–0444*), one of the most popular bars in Baja Norte, draws a young, energetic spring-break crowd for drinking and dancing on the beach and small stages.

BAJA NORTE: BORDER TOWNS

You'll find everything you'd expect from a border town in any of Baja's three major cities along the frontera. There are trinket stores, taco stands, morning lines of workers at the border crossing, and a general feeling of living in the shadow of a walled-off behemoth.

Tijuana has always been gritty: these days, a serious wave of violent crime has driven away many of the college-age partiers from Southern California. Mexicali is Tijuana's more industrial neighbor and the seat of the state government. Tecate remains a sleepy border town with a sunny plaza and the chugging towers of the eponymous brewery.

TIJUANA

29 km (18 mi) south of San Diego.

Over the course of the 20th century, Tijuana grew from a ranch populated by a few hundred Mexicans into a Prohibition retreat for boozing and gambling—then it morphed yet again into an industrial giant infamous for its proliferation of *maquiladoras* (sweatshops).

Gone are the glamorous days when Hollywood stars would frequent hot spots like the Agua Caliente Racetrack & Casino, which opened in 1929. When Prohibition was repealed, Tijuana's fortunes began to decline, and, in 1967, when the toll highway to Ensenada was completed, Tijuana ceased to be such a necessary pit stop on the overland route to the rest of Baja. Even the Jai-Alai Palace—which survived into the new millennium as the city's last bastion of gambling—is just a museum now.

In recent years, as drug violence has boomed along the U.S.–Mexico border, Tijuana has taken the brunt of it. Blatant street violence and firefights—though still rare—have taken places on city streets, and American visitors have become targets of some of the crime. Whatever glamour Tijuana may once have claimed is now gone, and those in search of bygone across-the-border thrills may find disappointment: even the party crowd has been scared away.

Apart from a handful of innovative restaurants featuring Mexican and international cuisine, there is very little to recommend Tijuana in its most recent state. Until the wave of crime subsides, the town is best seen from behind windows, en route to other destinations of the Baja Peninsula.

GETTING HERE AND AROUND

Most visitors to Baja Norte arrive in San Diego: there are few international flights into Tijuana, Baja Norte's only major airport. Aeropuerto Alberado Rodriguez (TIJ) is on Tijuana's eastern edge, near the Otay Mesa border crossing. Private taxis and *colectivos* (shared vans) serve the airport. Greyhound buses head to Tijuana from downtown San Diego several times daily. Buses to San Diego and Los Angeles depart from the Greyhound terminal in Tijuana 14 times a day. Mexicoach runs buses from the trolley depot in San Ysidro and the large parking lot on the U.S. side of the border to the Tijuana Tourist Terminal at

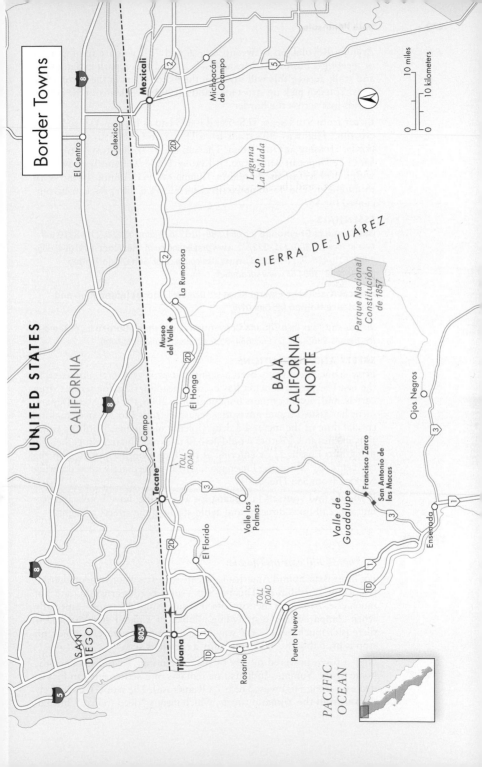

Avenida Revolución between Calles 6 and 7. If you are renting a car or meeting a bus on the Mexican side of the border, park in San Diego and walk across; this will save you the major waits in the automobile lines. You can pick up street food and cheap souvenirs from the artisan stands just across the border.

By car from San Diego, U.S. 5 and I–805 end at the San Ysidro border crossing; Highway 905 leads from U.S. 5 and I–805 to the Tijuana border crossing at Otay Mesa. The San Diego Trolley travels from the Santa Fe Depot in San Diego, at Kettner Boulevard and Broadway, to within 100 feet of the border in Tijuana every 15 minutes from 6 AM to midnight. The 45-minute trip costs $2.50; a day pass can be purchased for $5.

ESSENTIALS

Bus Contacts Greyhound (📠 664/688–0165 in Tijuana, 01800/710–8819 toll-free in Mexico, 800/231–2222 ⊕ www.greyhound.com). **Mexicoach** (📠 664/685–1440, 619/428–9517 in U.S. ⊕ www.mexicoach.com). **San Diego Trolley** (📠 619/233–3004 ⊕ www.sdcommute.com).

Medical Assistance Emergencies (📠 Dial 066). **Tourist Information and Assistance Hotline** (📠 Dial 078).

Visitor and Tour Info Tijuana Convention and Visitor's Bureau (✉ Paseo de los Héroes 9365-201 📠 664/684–0537 ⊕ www.tijuanaonline.org).

SAFETY AND PRECAUTIONS

Petty crime has always been a significant problem here; moreover, in the last few years, Tijuana has become headquarters for serious drug cartels, and violent crime is booming. Since 2008, the U.S. State Department has issued travel advisories regarding travel to Mexico, making special note of the increased drug violence in Tijuana. Until the situation ameliorates, visitors would do best to avoid Tijuana altogether (by flying into Ensenada or entering at the Tecate border), or to skip the city center by taking the Ensenada highway immediately upon entering Mexico from San Diego.

If you do find yourself in Tijuana for an evening, have hotels and restaurants call taxis directly, and avoid strolling the streets at night.

TECATE

62 km (38 mi) east of Tijuana.

For most Baja-bound Americans, Tecate serves as a convenient alternative to the northbound Tijuana–San Ysidro border crossing, and not much else. Although the town itself is sunny and pleasant—especially when compared to the sprawling jumbles of Tijuana and Mexicali—there isn't much here in the way of tourist infrastructure. A quick pit stop is probably the extent of many a traveler's stay.

Now a town powered mostly by manufacturing, Tecate was once the home of the Yumano Indians (the remains of a settlement can be visited east along Highway 2 near La Rumerosa). The name Tecate likely derives from the Yumano *zacate*, which means "deep trench." Indeed, the town itself is set in a dramatic bowl surrounded by tall mountains peppered with desert brush.

Modern-day Tecate began as the private ranch of Juan Bandani, a Peruvian who inherited 11,120 acres from the Mexican government. Bandani went on to become the mayor of San Diego (at that time still controlled by Mexico), and Tecate saw its heyday in the 1880s when the Valle de Guadalupe wine industry took off and the Bandani ranch headquarters became a supply stop for farmers heading south to plant grapes and olives. Eventually a town grew up around the ranch, and manufacturing blossomed on its outskirts, leaving the small-town atmosphere intact downtown. Tecate's best-known enterprise—the massive beer factory—however, is located just four blocks from the central plaza.

Free from Tijuana's grit and Mexicali's boomtime strip malls, Tecate is a homey place with local flavor and easygoing charm. Although there's been a mild increase in crime in the area, Tecate is neither a target nor a thoroughfare for drug violence, and most visitors will feel safe during daylight hours.

GETTING HERE AND AROUND
Tecate is small and easy to navigate. Highway 2 becomes Benito Juárez as it passes through town. Follow Calle Cárdenas straight out of town to the U.S.–Mexico border. If you're heading south to Baja, there's rarely a delay at the San Diego–Tijuana border, and crossing at Tijuana allows you the scenic drive down Highway 3. Northbound travelers, however, might opt for the Tecate crossing, as multiple-hour backups are not uncommon heading north into the United States from Tijuana. Even the Tecate crossing can get crowded in the early morning, however.

ESSENTIALS
Medical Assistance Emergencies (☎ *Dial 066*). **Tourist Information and Assistance Hotline** (☎ *Dial 078*).

SAFETY AND PRECAUTIONS
While there have been few reports of increased violence or crimes targeted at visitors, keep your wits about you in Tecate, lock your car, and don't venture out alone at night. The city's taxi drivers are mostly friendly and reliable, and upscale destinations will happily phone for a cab.

MEXICALI

146 km (91 mi) east of Tecate.

In some ways Tijuana's richer, more successful older brother, Mexicali is a border town founded on an economy that's less whimsical (agriculture, rather than tourism) and a seat of power that's real (the Baja statehouse). In place of trinket shops and taco stands, Mexicali's streetscape features Home Depots and Wal-Marts, and nary a luxury hotel is without its business center, conference rooms, Wi-Fi, and corporate stationery. Yet even with upscale digs and somewhat cleaner streets, Mexicali remains a border town, with all of the tensions and tragedies that accompany its walled divide from Calexico, California to the north.

Yet even before it was a border town, Mexicali was a Chinese settlement. In the late 19th and early 20th centuries, over 90% of the population consisted of Chinese laborers consigned to turn desert lands into farmable acreage. When the Imperial Canal—which diverts water from the Colorado River to irrigate California's Imperial Valley as well as Baja's northern desert—was completed in 1902 (largely by Chinese labor), and the land around Mexicali began to produce crops (again, planted largely by the Chinese), land-grant-following Mexicans started trickling into the region. Today, the basin around Mexicali is Baja's bread- and fruit-basket, and the capital's ethnic mix still reflects the history of the region. In La Chinesca, the city's Chinatown, numerous shops serve up *chau men* (a variation on chow mein), while others sell all of the expected gadgets from abroad.

GETTING HERE AND AROUND
ESSENTIALS
Medical Assistance Emergencies (☎ *Dial 066*). Tourist Information and Assistance Hotline (☎ *Dial 078*).

SAFETY AND PRECAUTIONS
Mexicali, like other border towns, has seen a rise in drug-related violence over the past several years. While there are few reports of increased crime directed at American tourists in Mexicali, additional caution is advised when traveling to the city. Most visitors head immediately down the coast rather that linger near the border, but if you do find yourself in Mexicali overnight, take the usual precautions: park your car in a secured hotel lot and avoid walking alone after dark. The city is generally safe, if not especially savory, during daylight hours.

UNDERSTANDING LOS CABOS AND THE BAJA PENINSULA

Vocabulary

SPANISH VOCABULARY

	ENGLISH	SPANISH	PRONUNCIATION
BASICS			
	Yes/no	Sí/no	see/no
	Please	Por favor	pore fah-**vore**
	May I?	¿Me permite?	may pair-**mee**-tay
	Thank you (very much)	(Muchas) gracias	(**moo**-chas) **grah**-see-as
	You're welcome	De nada	day **nah**-dah
	Excuse me	Con permiso	con pair-**mee**-so
	Pardon me	¿Perdón?	pair-**dohn**
	Could you tell me?	¿Podría decirme?	po-dree-ah deh-**seer**-meh
	I'm sorry	Lo siento	lo see-**en**-toh
	Good morning!	¡Buenos días!	**bway**-nohs **dee**-ahs
	Good afternoon!	¡Buenas tardes!	**bway**-nahs **tar**-dess
	Good evening!	¡Buenas noches!	**bway**-nahs **no**-chess
	Good-bye!	¡Adiós!/¡Hasta luego!	ah-dee-**ohss/ah** -stah **lwe**-go
	Mr./Mrs.	Señor/Señora	sen-**yor**/sen-**yohr**-ah
	Miss	Señorita	sen-yo-**ree**-tah
	Pleased to meet you	Mucho gusto	**moo**-cho **goose**-toh
	How are you?	¿Cómo está usted?	**ko**-mo es-**tah** oo-**sted**
	Very well, thank you.	Muy bien, gracias.	**moo**-ee bee-**en**, **grah**-see-as
	And you?	¿Y usted?	ee oos-**ted**
	Hello (on the telephone)	Diga	**dee**-gah
NUMBERS			
	1	un, uno	oon, **oo**-no
	2	dos	dos
	3	tres	tress
	4	cuatro	**kwah**-tro
	5	cinco	**sink**-oh

ENGLISH	SPANISH	PRONUNCIATION
6	seis	saice
7	siete	see-**et**-eh
8	ocho	**o**-cho
9	nueve	new-**eh**-vey
10	diez	dee-**es**
11	once	**ohn**-seh
12	doce	**doh**-seh
13	trece	**treh**-seh
14	catorce	ka-**tohr**-seh
15	quince	**keen**-seh
16	dieciséis	dee-**es**-ee-**saice**
17	diecisiete	dee-**es**-ee-see-**et**-eh
18	dieciocho	dee-**es**-ee-**o**-cho
19	diecinueve	**dee-es**-ee-new-**ev**-eh
20	veinte	**vain**-teh
21	veinte y uno/ veintiuno	**vain**-te-**oo**-noh
30	treinta	**train**-tah
32	treinta y dos	train-tay-**dohs**
40	cuarenta	kwah-**ren**-tah
43	cuarenta y tres	kwah-**ren**-tay-**tress**
50	cincuenta	seen-**kwen**-tah
54	cincuenta y cuatro	seen-**kwen**-tay **kwah**-tro
60	sesenta	sess-**en**-tah
65	sesenta y cinco	sess-**en**-tay **seen**-ko
70	setenta	set-**en**-tah
76	setenta y seis	set-**en**-tay **saice**
80	ochenta	oh-**chen**-tah
87	ochenta y siete	oh-**chen**-tay see-**yet**-eh
90	noventa	no-**ven**-tah

ENGLISH	SPANISH	PRONUNCIATION
98	noventa y ocho	no-**ven**-tah-**o**-choh
100	cien	see-**en**
101	ciento uno	see-**en**-toh **oo**-noh
200	doscientos	doh-see-**en**-tohss
500	quinientos	keen-**yen**-tohss
700	setecientos	set-eh-see-**en**-tohss
900	novecientos	no-veh-see-**en**-tohss
1,000	mil	meel
2,000	dos mil	dohs meel
1,000,000	un millón	oon meel-**yohn**

COLORS

black	negro	**neh**-groh
blue	azul	ah-**sool**
brown	café	kah-**feh**
green	verde	**ver**-deh
pink	rosa	**ro**-sah
purple	morado	mo-**rah**-doh
orange	naranja	na-**rahn**-hah
red	rojo	**roh**-hoh
white	blanco	**blahn**-koh
yellow	amarillo	ah-mah-**ree**-yoh

DAYS OF THE WEEK

Sunday	domingo	doe-**meen**-goh
Monday	lunes	**loo**-ness
Tuesday	martes	**mahr**-tess
Wednesday	miércoles	me-**air**-koh-less
Thursday	jueves	hoo-**ev**-ess
Friday	viernes	vee-**air**-ness
Saturday	sábado	**sah**-bah-doh

	ENGLISH	SPANISH	PRONUNCIATION

MONTHS

January	enero	eh-**neh**-roh
February	febrero	feh-**breh**-roh
March	marzo	**mahr**-soh
April	abril	ah-**breel**
May	mayo	**my**-oh
June	junio	**hoo**-nee-oh
July	julio	**hoo**-lee-yoh
August	agosto	ah-**ghost**-toh
September	septiembre	sep-tee-**em**-breh
October	octubre	oak-**too**-breh
November	noviembre	no-vee-**em**-breh
December	diciembre	dee-see-**em**-breh

USEFUL PHRASES

Do you speak English?	¿Habla usted inglés?	**ah**-blah oos-**ted** in-**glehs**
I don't speak Spanish	No hablo español	no **ah**-bloh es-pahn-**yol**
I don't understand (you)	No entiendo	no en-tee-**en**-doh
I understand (you)	Entiendo	en-tee-**en**-doh
I don't know	No sé	no seh
I am American/British	Soy americano (americana)/inglés(a)	soy ah-meh-ree- **kah**-no (ah-meh-ree- **kah**-nah)/in-**glehs(ah)**
What's your name?	¿Cómo se llama usted?	koh-mo seh **yah**-mah oos-**ted**
My name is...	Me llamo...	may **yah**-moh
What time is it?	¿Qué hora es?	keh **o**-rah es
It is one, two, three... o'clock.	Es la una./Son las dos, tres...	es la **oo**-nah/sohnahs dohs, tress
Yes, please/No, thank you	Sí, por favor/No, gracias	**see** pohr fah-**vor**/no **grah**-see-us
How?	¿Cómo?	**koh**-mo

ENGLISH	SPANISH	PRONUNCIATION
When?	¿Cuándo?	**kwahn**-doh
This/Next week	Esta semana/ la semana que entra	**es**-teh seh-**mah**- nah/ lah seh-**mah**-nah keh **en**-trah
This/Next month	Este mes/el próximo mes	**es**-teh mehs/el **proke**-see-mo mehs
This/Next year	Este año/el año que viene	**es**-teh **ahn**-yo/el **ahn**-yo keh vee-**yen**-ay
Yesterday/today/ tomorrow	Ayer/hoy/mañana	ah-**yehr**/oy/mahn-**yah**-nah
This morning/ afternoon	Esta mañana/ tarde	**es**-tah mahn-**yah**- nah/ **tar**-deh
Tonight	Esta noche	**es**-tah **no**-cheh
What?	¿Qué?	keh
What is it?	¿Qué es esto?	keh es **es**-toh
Why?	¿Por qué?	pore **keh**
Who?	¿Quién?	kee-**yen**
Where is…?	¿Dónde está…?	**dohn**-deh es-**tah**
the train station?	la estación del tren?	la es-tah-see-on del trehn
the subway station?	la estación del tren subterráneo?	la es-ta-see-**on** del trehn la es-ta-see-**on** soob-teh-**rrahn**-eh-oh
the bus stop?	la parada del autobus?	la pah-**rah**-dah del ow-toh-**boos**
the post office?	la oficina de correos?	la oh-fee-**see**- nah deh koh-**rreh**-os
the bank?	el banco?	el **bahn**-koh
the hotel?	el hotel?	el oh-**tel**
the store?	la tienda?	la tee-**en**-dah
the cashier?	la caja?	la **kah**-hah
the museum?	el museo?	el moo-**seh**-oh
the hospital?	el hospital?	el ohss-pee-**tal**
the elevator?	el ascensor?	el ah-**sen**-sohr
the bathroom?	el baño?	el **bahn**-yoh

ENGLISH	SPANISH	PRONUNCIATION
Here/there	Aquí/allá	ah-**key**/ah-**yah**
Open/closed	Abierto/cerrado	ah-bee-**er**-toh/ ser-**ah**-doh
Left/right	Izquierda/derecha	iss-key-**er**-dah/ dare-**eh**-chah
Straight ahead	Derecho	dare-**eh**-choh
Is it near/far?	¿Está cerca/lejos?	es-**tah sehr**-kah/ **leh**-hoss
I'd like...	Quisiera...	kee-see-ehr-ah
a room	un cuarto/una habitación	oon **kwahr**-toh/ **oo**-nah ah-bee- tah-see-**on**
the key	la llave	lah **yah**-veh
a newspaper	un periódico	oon pehr-ee-**oh**- dee-koh
a stamp	un sello de correo	oon **seh**-yo deh korr-ee-oh
I'd like to buy...	Quisiera comprar...	kee-see-**ehr**-ah kohm-**prahr**
cigarettes	cigarrillos	ce-ga-**ree**-yohs
matches	cerillos	ser-**ee**-ohs
a dictionary	un diccionario	oon deek-see-oh- **nah**-ree-oh
soap	jabón	hah-**bohn**
sunglasses	gafas de sol	**ga**-fahs deh sohl
suntan lotion	Loción bronceadora	loh-see-**ohn** brohn- seh-ah-**do**-rah
a map	un mapa	oon **mah**-pah
a magazine	una revista	**oon**-ah reh-**veess**-tah
paper	papel	pah-**pel**
envelopes	sobres	**so**-brehs
a postcard	una tarjeta postal	**oon**-ah tar-**het**-ah post-**ahl**
How much is it?	¿Cuánto cuesta?	**kwahn**-toh **kwes**-tah
It's expensive/ cheap	Está caro/barato	es-**tah kah**-roh/ bah-**rah**-toh

ENGLISH	SPANISH	PRONUNCIATION
A little/a lot	Un poquito/ mucho	oon poh-**kee**-toh/ **moo**-choh
More/less	Más/menos	mahss/**men**-ohss
Enough/too much/too little	Suficiente/ demasiado/ muy poco	soo-fee-see-**en**-teh/ deh-mah-see-**ah**- doh/ **moo**-ee **poh**-koh
Telephone	Teléfono	tel-**ef**-oh-no
Telegram	Telegrama	teh-leh-**grah**-mah
I am ill	Estoy enfermo(a)	es-**toy** en-**fehr**- moh(mah)
Please call a doctor	Por favor llame a un medico	pohr fah-**vor ya**-meh ah oon **med**-ee-koh

ON THE ROAD

Avenue	Avenida	ah-ven-**ee**-dah
Broad, tree-lined boulevard	Bulevar	boo-leh-**var**
Fertile plain	Vega	**veh**-gah
Highway	Carretera	car-reh-**ter**-ah
Mountain pass	Puerto	poo-**ehr**-toh
Street	Calle	**cah**-yeh
Waterfront promenade	Rambla	**rahm**-blah
Wharf	Embarcadero	em-bar-cah-**deh**-ro

IN TOWN

Cathedral	Catedral	cah-teh-**dral**
Church	Templo/Iglesia	**tem**-plo/ ee-**glehs**- see-ah
City hall	Casa de gobierno	kah-sah deh go-bee-**ehr**-no
Door, gate	Puerta portón	poo-**ehr**-tah por-**ton**
Entrance/exit	Entrada/salida	en-**trah**-dah/sah-**lee**- dah
Inn, rustic bar, or restaurant	Taverna	tah-**vehr**-nah

ENGLISH	SPANISH	PRONUNCIATION
Main square	Plaza principal	plah-thah prin- see-**pahl**

DINING OUT

Can you recommend a good restaurant?	¿Puede recomendarme un buen restaurante?	**pweh**-deh rreh-koh-mehn-**dahr**-me oon bwehn rrehs-tow- **rahn**-teh?
Where is it located?	¿Dónde está situado?	**dohn**-deh ehs-**tah** see-**twah**-doh?
Do I need reservations?	¿Se necesita una reservación?	seh neh-seh-**see**-tah **oo**-nah rreh-sehr- bah-**syohn**?
I'd like to reserve a table...	Quisiera reservar una mesa...	kee-**syeh**-rah rreh-sehr-**bahr oo**-nah **meh**-sah...
for two people.	para dos personas.	**pah**-rah dohs pehr- **soh**-nahs
for this evening.	para esta noche.	**pah**-rah **ehs**-tah **noh**-cheh
for 8 PM	para las ocho de la noche.	**pah**-rah lahs **oh**-choh deh lah **noh**-cheh
A bottle of...	Una botella de ...	**oo**-nah bo-**teh**-yah deh
A cup of...	Una taza de...	**oo**-nah **tah**-thah deh
A glass of...	Un vaso de...	oon **vah**-so deh
Ashtray	Un cenicero	oon sen-ee-**seh**-roh
Bill/check	La cuenta	lah **kwen**-tah
Bread	El pan	el pahn
Breakfast	El desayuno	el deh-sah-**yoon**-oh
Butter	La mantequilla	lah man-teh-**key**-yah
Cheers!	¡Salud!	sah-**lood**
Cocktail	Un aperitivo	oon ah-pehr-ee-**tee**-voh
Dinner	La cena	lah **seh**-nah
Dish	Un plato	oon **plah**-toh
Menu of the day	Menú del día	meh-**noo** del **dee**-ah
Enjoy!	¡Buen provecho!	bwehn pro-**veh**-cho

ENGLISH	SPANISH	PRONUNCIATION
Fixed-price menu	Menú fijo o turistico	meh-**noo** **fee**-hoh oh too-**ree**-stee-coh
Fork	El tenedor	el ten-eh-**dor**
Is the tip included?	¿Está incluida la propina?	es-**tah** in-cloo-**ee**-dah lah pro-**pee**-nah
Knife	El cuchillo	el koo-**chee**-yo
Large portion of savory snacks	Raciónes	rah-see-**oh**-nehs
Lunch	La comida	lah koh-**mee**-dah
Menu	La carta, el menú	lah **cart**-ah, el meh-**noo**
Napkin	La servilleta	lah sehr-vee-**yet**-ah
Pepper	La pimienta	lah pee-me-**en**-tah
Please give me	Por favor déme	pore fah-**vor deh**-meh
Salt	La sal	lah sahl
Savory snacks	Tapas	**tah**-pahs
Spoon	Una cuchara	**oo**-nah koo-**chah**-rah
Sugar	El azúcar	el ah-**thu**-kar
Waiter!/Waitress!	¡Por favor Señor/ Señorita!	pohr fah-**vor** sen- **yor**/ sen-yor-**ee**-tah

Travel Smart
Los Cabos

WORD OF MOUTH

"It's important for visitors new to [the Los Cabos] area to check a map first to see the lay of the land between the two different towns, and the Corridor in between."

—Suze

GETTING HERE AND AROUND

■ AIR TRAVEL

You can now fly nonstop to Los Cabos from Southern California, Atlanta, Chicago, Dallas-Fort Worth, Denver, Houston, Las Vegas, Mexico City, New York, Phoenix, Portland, Sacramento, San Diego, San Francisco, and Seattle. From most other destinations, you will have to make a connecting flight, either in the United States or in Mexico City. Via nonstop service, Los Cabos is about 2 hours from San Diego, about 2¼ hours from Houston, 3 hours from Dallas/Fort Worth, 2¼ hours from Los Angeles, and 2½ hours from Phoenix. Flying time from New York to Mexico City, where you must switch planes to continue to Los Cabos, is five hours. Los Cabos is about a 2½-hour flight from Mexico City.

Airlines and Airports Airline and Airport Links.com (⊕ www.airlineandairportlinks.com).

Airline Security Issues Transportation Security Administration (⊕ www.tsa.gov).

AIRPORTS

Aeropuerto Internacional de San José del Cabo (SJD) is 1 km (½) west of the Transpeninsular Highway (Highway 1), 13 km (8 mi) north of San José del Cabo, and 48 km (30 mi) northeast of Cabo San Lucas. The airport has restaurants, duty-free shops, and car-rental agencies. Los Cabos flights increase in winter with seasonal flights from U.S. airlines, and, despite growing numbers of visitors to the area, the airport manages to keep up nicely with the crowds.

Aeropuerto General Manuel Márquez de León serves La Paz. It's 11 km (7 mi) northwest of the Baja California Sur capital, which itself is 188 km (117 mi) northwest of Los Cabos.

Airport Information Aeropuerto Internacional Los Cabos (☎ 624/146–5111 ⊕ loscabos.aeropuertosgap.com.mx). Aeropuerto General Manuel Márquez de León

(☎ 612/112–0082). Aeropuerto Internacional de Loreto (⊕ loreto.asa.gob.mx).

FLIGHTS

AeroCalafia flies charter flights from Los Cabos for whale-watching. Aeroméxico has service to Los Cabos from San Diego; to Loreto from San Diego, Los Angeles, Hermosillo, and Mexico City; and to La Paz from Los Angeles, Tucson, Tijuana, and Mexico City.

Alaska Airlines flies nonstop to Los Cabos from Los Angeles, San Diego, Seattle, Portland, and San Francisco; twice weekly to Loreto from Los Angeles; and three times a week to La Paz from Los Angeles. Frontier flies nonstop from Denver. US Airways has nonstop service from Phoenix, San Diego, and Las Vegas. American flies nonstop from Dallas/Fort Worth, Chicago, Los Angeles, and New York JFK. British Airways and other European airlines fly to Mexico City, where connections are made for the 2½-hour flight to Los Cabos.

Continental has nonstop service from Houston. Delta flies to Los Cabos from Atlanta and Ontario, California, and has daily flights from Los Angeles to La Paz. Mexicana offers flights from Sacramento, Los Angeles, and Denver.

Airline Contacts AeroCalafia (☎ 624/143–4302 in Los Cabos ⊕ www.aereocalafia.com. mx). Aeroméxico (☎ 800/237–6639 in U.S., 624/146–5097 in Los Cabos, 612/124–6366 in La Paz, 613/135–1837 in Loreto ⊕ www. aeromexico.com). Alaska Airlines (☎ 800/426–0333, 800/252–7522, 624/146–5101 in Los Cabos ⊕ www.alaskaair.com). American Airlines (☎ 800/433–7300, 624/146–5303 in Los Cabos ⊕ www.aa.com). British Airways (☎ 800/247–9297 in U.S., 001/866-835-4133 in Mexico ⊕ www.britishairways.com). Continental Airlines (☎ 800/523–3273, 800/525–0280, 624/146–5040 in Los Cabos ⊕ www. continental.com). Delta Airlines (☎ 800/241–4141, 800/221–1212, 624/146–5005 in Los

Cabos ⊕ www.delta.com). **Frontier Airlines** (🖃 800/432–1359 ⊕ www.frontierairlines.com). **Mexicana** (🖃 800/531–7921, 624/146–5001 in Los Cabos ⊕ www.mexicana.com). **USAirways/ American West** (🖃 800/235–9292, 624/146–5380 in Los Cabos ⊕ www.usairways.com).

GROUND TRANSPORTATION

If you have purchased a vacation package from an airline or travel agency, transfers are usually included. Otherwise, only the most exclusive hotels in Los Cabos offer transfers. Fares from the airport to hotels in Los Cabos are expensive. The least expensive transport is by shuttle buses that stop at various hotels along the route; fares run $12 to $25 per person. Private taxi fares run from $20 to $70. Some hotels can arrange a pickup, which is much faster and might cost about the same as a shuttle. Ask about hotel transfers, especially if you're staying in the East Cape, La Paz, or Todos Santos and not renting a car—cab fares to these areas are astronomical.

If you're renting a car and driving say, to the East Cape, make sure you get detailed directions on how to locate where you'll be staying.

Unless you want to tour a time-share or real estate property, ignore the offers for free transfers when you first come out of customs. The scene can be bewildering for first timers. Sales representatives from various time-share properties compete vociferously for clients; often you won't realize you've been suckered into a time-share presentation until you get in the van. To avoid this situation, go to the official taxi booths inside the baggage claim or just outside the final customs clearance area and pay for a ticket for a regular shuttle bus. Private taxis, often U.S. vans, are expensive and not metered, so always ask the fare before getting in. Rates change frequently, but for one to four persons, it costs about $20 per person to get to San José del Cabo, $26 to a hotel along the Corridor, and $50 to Cabo San Lucas. After the fourth passenger, it's

about an additional $3 per person. Usually only vans accept more than four passengers. At the end of your trip, don't wait until the last minute to book return transport. Make arrangements a few days in advance for shuttle service, and then reconfirm the morning of your departure, or, again, at least a day in advance, sign up at your hotel's front desk to share a cab with other travelers, reconfirming the morning of your departure.

▌ BUS TRAVEL

In Los Cabos, the main Terminal de Autobus (Los Cabos Bus Terminal) is about a 10-minute drive west of Cabo San Lucas. Express buses with air-conditioning and restrooms travel frequently from the terminal to Todos Santos (one hour) and La Paz (three hours). One-way fare is $4 (payable in pesos or dollars) to Todos Santos, $14 to La Paz. From the Corridor, expect to pay about $25 for a taxi to the bus station.

SuburBaja can provide private transport for $60 between San José del Cabo and Cabo San Lucas.

In La Paz the main Terminal de Autobus is 10 blocks from the malecón. Bus companies offer service to Los Cabos (three hours), Loreto (five hours), and Guerrero Negro (the buses stop at the highway entrance to town). The Guerrero Negro trip takes anywhere from six to nine hours, and buses stop in Santa Rosalia and San Ignacio.

Bus Information Los Cabos Terminal de Autobus (🖃 Hwy. 19 🖃 624/143–5020 or 624/143–7880). **SuburBaja** (🖃 624/146–0888).

▌ CAR TRAVEL

Rental cars come in handy when exploring Baja. Countless paved and dirt roads branch off Highway 1 like octopus tentacles beckoning adventurers toward the mountains, ocean, and sea. Baja Sur's highways and city streets are under constant improvement, and Highway 1 is usually in good condition except during heavy rains. Four-wheel drive comes in handy for hard-core backcountry explorations, but isn't necessary most of the time. Just be aware that some car-rental companies void their insurance policies if you run into trouble off paved roads. Even if you are even slightly inclined to impromptu adventures, it's best to find out what your company's policy is before you leave the pavement.

GASOLINE

Pemex (the government petroleum monopoly) franchises all gas stations in Mexico. Stations are to be found in both towns as well as on the outskirts of San José del Cabo and Cabo San Lucas and in the Corridor, and there are also several along Highway 1. Gas is measured in liters. Gas stations in Los Cabos may not accept credit cards. Prices run higher than in the United States. Premium unleaded gas (*magna premio*) and regular unleaded gas (*magna sin*) is available nationwide, but it's still a good idea to fill up whenever you can. Fuel quality is generally lower than that in the United States and Europe. Vehicles with fuel-injected engines are likely to have problems after driving extended distances.

Gas-station attendants pump the gas for you and may also wash your windshield and check your oil and tire air pressure. A tip of 5 or 10 pesos (about 50¢ or $1) is customary depending on the number of services rendered, beyond pumping gas.

ROAD CONDITIONS

Mexico Highway 1, also known as the Carretera Transpeninsular, runs the entire 1,700 km (1,054 mi) from Tijuana to Cabo San Lucas. Do not drive the highway at high speeds or at night—it is not lighted and is very narrow much of the way.

Highway 19 runs between Cabo San Lucas and Todos Santos and is currently being widened to two lanes in each direction, albeit slowly, joining Highway 1 below La Paz. The four-lane road between San José del Cabo and Cabo San Lucas is usually in good condition. Roadwork along the highway is common and commonly frustrates locals and visitors alike. Take your time and don't act rashly if encountering delays or if you need to drive several miles out of your way to turn around and re-approach a missed turnoff.

In rural areas, roads tend to be iffy and in unpredictable condition. Use caution, especially during the rainy season, when rock slides and potholes are a problem, and be alert for animals—cattle, goats, horses, coyotes, and dogs in particular—even on the highways. If you have a long distance to cover, start early, fill up on gas, and remember to keep your tank full as gas stations are simply not as abundant here as they are in the United States or Europe. Allow extra time for unforeseen obstacles.

Signage is not always adequate in Mexico, and the best advice is to travel with a companion and a good map. Take your time. Always lock your car, and never leave valuable items in the body of the car (the trunk will suffice for daytime outings, but be smart about stashing expensive items in there in full view of curious onlookers).

The Mexican Tourism Ministry distributes free road maps from its tourism offices outside the country. Guía Roji and Pemex publish current city, regional, and national road maps, which are available in bookstores and big supermarket chains for under $10; but stock up on every map your rental-car company has, as gas stations generally do not carry maps.

ROADSIDE EMERGENCIES

The Mexican Tourism Ministry operates a fleet of more than 350 pickup trucks, known as the Angeles Verdes, or Green Angels. Bilingual drivers provide mechanical help, first aid, radio-telephone communication, basic supplies and small parts, towing, tourist information, and protection. Services are free; spare parts, fuel, and lubricants are provided at cost. Tips are always appreciated ($5–$10 for big jobs, $2–$3 for minor repairs). The Green Angels patrol sections of the major highways daily 8–8 (later on holiday weekends). If you break down, **pull off the road as far as possible,** lift the hood of your car, hail a passing vehicle, and ask the driver to **notify the patrol.** Most bus and truck drivers will be quite helpful. If you witness an accident, do not stop to help—it could be a ploy to rob you or could get you interminably involved with the police. Instead, notify the nearest official.

Contacts Federal Highway Patrol (☎ 624/122-5735 or 624/125-3584). **Green Angels, La Paz** (☎ 612/125-9677).

SAFETY ON THE ROAD

The mythical *banditos* are not a big concern in Baja. Still, **do your very best to avoid driving at night,** especially in rural areas. Cows and burros grazing alongside the road can pose as real a danger as the ones actually *in* the road—you never know when they'll decide to wander into traffic. Other good reasons for not driving at night include potholes, cars with no working lights, road-hogging trucks, and difficulty with getting assistance. Despite the temptation of margaritas and cold *cervezas,* do not drink and drive; choose a designated driver. Plan driving times, and if night is falling, find a nearby hotel or at least slow down your speed considerably.

Though it isn't common in Los Cabos, police may pull you over for supposedly breaking the law, or for being a good prospect for a scam. If it happens to you, remember to **be polite**—displays of anger will only make matters worse—tell the officer that you would like to talk to the police captain when you get to the station. The officer will usually let you go. If you're stopped for speeding, the officer is supposed to hold your license until you pay the fine at the local police station. But he will always prefer taking a *mordida* (small bribe) to wasting his time at the

police station. Corruption is a fact of life in Mexico, and the $10 or $20 it costs to get your license back is supplementary income for the officer who pulled you over with no intention of taking you to police headquarters.

RENTAL CARS

When you reserve a car, ask about cancellation penalties, taxes, drop-off charges (if you're planning to pick up the car in one city and leave it in another), and surcharges (for being under or over a certain age, for additional drivers, or for driving across state or country borders or beyond a specific distance from your point of rental). All these things can add substantially to your costs. Request car seats and extras such as GPS when you book.

Rates are sometimes—but not always—better if you book in advance or reserve through a rental agency's Web site. There are other reasons to book ahead, though: for popular destinations, during busy times of the year, or to ensure that you get certain types of cars (vans, SUVs, exotic sports cars). We've also found that car-rental prices are much better when reservations are made ahead of travel, from the United States. Prices can be as much as 50% more when renting a car upon arrival in Los Cabos.

■**TIP**→ Make sure that a confirmed reservation guarantees you a car. Agencies sometimes overbook, particularly for busy weekends and holiday periods.

Taxi fares are especially steep in Los Cabos, and a rental car can come in handy if you'd like to dine at the Corridor hotels; travel frequently between the two towns; stay at a hotel along the Cabo Corridor; spend more than a few days in Los Cabos; or plan to see some of the sights outside Los Cabos proper, such as La Paz, Todos Santos, or even farther afield. If you don't want to rent a car, your hotel concierge or tour operator can arrange for a car with a driver or limousine service.

Convertibles and jeeps are popular rentals, but beware of sunburn and windburn and remember there's nowhere to stash your belongings out of sight. Specify whether you want air-conditioning and manual or automatic transmission. If you rent from a major U.S.-based company, you can find a car for about $40 per day ($280 per week), including automatic transmission, unlimited mileage, and 10% tax; however, having the protection of complete coverage insurance will add another $19 to $25 per day, depending on the company, so you should figure the cost of insurance into your budget. You will pay considerably more (probably double) for a larger or higher-end car. Most vendors negotiate considerably if tourism is slow; ask about special rates if you're renting by the week.

To increase the likelihood of getting the car you want and to get considerably better car-rental prices, make arrangements before you leave for your trip. You can sometimes, but not always, find cheaper rates on the Internet. No matter how you book, rates are generally much lower when you reserve a car in advance outside Mexico.

In Mexico your own driver's license is acceptable. In most cases, the minimum rental age is 25, although some companies will lower it to 22 for an extra daily charge. A valid driver's license, major credit card, and Mexican car insurance are required.

CAR-RENTAL INSURANCE

Everyone who rents a car wonders whether the insurance that the rental companies offer is worth the expense. No one—including us—has a simple answer. It all depends on how much regular insurance you have, how comfortable you are with risk, and whether or not money is an issue. Just to be on the safe side, agree to at least the minimum rental insurance. It's best to be completely covered when driving in Mexico.

If you own a car, your personal auto insurance may cover a rental to some degree, though not all policies protect you abroad; always read your policy's fine print. If you don't have auto insurance, then seriously consider buying the collision- or loss-damage waiver (CDW or LDW) from the car-rental company, which eliminates your liability for damage to the car. Some credit cards offer CDW coverage, but it's usually supplemental to your own insurance and rarely covers SUVs, minivans, luxury models, and the like. If your coverage is secondary, you may still be liable for loss-of-use costs from the car-rental company. But no credit-card insurance is valid unless you use that card for *all* transactions, from reserving to paying the final bill. All companies exclude car rental in some countries, so be sure to find out about the destination to which you are traveling.

■**TIP➜** American Express offers primary CDW coverage on all rentals reserved and paid for with the card. This means that the American Express company—not your own car insurance—pays in case of an accident. It *doesn't* mean your car-insurance company won't raise your rates once it discovers you had an accident—but it provides a welcome amount of security for travelers.

Most rental agencies require you to have CDW coverage; many will even include it in quoted rates. All will strongly encourage you to buy CDW—making it difficult to discern whether they are recommending or requiring it—so be sure to ask about such things before renting. In most cases it's cheaper to add a supplemental CDW plan to your comprehensive travel-insurance policy than to purchase it from a rental company. That said, you don't want to pay for a supplement if you're required to buy insurance from the rental company.

If you are going to drive in Mexico you must **carry Mexican auto liability insurance**. This coverage is automatically added to your rental car fees, but if you are driving your own vehicle down, you must arrange for Mexican liability on your own. If you're an AAA (American Automobile Association) member, you can purchase

Mexican insurance in advance; call your local AAA office for details. If you injure anyone in an accident, you could well be jailed—whether it was your fault or not—unless you have insurance. It is difficult to arrange bail once you are jailed, and it can take months for your case to be heard by the courts.

▌TAXI TRAVEL

Taxis are plentiful throughout Baja Sur, even in the smallest towns. Government-certified taxis have a license with a photo of the driver and a taxi number prominently displayed. Fares are exorbitant in Los Cabos, and the taxi union is very powerful. Some visitors have taken to boycotting taxis completely, using rental cars and buses instead, the latter of which can be most time-consuming. The fare between Cabo San Lucas and San José del Cabo runs about $50–$60—more at night. Cabs from Corridor hotels to either town run at least $30 each way. Expect to pay at least $30 from the airport to hotels in San José, and closer to $65 to Cabo.

In La Paz, taxis are readily available and inexpensive. A ride within town costs under $5; a trip to Pichilingue costs between $7 and $10. Illegal taxis aren't a problem in this region.

ESSENTIALS

■ COMMUNICATIONS

INTERNET

You'll find little Internet cafés throughout the region, and many hotels have public terminals to use for free, or for a small fee. Cabo Mail Internet in Cabo San Lucas has several computers and charges $10 an hour. Trazzo Digital in San José del Cabo offers access for $10 an hour. Baja Net in La Paz has ports for laptops along with many computer terminals, also for about $10 an hour.

Contacts Baja Net (✉ Av. Madero 430, La Paz ☎ 612/125–9380). **Cabo Mail Internet** (✉ Av. Cárdenas, Cabo San Lucas ☎ 624/143–7797). **Cybercafes** (🌐 www.cybercafes.com) lists more than 4,000 Internet cafés worldwide. **Trazzo Digital** (✉ Zaragoza 24, San José del Cabo ☎ 624/142–0303).

PHONES

Los Cabos is on U.S. Mountain Time. The region has good telephone service, with pay phone booths along the streets and the Corridor, and wide cell-phone reception. Most phones have Touch-Tone (digital) circuitry. Phone numbers in Mexico change frequently; a recording may offer the new number, so it's useful to learn the Spanish words for numbers 1 through 9. Beware of pay phones and hotel-room phones with signs saying "Call Home" and other enticements. Some of these phone companies charge astronomical rates.

The country code for Mexico is 52. When calling a Mexico number from abroad, dial the country code and then the area code and local number. At this writing, the area code for all of Los Cabos is 624. All local numbers now have seven digits.

CALLING WITHIN MEXICO

For local or long-distance calls, one option is to find a *caseta de larga distancia,* a telephone service usually operated out of a small business; look for the phone symbol on the door. Casetas have become less common as pay phones have begun to appear even in the smallest towns and increasing numbers of people have cell phones. Rates at casetas seem to vary widely, so shop around. Sometimes you can make collect calls from casetas, and sometimes you cannot, depending on the operator and possibly your degree of visible desperation. Casetas generally charge 50¢–$1.50 to place a collect call (some charge by the minute); it's usually better to call *por cobrar* (collect) from a pay phone.

CALLING OUTSIDE MEXICO

To make a call to the United States or Canada, dial 001 before the area code and number. For operator assistance in making an international call dial 090.

AT&T, MCI, and Sprint access codes make calling long-distance relatively convenient, but you may find the local access number blocked in many hotel rooms. First ask the hotel operator to connect you. If the hotel operator balks, ask for an international operator, or dial the international operator yourself. One way to improve your odds of getting connected to your long-distance carrier is to travel with more than one company's calling card (a hotel may block Sprint, for example, but not MCI). If all else fails, call from a pay phone.

Access Codes AT&T Direct (☎ 01–800/462–4240). **MCI WorldPhone** (☎ 01–800/674–7000). **Sprint International Access** (☎ 01–800/877–8000).

DIRECTORY AND OPERATOR ASSISTANCE

Directory assistance in Mexico is 040 nationwide. For international assistance, dial 020 first for an international operator and most likely you'll get one who speaks English; indicate in which city, state, and country you require directory assistance and you will be connected with directory assistance there.

MOBILE PHONES

If you have a multiband phone (some countries use different frequencies from what's used in the United States) and your service provider uses the world-standard GSM network (as do T-Mobile, Cingular, and Verizon), you can probably use your phone abroad. Roaming fees can be steep, however: 99¢ a minute is considered reasonable. And overseas you normally pay the toll charges for incoming calls. It's almost always cheaper to send a text message than to make a call, since text messages have a very low set fee (often less than 5¢). Verizon offers very reasonable Mexican calling plans that can be added to your existing plan.

If you just want to make local calls, consider buying a new SIM card (note that your provider may have to unlock your phone for you to use a different SIM card) and a prepaid service plan in the destination. You'll then have a local number and can make local calls at local rates. If your trip is extensive, you could also simply buy a new cell phone in your destination, as the initial cost will be offset over time.

■**TIP→** If you travel internationally frequently, save one of your old mobile phones or buy a cheap one on the Internet; ask your cell phone company to unlock it for you, and take it with you as a travel phone, buying a new SIM card with pay-as-you-go service in each destination.

There are now companies that rent cell phones (with or without SIM cards) for the duration of your trip. You get the phone, charger, and carrying case in the mail and return them in the mailer.

Contacts Cellular Abroad (🕾 *800/287–5072* ⊕ *www.cellularabroad.com*). **Daystar** (🕾 *888/908-4100* ⊕ *www.daystarwireless. com*). **Mobal** (🕾 *888/888-9162* ⊕ *www.mobalrental.com*). **Planet Fone** (🕾 *888/988-4777* ⊕ *www.planetfone.com*).

PUBLIC PHONES

Occasionally you'll see traditional black, square pay phones with push buttons or dials; although they have a coin slot on top, local calls are free. However, these coin-only pay phones are usually broken. Newer pay phones have an unmarked slot for prepaid phone cards called Telmex cards. The cards are sold in 30-, 50-, or 100-peso denominations at newsstands or pharmacies. Credit is deleted from the Telmex card as you use it, and your balance is displayed on a small screen on the phone. Some phones have two unmarked slots, one for a Telmex card and the other for a credit card. These are primarily for Mexican bank cards, but some accept Visa or MasterCard.

TOLL-FREE NUMBERS

Toll-free numbers in Mexico start with an 800 prefix. To reach them, you need to dial 01 before the number. In this guide, Mexico-only toll-free numbers appear as follows: 01–800/123–4567 (numbers have seven digits). Most of the 800 numbers in this book work in the United States only and are listed simply: 800/123–4567; you cannot access a U.S. 800 number from Mexico. Some U.S. toll-free numbers ring directly at Mexican properties. Don't be deterred if someone answers the phone in Spanish. Simply ask for someone who speaks English. Toll-free numbers that work in other countries are labeled accordingly.

■ CUSTOMS AND DUTIES

Upon entering Mexico, you'll be given a baggage declaration form and asked to itemize what you're bringing into the country. You are allowed to bring in 3 liters of spirits or wine for personal use; 400 cigarettes, 25 cigars, or 200 grams of tobacco; a reasonable amount of perfume for personal use; one video camera and one regular camera and 12 rolls of film for each; and gift items not to exceed a total of $300. If driving across the U.S. border, gift items shouldn't exceed $50, although foreigners aren't usually hassled about this. ⚠ Although the much-publicized border violence doesn't usually affect travelers, it is real. To be safe don't linger long at the border.

You aren't allowed to bring firearms, ammunition, meat, vegetables, plants, fruit, or flowers into the country. You can bring in one of each of the following items without paying taxes: a cell phone, a beeper, a radio or tape recorder, a musical instrument, a laptop computer, and portable copier or printer. Compact discs and/or audio cassettes are limited to 20 total and DVDs to five.

Mexico also allows you to bring one cat or dog, if you have two things: (1) a pet health certificate signed by a registered veterinarian in the United States and issued not more than 72 hours before the animal enters Mexico; and (2) a pet vaccination certificate showing that the animal has been treated (as applicable) for rabies, hepatitis, distemper, and leptospirosis.

For more information or information on bringing other animals or more than one type of animal, contact the Mexican consulate, which has branches in many major American cities as well as border towns. To find the consulate nearest you, check the Ministry of Foreign Affairs Web site (go to the "Servicios Consulares" option).

Information in Mexico Mexican Embassy (☎ 202/728–1600 ⊕ www.embassyofmexico. org). **Ministry of Foreign Affairs** (⊕ portal.sre. gob.mx/eua).

U.S. Information U.S. Customs and Border Protection (⊕ www.cbp.gov).

▌ELECTRICITY

For U.S. and Canadian travelers, electrical converters are not necessary because Mexico operates on the 60-cycle, 120-volt system; however, many Mexican outlets have not been updated to accommodate three-prong and polarized plugs (those with one larger prong), so to be safe bring

an adapter. If your appliances are dual-voltage you'll need only an adapter. Don't use 110-volt outlets, marked FOR SHAVERS ONLY, for high-wattage appliances such as blow dryers. Most laptops operate equally well on 110 and 220 volts and so require only an adapter. It is well worth bringing a small surge protector if you're going to be plugging in your laptop.

▌EMERGENCIES

The state of Baja California Sur has instituted an emergency number for police and fire: 060. A second number, 065, is available to summon medical assistance. Both numbers can be used throughout the state, and there are English-speaking operators. For medical emergencies, Tourist Medical Assist Co. operates Balboa Hospital & Walk-In Clinic in Cabo San Lucas. Another option is air medical services, find a provider through the Association of Air Medical Services (AAMS); several of the U.S.-headquartered operations have bases around Mexico, so they can reach you more quickly.

Emergency Services AAMS (☎ 703/836–8732 ⊕ www.aams.org). **Highway Patrol** (☎ 624/146–0573 in Los Cabos, 612/122–0369 in La Paz). **Police** (☎ 624/142–0361 in San José del Cabo, 624/143–3977 in Cabo San Lucas, 612/122–0477 in La Paz). **Balboa Hospital & Walk-In Clinic** (✉ 911 Lazaro Cárdenas Av., Cabo San Lucas ☎ 624/143–5911).

Foreign Consulates Consular Agent in Cabo San Lucas (✉ Blvd. Marina, Local C-4, Plaza Nautica, Cabo San Lucas ☎ 624/143–3566). **Consulate General Tijuana** (✉ Av. Tapachula 96, Colonia Hipodromo, Tijuana ☎ 664/622–7400 ⊕ tijuana.usconsulate.gov).

Hospitals and Clinics AmeriMed (✉ Av. Cárdenas at Paseo Marina, Cabo San Lucas ☎ 624/143–9670). **Centro de Especialidades Médicas** (✉ Calle Delfines 110, La Paz ☎ 612/124–0400).

Pharmacies Farmacia Baja California (✉ Calle Independencia at Av. Madero, La Paz ☎ 612/122–0240).

▌HEALTH

FOOD AND DRINK

Despite concerns raised by the H1N1 influenza outbreak of early 2009, in Mexico the biggest health risk is *turista* (traveler's diarrhea) caused by consuming contaminated fruit, vegetables, or water. To minimize risks, avoid questionable-looking street stands and bad-smelling food even in the toniest establishments; and if you're not sure of a restaurant's standards, pass up ceviche (raw fish cured in lemon juice) and raw vegetables that haven't been or can't be, peeled (e.g., lettuce and tomatoes).

In general, Los Cabos does not pose as great a health risk as other parts of Mexico. Nevertheless, watch what you eat and drink only bottled water or water that has been boiled for a few minutes. Water in most major hotels is safe for brushing your teeth, but to avoid any risk, use bottled water. Hotels with water-purification systems will post signs to that effect in the rooms.

When ordering cold drinks at establishments that don't seem to get many tourists, skip the ice: *sin hielo*. (You can usually identify ice made commercially from purified water by its uniform shape.)

Stay away from uncooked food and unpasteurized milk and milk products. Mexicans excel at grilling meats and seafood, but be smart about where you eat—ask locals to recommend their favorite restaurants or taco stands, and if you have the slightest hesitation about cleanliness or freshness, then skip it. This caution must extend to ceviche—raw fish cured in lemon juice—which is a favorite appetizer, especially at seaside resorts. The Mexican Department of Health warns that marinating in lemon juice does not constitute the "cooking" that would make the shellfish safe to eat. Fruit and *licuados* (smoothies) stands are wonderful for refreshing treats, but again, ask around, be fanatical about freshness, and watch to see how the vendor handles the food.

Mexico is a food-lover's adventureland, and many travelers wouldn't dream of passing up the chance to try something new and delicious.

Mild cases of turista may respond to Imodium (known generically as loperamide), Lomotil, or Pepto-Bismol (not as strong), all of which you can buy over the counter; keep in mind, though, that these drugs can complicate more serious illnesses. You'll need to replace fluids, so drink plenty of purified water or tea.

Chamomile tea (*té de manzanilla*) and peppermint tea (*té de menta/hierbabuena*) can be good for calming upset stomachs, and they're readily available in restaurants throughout Mexico.

It's smart to bring down a few packets of drink mix, such as EmergenC, when you travel to Mexico. You can also make a salt-sugar solution (½ teaspoon salt and 4 tablespoons sugar per quart of water) to rehydrate. If your fever and diarrhea last longer than a day or two, see a doctor—you may have picked up a parasite or disease that requires prescription medication.

DIVERS' ALERT
⚠ Do not fly within 24 hours of scuba diving.

SHOTS AND MEDICATIONS

According to the U.S. National Centers for Disease Control and Prevention (CDC), there's a limited risk of dengue fever and other insect-carried or parasite-caused illnesses in some rural parts of Mexico, though Baja California Sur is not one of the major areas of concern.

Health Information National Centers for Disease Control & Prevention (*CDC* ☎ *877/394–8747 international travelers' health line* ⊕ *www.cdc.gov/travel*). **World Health Organization** (*WHO* ⊕ *www.who.int*).

MEDICAL INSURANCE AND ASSISTANCE

Consider buying trip insurance with medical-only coverage. Neither Medicare nor some private insurers cover medical expenses anywhere outside the United

States. Medical-only policies typically reimburse you for medical care (excluding that related to pre-existing conditions) and hospitalization abroad, and provide for evacuation. You still have to pay the bills and await reimbursement from the insurer, though.

Another option is to sign up with a medical-evacuation assistance company. Membership gets you doctor referrals, emergency evacuation or repatriation, 24-hour hotlines for medical consultation, and other assistance. International SOS Assistance Emergency and AirMed International provide evacuation services and medical referrals. MedjetAssist offers medical evacuation.

Medical Assistance Companies AirMed International (⊕ www.airmed.com).**International SOS Assistance Emergency** (⊕ www.intsos.com).**MedjetAssist** (⊕ www.medjetassist.com).

Medical-Only Insurers International Medical Group (☎ 800/628–4664 ⊕ www.imglobal.com). **Wallach & Company** (☎ 800/237–6615 or 540/687–3166 ⊕ www.wallach.com).

■ HOLIDAYS

Mexico is the land of festivals; if you reserve lodging well in advance, they present a golden opportunity to have a thoroughly Mexican experience. Banks and government offices close during Holy Week (the week leading to Easter Sunday) and on Cinco de Mayo, Día de la Raza, and Independence Day. Government offices usually have reduced hours and staff from Christmas through New Year's Day. Some banks and offices close for religious holidays.

Official holidays include New Year's Day (January 1); Constitution Day (February 5); Flag Day (February 24); Benito Juárez's Birthday (March 21); Good Friday (Friday before Easter Sunday); Easter Sunday (the first Sunday after the first full moon following spring equinox); Labor Day (May 1); Cinco de Mayo (May 5); St.

John the Baptist Day (June 24); Independence Day (September 16); Día de la Raza (Day of the Race; October 12); Dia de los Muertos (Day of the Dead; November 2); Anniversary of the Mexican Revolution (November 20); Christmas (December 25).

Festivals include Carnaval (February and March, before Lent); Semana Santa (Holy Week; week before Easter Sunday); Día de Nuestra Señora de Guadalupe (Day of Our Lady of Guadalupe; December 12); and Las Posadas (pre-Christmas religious celebrations; December 16–25).

■ HOURS OF OPERATION

Banks are usually open weekdays 8:30–3 (although sometimes banks in Cabo and San José stay open until 5). Government offices are usually open to the public weekdays 8–3; they're closed—along with banks and most private offices—on national holidays. Stores are generally open weekdays and Saturday from 9 or 10 to 7 or 8. In tourist areas, some shops don't close until 10 and are open Sunday. Some shops close for a two-hour lunch break, usually from 2 to 4. Shops extend their hours when cruise ships are in town.

■ MAIL

Airmail letters from Baja Sur can take up to two weeks and often much longer to reach their destination. The *oficina de correos* (post office) in San José del Cabo is open 8–7 weekdays (with a possible closure for lunch) and 9–1 Saturday. Offices in Cabo San Lucas, La Paz, and Loreto are open 9–1 and 3–6 weekdays; La Paz and San Lucas offices are also open 9–noon on Saturday.

Post Offices Cabo San Lucas Oficina de Correo (✉ Av. Cárdenas s/n ☎ 624/143–0048). **San José del Cabo Oficina de Correo** (✉ Mijares and Margarita Maya de Juárez ☎ No phone).

SHIPPING PACKAGES

FedEx does not serve Los Cabos area. DHL has express service for letters and packages from Los Cabos to the United States and Canada; most deliveries take three to four days (overnight service is not available). To the United States, letters take three days and boxes and packages take four days. Cabo San Lucas, San José del Cabo, and La Paz have a DHL drop-off location. Mail Boxes Etc. can help with DHL and postal services.

Major Services **DHL Worldwide Express** (✉ *Plaza los Portales, Hwy. 1, Km 31.5, Local 2, San José del Cabo* ☎ *624/142–2148* ✉ *Hwy. 1, Km 1, Centro Comercial Plaza Copan, Local 18 and 21, Cabo San Lucas* ☎ *624/143–5202*). **Mail Boxes Etc.** (✉ *Plaza las Palmas, Hwy. 1, Km 31, San José del Cabo* ☎ *624/142–4355* ✉ *Blvd. Marina, Plaza Bonita, Local 44-E, Cabo San Lucas* ☎ *624/143–3032*).

▋ MONEY

Mexico has a reputation for being inexpensive, but Los Cabos is one of the most expensive places to visit in the country. Prices rise from 10% to 18% annually and are comparable to those in Southern California.

Prices in this book are quoted most often in U.S. dollars, which are readily accepted in Los Cabos (although you should always have pesos on you if you venture anywhere beyond the walls of a resort). ⇨ *For information on taxes, see Taxes.*

Prices throughout this guide are given for adults. Substantially reduced fees are almost always available for children, students, and senior citizens.

ATMS AND BANKS

ATMs (*cajas automáticas*) are commonplace in Los Cabos and La Paz; Loreto and Mulege also have an ATM. If you're going to a less-developed area, though, go equipped with cash. Cirrus and Plus cards are the most commonly accepted. The ATMs at Banamex, one of the oldest nationwide banks, tend to be the most

reliable. Bancomer is another bank with many ATM locations.

Many Mexican ATMs cannot accept PINs with more than four digits. If yours is longer, change your PIN to four digits before you leave home. If your PIN is fine yet your transaction still can't be completed, chances are that the computer lines are busy or that the machine has run out of money or is being serviced. Don't give up.

CREDIT CARDS

Throughout this guide, the following abbreviations are used: **AE,** American Express; **D,** Discover; **DC,** Diners Club; **MC,** MasterCard; and **V,** Visa.

When shopping, you can often get better prices if you pay with cash, particularly in small shops. But you'll receive wholesale exchange rates when you make purchases with credit cards. These exchange rates are usually better than those that banks give you for changing money. The decision to pay cash or to use a credit card might depend on whether the establishment in which you are making a purchase finds bargaining for prices acceptable, and whether you want the safety net of your card's purchase protection. To avoid fraud or errors, it's wise to make sure that "pesos" is clearly marked on all credit-card receipts.

Before you leave for Mexico, contact your credit-card company to get lost-card phone numbers that work in Mexico; the standard toll-free numbers often don't work abroad. Carry these numbers separately from your wallet so you'll have them if you need to call to report lost or stolen cards. American Express, MasterCard, and Visa note the international number for card-replacement calls on the back of their cards.

CURRENCY AND EXCHANGE

The currency in Los Cabos is the Mexican peso (MXP), though prices are often given in U.S. dollars. Mexican currency comes in denominations of 20-, 50-, 100-, 200-, and 500-peso bills. Coins come in denominations of 1, 2, 5, 10, and 20 pesos and 20 and 50 centavos (20-centavo coins are only rarely seen). Many of the coins are very similar, so check carefully; bills, however, are different colors and easily distinguished.

At this writing, US$1 was equivalent to approximately MXP 12.76

■ PASSPORTS AND VISAS

A passport, or other WHTI (Western Hemisphere Travel Initiative) compliant document, is now required of all visitors to Mexico, including U.S. citizens who may remember the days when only driver's licenses were needed to cross the border. Upon entering Mexico all visitors must get a tourist card. If you're arriving by plane from the United States or Canada, the standard tourist card will be given to you on the plane. They're also available through travel agents and Mexican consulates and at the border if you're entering by land.

■ **TIP→** You're given a portion of the tourist card form upon entering Mexico. Keep track of this documentation throughout your trip: you will need it when you depart. You'll be asked to hand it, your ticket, and your passport to airline representatives at the gate when boarding for departure.

If you lose your tourist card, plan to spend some time (and about $60) sorting it out with Mexican officials at the airport on departure.

A tourist card costs about $20. The fee is generally tacked onto the price of your airline ticket; if you enter by land or boat you'll have to pay the fee separately. You're exempt from the fee if you enter by sea and stay less than 72 hours, or by land and do not stray past the 26- to 30-km (16- to 18-mi) checkpoint into the country's interior.

Tourist cards and visas are valid from 15 to 180 days, at the discretion of the immigration officer at your point of entry (90 days for Australians). Americans,

Canadians, New Zealanders, and the British may request up to 180 days for a tourist card or visa extension. The extension fee is about $20, and the process can be time-consuming. There's no guarantee that you'll get the extension you're requesting. If you're planning an extended stay, plead with the immigration official for the maximum allowed days at the time of entry. It will save you time and money later.

■ **TIP→** Mexico has some of the strictest policies about children entering the country. Minors traveling with one parent need notarized permission from the absent parent.

If you're a single parent traveling with children up to age 18, you must have a notarized letter from the other parent stating that the child has his or her permission to leave his or her home country. The child must be carrying the original letter—not a facsimile or scanned copy—as well as proof of the parent/child relationship (usually a birth certificate or court document), and an original custody decree, if applicable. If the other parent is deceased or the child has only one legal parent, a notarized statement saying so must be obtained as proof. In addition, you must fill out a tourist card for each child over the age of 10 traveling with you.

Info Mexican Embassy (🕾 202/728–1600 ⊕ portal.sre.gob.mx/usa).

U.S. Passport Information U.S. Department of State (🕾 877/487–2778 ⊕ travel.state.gov/passport).

■ RESTROOMS

Expect to find clean flushing toilets, toilet tissue, soap, and running water in Los Cabos. An exception may be small roadside stands or restaurants in rural areas. If there's a bucket and a large container of water sitting outside the facilities, fill the bucket and use it for the flush. Some public places, such as bus stations, charge 1 or 2 pesos for use of the facility, but toilet paper is included in the fee. Still, it's always a good idea to carry some tissue. Throw your toilet paper and any other materials into the provided waste bins rather than the toilet. Mexican plumbing simply isn't equipped to deal with the volume of paper Americans are accustomed to putting in toilets.

SAFETY

Although Los Cabos area is one of the safest in Mexico, it's still important to be aware of your surroundings and to follow normal safety precautions. Everyone has heard some horror story about highway assaults, pickpocketing, bribes, or foreigners languishing in Mexican jails. Reports of these crimes apply in large part to Mexico City and other large cities; in Los Cabos, pickpocketing is usually the biggest concern.

General Information and Warnings Transportation Security Administration (*TSA* ⊕ *www.tsa.gov*). **U.S. Department of State** (⊕ *www.travel.state.gov*).

TAXES

Mexico charges a departure and airport tax of about US$13 and US$8.50, or the peso equivalent, respectively, when you leave the country. This tax is almost universally included in the price of your ticket, but check to be certain. Traveler's checks and credit cards are not accepted at the airport as payment for this fee.

A 2% tax on accommodations is charged in Los Cabos, with proceeds used for tourism promotion.

Baja California Sur has a value-added tax of 10%, called I.V.A. (*impuesto de valor agregado*), which is occasionally (and illegally) waived for cash purchases. Other taxes and charges apply for phone calls made from your hotel room.

TIME

Baja California Sur is on Mountain Standard Time, Baja California is on Pacific Standard Time. And the unofficial standard for behavior is "Mexican time"— meaning stop rushing, enjoy yourself, and practice being *tranquilo*.

TIPPING

When tipping in Baja, remember that the minimum wage is equivalent to a mere $4.50 a day, and that the vast majority of workers in the tourist industry of Mexico live barely above the poverty line. However, there are Mexicans who think in dollars and know, for example, that in the United States porters are tipped about $2 a bag; many of them expect the peso equivalent from foreigners but are sometimes happy to accept 5 pesos (about 50¢) a bag from Mexicans. They will complain either verbally or with a facial expression if they feel they deserve more—you and your conscience must decide. Following are some guidelines. Naturally, larger tips are always welcome.

For porters and bellboys at airports and at moderate and inexpensive hotels, $1 (about 13 pesos) per bag should be sufficient. At expensive hotels, porters expect at least $2 (about 26 pesos) per bag. Leave at least $1 (10 pesos) per night for maids at all hotels. The norm for waiters is 10% to 15% of the bill, depending on service (make sure a 10%–15% service charge hasn't already been added to the bill, although this practice is more common in resorts). Tipping taxi drivers is necessary only if the driver helps with your bags; 50¢ to $1 (6 to 13 pesos) should be enough, depending on the extent of the help. Tip tour guides and drivers at least $1 (13 pesos) per half day or 10% of the tour fee, minimum. Gas-station attendants receive 30¢ to 50¢ (4 to 6 pesos), more if they check the oil, tires, etc. Parking attendants—including those at restaurants with valet parking—should be tipped 50¢ to $1 (6 to 13 pesos).

∎ TRIP INSURANCE

Comprehensive trip insurance is valuable if you're booking a very expensive or complicated trip (particularly to an isolated region) or if you're booking far in advance. Comprehensive policies typically cover trip-cancellation and interruption, letting you cancel or cut your trip short because of a personal emergency, illness, or, in some cases, acts of terrorism in your destination. Such policies also cover evacuation and medical care. (For trips abroad you should at least have medical-only coverage). Some also cover you for trip delays because of bad weather or mechanical problems as well as for lost or delayed baggage.

Another type of coverage to look for is financial default—that is, when your trip is disrupted because a tour operator, airline, or cruise line goes out of business. Generally you must buy this when you book your trip or shortly thereafter, and it's only available to you if your operator isn't on a list of excluded companies.

Always read the fine print of your policy to make sure that you are covered for the risks that are of most concern to you. Compare several policies to make sure you're getting the best price and range of coverage available.

Insurance Comparison Sites Insure My Trip. com (☎ 800/487-4722 ⊕ www.insuremytrip. com). **Square Mouth.com** (☎ 800/240-0369 ⊕ www.squaremouth.com).

Comprehensive Travel Insurers Access America (☎ 800/284-8300 ⊕ www. accessamerica.com). **AIG Travel Guard** (☎ 800/826-4919 ⊕ www.travelguard.com). **CSA Travel Protection** (☎ 800/711-1197 ⊕ www.csatravelprotection.com). **Travelex Insurance** (☎ 800/228-9792 ⊕ www.travelex-insurance.com). **Travel Insured International** (☎ 800/243-3174 ⊕ www.travelinsured.com).

∎ VISITOR INFORMATION

Avoid tour stands on the streets; they are usually associated with time-share operations. In Todos Santos, pick up a copy of *El Calendario de Todos Santos* for information on local events. The *Gringo Gazette* newspaper and the pocket-size *Cabo Noche* are good guides for the Cabo scene. These publications are free and easy to find in hotels and restaurants throughout the region. Discover Baja, a membership club for Baja travelers, has links and info at its Web site. Planeta. com has information about ecotourism and environmental issues.

The Baja California Sur State Tourist Office is in La Paz about a 10-minute drive north of the *malecón*, the seaside promenade. It serves as both the state and city tourism office. There's also an information stand on the malecón (no phone) across from Los Arcos hotel. The booth is a more convenient spot, and it can give you info on La Paz, Scammon's Lagoon, Santa Rosalia, and other smaller towns. Both offices and the booth are open weekdays 9–5.

Contacts Baja California Sur State Tourist Office (✉ Mariano Abasolo s/n, La Paz ☎ 612/124-0100 or 612/122-5939 ⊕ www. vivalapaz.com). **Discover Baja** (⊕ www. discoverbaja.com). *El Calendario de Todos Santos* (⊕ www.elcalendariodetodossantos. com). *Gringo Gazette* (⊕ www.gringogazette. com). **Los Cabos Convention & Visitors Bureau** (☎ 866/LOS-CABOS ⊕ www.visitloscabos.org and www.experienceloscabos.com). **Mexican Government Tourist & Promotion Board** (☎ 800/446-3942 from U.S. and Canada ⊕ www.visitmexico.com). **Planeta.com** (⊕ www.planeta.com). **TodosSantos-Baja.com** (⊕ www.todossantos-baja.com).

INDEX